# 2005 Edition

# A GUIDE TO CANADIAN MONEY LAUNDERING LEGISLATION

Alison Manzer, B.Sc. LL.B., M.B.A., LL.M.

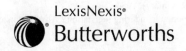
LexisNexis®
Butterworths

**A Guide to Canadian Money Laundering Legislation, 2005 Edition**
© LexisNexis Canada Inc. 2004
October 2004

**Members of the LexisNexis Group worldwide**

| | |
|---|---|
| **Canada** | LexisNexis Canada Inc, 123 Commerce Valley Drive East, MARKHAM, Ontario |
| **Argentina** | Abeledo Perrot, Jurisprudencia Argentina and Depalma, BUENOS AIRES |
| **Australia** | Butterworths, a Division of Reed International Books Australia Pty Ltd, CHATSWOOD, New South Wales |
| **Austria** | ARD Betriebsdienst and Verlag Orac, VIENNA |
| **Chile** | Publitecsa and Conosur Ltda, SANTIAGO DE CHILE |
| **Czech Republic** | Orac sro, PRAGUE |
| **France** | Éditions du Juris-Classeur SA, PARIS |
| **Hong Kong** | Butterworths Asia (Hong Kong), HONG KONG |
| **Hungary** | Hvg Orac, BUDAPEST |
| **India** | Butterworths India, NEW DELHI |
| **Ireland** | Butterworths (Ireland) Ltd, DUBLIN |
| **Italy** | Giuffré, MILAN |
| **Malaysia** | Malayan Law Journal Sdn Bhd, KUALA LUMPUR |
| **New Zealand** | Butterworths of New Zealand, WELLINGTON |
| **Poland** | Wydawnictwa Prawnicze PWN, WARSAW |
| **Singapore** | Butterworths Asia, SINGAPORE |
| **South Africa** | Butterworth Publishers (Pty) Ltd, DURBAN |
| **Switzerland** | Stämpfli Verlag AG, BERNE |
| **United Kingdom** | Butterworths Tolley, a Division of Reed Elsevier (UK), LONDON, WC2A |
| **USA** | LexisNexis, DAYTON, Ohio |

**Library and Archives Canada Cataloguing in Publication**
Manzer, Alison R. (Alison Rosemary), 1954-
    A guide to Canadian money laundering legislation / Alison Manzer. — 2005 ed.

Includes index.
ISBN 0-433-44772-9

        1. Money laundering—Canada. 2. Money—Law and legislation—Canada—Criminal provisions. I. Title.

| | | |
|---|---|---|
| KE1024.R42M35 2004 | 345.71'0268 | C2004-904938-0 |
| KF1030.R3M35 2004 | | |

Printed and bound in Canada

## ABOUT THE AUTHOR

Alison R. Manzer, B.Sc.(Hon)., LL.B., M.B.A., LL.M., is a partner in the financial services group at Cassels Brock & Blackwell in Toronto. Her practice encompasses a broad range of commercial practice in the financial services sector, including financial institution regulation, corporate and commercial lending, syndication, and related areas, and a significant part of her practice involves multi-jurisdictional transactions. Ms. Manzer was named as a leading banking lawyer by Euromoney's Legal Media Group in its *2003 Guide to the World's Leading Banking Lawyers* and is named a leading practitioner in *Canadian Legal LEXPERT® Directory* 2004.

# PREFACE

The materials in this book have been prepared to provide a comprehensive, although high level, guide to the legislation and related regulations dealing with the identification and reporting of potential money laundering activities in Canada. In order to provide as comprehensive a guide as possible, while remaining efficient, duplication has been reduced by choosing not to repeatedly publish overlapping, identical, sections to guidelines, and similar materials. The elimination of duplication is noted in the materials provided, and in all instances, the readily available web site sources for these materials have been noted.

The law in Canada, relating to the identification and publication of information and activities intended to record and report, and if possible reduce, money laundering activity was recently enacted. As a result, it is subject to ongoing change, and regulations and guidelines issued continue to be under regular review and change, as experience and industry input indicates a need for amendment. The materials in this book have been made as up to date as possible, at the time of preparation, however, in the event that specific matters are being reviewed, reference to up to date publications, to ensure that there has not been amendment as to the matter under consideration, should be conducted. While material changes to the general scope and intent of the legislation, and its supporting regulations, has not occurred, fine tuning, particularly relating to industry-specific application, has been an ongoing exercise.

*A Guide to Canadian Money Laundering Legislation, 2005 Edition* was prepared using a guideline and legislation reproduction format. The guideline is intended to provide a plain language explanation of the intent and working of the legislation and its related regulations.

Many of my views as to the application and effect of the legislation have been included. These comments have been included to substitute for commentary which would be derived from applicable case law. To date, the only case law available are the constitutional challenges considered by several of the provincial courts, with regard to the application of the legislation to the legal profession. As the courts consider this legislation, and its application to the various reporting entities, more conclusive, and focused, commentary will be possible.

This book represents the most recent update of materials that were initially formulated for lectures given during the years 2000 and 2001. The materials have been substantially amended and updated to reflect the most recent information available. The reader must recognize that this is law in a state of flux, and that revisions to regulations, additional regulations, guidelines and commentary, will be issued over the course of the next year. An updated version of these materials will be prepared when the time is suitable. I want to express my thanks to Brian Koscak and Eric Kupka for their thoughts in the initial conceptualization of these materials.

Alison Manzer
September 2004

# GENERAL TABLE OF CONTENTS

*Page*

*About the Author*..............................................................................................iii

*Preface*...............................................................................................................v

Chapter 1.  Introduction ......................................................................................1

Chapter 2.  An Effective Compliance Regime..................................................11

Chapter 3.  FINTRAC........................................................................................15

Chapter 4.  Reporting and Record Keeping Requirements ..............................19

Chapter 5.  Ascertaining Identity .....................................................................43

Chapter 6.  Record Keeping Requirements.......................................................49

Chapter 7.  Search and Seizure .........................................................................51

Chapter 8.  Offences .........................................................................................57

Chapter 9.  Immunity from Legal Action on Compliance ................................61

Chapter 10. Compliance Regimes......................................................................63

Proceeds of Crime (Money Laundering) and Terrorist Financing Act ............69

Proceeds of Crime (Money Laundering) and Terrorist
    Financing Suspicious Transaction Reporting Regulations .......................105

Proceeds of Crime (Money Laundering) and Terrorist
    Financing Regulations ..............................................................................111

Cross-border Currency and Monetary Instruments Reporting Regulations..................140

United Nations Suppression of Terrorism Regulations....................................147

Guideline 1: Backgrounder................................................................................151

Guideline 2:  Suspicious Transactions .............................................................169

Guideline 3A:  Submitting Suspicious Transaction Reports to FINTRAC
    Electronically.............................................................................................185

Guideline 3B:  Submitting Suspicious Transaction Reports to FINTRAC
    by Paper.....................................................................................................197

Guideline 4:  Implementation of a Compliance Regime...................................205

Guideline 5:  Submitting Terrorist Property Reports to FINTRAC................219

Guideline 6:  Record Keeping and Client Identification for
    Life Insurance Companies, Brokers and Agents ......................................229

Guideline 7A:  Submitting Large Cash Transaction Reports to
    FINTRAC Electronically ..........................................................................241

Guideline 7B:  Submitting Large Cash Transaction Reports to
    FINTRAC by Paper ..................................................................................253

Guideline 8:  Submitting Electronic Funds Transfers to
    FINTRAC ..................................................................................................263

Table of Contents

Guideline 9:  Submitting Alternative to Large Cash Transaction Reports
    to FINTRAC ...................................................................................................275
OSFI's Draft Revised Guideline B-8 on Deterring and Detecting Money
    Laundering and Terrorist Financing .......................................................287
Glossary ...........................................................................................................301
Reference Web Sites .........................................................................................305
Written Materials Useful for Review .................................................................307
Index  ...............................................................................................................309

# TABLE OF CONTENTS

*Page*

*About the Author*................................................................................. iii

*Preface*................................................................................................... v

*General Table of Contents*................................................................ vi

1.  **Introduction**.......................................................................... 1

    A.   The Origins and Status of Canada's Anti-Money
           Laundering Efforts ...........................................................1

    B.   What is Money Laundering? .................................................3

    C.   Overview of the 2000 Act......................................................5

    D.   An Overview of the Regulations ..........................................8

2.  **An Effective Compliance Regime** .................................... 12

3.  **FINTRAC** ............................................................................... 15

    A.   Introduction ........................................................................15

    B.   Organization and Collection of Information........................17

4.  **Reporting and Record Keeping Requirements**..................... 19

    A.   Suspicious Transactions.....................................................19

    B.   Suspicious Transaction Reporting .....................................

    C.   Prescribed Transactions – Large Cash Transactions..........30

    D.   Cross-Border Movements of Currency and
           Monetary Instruments .....................................................35

    E.   Anti-Terrorism Act and the Public
           Safety Act, 2002..............................................................37

    F.   Reporting Procedures.........................................................40

5.  **Ascertaining Identity** ........................................................... 43

    A.   When One Must Ascertain Identity ....................................43

    B.   How One Must Ascertain Identity ......................................47

6.  **Other Record Keeping Requirements** ............................... 49

7.  **Search and Seizure**............................................................... 51

    A.   Customs Officers ...............................................................51

    B.   Fintrac's Search Powers.....................................................54

    C.   Release of Information .......................................................54

8.  **Offences**.................................................................................. 57

9.  **Immunity from Legal Action on Compliance**........................ 61

Table of Contents

**10.   Compliance Regimes**............................................................... **63**
    A.   General........................................................................63
    B.   Compliance Officer ...............................................64
    C.   Compliance Policies and Procedures...............................66
    D.   Review of Compliance Policies and Procedures.............67
    E.   Compliance Training for Relevant Employees.................68

**PROCEEDS OF CRIME (MONEY LAUNDERING) AND
TERRORIST FINANCING ACT**

**S.C. 2000, c. 17**

*Page*
1.   Short title............................................................................... 69
2.   Definitions.............................................................................. 69
3.   Object...................................................................................... 70
4.   Binding on Her Majesty ........................................................ 71

**PART 1**

RECORD KEEPING AND REPORTING OF
SUSPICIOUS TRANSACTIONS

5.   Application of Part................................................................. 71
6.   Duties ..................................................................................... 72
7.   Transactions if reasonable grounds to suspect ...................... 72
7.1   Disclosure ............................................................................. 72
8.   No disclosure of reports ........................................................ 72
9.   Prescribed financial transactions........................................... 72
9.1   Reports under other Acts....................................................... 73
10.   Immunity................................................................................ 73
11.   Solicitor-client privilege ...................................................... 73

# PART 2

## REPORTING OF CURRENCY AND MONETARY INSTRUMENTS

*Page*

12.  Currency and monetary instruments ............................................... 73
13.  Decision not to proceed with importing or exporting ...................... 74
14.  Temporary retention..................................................................... 74
15.  Search of the person..................................................................... 75
16.  Search of conveyance ................................................................... 75
17.  Examination and opening of mail .................................................. 76
18.  Seizure and forfeiture................................................................... 76
19.  Power to call in aid...................................................................... 77
19.1 Recording of reasons for decision................................................. 77
20.  Report to Commissioner and the Centre ........................................ 77
21.  Mail to be made available to an officer.......................................... 77
22.  When forfeiture under s. 14(5)...................................................... 78
23.  Time of forfeiture........................................................................ 78
24.  Review of forfeiture ..................................................................... 78
25.  Request for Minister's decision ..................................................... 78
26.  Notice of Commissioner ............................................................... 78
27.  Decision of the Minister................................................................ 78
28.  If there is no contravention .......................................................... 79
29.  If there is a contravention............................................................. 79
30.  Appeal to Federal Court................................................................ 79
31.  Service of notices......................................................................... 80
32.  Interest as owner ......................................................................... 80
33.  Order .......................................................................................... 80
34.  Appeal ........................................................................................ 81
35.  Delivery after final order............................................................... 81
36.  Prohibition................................................................................... 81
37.  Use of information ....................................................................... 82
38.  Agreements with foreign states...................................................... 82
39.  Minister's duties........................................................................... 83

# PART 3

## FINANCIAL TRANSACTIONS AND REPORTS ANALYSIS CENTRE OF CANADA

*Page*

40. Object ................................................................................................ 83
41. Centre established ............................................................................. 84
42. Minister is responsible ..................................................................... 84
43. Appointment of Director ................................................................... 84
44. Accident compensation ..................................................................... 84
45. Director's powers .............................................................................. 84
46. Employees ......................................................................................... 85
47. Remuneration .................................................................................... 85
48. Head office ........................................................................................ 85
49. Personnel ........................................................................................... 85
50. Political partisanship ........................................................................ 85
51. Authority to provide services ........................................................... 86
52. Director to report to Minister ........................................................... 86
53. Limitation ......................................................................................... 86
54. Reports and information .................................................................... 86
55. Disclosure by Centre prohibited ....................................................... 87
55.1 Disclosure of information to the Canadian
     Security Intelligence Service ......................................................... 88
56. Agreements and arrangements ........................................................... 89
56.1 Disclosure to foreign agencies ........................................................ 89
57. Use of information ............................................................................ 91
58. Feedback, research and public education .......................................... 91
59. Immunity from compulsory processes ............................................. 91
60. Limitation on orders for disclosure of information .......................... 92
60.1 Application for production order ..................................................... 94
60.2 Hearing of applications .................................................................... 96
61. Certain provisions not applicable ..................................................... 97
62. To ensure compliance ....................................................................... 97
63. Warrant required to enter dwelling-house ........................................ 97
64. Definition of "judge" ....................................................................... 98
65. Disclosure to law enforcement agencies .......................................... 99
66. Power to enter into ........................................................................... 100
67. Choice of service providers .............................................................. 100

Table of Contents

*Page*

68. Centre ................................................................................ 100
69. No liability ......................................................................... 100
70. Audit .................................................................................. 101
71. Annual report ..................................................................... 101
72. Review of Act by parliamentary committee ......................... 101

## PART 4

## REGULATIONS

73. Regulations ......................................................................... 101

## PART 5

## OFFENCES AND PUNISHMENT

74. General offences ................................................................. 102
75. Reporting — sections 7 and 7.1 .......................................... 102
76. Disclosure .......................................................................... 102
77. Reporting — section 9 ........................................................ 103
78. Liability of officers and directors ....................................... 103
79. Offence by employee or agent ............................................ 103
80. Exemption .......................................................................... 103
81. Time limitation ................................................................... 103
82. Venue ................................................................................. 103

## PART 6

## TRANSITIONAL PROVISION, CONSEQUENTIAL AND CONDITIONAL AMENDMENTS, REPEAL AND COMING INTO FORCE

83. Regulations remain in effect ............................................... 104

Table of Contents

# PROCEEDS OF CRIME (MONEY LAUNDERING) AND TERRORIST FINANCING SUSPICIOUS TRANSACTION REPORTING REGULATIONS

## SOR/2001-317

*Page*

| | | |
|---|---|---|
| 1.-2. | Interpretation | 105 |
| 3.-9. | Application of Part 1 of the Act | 107 |
| 10. | Report Made Under Section 83.1 of the Criminal Code | 108 |
| 11. | Exemption | 108 |
| 12. | Sending | 108 |
| 13. | Prescribed Information | 108 |

# PROCEEDS OF CRIME (MONEY LAUNDERING) AND TERRORIST FINANCING REGULATIONS

## SOR/2002-184

| | | |
|---|---|---|
| 1. | Interpretation | 111 |
| 2. | Foreign Currency | 114 |
| 3. | Single Transactions | 114 |
| 4. | Sending Reports | 115 |
| 5. | Reporting Time Limits | 115 |
| 6.-7. | Transactions Conducted by Employees or Agents | 115 |
| 8.-11. | Third Party Determination | 115 |
| 12.-15. | Financial Entities | 118 |
| 16.-20. | Life Insurance Companies and Life Insurance Brokers or Agents | 120 |
| 21.-23. | Securities Dealers | 120 |
| 24.-26. | Persons or Entities Engaged in the Business of Foreign Exchange Dealing | 121 |
| 27.-30. | Money Services Businesses | 122 |
| 31.-33. | [Repealed] | 124 |
| 34.-36. | Accountants and Accounting Firms | 124 |
| 37.-39. | Real Estate Brokers or Sales Representatives | 124 |
| 40.-44. | Casinos | 125 |
| 45. | Acceptance of Deposit Liabilities | 126 |

Table of Contents

46.-49.  Sale or Redemption of Money Orders ............................................... 126

50-52.  Exceptions ................................................................................... 127

53.  Persons or Entities Required to Keep Large Cash Transaction
       Records .................................................................................. 129

54.-55.  Financial Entities ......................................................................... 129

56.  Life Insurance Companies and Life Insurance Brokers or Agents.... 130

57.  Securities Dealers ........................................................................... 130

58.  Persons or Entities Engaged in the Business of
       Foreign Exchange Dealing .............................................................. 131

59.  Money Services Businesses ................................................................ 132

60.  Casinos ........................................................................................... 132

61.  Departments or Agents of Her Majesty in Right of Canada or
       of a Province that Sell Money Orders............................................. 133

62.-71.  Exceptions to Ascertaining Identity .................................................. 133

## CROSS-BORDER CURRENCY AND MONETARY INSTRUMENTS REPORTING REGULATIONS

### SOR/2002-412

1.  Interpretation ................................................................................. 139

2.-14.  Reporting of Importations and Exportations ..................................... 140

15.  Exception Applicable to the Bank of Canada.................................... 144

15.1  Exception Applicable to Imported Shares.......................................... 144

16.-17.  Retention ...................................................................................... 144

18.  Penalties ........................................................................................ 145

19.-23.  Amendments to these Regulations .................................................... 145

24.  Coming into Force.......................................................................... 145

## UNITED NATIONS SUPPRESSION OF TERRORISM REGULATIONS

### SOR/2001-360

1.  Interpretation ................................................................................. 147

2.  List ................................................................................................ 147

3.  Providing or Collecting Funds ......................................................... 148

*Page*

| | | |
|---|---|---|
| 4.-5. | Freezing Property | 148 |
| 6. | Causing, Assisting or Promoting | 148 |
| 7. | Duty to Determine | 148 |
| 8. | Disclosure | 149 |
| 9.-10. | Offences and Punishment | 149 |
| 11. | Certificate | 149 |
| 12. | Coming into Force | 149 |

## GUIDELINES

| | | |
|---|---|---|
| Guideline 1 | Backgrounder | 151 |
| Guideline 2 | Suspicious Transactions | 169 |
| Guideline 3A | Submitting Suspicious Transaction Reports to Fintrac Electronically | 185 |
| Guideline 3B | Submitting Suspicious Transaction Reports to Fintrac by Paper | 197 |
| Guideline 4 | Implementation of a Compliance Regime | 205 |
| Guideline 5 | Submitting Terrorist Property Reports to Fintrac | 219 |
| Guideline 6 | Record Keeping and Client Identification for Life Insurance Companies, Brokers and Agents | 229 |
| Guideline 7A | Submitting Large Cash Transaction Reports to FINTRAC Electronically | 241 |
| Guideline 7B | Submitting Large Cash Transaction Reports to FINTRAC by Paper | 253 |
| Guideline 8 | Submitting Electronic Funds Transfers to FINTRAC | 263 |
| Guideline 9 | Submitting Alternative to Large Cash Transaction Reports to FINTRAC | 275 |

| | |
|---|---|
| OSFI's Draft Revised Guideline B-8 on Deterring and Detecting Money Laundering | 287 |
| Glossary | 301 |
| Reference Web Sites | 305 |
| Written Materials Useful for Review | 307 |
| Index | 309 |

# 1.

# INTRODUCTION

## A. THE ORIGINS AND STATUS OF CANADA'S ANTI-MONEY LAUNDERING EFFORTS

In recent years, law enforcement agencies around the world have focused on money laundering as a tool in crime prevention, seeking greater sanctions and increased reporting by non-police entities in an attempt to discourage further criminal activity by depriving the perpetrators of the profits gained through said criminal activity.

The G-7 countries[1] established the Financial Action Task Force on Money Laundering (the "Task Force") in 1989 as a result of proposals put forward by the United States of America, proposals that were based on the idea that stopping the ability to benefit from the profit of crime would reduce criminal activity. The Task Force was an inter-governmental body consisting of 29 countries and two international organizations[2] whose purpose was to develop and promote policies to generate a global attack on money laundering. In 1990, the Task Force released a report with 40 recommendations (the "Task Force Recommendations") which has formed the basis of anti-money laundering legislation in most countries which are members of the World Trade Organization.[3]

The Task Force Recommendations, among other things, recommended the adoption of local measures to enable law enforcement and other authorities to more readily confiscate laundered property by: (a) identifying, tracing and evaluating property which could be traced to criminal activity and therefore subject to confiscation; (b) carrying out provisional measures such as freezing and seizing property which is reasonably identified as relating to criminal activity to prevent any dealing, transfer or disposal of such property; and (c) taking investigative measures to improve the identification and reporting of financial activity which utilizes proceeds of criminal activity.[4] Other of the Task Force Recommendations recommended passing legislation requiring financial institutions to: (a) take reasonable measures to obtain information about the true identity of the persons on whose behalf a banking or securities account is opened or financial transactions are conducted, and to determine whether the clients, or customers, are acting on their own behalf or for another;[5] (b) report financial transactions to competent authorities where there is suspicion that the

---

[1] The G-7 countries are: Canada, France, Germany, Italy, Japan, the United Kingdom and the United States.

[2] Financial Action Task Force, "*The Forty Recommendations*", released 1990, Task Force Recommendation, p. 1.

[3] *Ibid.*

[4] *Ibid.*, p. 2.

[5] *Ibid.*, p. 3

funds may stem from a criminal activity;[6] and (c) develop programs to assist in countering money laundering, including (i) the development of internal policies, procedures and controls requiring the obtaining of customer information, identifying the source of funds and reporting suspicious transactions, (ii) the implementation of ongoing employee training programs to educate employees as to these requirements, and (iii) an audit process to test the effectiveness of the procedures developed.[7]

Canada was a signatory to the Task Force Recommendations and agreed to implement legislation effectively encompassing these recommendations. Canada first enacted legislation to respond to the Task Force money laundering recommendations on October 10, 1991, when *The Proceeds of Crime (Money Laundering) Act* (the "1991 Act"), was proclaimed in force. The 1991 Act operated together with the Canadian *Criminal Code*[8] provisions related to money laundering, which made it a crime to further activity which was related to money laundering. Voluntary measures largely in keeping with the Task Force Recommendations were adopted by the Canadian chartered banks at that time. The 1991 Act and those additional measures remained in effect until June 19, 2000, when the 1991 Act was replaced by new legislation[9] having the same name but with significantly expanded scope (the "2000 Act").

The 1991 Act was replaced by the 2000 Act for several reasons. The 1991 Act applied to only a limited number of the types of persons who it was perceived might be in a position to identify and report money laundering activity (for example, it applied to banks and securities dealers, but not accountants). It was believed that expansion of the types of persons required to report would enhance effectiveness. The lack of mandatory reporting requirements was also identified as a matter of concern. A further shortcoming was the lack of a central agency to collect information from reporting requirements and to coordinate anti-money laundering activities outside of law enforcement. Under the 2000 Act, Canada's legislative requirements are now generally consistent with those in place in the rest of the G-8 countries, and particularly those in the United States, and includes measures to eliminate those perceived shortcomings of the 1991 Act.

The stated objects of the 2000 Act are to: (a) implement specific measures to detect and deter money laundering and to facilitate the investigation and prosecution of money laundering offences; (b) respond to the threat posed by organized crime by providing law enforcement officials with the information they need to deprive criminals of the proceeds of their criminal activities, while ensuring that appropriate safeguards are put in place to protect the privacy of persons regarding personal information about themselves; and (c) assist in fulfilling Canada's international commitments to participate in the fight against

---

[6]   *Ibid.*, p. 4.

[7]   *Ibid.*, p. 5.

[8]   R.S.C. 1985, c. C-46. Section 462.31 states that it is an offence to use, transfer, possess, *etc.*, any proceeds or property with intent to conceal or convert that property knowing or believing it is a result of enterprise crime or designated substance offence.

[9]   *The Proceeds of Crime (Money Laundering) and Terrorist Financing Act*, S.C. 2000, c. 17.

trans-national crime, particularly money laundering. The objectives have been expanded by amendments enacted under the *Anti-terrorism Act*, in December, 2001 (discussed below) which has added provisions intended to deter terrorist activity by cutting off the sources of funding to terrorist linked groups.

On October 7, 2003, *An Act to Amend Certain Acts of Canada and to Enact Measures for Implementing the Biological and Toxin Weapons Convention*[10] was adopted by the House of Commons. Commonly known as the *Public Safety Act, 2002*, it amends the *Proceeds of Crime (Money Laundering) and Terrorism Financing Act* at Part 19 by extending the types of government databases from which the Financial Transactions and Report Analysis Centre of Canada ("FINTRAC") may collect information which is considered relevant to money laundering or terrorist financing, this expansion allows FINTRAC access to national security databases. The amendments also authorized FINTRAC to exchange information related to compliance with Part I of the 2000 Act with regulators and supervisors of persons and entities that are subject to the 2000 Act. It is stated that this expansion of access to information, including the expanded requirement to provide information has been enacted in order to facilitate FINTRAC's compliance responsibilities under the 2000 Act. The relevant sections of the *Public Safety Act* were proclaimed in force effective on June 1, 2004.

To supplement the legislative and regulatory requirements, FINTRAC, the federal agency created to monitor money laundering in Canada, issues guidelines as to expected standards for compliance. The guidelines do not have the force of law, and are not equivalent to regulations; they are designed to assist reporting entities to better understand and fulfil their obligations under the 2000 Act.

## B.   WHAT IS MONEY LAUNDERING?

The 2000 Act defines a "money laundering" offence by reference to the *Criminal Code*. Money laundering is generally defined as "the process whereby 'dirty money', produced through criminal activity, is transformed into 'clean money' whose criminal origin is difficult to trace."[11] Criminals do this by disguising sources, changing the form, or moving funds to a place or places where they are less likely to attract attention.

Section 7 of the 2000 Act requires reporting of any financial transaction which, in addition to appearing suspicious, is related to a money laundering offence. The definition of a money laundering offence is relatively narrow and includes only those offences which fall under the specific listing of criminal activities. If the suspected activity appears to be illegal but is not on the specific list of criminal activities, it is not a money laundering offence.

Offences listed in section 462.31(1) of the *Criminal Code* means this is a section which provides that it is an offence for a person to deal with property with the intent to conceal or convert that property, knowing or believing that it

---

[10]   Bill C-7 of the Third Session, 37th Parliament, 52-53 Elizabeth II, 2004.
[11]   See the FINTRAC discussion in the FAQ section, online at http://www.fintrac.gc.ca/.

was obtained or derived as a result of (i) an enterprise crime offence, which covers numerous listed offences associated with organized crime, or (ii) a drug related offence.

The *Public Safety Act, 2002* has made amendments[12] to the *Criminal Code*, expanding the definition of an "Offence", to include section 462.31, (Laundering Proceeds of Crime), and includes any other offence where there are reasonable grounds to believe there is a criminal organization offence or any other "Terrorism Offence."

There are three stages generally involved in the money laundering process. First, there is placement, whereby the proceeds of crime are placed in the financial system. This might be done by breaking up large amounts of cash into less conspicuous sums that are then deposited in various bank accounts or other depositories. Alternatively, a series of monetary instruments such as cheques and money orders may be purchased and then deposited into accounts at other locations. The concept is that monetary instruments must be of a nature where the source and the holder of those instruments is not generally traceable. This requires that they be instruments of a money-like quality, that is, those which can be tendered and cash received or a monetary exchange completed by any person who tenders the instrument without identification and proof of entitlement. The monetary instrument must effectively be a direct substitute for the bills and coins which constitute cash.

Second, there is layering, whereby the proceeds of crime are converted into another form. This usually occurs through a series of complex layers of financial transactions that are created to disguise the source and ownership of funds and make it difficult to trace by any audit trail. For example, funds might be wired through a series of different accounts throughout the world. The use of a sequence of wire transfers of funds has been one of the most prevalent methods of carrying out money laundering. The ability to rapidly complete back-to-back transfers is perfect for the purpose of money laundering, which is to disguise the source, and ultimately the destination, of the funds which have been gained from criminal activity. Electronic transfers of funds can result in cross-border transfers several times in a day, effectively, by the speed of transfer disguising the original source of the funds as it becomes increasingly difficult to trace the funds back to the origin.

Third, there is integration, which occurs when the laundered proceeds are placed back in the economy to create the perception of legitimacy. Typically, the funds are invested into real estate, luxury assets, or business ventures.[13] Initially, money laundering must involve investment into assets which can be rapidly reconverted to cash or will generate large cash returns. The essence of money laundering is the rapid turnover of the original cash, such that its source, arising from criminal activities, is disguised. Ultimately, when the source has been effectively blurred or disguised, the funds can be invested into assets which, generally, will be subsequently, resold. The essence of money laundering is not

---

[12] See s. 183.

[13] Financial Action Task Force, *Policy Brief* (July 1999), p. 2.

the use of the assets by the criminals benefiting, but the transfer of the assets in a manner which will hide them as having been proceeds of criminal activity and re-conversion to cash. The provisions of section 462.31 of the *Criminal Code* clearly establish this by making the essence of the offence the intent to conceal or convert the proceeds or property arising from the named criminal acts.

Money launderers will use either a knowing participant (*i.e.*, an active accomplice) or an unknowing participant to assist in furthering the money laundering scheme. Generally, the money launderer must make arrangements to convert cash which has been received from crime into an asset, generally a monetary instrument or a similar non-traceable asset or into an asset which will not attract attention as arising from proceeds of crime.

Money laundering requires that the end result of the series of activities is that the origin of the money, both as to the person and as to the activity, is effectively disguised. The money must appear, at the end of the money laundering chain, to be legitimate funds in the hands of the persons then using them for business or personal purposes. It is the rapid turnover, moving of the funds through a number of hands, which best disguises the original source of the monies as criminal. Those who initiated the money laundering process do not wish to be associated with funds which in any manner can be traced back to the criminal activity. Although the funds may ultimately end up back in the hands of those involved in the criminal activity, at that point in time it is apparently legitimate funds which they are receiving.

## C.   OVERVIEW OF THE 2000 ACT

The 2000 Act is divided into five parts. Part 1 establishes mandatory reporting and record-keeping measures to detect and deter money laundering, and to facilitate the investigation and prosecution of money laundering offences. Part 2 requires all persons or entities importing into or exporting from Canada currency and monetary instruments in excess of the prescribed amount to file a report with the "officers" in the named circumstances. "Officers" are customs officers and the Royal Canadian Mounted Police. Failure to report will result in seizure and forfeiture of the amount imported or exported, and various criminal sanctions. Part 3 establishes the new agency responsible to carry out the objects of Part 1 of the 2000 Act, the "Financial Transactions and Reports Analysis Centre of Canada", known as FINTRAC. Part 4 authorizes the Governor-in-Council to make regulations for carrying out the purposes and provisions of the 2000 Act. Part 5 creates offences for failing to report suspicious financial transactions and for the inappropriate disclosure or use of information under the control of FINTRAC, and the sanctions for these offences.

The reporting and recordkeeping provisions of the 2000 Act apply to a wide variety of persons. They are listed in section 5 of the 2000 Act, including domestic and foreign banks, co-operative credit societies, savings and credit unions, casinos, government departments and agencies, foreign exchange dealers, life insurance companies, life insurance brokers and agents and securities dealers. In addition, section 5 provides that persons engaged in any "business, profession or activity" may be added to the list by designation by virtue of the power to make regulations under section 73(1)(a) and (b) of the 2000 Act. The expansion of the list of reporting entities from financial institutions who traditionally deal in the transfer of funds, is designed to add persons who primarily, or as part of other services, engage in financial intermediation. This expanded list includes the life insurance industry, securities industry, accountants, and similar persons.

Only financial transactions are the subject matter of the recording and reporting requirements under the 2000 Act, however, "financial transaction" is not a defined term in the 2000 Act. It is expected that a financial transaction should be defined considering the basic scheme of the 2000 Act which deals with the receipt and transfer of cash and monetary instruments in specific circumstances. A financial transaction should in the ordinary sense involve the transfer of cash or monetary instruments. It is difficult to offer a precise definition of a concept which is not generally used in business or considered in law. No legal definition of "financial transaction" was found in the commonly used legal dictionaries, however, a "financial intermediary" was defined, generally as an entity that "advances the transfer of funds". This arises both as a consequence of the context in which the expression is used, and as a consequence of its use with the requirement that the financial transaction relate to a money laundering offence. The exchange of monies, or monetary equivalent, is necessarily required for an activity to amount to "money laundering".

This definition is somewhat expanded by the *Anti-terrorism Act*[14] amendments, which add to the offences which are subject to the 2000 Act transactions relating to the financing of terrorist activity. The *Anti-terrorism Act* amends the 2000 Act, renaming the 2000 Act *The Proceeds of Crime (Money Laundering) and Terrorist Activity Financing Act* and including, along with money laundering offences, under effectively every section of the 2000 Act, a terrorist activity financing offence as if it was money laundering. A terrorist activity financing offence is an offence under sections 83.02, 83.03 and 83.04 of the *Criminal Code*, or an offence under section 83.12 of the *Criminal Code*, and includes threats to the security of Canada. The *Anti-terrorism Act* adds the financing of terrorist activities to all sections of the 2000 Act where reference is made to money laundering, by addition.

The phrase "Terrorist activities financing offences" is defined in new section 83.01 of the *Criminal Code*, where it is given a fairly vague definition, and a significant number of offences are incorporated from other Canadian and international statutes. The general definition of terrorist activity is found in section 83.01(b) which describes it as activity being undertaken for political, religious or ideological purposes with the purpose or intention of the activity to intimidate the public or a segment of the public. Comment has been made by several pundits that the definition of a "terrorist activity" is extremely vague and therefore the offence of "terrorist activity financing offence" is so broad as to be incapable of any reasonable definition.

---

[14] S.C. 2001, c. 41.

There are provisions in criminal law under the *Criminal Code*, which create other compliance requirements for money laundering activity. The *Criminal Code* provides that a person cannot knowingly assist in the conduct of a criminal offence, including where related to money laundering activities.[15]

The destination of funds which are transferred or transformed in a financial transaction should also now be considered. The need to review the use and recipient of the funds relates to both money laundering and anti-terrorism reporting. If funds are designated to be transferred in bearer form or to be transferred to a third party where there is no apparent business relationship, then this may give rise to suspicion there is money laundering activity. If funds are coming from any source (even if openly disclosed and legitimate) and are directed to any one of a named list of terrorist linked organizations or countries, then anti-terrorism reporting requirements may be applicable.

Because the definitions of both "terrorist activity" and "terrorist activity financing offences" are extremely vague, persons dealing with receipt and disbursement of funds will need to be aware of the prescribed list of suspected organizations. The only practical way of identifying terrorist financing activity, given the broad definition, is to use the list of suspected terrorist organizations which will be issued by authority of the *Anti-terrorism Act*. The organizations are updated periodically and are listed on the FINTRAC website, among other sites. Although reference to this list will not be definitive as to whether terrorist financing is involved, in general, a person receiving and disbursing funds will be in a poor position to determine whether they are being used for political, religious or ideologic activities, and will not be in a position to directly be aware of whether they are intended to be used for intimidation. It would appear that the only practical way of identifying terrorist activity financing is to use the list of suspected organizations.

The 2000 Act has been designed to rely extensively on regulation; the statute is brief, broadly drafted and includes frequent reference to matters prescribed by regulation. In addition, FINTRAC has issued guidelines which do not have the legal authority of statute or regulation but have been drafted to act as policy commentary to assist reporting entities in understanding the basics of the reporting requirements and of establishing and administering a compliance regime. FINTRAC has expressly stated that the guidelines are not intended to form law, however, as a practical matter, it will be necessary to ensure that there is compliance with the basic outline of the suggested compliance regime and reporting forms and to ensure there is recognition in any compliance program of the listed indicators set out in the guidelines as comprising elements of suspicious transactions.

The compliance recommendations of the guidelines are likely to constitute the base level of performance that will be expected under the 2000 Act. It would appear that the closest parallel to the nature and effect of the FINTRAC Guidelines would be the issuance of "Interpretation Bulletins" by the Canada Customs and Revenue Agency. Any court looking to determine whether

---

[15] See s. 462.31 (as to dealing with proceeds of certain crimes) and s. 21 (as to aiding and abetting).

someone has appropriately complied with the legislative requirements of the 2000 Act is likely to look to the guidelines, and would generally find that the guidelines represent not the entire scope of responsibility but at least the minimum scope of responsibility. In general, compliance will require at least the recognition of, and the education of employees as to, the contents of the guidelines. The guidelines will necessarily form a basic part of any compliance program, and recognition of the key indicators as to what constitutes a suspicious transaction and terrorist financing activity will need to be taken into account in any education and compliance program.

The money laundering legislation has a focus on individual responsibility for identification and reporting of money laundering. Effectively, regardless of how they may be associated with the reporting entity, individuals who have a connection with a reporting entity, are individually responsible for the recording and reporting as required under the legislation. Further, there is a very high level of responsibility placed upon persons who do not directly have the ability to control this recording and reporting, being senior officers and directors. Although due diligence is a defence, it will be necessary to meet very high standards as to education of employees, and as to the enunciation of corporate policy and the provision of effective means for recording. The difficulty of establishing personal responsibility for reporting, while maintaining obligation and liability at the employer level, was addressed in the November 2003 amendments to the Regulation. However, section 6 of the Regulation, relating to employees or agents, was considerably expanded from the initial version and clarifies that it is the employer rather than the employee who is responsible for meeting requirements in the vast majority of cases.

## D.   AN OVERVIEW OF THE REGULATIONS

Three regulations, on a consolidated basis, have now been enacted pursuant to the 2000 Act. The first is the *Proceeds of Crime (Money Laundering) and Terrorist Financing Regulations* ("The Regulation")[16] which generally deals with large cash transactions, providing the necessary definitions and reporting requirements, and provides certain general provisions which supplement the terms of the 2000 Act. The Regulation provides for some of the basic interpretative terms required to supplement the definitions and application of the 2000 Act. It also generally outlines the requirements for reporting of large cash transactions, including transfers made by electronic wire transfer. Amendments made subsequent to initial enactment of the Regulation provide a useful illustration of the intentions of the regulation, specific issues which were identified subsequent to initial enactment.

The general provisions of the Regulation include basic provisions for currency conversion for the purposes of providing currency equivalents to Canadian funds, the definition of a "single transaction" for the purpose of providing for reporting of large cash transactions, a requirement that reporting be done in electronic format, and outlining the specific responsibilities of

---

[16]   SOR/2002-184.

employees. The Regulation also enhances the requirements for delivery of information as to whether a transaction is being carried out for a third party.

In general, the Regulation provides the detail of the reporting requirements for large cash transactions, including the electronic transfer of large amounts of cash. "Large amounts of cash" are defined as $10,000, Canadian, in a "single transaction" (a single transaction is any transaction occurring over a 24 hour period). The contents and transactions triggering reporting requirements are specific by industry, with different types of reporting entities being required to report to different transactions and in somewhat different ways. Exceptions to reporting requirements are also included in the Regulation.

A number of the sections of the Regulation are provisions setting out when it is necessary to ascertain the identity of a person in relation to a financial transaction, again this is segregated and differentiated by industry type, and sets the basic standards and identification to be reviewed in ascertaining identity. The Regulation also sets out the basic requirements for the retention of records.

The Regulation establishes the need to establish a compliance regime, which is discussed in considerably more detail elsewhere in these materials. The most significant portion of the Regulation is a specific outline of the required format of the reports to be provided relating to large cash transactions, including electronic transfers of funds. Schedules 1 to 6 of the Regulation provide for the specific contents of the reports required to be submitted.

The *Proceeds of Crime (Money Laundering) and Terrorist Financing Suspicious Transaction Reporting Regulations* (the "Suspicious Transaction Reporting Regulation")[17] establishes the requirements for suspicious transactions identification and reporting, which is outlined in significant detail elsewhere in these materials. The Suspicious Transaction Reporting Regulation outlines the activities which would give rise to the need to consider a transaction suspicious and generate a report. This regulation also establishes the basic nature of the reporting requirements for this type of transaction. The guidelines, as is discussed elsewhere, give more detail as to the expected details and contents of the required report and the judgements needed to be made in connection with suspicious transactions reporting.

The *Suspicious Transaction Reporting Regulations* provide the regulatory requirement as to how to send reports of suspicious transactions to FINTRAC, essentially by electronic reporting requirements. It also outlines the required information to be included in the reports. Schedule 1 to the Suspicious Transaction Reporting Regulation provides for the details of a suspicious transaction report and Schedule 2 the details of a terrorist group property report.

The *Cross-Border Currency and Monetary Instruments Reporting Regulations*[18] ("the Cross-Border Reporting Regulation"), the third set of regulations under the 2000 Act, provide the definitions clarifying the nature of monetary instruments that will require reporting on a cross-border transfer.

---

[17]  SOR/2001-317.
[18]  SOR/2002-412.

"Monetary instruments", for the purposes of this regulation, means "instruments in bearer form or in such other form as title to them passes on delivery" for example, securities, including stocks, bonds, debentures and treasury bills, and negotiable instruments. The definition does not, however, apply to securities or negotiable instruments that bear restrictive endorsements, stamped for the purpose of clearing or made payable to a named person that have not been endorsed into bearer form. The definitions also include "conveyance", "commercial passenger conveyance" and "non-commercial passenger conveyance" to identify the manner of transportation which may be subject to the Cross-Border Reporting Regulation requirements.

The *Cross-Border Currency and Monetary Instruments Reporting Regulations* establish the basis for the reporting of importations and exportations of currency, at present, involving transfers of $10,000, Canadian, or more to and from Canada. Exceptions to the reporting requirements are then outlined, including specifically importation and exportation by the Bank of Canada, and if relating to shares, excluding those with identifiable ownership. Retention of records requirements and penalties are also outlined. Schedules 1 to 3 of the *Cross-Border Reporting Regulations* outlines the information required to be given by a person engaging in the import or export of currency from Canada.

# 2.

# AN EFFECTIVE COMPLIANCE REGIME

The requirement to establish a compliance regime under the 2000 Act is set out at section 71 of the *Proceeds of Crime (Money Laundering) and Terrorist Financing Regulations* ("The Regulation"),[1] which provide that, for the purpose of paragraph 3(a) of the 2000 Act, and to assist FINTRAC in carrying out its mandate under paragraph 40(e) of the 2000 Act, every person or entity to which any of paragraphs 5(a) to (l) of the 2000 Act applies shall implement a regime for complying with the 2000 Act[2] and any regulations made under the 2000 Act. The Regulation goes on to provide that the compliance regime shall include, as far as practicable, the appointment of a person who is to be responsible for implementation of the regime, the development and application of compliance policies and procedures, a periodic review of the policies and procedures and an ongoing compliance training program. These requirements have been enhanced by the requirements of FINTRAC Guideline 4,[3] which provides guidance as to FINTRAC's expectation as to what will be included in an effective compliance regime.

A compliance program would appear to require the following:

1. The reporting entity must ensure that they can properly file the electronic filing required by the 2000 Act and regulations. This will entail review of the systems and software available to the reporting entity, and a review of the security requirements, including specifically the browser requirements necessary for reporting. These can be reviewed by way of reviewing the reporting requirements as outlined on the FINTRAC website. If electronic reporting is not possible as a consequence of the inability of the computer system and software of the entity to communicate with FINTRAC, paper reporting is permitted. If paper reporting must be used, then the appropriate forms for reporting must be prepared based upon the reporting requirements. These are set out at the schedules to the regulations and clarified in the Guidelines.

2. Information appropriate to the needs of the reporting entity outlining the requirements of the 2000 Act and the regulations must be prepared, and circulated, to all employees. This should include circulation to all officers, directors, management, supervisory personnel and to all persons who would have a client interface in a manner which would put them in a position to see, and potentially identify, a suspicious or large cash transaction. It is suggested that this information and notification of the requirements to report must be in writing, and must have been adequately

---

[1] SOR/2002-184.

[2] S.C. 2000, c. 17.

[3] FINTRAC, *Guideline 4: Implementation of a Compliance Regime* (November 2003), available online at http://www.fintrac.gc.ca/publications/guide/guide_e.asp.

circulated so as to bring the requirements for reporting to the attention of all employees who would be in a position to identify a transaction which is required to be reported.

3. The reporting entity must prepare, they can use the guidelines as a basic outline, an outline of the applicable reporting requirements including the information which must be gathered and retained as to the customer and as to the transaction. It is suggested that all client contact forms must include the information required for a report as to the customer, any third parties they may be acting for, and the basis of the transaction. Employees should not be permitted to initiate a transaction unless they have obtained the compulsory information regarding the client and any third party involved and can record the details of the transaction. Electronic or paper based forms must be prepared and circulated, such that individuals have an appropriate format in which to record and forward the information. Restrictions on the commencement of a new client relationship, or a specific transaction relationship, unless the information is obtained, should be imposed.

4. Persons dealing with customers need to be provided with a specific, as clear as possible, handbook on the identification of a transaction which must be reported. This must include the general criteria for a suspicious, large cash or cross-border transaction reporting requirement. The outline should specifically and clearly state the nature of the transactions which are required to be reported, and, for suspicious transactions, the criteria for those transactions which should be considered a suspicious transaction.

5. Employees should be provided with a brief training manual which indicates the basis for identification of a reportable transaction, the general criteria or indicators which should give rise to a concern that a financial transaction may be a suspicious transaction, and listing the industry-specific indicators for the reporting entity.

6. A compliance officer needs to be appointed and the specific instructions as to how the transaction is to be reported, preferably through a central office or individual, must be established. Employees must know to whom, how, and when they make the report. The employees must have an appropriate form to complete with the information required for the report.

7. The reporting system must provide a means for the reporting information to be provided to the individual responsible for reporting within the time frames for reporting, and that individual must have the means of providing the report to FINTRAC.

FINTRAC Guideline 4, in Part II, initially outlines who has to implement a compliance regime. This is done on the basis of outlining types of reporting entities, and listing the basic requirements for compliance. The entities which are listed are financial entities, life insurance companies, brokers and independent agents, securities dealers, portfolio managers and investment counsellors, casinos, real estate brokers or sales representatives, agents of the Crown that sell or redeem money orders, foreign exchange dealers, money services businesses and accountants and accounting firms. Each of these outlines indicate the activities in relation to which the compliance regime needs to be established, and the respective roles for employees and employers. The discussion of what is a compliance regime, notes that the compliance regime needs to be tailored to fit the individual needs of the reporting entity. The compliance regime needs to specifically reflect the nature, size and complexity of the operations.

The basics of a compliance regime, outlined at Part IV, start with the requirement for the appointment of a compliance officer. Specific note is made that the compliance officer must have the authority and the resources necessary to discharge responsibilities effectively. The compliance officer, on a regular basis, needs to report to a senior level such as the board of directors, senior management or the owner or chief operator. An appropriate compliance regime must include policies and procedures, and clearly state the commitment to prevent, detect and address non-compliance. Again, note is made that the degree of detail, specificity and formality will vary according to the issues and transactions involved.

An essential part of an effective compliance policy is communication, and assurance that the policies are understood by and will be adhered to on the part of anyone who will deal with clients and property owned or controlled by clients. A compliance regime now must also include education and the requirement to be alert to transactions which might involve countries or territories who are on the list of non-cooperative countries, or persons identified by regulation as being identified for terrorist financing purposes. At the very least, reporting obligations relating to terrorist property or suspicions of terrorist financing policies and procedures must reflect the need to check a new customer against the suspected terrorist organization lists published in Canada.

Periodic reviews of the policies and compliance program will need to be undertaken, and specific review can be triggered by factors such as changes in legislation, identification of a non-compliance issue or the introduction of new services or products. Review of the compliance regime must be conducted on an audit basis, and should include interviews with those employees actually handling transactions on an interface with the public.

The standards for the frequency and method of compliance training needs to be regularly reviewed. New employees must be trained before they begin to deal with customers and all employees should be periodically informed of changes. Employee training must include sensitization to the requirements for reporting and identification, and the policies and procedures required to be followed for obtaining customer information, reporting and recording of reportable transactions.

FINTRAC has a specific responsibility to monitor and ensure compliance with the legislative requirements under the 2000 Act. FINTRAC at any time can examine compliance regime and records, and can provide feedback about the adequacy of the program.

The appendices to Guideline 4 include reporting, record keeping, client identification, third party determination requirements by the reporting person or reporting entity sector. The appendices present summaries of these requirements which can be used to assist in formulating the compliance regime.

# 3.

# FINANCIAL TRANSACTIONS AND REPORTS CENTRE OF CANADA

## A.  INTRODUCTION

In creating the Financial Transactions and Reports Centre of Canada ("FINTRAC"), the 2000 Act[1] envisaged a new agency that is intended to lead the fight against money laundering in Canada, albeit not as a criminal authority.[2] The Financial Transactions and Reports Centre of Canada is established under section 40 of the 2000 Act. The Director of FINTRAC reports directly to the Minister of Finance who is designated as being responsible for FINTRAC, and the Minister is given the statutory power under section 42 to direct FINTRAC "on any matter that in the Minister's opinion materially affects public policy or the strategic direction" of FINTRAC. The Governor-in-Council appoints a director of FINTRAC, who may hold the office for not more than five-year terms under section 43 of the 2000 Act. The term may be renewed, but only up to ten years in aggregate.[3]

FINTRAC is required, through its director, to report to the Minister of Finance from time to time on the exercise of the duties and functions under the Act. The director also must keep the Minister of Finance informed of any matter that could materially affect public policy relating to FINTRAC. The director is also required at the Minister's request to disclose to the Minister any information that the Minister of Finance considers relevant for the purpose of carrying out the powers and duties under the 2000 Act, excluding information that could directly identify an individual reporting, or being reported on. The powers and duties granted to the Minister of Finance and FINTRAC under the 2000 Act are broad. The object of the 2000 Act is to establish record keeping and client identification requirements, requiring the reporting of certain transactions, to respond to threats posed by organized crime, and now by terrorist activity, by providing law enforcement officials with information and to fulfil international commitments. FINTRAC, despite the statements in the guidelines and written materials provided to date, is required to release information, without significant limitations, and to respond to requests of the Minister of Finance, given under the broad and vague set of powers and purposes.

FINTRAC is specifically, under section 54, to receive the reports which are made under the 2000 Act, to collect the information it considers relevant from other reports and public sources, and to analyze and assess the reports and

---

[1]  S.C. 2000, c . 17.
[2]  See the stated purpose of the Centre which says it is intended to operate outside of law enforcement.
[3]  Subsection 43(3).

information. The only specific powers and duties of FINTRAC, other than the provision of information reports to the Minister of Finance, are that FINTRAC, where it has reasonable grounds to suspect that the information would be relevant to investigating or prosecuting a money laundering offence, and now terrorist activity financing offence, may disclose the information to criminal authorities, including foreign authorities. Otherwise, there is no stated purpose for, or basis for the use of, the information which is gathered and analyzed by FINTRAC. Accordingly, FINTRAC's roles and responsibilities are vague, but it appears to be a centre for providing materials and information to the Minister, for undefined purposes related to public policy, and to inform police authorities on a national and international basis.

FINTRAC's powers and responsibilities are described in Part 3 of the 2000 Act. Section 40 describes its general responsibilities as follows:

(a) acts at arm's length from law enforcement agencies and other entities to which it is authorized to disclose information;

(b) collects, analyzes, assesses and discloses information in order to assist in the detection, prevention and deterrence of money laundering and of the financing of terrorist activities;

(c) ensures that personal information under its control is protected from unauthorized disclosure;

(d) operates to enhance public awareness and understanding of matters related to money laundering; and

(e) ensures compliance with Part 1.

FINTRAC is the central repository for information in Canada about suspected money laundering activities. [4] It will advise the government regarding the nature and scope of money laundering in Canada, and regarding any new or emerging trends that may require legislative amendment.[5] FINTRAC also has a role in informing and educating client groups and the public in its role and mandate, as well as on the extent of money laundering in Canada.[6] FINTRAC is to operate at arm's length from law enforcement agencies and will disclose only specified information that identifies an individual's identity and certain transaction-related information.[7] However, FINTRAC is able to disclose this information, gathered from its investigative powers and reporting, to a broad range of criminal and quasi-criminal authorities, both within Canada and internationally. FINTRAC representatives in speeches and statements have said that FINTRAC "should be seen as a buffer between individual privacy concerns and law enforcement needs."

---

[4] Patricia Smith, *FINTRAC's Role in the Fight Against Money Laundering in Canada* (2000: FINTRAC), p. 5.

[5] *Ibid.*

[6] *Ibid.*, p. 6.

[7] *Ibid.*, s. 55(7) of the 2000 Act.

## B.    ORGANIZATION AND COLLECTION OF INFORMATION

The Minister of Finance[8] is responsible for FINTRAC and may direct it on any matter that, in his or her opinion, materially affects public policy or its strategic direction.[9] FINTRAC is headed by a Director who is its chief executive officer[10] and who is appointed for terms of five years and not more than ten years in the aggregate.[11]

One of the principal functions of FINTRAC is to collect and review information that is provided by reporting entities and to disclose certain information as permitted under the 2000 Act.[12] FINTRAC also receives reports from other law enforcement agencies, government institutions and agencies of other nations similar to FINTRAC as well as any information voluntarily provided. FINTRAC may also collect publicly available information that it considers relevant to money laundering activities. FINTRAC has the duty to analyze and assess all of this information, and will keep it for a minimum of five years and a maximum of eight years after it is received. The exchange of information with foreign authorities will be done under bilateral accords with "suitable" agencies in these foreign jurisdictions. The purpose of this analysis of information by FINTRAC is unclear, but seems to be for the purpose of public education, legislative change and delivery to law enforcement, revenue and customs authorities.

---

[8]   For the purposes of ss. 25 to 39 of the 2000 Act, "Minister" means the Minister of Finance.

[9]   Sections 42(1) and 42(2) of the 2000 Act.

[10]   Section 45(1) of the 2000 Act.

[11]   Section 43 of the 2000 Act.

[12]   Section 54 of the 2000 Act.

# 4.

# REPORTING AND RECORD KEEPING REQUIREMENTS

The reporting requirements imposed on the reporting entities are the central provisions of the 2000 Act.[1] It is important for reporting entities to familiarize themselves with these requirements because they may significantly affect the way they obtain and record information in their business. There are three different types of transactions that must be reported to FINTRAC: (a) suspicious transactions (section 7 of the 2000 Act); (b) prescribed transactions (currently large cash and electronic funds transfers transactions of $10,000 or more, section 9 of the 2000 Act, as a prescribed transaction in the regulations); and (c) cross-border movements of currency and monetary instruments in excess of a prescribed amount (section 12 of the 2000 Act).[2]

## A. SUSPICIOUS TRANSACTIONS

Reporting entities are required to inform FINTRAC whenever they encounter, in the course of their business activities, a transaction that they suspect may be related to money laundering or the financing of terrorist activity. Section 7 of the 2000 Act requires a report if there are reasonable grounds to suspect that the financial transaction is related to the commission of a money laundering offence.

There is no threshold, as to dollar amount, with regard to the requirement to report a suspicious transaction. There is often confusion between the large cash transactions reporting and the suspicious transactions reporting. Large cash transactions reporting requires reporting of the movement of cash where the amount is, under current regulation, $10,000 or more. It is necessary to report a financial transaction as suspicious where there are reasonable grounds to suspect the transaction is related to money laundering regardless of the dollar amount of the transaction.

The 2000 Act and the regulations, particularly the *Suspicious Transaction Reporting Regulations*[3] place significant emphasis on identifying whether the transaction is being undertaken for or on behalf of a third party. The requirement to identify transactions undertaken on behalf of a third party, and the details of third party information required to be gathered are extensively set out. The concept of reasonable measures to determine whether the account or transaction is being undertaken for a third party have been maintained, but a more extensive

---

[1]   S.C. 2000, c. 17.

[2]   Section 1(1) of the *Cross-Border Currency and Monetary Instruments Reporting Regulations*, SOR/2002-412, defines monetary instruments as:

   ...the following instruments in bearer form or in such other form as title to them passes on delivery, namely,

   (a)   securities, including stocks, bonds, debentures and treasury bills; and

   (b)   negotiable instruments, including bank drafts, cheques, promissory notes, travellers' cheques and money orders, other than warehouse receipts or bills of lading.

[3]   SOR/2001-317.

regime for requesting or requiring information, and the gathering and maintaining of information regarding third parties has been included.

Suspicious transactions must be looked at as to the transaction and the persons involved as a whole. Note is made at Section 3.1 of Guideline 2[4] that a suspicious transaction may involve several factors that seem individually insignificant but together may raise suspicion that the transaction is related to the commission of a money laundering offence. The most significant factor is to consider the context in which the transaction occurs. The reporting entity will need to be able to identify that the transaction is outside of the ordinary course of business, such that it does not appear to be in keeping with normal industry practices. Assessment of the suspicion should be based on a reasonable evaluation of relevant factors. Knowledge of the customer, the customer's business and financial circumstances will also be relevant.

A suspicious transaction is, by the definition in section 7 of the 2000 Act, a financial transaction that the reporting entity has "reasonable grounds to suspect" is related to the commission of a money laundering offence. Initially, the transaction must be a financial transaction, that is, it must involve the transfer of money, or the exchange of money for an asset. Other transactions which are not financial in nature do not fall under the requirements. This is not necessarily the case with the transactions required to be reported under the amendments made by the *Anti-terrorism Act*.[5] The *Suspicious Transaction Reporting Regulations* provide the details as to the persons, activities and basic nature of reporting of suspicious transactions. As is the case throughout the 2000 Act and the regulations, the reporting requirements extend to and include suspicion that there is financing of terrorist activity.

Reporting under section 7 of the 2000 Act is only required for "financial transactions". The 2000 Act, the regulation and the guidelines do not define a "financial transaction". The statute and the regulations were drafted to be as broad and vague as possible to capture a concept and not a narrow list of transactions. It would, however, seem that a financial transaction necessarily involves the transfer of money, otherwise the concepts necessary for the transaction to be related to money laundering do not exist. If the transaction trades money for an asset, that probably is a financial transaction. If you are trading two assets, but it is clear that these assets are of a monetary nature, for example, bearer bonds, that is likely a financial transaction because the 2000 Act includes monetary instruments as an equivalent to cash for many purposes. The regulation defines monetary instruments as those that are effectively used in the same manner as, or are equivalent to, cash. If the transaction is a trade of assets that are not equivalent to money, it is probably not a financial transaction. It is necessary initially to determine if the transaction is a financial transaction because only financial transactions are included in the 2000 Act for reporting of suspicious transactions.

---

[4]   FINTRAC, *Guideline 2: Suspicious Transactions* (March 24, 2003), online at http://www. fintrac.gc.ca/publications/guide/guide_e.asp.

[5]   S.C. 2001, c. 41.

The *Suspicious Transaction Reporting Regulations* establish the required report form and contents, but the requirement to report is under section 7 of the 2000 Act. There is a series of considerations and judgements that must be made to determine if a report is required. The first consideration is the application of the provision to determine if there is reasonable grounds to "suspect". The overall starting point to considering if there is "suspicion" for the purpose of the 2000 Act should be suspicion as to the source of the funds, because reporting relates only to financial transactions relating to money laundering offences which requires the funds to have arisen from a specific list of criminal activities. The anti-terrorism amendments add the responsibility of considering the identity of the recipient of the funds. In addition to money laundering, the *Anti-terrorism Act* adds the financing of terrorist activities to the activities which require reporting.

Where there are any grounds to have concern about the source of the funds, the purpose of the movement of funds through a sequence of entities should be reviewed. Money laundering schemes will involve the movement of funds through a number of entities, ultimately intended to disguise the original source of the funds. If there is an appropriate explanation, and particularly where the transfer of funds is through a closed loop of identified related entities, it is unlikely that this should give rise to "suspicion". The typical tax-structured arrangement moves monies through different types of entities, but all of which have a common ownership or control or identified business relationships. Money laundering efforts would need to move monies through unrelated or disguised entities to effectively disguise the source of the funds. The entire concept behind money laundering is that the original source, arising from criminal activity, is disguised. If the monies are moved in a manner which permits the clear identification of the source of those monies then the purpose of money laundering is not achieved.

The next concept in the definition is that the transaction is one that occurs "in the course of their activities". There is some lack of clarity to that portion of the section, and it is difficult to determine whether "in the course of their activities" means the usual and ordinary course of business, so if you have a highly unusual request before you that that is not included. It would seem it is more likely that this phrase means anything that you might be doing that relates to the financial transaction or that relates to doing business in general that is in the course of business or employment duties. This is another example of the vague drafting of this statute. It is clear that the financial transaction must occur in the course of the general undertaking of the business of the reporting entity, but what it is intended to exclude is far from clear.

If a transaction request is made that you chose not to do, the request does not give rise to a reporting requirement. Reporting is only required where the transaction is completed; if a transaction is not completed you do not need to report it.[6] Therefore "in the course of their activities" probably means that anything that generally has a business guise, and that is part of the business of

---

[6] See Section 2.4 of Guideline 2.

21

the reporting entity is likely in the course of your activities. Inclusion of a concept limiting requirements to report to activities in the course of their activities is unusual and there is no directly applicable legislation to give guidance as to its meaning. It should be anticipated, however, that it will require that the necessity of recording and reporting extend to any activities actually done in the course of employment or business and not be limited to those in the usual course of employment or business.

The wording of section 7 of the 2000 Act next requires that the reporting entity have "reasonable grounds" for suspicion, before the obligation to report arises. What does reasonable grounds mean? Reasonable grounds is a difficult concept to deal with in law. Attempts to define the reasonable man, reasonable judgment, reasonable anything, have been going on for hundreds of years, the best the courts have developed is the concept that a reasonable man is someone who is reasonable.[7] The answer in law is that there is no clear objective meaning to the word "reasonable". The expression "grounds" has the legal meaning "reasons", while "reasonable grounds" has been defined as "probable cause" which means "a reasonable ground to suspect" that person has committed a crime. This is generally more than bare suspicion but less than evidence that would justify a conviction (this is the general standard for issuing a search warrant).[8]

The issue is that an entity is only required to report a transaction if there are reasonable grounds, but the law does not clearly define what reasonable grounds are. Does reasonable mean that something is apparent beyond a reasonable doubt, or is something reasonable when there is only a vague concern. The legal definition as to what are reasonable grounds will evolve as the courts decide when a report should or should not have been made. The exercise of judgment which will need to be made in the meantime are whether the indicators are sufficient that you reasonably should have identified the relation to money laundering. This is a statutory drafting attempt to avoid wilful blindness; to ensure that there is something less than an absolute certainty that a transaction is a suspicious transaction before reporting is required.

When asked the question of what constitutes reasonable grounds, FINTRAC representatives, in public speaking forums, have stated "when in doubt, report". That does not properly address the requirements of reporting entities who are balancing the rights of their clients to confidentiality and the need to report. The statute is stated to be for the purpose of assisting in law enforcement but is not a part of the *Criminal Code*,[9] therefore one must assume that the accusation inherent in a report does not require the criminal test of beyond a reasonable doubt, which assumption is supported by the more common definition of "reasonable grounds" as having "probable cause". Therefore, a best guess as to reasonable grounds is that there are enough surrounding indications

---

[7] A reasonable person is one who acts sensibly, does things without serious delay and takes proper but not excessive precautions.

[8] *Black's Law Dictionary*, 7th ed. (St. Paul, Minnesota: West Publishing Co., 1990). These definitions are United States derived.

[9] R.S.C. 1985, c. C-46. See objects of the 2000 Act at s. 3.

that something is outside of the ordinary course in the transaction, that doesn't amount to an absolute certainty but is more than a vague inkling. Not a great legal definition, but that is the one that we have to cope with for the present.

Reference must be made to the *Suspicious Transaction Reporting Regulations* to determine the extent and nature of the reporting requirements pursuant to the 2000 Act. A suggestion is made that while the 2000 Act and regulations do not require an automated system for detecting suspicious transactions, such a system may be beneficial to the business. The reason for the "beneficial" nature of an automated system arises most specifically from the concept that the indicators may not be seen all at the same instance, for example, at the presentation of an instrument at a counter or desk. An automated system would permit individual indicators to be easily aggregated with regard to a specific client. An automated system would record, and would highlight to a compliance officer, repeated, smaller transactions which would indicate an unusual pattern of commercial activity.

## B.    SUSPICIOUS TRANSACTION REPORTING

Effective November 8, 2001 all persons required to report under the 2000 Act were required to have implemented suspicious transactions reporting as required under the *Suspicious Transaction Reporting Regulations*.

The *Suspicious Transaction Reporting Regulations* impose both individual and institutional responsibility. The regulation specifically states that an individual undertaking activities in the course of their employment will be deemed to be acting on behalf of their employer, except in very limited circumstances, which imposes responsibility on the entity for the activities of the employee. The legislation imposes responsibility on individuals, while requiring an institutional compliance regime, with responsibility laying with the reporting entity under the supervision of its directors and officers, to implement the compliance regime. This has been the pattern for compliance orientated legislation, such as the oversight of conflict of interest and investment policy for federal financial regulations, for some time. In this case, the legislation applies to each individual involved with a reporting entity, such that each individual who may encounter a transaction which is prescribed under the legislation to require reporting, including large cash transactions and suspicious transactions, is personally responsible for the recording and reporting, and personally liable for the sanctions under the 2000 Act. Employees can effectively discharge their duties and responsibilities by internal reporting to a superior within the organization. Persons who are not employees cannot comply, as to legal responsibility, using internal reporting.

A number of new reporting entities have been included under the 2000 Act as being required to record and report, although in some instances only for specified activities, under the concept that it is only financial transactions which are the subject matter of the requirement to report under the 2000 Act. As a consequence, reporting entities who would deal with other types of transactions on a routine basis have generally been required to undertake reporting only in relation to that part of their activities which would constitute financial intermediation, and in relation to financial transactions. In each instance, the listing of activities which has been included are those where the entity was considered by the legislative draftsman to be engaged in financial intermediation. Each of the reporting entities is required to ensure there is compliance as to reporting under Part I of the 2000 Act only as to that portion of their business which is directly described as being a listed activity for that reporting entity in the regulation.

The reporting of suspicions of terrorist financing, as well as any holding or control of terrorist property, forms part of the reporting regulations. The time period for reporting is included in the Regulations at sections 9 and 10, and the form and manner at sections 9, 10 and 12. In addition to the other reporting requirements under the *Suspicious Transaction Reporting Regulations*, reports must be submitted to FINTRAC 30 days after the entity first detects reasonable grounds to suspect that the transaction is related to terrorist financing. There has been no change as to the identity of reporting entities, as a consequence of the *Anti-Terrorism Act* amendments, and the related amended regulations.

The *United Nations Act*[10] gives the Governor-in-Council the power to enact regulations to give effect to measures passed by the Security Council of the United Nations. The *United Nations Suppression of Terrorism Regulations*[11] was passed by the authority of that Act to create a list of persons where there is a reasonable ground to believe that the person is engaged in a number of activities relating to terrorist activity. The *Suspicious Transaction Reporting Regulations* prohibits a person in Canada or a Canadian outside of Canada from knowingly providing or collecting by any means funds with the intention that the funds will be used, or having the knowledge that the funds will be used, by a listed person. In addition, no person in Canada and no Canadian outside of Canada is permitted to deal directly or indirectly with any property of a listed person.

There is a requirement under section 7 of the *Suspicious Transaction Reporting Regulations* for a Canadian financial institution within the meaning of section 2 of the *Bank Act* to determine whether it is in possession or control of property owned or controlled by or on behalf of a listed person. Under section 8, every person in Canada and every Canadian outside of Canada is required to disclose to the Royal Canadian Mounted Police and to the Canadian Security Intelligence Service the existence of any property which is owned or controlled by or on behalf of a listed person. These provisions supplement the requirement to report under the 2000 Act, and related regulations, any dealing in funds which are reasonably believed to relate to a terrorist financing activity offence. The listing of persons, for the purposes of the regulations, are posted on the web site maintained by the Department of Foreign Affairs and International Trade, and those of FINTRAC and the Office of the Superintendent of Financial Institutions ("OSFI").

Section 9 of the *Suspicious Transaction Reporting Regulations* requires that where there are reasonable grounds to suspect that the transaction is related

---

[10]  R.S. 1985, c. U-2.
[11]  SOR/2001-360.

to the commission of a money laundering offence or a terrorist activity financing offence a report must be made which will contain the information set out in the schedules to that regulation. The reporting information required to be included is divided into two sections, that marked with an asterisk and that which is not. That which is marked with an asterisk must be obtained and reported. That which is not marked with an asterisk requires that the person or entity only take reasonable measures to obtain the information under section 52(1) of the regulation.[12]

All sections of the 2000 Act which involve a "money laundering offence" now also include the "financing of terrorist activities" as an offence. As an example, the requirement under section 7 to report where there are reasonable grounds to suspect a transaction relating to a money laundering offence now includes reporting of the activity of a "terrorist activity financing offence". Similar changes are made to effectively every section of the 2000 Act which involves a money laundering offence. Therefore, in considering whether there has been a transaction which gives rise to the need to make a report under section 7 of the 2000 Act, in addition to considering funds which appear to be related to a money laundering offence, it is also necessary to consider whether, on reasonable grounds, the transaction may involve the financing of terrorist activity, which falls under the definition of a terrorist activity financing offence.

Under section 10 of the *Suspicious Transaction Reporting Regulations*, suspicious transactions reports must be sent to FINTRAC within 30 days after the person first detects a fact respecting the transaction that constitutes reasonable grounds to suspect the transaction is related to the commission of the money laundering offence.

FINTRAC has set up an electronic reporting system, and other than if the person or entity does not have the technical capability to send the report electronically, it must send reports to FINTRAC electronically. If the person or entity does not have the technical capability, then they may use a paper reporting format. The technical capability for reporting requires only that computer hardware and software meet the minimum standard which will support the privacy protocols which have been established by FINTRAC. If this type of hardware and software support is available, then the entity must use electronic reporting. The legislation does not however require that entities that do not have computer hardware and software which is capable of communicating with the FINTRAC computer, and of maintaining the confidentiality protocols, be required to obtain the hardware or software, rather they will be able to use paper reporting. The standards and levels of computer hardware and software support are relatively common, and it is anticipated that most reporting entities will have the appropriate support for electronic reporting. The FINTRAC website has made available programs necessary to ensure that confidentiality of the reports is maintained, and these can be downloaded from the FINTRAC website as required.

---

[12] The form appended to the *Suspicious Transaction Reporting Regulations* is mandatory, and reporting will only satisfy the regulatory requirements if filed in that form and fully completed.

Prescribed information must be included in providing a report of a suspicious transaction. This requires two sets of information, one describing the client or any third party that the client is acting for in the transaction, and the other describing the financial transaction. Section 12 of the *Suspicious Transaction Reporting Regulations* sets out the information to be recorded and the schedule to the regulation, at section 9, sets out the details of the form of report that must be used. The asterisked items must be included in the report while the non-asterisked items merely require reasonable due diligence be exercised to obtain and include that information.

The *Suspicious Transaction Reporting Regulations* and FINTRAC Guideline 2 outline the standards to be followed with regard to obtaining the identification information which must be provided with the filing of a report. The standards which have been enunciated only give guidance as to the nature of the identification which must be reviewed. The difficulty for the majority of reporting entities will be determining the level and extent of inquiry which they must make behind apparently official identification. The majority of employees of a reporting entity will have no experience in identifying falsified identification. It would seem that a visual examination of the identification provided should suffice. This is, however, not clear and the standard of inquiry has not been clearly enunciated. The reasonable expectation will be that an obvious alteration to the identification should not be accepted as required official identification. Short of an obvious alteration, it would appear that the reporting entity can accept a presented, apparently valid, identification documentation. However, care must be taken to ensure that the required identification has been reviewed; the regulations and guidelines together provide an outline of the acceptable identification, which differs as to individuals and different types of legal entities.

Simply using the guideline indicators to identify suspicious transactions will not provide assurance of compliance to financial intermediaries with regard to the obligations to report and record suspicious transactions. If the financial intermediary determines to record and report only those transactions which appear to include the listed indicators under the guidelines, they could still be found to be in breach of the statute by failing to identify other, different, financial transactions that should have been noted as suspicious. It will be interesting to see whether, when funds are traced through financial intermediaries, and are found in the end result to arise from money laundering activities, there will be a *prima facie* assumption that suspicion requiring a report should have arisen.

There are no explicit statutory provisions providing objective requirements to report, which would give rise to the ability of financial intermediaries to point to those statutory requirements and indicate a compulsion to report. There will be a significant exercise of judgment in determining whether to report a suspicious transaction. The regulations are not prescribing specific requirements, and the guidelines are purely that, guidelines. It would appear fairly clear that if a report is made based upon indicators set out in the guidelines, that should give rise to the argument that reasonable judgment has been exercised. This, however, is not stated and there will not be statutory protection such as would arise from objective standards as to compulsory reporting.

Although the money laundering legislation provides protection from legal claims arising as a result of a report, the question which will be raised by plaintiffs is likely to be whether the report was required to be made in the first place. Because a judgment call has to be made as to (a) whether there are reasonable grounds to suspect, (b) whether the transaction is a financial transaction, (c) whether it is related to a money laundering offence or financing terrorist activities and (d) whether it is suspicious, a plaintiff would appear to have the ability to claim that there was no mandatory requirements for making a report, and, accordingly, the report was inappropriately made. If inappropriately made, then the protections of the statute may not be available despite the clear wording of the statute. The 2000 Act requires only that a report be made in "good faith" standard for protection from liability for making a report, but there are significant legal and constitutional questions as to the effectiveness of that provision.

FINTRAC has issued Guideline 2 to assist reporting entities with identifying situations when a suspicious transaction should be reported. Guideline 2 lists a number of general indicators of suspicious transactions and a listing which are grouped according to reporting entity.[13] The guidelines presuppose industry knowledge of usual commercial practice, and indicate that transactions undertaken outside of usual commercial practice generally indicate that the funds being utilized may have originated from a criminal source, or are being channelled to terrorist activity, which gives rise to the requirement to report. Unfortunately, the guidelines cannot be taken as a complete and exclusive listing of transaction characteristics which must lead to suspicion of the transaction.

The listing of general indicators includes matters such as (a) the client admitting or making statements about the involvement in criminal activities, (b) the desire of the client not to have correspondence sent to a home address, (c) the client has vague knowledge or presents confusing details about the transaction, (d) the client is secretive and reluctant to meet in person, among others. These generally indicate a client who appears to have a cavalier attitude as to the transaction or the funds or is nervous or suspicious of normal transaction enquiries or procedures. Section 4.2 indicators include an uncommon knowledge of money laundering reporting requirements. At Section 4.3 of the guideline, there is a list of indicators which generally relate to the client not promptly, and effectively, providing identification. The obtaining of personal identification with regard to the client is a necessary component to money laundering recording and reporting. Other general indicators are listed in Section 4.4 which indicates an unusual pattern of cash transactions and 4.5 which

---

[13]   As an example, see Guideline 2, p. 14. Section 5.4 of Guideline 2 specifically lists indicators that life insurance companies and life insurance brokers and agents should consider as indicating a suspicious transaction. These include indicators such as a client who requests an insurance product that has no discernible purpose, a client who cancels an investment soon after purchase, and a client whose first or single premium is paid for from a bank account outside the country.

provides a series of indicators generally related to there being no sound or usual economic purpose to the transaction. Sections 4.6 and 4.7 provide more general indicators, the first relating to unusual account opening and use activity and the latter being the use of international transfer of funds, where it does not appear to be required in commercial transactions. Finally, Section 4.8 alerts the reporting entity to the suspicious nature of certain offshore business activity, such as frequent transfer of funds to offshore accounts or persons, where that does not appear to be a necessary part of the client's business.

Guideline No. 2 sets out industry specific indicators that are intended to provide a basic means of identifying suspicious transactions which are most likely to occur in transactions of a reporting entity. It is suggested that if the compliance regime, and employee training, includes this listing of indicators from the guidelines, and if identification of transactions follows the recommendation of this list of indicators, that it is likely the reporting entity will be considered to have acted reasonably, and with an acceptable level of due diligence.

The 2000 Act states that the reasonable grounds must be to suspect. Again, it is a poorly defined concept as to what is suspicion or "to suspect". To suspect is likely less than "I am absolutely sure this is the case" but is somewhat more than "this does not feel right but there is nothing out of the ordinary". Suspicion is a very low standard for reporting, but it does have to be read in conjunction with the need for reasonable grounds. Next, the suspicion must be that the transaction is involved with money laundering, reporting is only required if the transaction is related to "the commission of a money laundering offence" or is related to a "terrorist activity financing offence". The definition of a money laundering offence does seem to be fairly clear as it is defined in the statute. A money laundering offence is defined as an "offence" under subsection 462.31(1) of the *Criminal Code*.[14]

The listing of offences under section 462.31 of the *Criminal Code* is extensive and specifically lists criminal offences that constitute the money laundering offences.[15] It is a specific list, but the list is extensive, and it will be necessary to have some understanding of the criteria of these offences to know if the indicators involve an offence listed in that section of the *Criminal Code*. A course of action is only a money laundering offence if it falls under the specific list of criminal activity. Also, the offences under statutes other than the *Criminal Code* are included and must be understood.

The *Anti-terrorism Act* added an amendment providing that reporting under section 7 must also be made where the transaction is related to the commission of a terrorist activity financing offence.[16] A terrorist activity financing offence means an offence under section 83.02, 83.03 or 83.04 of the *Criminal Code* or an offence under section 83.12 of the *Criminal Code* arising

---

[14] These criminal offences are primarily those which involve activities such as drug dealing and which involve the obtaining of funds from an illegal activity and the subsequent act to hide that source of funds.

[15] See also the definitions at s. 462.3 of the *Criminal Code*.

[16] See also the provisions regarding threats to the security of Canada.

out of a contravention of section 83.08 of that Act. The *Anti-terrorism Act* added sections to the *Criminal Code*, as section 83.01 and following. Those sections define "terrorist activity" and create offences, particularly at sections 83.01 to 83.05. As an example, section 83.02 provides that everyone who directly or indirectly provides or collects property intending that it be used or knowing that it will be used in whole or in part to carry out a terrorist activity, or any other act or omission intended to cause death or serious bodily harm if the purpose is to intimidate the public or to compel government or international organizations to do or refrain from doing any act is guilty of an indictable offence. Terrorism offences under the *Criminal Code* relate to the obtaining of money or property and providing it for an activity which will meet the definition of "terrorist activity".

A "terrorist activity" is a violent act for the purpose of intimidation of the public or a government or international agency. The definition in the *Anti-terrorism Act* defines a terrorist activity as having the same meaning as in subsection 83.01(1) of the *Criminal Code*. A "terrorist activity financing offence", which is the direct equivalent to a money laundering offence for the purpose of the 2000 Act, means an offence under sections 83.02, 83.03 and 83.04 of the *Criminal Code* or an offence under section 83.12 of the *Criminal Code*. A terrorist activity also includes, in the sections amending the 2000 Act, threats to the security of Canada, which is given the same meaning as in section 2 of the *Canadian Security Intelligence Service Act*.[17] The *Anti-terrorism Act* amends the *Criminal Code* by adding a new Part after section 83, entitled "Part 11.1 Terrorism" and under section 83.01, defines the various activities which are deemed to be "terrorist activity". This provides for an extensive list of activities that will constitute terrorist activity.

The provisions of section 83 of the *Criminal Code* define the offences by description of the sanctioned activity and grant powers and sanctions under the *Criminal Code* in relation to the investigation and suppression of these activities. Terrorist activity is defined as an act or omission committed inside or outside Canada, under a specified list of statutes, including matters such as aircraft hijacking, crimes against internationally protected persons, the taking of hostages and similar. The definition also includes an act or omission inside or outside of Canada "in whole or in part for a political, religious or ideological purpose, objective or cause" with the "intention of intimidating the public, or a segment of the public with regard to its security, including its economic security, or compelling a person, a government or a domestic or an international organization to do or refrain from doing any act" and that intentionally causes death or serious bodily harm, or creates dangers that cause serious risk to health or safety, causes substantial damage or causes serious interference with or disruption of an essential service facility or system. Conspiracy, attempt or threats to commit any such acts are also included.

Once a reporting entity files a suspicious transaction report with FINTRAC, the reporting entity is expressly prohibited from disclosing that it has

---

[17]   R.S.C. 1985, c. C-23.

made such a report. Section 8 of the 2000 Act states that "no person or entity shall disclose that they have made a report under section 7 [of the 2000 Act], or disclose the contents of such a report, with the intent to prejudice a criminal investigation, whether or not a criminal investigation has begun." This provision prohibits reporting entities from telling their clients that they have "snitched" on them. As will be seen below, a violation of section 8 of the 2000 Act is an offence that can lead to up to two years of imprisonment.

It is impossible to predict the standards that the courts will set in dealing with the violation of section 8. The *Criminal Code* provides that a person cannot, at risk of criminal sanction, further criminal activity. The criminal activities which are contemplated by the relevant section of the *Criminal Code* includes money laundering. Accordingly, if a person suspects that there is a money laundering connection to a transaction, and reports it as a suspicious transaction, they have a simultaneous obligation under the *Criminal Code* not to further that suspected criminal activity.[18] In such an event, it would appear that the reporting entity should withdraw from any transaction involving that person, or those activities, to avoid *Criminal Code* sanctions. If the transaction is not completed with the involvement of the reporting entity, then the reporting entity does not need to file the suspicious transaction report, based on the comments in Guideline 2. Guideline 2 issued by FINTRAC, in Section 2.4 states that the requirement to report a suspicious transaction applies only when the transaction has been completed, if the reporting entity, or the client, decides not to complete transaction there is no obligation to report.

## C.  PRESCRIBED TRANSACTIONS – LARGE CASH TRANSACTIONS

Section 9(1) of the 2000 Act states that every reporting entity shall report to FINTRAC every *prescribed* financial transaction that occurs in the course of their activities, subject to certain exceptions described in the regulations.[19] "Prescribed" means that a regulation has listed the transaction as a type of transaction to be reported. If a transaction is "prescribed" as requiring reporting, it must be reported unless the transaction falls under an exception, in which case the reporting entities must keep a list of clients in respect of whom a report would have been required under section 9(1) of the 2000 Act were it not for the exception.[20] The exceptions that are included are reasonably limited, and include clients such as a retail client who would normally be receiving large volumes of cash in the ordinary course of their business. The prescribed transactions can and do vary by type of reporting entity.

Changes were made to the initial draft Large Cash Transaction section of the *Proceeds of Crime and Terrorist Financing Regulations*[21] to better reflect the nature of the business undertaken by reporting entities. Examples of this are the exclusion of charity casinos from the definition of "casino", and the

---

[18]  Section 43 of the 2000 Act.
[19]  Section 9(2) of the 2000 Act.
[20]  Section 9(3) of the 2000 Act.
[21]  SOR/2002-184.

inclusion of financial entities when they carry out various services for a person other than an account holder that would otherwise fall under the definition of another reporting entity such as a money services business. Clarification has also been included for accountants, resulting in reporting requirements being placed at the firm level, rather than the individual member of the firm. The purpose of the changes made in November of 2003 were to specifically deal with industry-specific matters of application which were identified in consultation with reporting entities. They were to clarify the application of specific regulatory requirements to industries, and in many instances to add exceptions and make compliance functional for certain of the industry sectors for reporting entities.

Also included in the regulations are provisions requiring the reporting of electronic funds transfers, focusing initially on SWIFT, the Society for Worldwide Interbank Financial Telecommunication, transfer systems, and thereafter other electronic transmission methods. Generally, similar concepts to those which were included in the Regulation for the reporting of large cash transactions have been extended to electronic funds transfers, and the similar amount of $10,000 or more has been included for the threshold for reporting of electronic funds transfers. The reporting of electronic funds transfers does include a more rapid reporting requirement, with electronic funds transfers being required to be reported in five working days, whereas a large cash transaction record is required to be sent within 30 days after any transaction occurring within 12 months after the regulation comes into force and 15 days after the transaction occurs once the one-year period expires.

The Large Cash Transaction portion of the *Proceeds of Crime and the Terrorist Financing Regulations* establishes a series of exceptions to the reporting requirements. These exceptions are generally specific to the reporting entity and to specific financial transactions. The most significant exception is the exception to reporting of transactions in circumstances where the funds otherwise required to be reported have been received from another reporting entity with the responsibility to report.

Section 12 of the Regulation establishes the reporting requirements for financial entities, and the sections following thereafter clarify these requirements and add those for other reporting entities. For a financial entity, the requirement is to report receipt from a client of an amount in cash of $10,000 or more, the sending out of Canada at the request of a client of an electronic funds transfer of $10,000 or more and the receipt from outside of Canada of an electronic funds transfer sent at the request of a client at $10,000 or more. The reporting requirement does not apply to a financial entity sending an electronic funds transfer to a person or entity in Canada, even if the final recipient is outside of Canada. There is a specific exemption where cash is received from another financial entity or public body. The details have been included as to the records which are required to be kept. Similar requirements have been included for other reporting entities, but in several instances deleting the requirement to report electronic funds transfers.

Reporting entities have been segregated by type of entity, and specific requirements have been included based upon the types of transaction and the nature of the customer that those reporting entities would be dealing with. Each type of reporting entity is specifically dealt with, with an outline of the transactions to which reporting requirements apply, the contents of the reports required, and the exceptions which are available for that reporting entity. Amendments were made to the Regulation in 2003 in order to tailor the reporting requirements to the nature of the financial transactions that would be undertaken by each reporting entity. As an example, only financial entities which directly initiate or receive an electronic transfer of funds need report these transactions and only casinos have the need for specifically tailored requirements relating to the sale of chips or the use of casino cheques. Expanded provisions have been included relating to a department or agency of the federal or provincial government where they accept deposit liabilities in the course of providing financial services to the public.

Section 50 of the Regulation includes a number of exceptions from reporting, primarily relating to retail businesses. These permit reporting entities to identify significant retailers, that they have dealt with for some time, where there is a routine deposit of cash in the course of business and except those deposits from large cash transaction reporting. These exemptions do not include businesses particularly prone to money laundering such as pawn brokering, or those engaged in retailing of luxury assets which have been identified as being frequent acquisitions using laundered funds.

The requirements for the ascertaining of identity of clients, commencing at section 53 of this regulation have been expanded from the initial draft, to clarify the nature of the required proof of identity, and to deal with matters such as minors and the settlors of an *inter vivos* trust, among others. Industry-specific requirements have been included for the ascertaining of identity, and these specifically relate to the nature and type of business being undertaken, and client dealing with that particular reporting entity. Exceptions to ascertaining identity are included at section 63, and generally relate to insurance industry product purchases, or to persons who are readily identifiable from other sources or from dealings with other reporting entities.

The measures for ascertaining identity at section 64 of the Regulation permit reliance on listed forms of identification, or the use of a cleared cheque by a reporting financial entity, confirming the focus of the regulations which permits reliance on identification, records or deposits by another reporting entity. The time for undertaking identification has also been specifically included at section 63 and the record keeping requirements arising from the review of identification at section 67.

The general requirements as to the nature of the reporting, such as requiring electronic filing, under section 4, the time limits for reporting set out at section 5, the requirement to determine whether a third party is involved in the transaction at section 7, and similar are applicable to all reporting entities. The specific reports for financial transactions and record keeping is under the sections relating to specified reporting entities; for example, at section 12 financial entities are required to report any receipt from a client of an amount in cash of $10,000 or more, the sending of an electronic funds transfer of $10,000 or more, the receipt of an electronic funds transfer of $10,000 or more. The records to be kept by financial entities are specified under section 14 and include the requirement to maintain records regarding cleared cheques. Other reporting entities require the reporting of only some specific transactions, as illustrated by the requirements for life insurance and securities dealers described later. For some reporting entities, the nature of the activities which imposes the requirement to report under the 2000 Act is limited, as it is with accountants, to financial intermediation. The intention is that the list of reporting requirements is intended to focus on the financial intermediation activities of the reporting entity.

The Large Cash Transaction section also has separate, by type of reporting entities, requirements as to the ascertaining of the identity of clients. These are again intended to provide for identification requirements which are specifically oriented to the relationship which would be usual between the reporting entity and the customer.

Section 1 of the *Proceeds of Crime (Money Laundering) and Terrorist Financing Regulations* defines cash as notes or bills used as currency and coins. Monetary instruments are defined in the regulation. Funds is defined to include negotiable instruments such as securities, travellers cheques, blank endorsed certified cheques, and similar. These are effectively cash or an equivalent to cash, being able to be used as currency by any person because it is not in registered form, it is freely negotiable and tenderable as a close equivalent to cash. These instruments are of such nature that the person presenting the instrument can, without proving ownership, or identification, other than that which may be required under the provisions of the 2000 Act, receive replacement proceeds consisting of cash or another monetary instrument, or use the instrument for the purchase of other assets.

To deal with the compliance burden, it was decided that most reporting entities have to report cash transactions only, thereby eliminating monetary instruments and electronic funds transfers which would be the more common way of dealing with larger value transfers. The use of cash only reporting places the majority of the burden on monitoring anything other than the proverbial "suitcase of cash" on the banking institutions, who more routinely deal with monetary instruments. Reporting requirements are generally limited to financial activities.

Some reporting entities are required only to report cash and others both cash and electronic funds transfers or foreign currency exchanges. In general, financial institutions will be required to report both cash and electronic funds transfers, while reporting entities which have limited financial intermediation, such as real estate agents and accountants, will be required to report cash receipts only.

The Large Cash Transaction section of the Regulation also prescribes the large cash transaction record keeping requirements. Section 1(2) of the Regulations defines a large cash transaction record as a record that indicates the receipt of $10,000 or more in cash in the course of a single transaction[22] and that contains the following information: (a) the name of each person or entity for whom the amount is deposited, or the name, address and principal business or occupation of the individual who gives the amount; (b) the nature of the transaction; (c) the time of the deposit, if it is made during business hours, or, if the deposit is made outside business hours, an indication that it was a night deposit; (d) the number and type of any account affected by the transaction, and the name of the person or entity who holds such account; (e) the purpose and details of the transaction; (f) whether the cash is received by armoured car, in person, by mail or in any other way; and (g) the amount and currency of the cash received. The requirements for the large cash transaction report must be read together with the industry-specific requirements of the regulation as to transactions that are to be reported, and the nature of the records which must also be made and kept by that reporting entity with regard to the customer and the transaction.

Compliance requirements with regard to electronic funds transfer are included under the Regulation. An electronic funds transfer means the transmission, through any electronic, magnetic or optical device, telephone instrument or computer of instructions for the transfer of funds, other than a transfer of funds within Canada. In the basic reporting requirements, set out on a reporting entity by reporting entity basis, some reporting entities are required to report cash only, while others are also required to report the sending of electronic funds transfers. Essentially those required to report and record electronic funds transfers are those which would actively engage in the electronic transaction.

Most reporting entities will be entitled to rely on the financial institutions that are the generators and recipients of monetary instruments or electronic transfer of funds to report. This is the concept behind requiring most reporting entities to report based upon cash receipts only. Section 52(1) of the Regulation states that a reporting entity does not have to keep or retain a separate large cash transaction record if the information that must be reported to FINTRAC is readily obtainable from other records that the reporting entity must keep or retain under the regulation.

Exceptions as to the reporting of a transaction are set out at section 50 of the Large Cash Transaction portion of the Regulation. These provisions state that a reporting entity is not required to report transactions in respect of the business of a client where specifically listed conditions are met. These

---

[22] Section 3 of the Regulations states that:

...two or more cash transactions or electronic funds transfers of less than $10,000 each that are made within 24 consecutive hours and that total $10,000 or more are considered to be a single transaction of $10,000 or more if

(a) where a person is required to keep a large cash transaction record or to report an electronic funds transfer in accordance with these Regulations, the person knows that the transactions or transfers are conducted by, or on behalf of, the same person or entity; and

(b) where an entity is required to keep a large cash transaction record or to report an electronic funds transfer in accordance with these Regulations, an employee or a senior officer of the entity knows that the transactions or transfers are conducted by, or on behalf of, the same person or entity.

exceptions generally relate to consistency with usual practice for the customer in the movement of funds and requires the maintenance of a list and periodic reporting of changes in practice. Exceptions are also set out in the regulation as to the need to ascertain identity of a customer.[23] These generally relate to the acquisition of life insurance and pension products.

Reporting entities who receive from a client, an amount *in cash* of $10,000 or more in the course of a "Single Transaction", a defined term under the regulation at section 3, must report it to FINTRAC according to the form set out in Schedule 2 of the Regulations.[24] A "Single Transaction" is defined in section 3 of the regulation which requires reporting entities to recognize and aggregate cash transactions made by a client in a 24 hour period. The standard for recognizing that more than one transaction has occurred to aggregate $10,000 or more, is the knowledge of an employee or senior officer that is relevant. The guidelines do not give clear indication as to the level of diligence which will be required. Obviously, with extensive multi-branch financial institutions, it can be difficult to determine that this has occurred, even with prompt recording and reporting. It would seem that FINTRAC should only expect detection if it would be detected in the normal course of the undertaking of business. Any other standard of expectation would result in a requirement to engage in investigation and inquiry beyond that which appears to be contemplated by the legislation.

## D.   CROSS-BORDER MOVEMENTS OF CURRENCY AND MONETARY INSTRUMENTS

Money laundering and terrorist activity is global in scope and much of the success of these activities depends on moving funds in and out of different countries. Therefore, section 12(1) of the 2000 Act mandates that persons and entities must report to a customs officer (not to FINTRAC) "the importation or exportation of currency or monetary instruments of a value equal to or greater than the prescribed amount.[25] The specific wording of section 12(1) is that the report must be made to an "officer", and section 12(3) specifically lists the persons who must report the import or export of currency or monetary instruments. Note should be made that section 12 includes more than the reporting of cash, and specifically includes the import and export of monetary instruments. An officer is defined as having the same meaning as in subsection 2(1) of the *Customs Act*, which means a person employed in the administration and enforcement of the *Customs Act* and includes any member of the Royal Canadian Mounted Police.

The dollar amount prescribed of cross-border movement of funds is currently $10,000.

---

[23]   Section 62.

[24]   Section 17 of the Regulations.

[25]   Section 2 of the Regulations states that the term "officer" is used in the Regulations as such term is defined in s. 2(1) of the *Customs Act*, which reads as follows: "'officer' means a person employed in the administration or enforcement of this Act, the *Customs Tariff* or the *Special Import Measures Act* and includes any member of the Royal Canadian Mounted Police."

Section 12 of the 2000 Act was amended by the *Anti-Terrorism Act*, providing a concept that reporting is required where currency or monetary instruments are imported or exported having a value *equal to* or greater than the stated amount, whereas previously the reference was only to *greater than*. The purpose of this, is somewhat unclear. It merely moves by naming a dollar amount, the dollar amount as to the requirement down by a dollar, or so, but may be intended to add certainty as to the cutoff point.

An amendment was made at section 12(3)(a), requiring currency or monetary instruments that are in the possession of a person arriving or departing, or which forms part of their baggage, must be reported as import or export and made by that person or in prescribed circumstances by the person in charge of the conveyance. The addition is the extension of responsibility to persons in charge of a conveyance to make a report for a passenger. It is difficult to determine what would be a suitable level or nature of declaration which should be obtained from passengers by the operators of buses, ships, railway or aircraft. It is not practical to require persons operating export or transportation systems to undertake more than a reasonable inquiry of their passengers, and it is downloading an unreasonable level of police type investigative powers if enquiry extends beyond that of a simple written declaration form. This is, however, an important change expanding the duties and responsibilities being placed on others to effectively do the job of identifying and reporting money laundering and terrorist activity.

An interesting amendment under the *Anti-Terrorism Act* is at section 22(1). Section 22(1) under the 2000 Act required that an officer who retained money or monetary instruments forfeited under the 2000 Act should without delay send them to the Minister of Public Works and Government Services. The expression "without delay" has now been deleted by the amendments under the *Anti-terrorism Act*. One amendment which has been included, likely to some practicable purpose, is the amendment to section 25, which extends the appeal period for a person whose currency or monetary instruments are seized from 30 days, under the 2000 Act, to 90 days after the date of seizure. A similar extension of the appeal period was made at section 32(1), extending the 60-day appeal period by third parties entitled to claim seized funds to 90 days after the seizure.

The 2000 Act requires that any currency or monetary instruments in the actual possession of a person coming to or leaving Canada, that is imported or exported by courier or mail, or that is on board a conveyance arriving or leaving Canada must be reported to an officer.[26] The person reporting must truthfully answer any questions the officer poses with respect to the information contained in the report and must, on request of the officer, present the currency or monetary instruments in question.[27] It is important to note that the requirement to report currency or monetary instruments applies to all importing or exporting persons and not just reporting entities.

---

[26] Section 12(3) of the 2000 Act.

[27] Section 12(4) of the 2000 Act.

## E.    ANTI-TERRORISM ACT AND THE PUBLIC SAFETY ACT, 2002[28]

The 2000 Act was amended by an *Act to amend the Criminal Code, the Official Secrets Act, the Canada Evidence Act, the Proceeds of Crime (Money Laundering) Act and other Acts, and to enact measures respecting the registration of charities, in order to combat terrorism*, pursuant to Bill C-36 which was assented to on December 18, 2001. Under Part IV of that legislation, entitled *"Proceeds of Crime (Money Laundering) Act*, various provisions were enacted to amend the *Proceeds of Crime (Money Laundering) Act.* Both the long and short title of the 2000 Act were amended, with the short title of the 2000 Act being amended to the *Proceeds of Crime (Money Laundering) and Terrorist Financing Act.*

Various changes were made to the money laundering legislation, most to include wherever the concept of a money laundering offence had been referenced in the 2000 Act, the additional reference of the offence of terrorist activity financing. In addition, there were a number of technical amendments made to several of the technical terms of the 2000 Act. These were not made to import the anti-terrorism provisions, but to deal with minor technical matters that had been identified in the review of the 2000 Act. As an example, the definition of "client" was amended in the latter part to delete the portion reading "and includes a person or an entity on whose behalf the person who engages in the transaction or activity is acting" with the phrase "and includes a person or an entity on whose behalf the person or the entity that engages in the transaction or activity is acting". Effectively, the reference to "or entity" had been excluded from the prior drafting. Similarly, "courier" was defined in the 2000 Act as having the same meaning as subsection 2(1) of the *Customs Act*, whereas under the amendments, "courier" is defined to mean a courier as defined by regulation under this legislation.

The primary purpose of the changes arising from the amendments under the anti-terrorism legislation was to add the concept that the financing of terrorist activities is an offence to be dealt with in similar manner to money laundering offences, for the purposes of the money laundering legislation. Terrorist activity financing offences are defined in the amendments, and specifically means an offence under section 83.02, 83.03 or 83.04 of the *Criminal Code*, or an offence under section 83.12 of the *Criminal Code* arising out of a contravention of section 83.08 of that Act. The offences referenced under the *Criminal Code* are amendments to the *Criminal Code* which were included in the *Anti-Terrorism Act*. The *Criminal Code* now, at section 83.02, provides that it is an offence for:

> Every one directly or indirectly, wilfully and without lawful justification or excuse, provides or collects property intending that it be used, or knowing that it will be used, in whole or in part, in order to carry out (a) an act or omission that constitutes an offence referred to in . . . the definition of "terrorist activity", or (b) any other act or omission intended to cause death or serious bodily harm to a civilian or to any other person not taking an active part in the hostilities in a situation of armed conflict, if the purpose of

---

[28]    Bill C-7 of the Third Session, 37th Parliament, 52-53 Elizabeth II, 2004.

that act or omission, by its nature or context, is to intimidate the public or to compel a government or an international organization to do or refrain from doing any act.

This is an indictable offence and is liable to prison for a term of not more than ten years.

"Terrorist activity" has an extensive definition under section 83.01, but basically includes acts or omissions committed inside or outside of Canada involving the seizure or the affecting of the safety of aircraft; crimes against protected persons; the taking of hostages; matters relating to nuclear material; violence relating to aircraft or maritime navigation (piracy); oil rigs; and matters relating to issues such as terrorist bombing and the international conventions on the financing of terrorism. Section 83.01 goes on to include at subparagraph (b) an act or omission in or outside of Canada that in whole or in part, for a political, religious or ideological purpose, objective or cause, is undertaken for the intention, "in whole or in part, of intimidating the public . . . with regard to its security, including its economic security, or compelling a person, a government or a domestic or an international organization to do or refrain from doing any act", and that intentionally causes death or serious bodily harm, or endangers or causes serious risk. Conspiracy, attempts or threats are also included under the offence.

Section 83.03 makes it an offence to directly or indirectly collect property, provide or invite a person to provide or make available financial or other related services intending that they be used or knowing that they will be used for the purpose of facilitating or carrying out a terrorist activity, or knowing that they will be used by or will benefit a terrorist group. "Terrorist group" is defined as "an entity that has as one of its purposes or activities facilitating or carrying out any terrorist activity or [is] a listed entity". Organizations that are identified as being suspected of carrying out political, religious or ideological terrorist activity are added to the published lists. The list created under this section is referred to in the discussion of compliance requirements as a list which must be periodically reviewed and updated. This is also an indictable offence, with the offender being liable to imprisonment. Section 83.04 makes it an offence for anyone to use "property, directly or indirectly, in whole or in part, for the purpose of facilitating or carrying out a terrorist activity" or being in possession of property intending that it be used or knowing it will be used for such purpose. This is again an indictable offence.

At section 83.05, the Governor-in-Council is given the power to establish a list on which it will place the entities which will then be constituted as listed entities known as terrorist groups. If the Governor-in-Council is satisfied there are reasonable grounds to believe that "the entity has knowingly carried out, attempted to carry out, participated in or facilitated a terrorist activity, or the entity is knowingly acting on behalf of, at the direction of or in association" with such an entity, it may be added to the list and will then be considered a "terrorist group". This list will provide guidance as to when a transaction will need to be reported; under these anti-terrorism amendments the sending of any money, or receipt of money, with or in association with one of the listed entities would require reporting. The definition of "terrorist" group is, however, broader than just a list of names and will require that some attention be made to the nature of entities other than those specifically listed. Simply relying upon the list published in the regulations as to what is a "terrorist group" will not be sufficient. The definition of terrorist group is not limited to the "list" but also includes an entity that has as one of its purposes or activities facilitating or carrying out terrorist activity and includes association with such groups. The requirement to determine if funding is being sent to such a group is very unclear at present.

The general basis for identifying that a transaction may relate to a terrorist activity financing offence will require being familiar with the list of named terrorist organizations (under section 83.05 of the *Criminal Code*) or countries known for the harbouring of terrorists and terrorist activity. Preparation of the list of named terrorist organizations which will fall under the definition of terrorist group will be under section 83.05 of the *Criminal Code*. The list is published in several government sources of information, readily available to the public, including the FINTRAC website. Reporting entities will need to become familiar with, and check periodic changes to, the list of terrorist groups for the purpose of complying with the anti-terrorism portions of the 2000 Act. There are fairly extensive provisions now included in the amendments to the *Criminal Code*, underlying the basis for the preparation of the list of terrorist groups. If the monies are destined for one of the listed terrorist organizations, or for a country which is listed as being a haven for terrorist activity on the FINTRAC site, then it is likely that a report will be needed because of the broad definitions in the *Criminal Code*.

The *Suspicious Transaction Reporting Regulations* provide for the requirement to report a terrorist activity financing offence at section 9.

There are significant amendments in the section of the *Anti-terrorism Act* dealing with the money laundering amendments. Section 7, the suspicious transactions reporting requirement, has been amended by adding to it the requirement to report every financial transaction that occurs in the course of their activities and in respect of which there are reasonable grounds to suspect that the transaction is related to a terrorist activity financing offence. In addition, section 7.1 has been added, which adds the additional requirement stating that any person or entity that is required to make a disclosure under the new section 83.1 of the *Criminal Code* shall also make a report on it to FINTRAC in the prescribed form and manner. Section 83.1 of the *Criminal Code* provides that:

> Every person in Canada and every Canadian outside Canada shall disclose forthwith to the Commissioner of the Royal Canadian Mounted Police and to the Director of the Canadian Security Intelligence Service (a) the existence of property in their possession or control that they know is owned or controlled by or on behalf of a terrorist group; and (b) information about a transaction or proposed transaction in respect of [that] property. . .

Section 9 of the 2000 Act, the general reporting section which requires every person or entity to report to the Centre in the prescribed form and manner every financial transaction that occurs in the course of their activities, was amended by adding section 9.1. Section 9.1 requires that every person or entity that is required to make a report to FINTRAC under any Act of parliament or any regulations shall make it in the form and manner prescribed under the 2000 Act for the report under that other act of parliament. Note should be made that reporting forms are largely dictated by FINTRAC electronic report requirements. These have been most recently changed on March 29, 2004.

The immunity section of the 2000 Act, section 10, which provides that no criminal or civil proceedings lie against a person or entity who makes a report under section 7 or 9 in good faith regarding their suspicions about money laundering or the financing of terrorist activities, has been amended, to add section 7.1. Interestingly, the amendment has not added section 9.1 to the list of protected reports and therefore the extent and scope of the civil and criminal immunity, difficult to determine at the best of times, because of the lack of constitutional authority and the uncertainty of the requirement for good faith, specifically will not extend to the reports which are required to be filed under Acts of parliament other than the 2000 Act. The purpose of this omission is unclear.

## F. REPORTING PROCEDURES

The regulations and guidelines contain the technical provisions regarding the form of reports required to be filed. At present, nine guidelines have been issued by FINTRAC, supplementing the requirements of the 2000 Act and the regulations under that Act. Guideline 1 is a backgrounder, which explains money laundering and terrorist financing, including alerting the reader to the international nature of the concern. This guideline provides an outline of legislative requirements, and an overview of FINTRAC's mandate and responsibilities, with a view to providing a simple, plain language, guide to the view of FINTRAC as to the extent and nature of the statutory provisions. Guideline 4 outlines the basic requirements for the implementation of an acceptable compliance regime.

Guideline 2, "Suspicious Transactions", includes the detailed guidance as to how to identify a suspicious transaction. It includes general and industry-specific indicators. These can be used to help identify, conduct, and evaluate transactions which may involve a necessity for a suspicious transaction report.

The remaining guidelines all outline the requirements for the submission of reports, and provide the details as to the method of transmission and the contents of those reports. This includes Guideline 3, "Submitting Suspicious Transaction Reports to FINTRAC", Guideline 5, "Submitting Terrorist Property Reports to FINTRAC", Guideline 6, "Record Keeping and Client Identification", Guideline 7, "Submitting Large Cash Transaction Reports to FINTRAC", Guideline 8, "Submitting Electronic Funds Transfer Reports to FINTRAC" and Guideline 9, "Submitting Alternative to Large Cash Transaction Reports to FINTRAC".

FINTRAC has stated it will assist reporting entities in organizing their responsibilities to complete electronic filing. The process of filing, the electronic requirements, and the confidentiality and security requirements of the browsers, are fully explained in the FINTRAC website materials. FINTRAC assists by providing downloadable browsers which will provide the appropriate level of security for the reporting process.

The electronic filing requirements are dictated initially by the nature of the reports. The report contents will dictate what must be provided, and the format for the provision of that information. The format for reports is included in the regulations and guideline information assists in completion. The detailed contents of the reports are included in the regulations by including the report form, and this is supplemented by the guideline information. A number of the fields in the reports require mandatory completion. Failure to fully complete the report can constitute an offence because it will not constitute an appropriate filing of the report. FINTRAC has indicated in publicly issued statements that they will, at first, assist reporting entities in ensuring the reports are fully and properly completed. It should, however, be anticipated that the requirements will necessitate that the records of the reporting entity include the information necessary to complete the reports, and that the assistance will relate only to the appropriate format, and technological requirements, for a completion of the filing. The filing requirements have been amended as of March 29, 2004 and reference should be had to the FINTRAC web site for a review of technical filing requirements.

# 5.

# ASCERTAINING IDENTITY

## A.    WHEN ONE MUST ASCERTAIN IDENTITY

An important aspect in the fight against money laundering is ensuring financial intermediaries are aware of who is conducting financial transactions and who is behind those persons. To that end, the Regulation, entitled *Proceeds of Crime (Money Laundering) and Terrorist Financing Regulations* ("the Regulation")[1] set out a number of "know your client" rules that require reporting entities to ascertain and verify the identity of their clients. The specific requirements differ somewhat by type of reporting entity.[2] However, generally, a reporting entity must ascertain the identity of any individual who conducts a transaction, on his or her own behalf or on behalf of a third party, for which a "client information record"[3] must be retained under section 19 of the Regulation. The same requirement is made in respect of clients that are corporations, or that are neither individuals nor corporations (*i.e.*, trusts or partnerships).[4] This requirement is waived if the person's identity was already ascertained by another reporting entity in respect of the same transaction or series of transactions, or if any of the record exceptions apply.[5]

The tone of the Regulation is such that it appears that the reporting entity can rely on information provided by the customer, without need to officially or extensively verify, but reporting entities will need to ensure that they are making appropriate enquiries. It is suggested that the paperwork initiating any transaction include specific inquiries of the customer as to their identity, which must be verified by a review of publicly issued identification documents, and to determine whether the transaction is being conducted on behalf of a third party. It does appear that the due diligence defences under the 2000 Act will protect the reporting entity which makes these inquiries, in written form, in the client application initiating the transaction. This list of required information can be taken from the compulsory elements of the required form of report. The compulsory information is clearly noted in the reporting forms included in the

---

[1]    SOR/2002-184.

[2]    See the "know your client" rules for financial entities and casinos at ss. 53 and 54 of the Regulation; persons engaged in foreign exchange dealing at s. 58 of the Regulation, money services businesses at s. 59 of the Regulation, casinos at s. 60 of the Regulation and government departments and agencies at s. 61 of the Regulation.

[3]    Section 1(2) of the Regulation defines "client information record" as a record that sets out the client's name, address and nature of the client's business or occupation.

[4]    Sections 56(3) and (4) of the Regulation.

[5]    In ss. 56(1) and (2) of the Regulation, provided by way of example only for the life insurance industry, the exceptions which are included in the proposed regulations generally will exclude from the need to record and report information regarding client, or transaction, where that information would be readily available in other records of the reporting entity, or would be available in the records of another reporting entity involved with that client and transaction.

regulations. The information obtained for record purposes must include the compulsory reporting information for all transactions to be reported.

The Regulation specifies the detail of the reporting requirements, including the nature and form of report, and the contents of the report, appending the report forms as schedules. The Regulation sets out certain limited exceptions from recording and reporting which would otherwise be required, generally relating to information which would be included in the records and reports of another reporting entity. The reporting entity must confirm the identity of every individual who is authorized to give instructions in respect of an account for which a record must be kept under section 23(1)[6] of the Regulation. The same requirement is made of clients that are corporations, or that are neither individuals nor corporations (*i.e.*, trusts or partnerships).[7] The requirement does not apply to: (a) corporate accounts where the securities dealer has already identified at least three individuals authorized to give instructions; (b) accounts opened for the deposit and sale of shares from a corporate demutualization, an employee stock purchase plan or the privatization of a Crown corporation; (c) registered plan accounts; and (d) accounts in the names of foreign affiliates of a financial entity.[8]

There are also client identification requirements under the Suspicious Transaction Report Regulation. The reporting entity will need to obtain the customer identification necessary to complete these reports, if and when required to be filed. Those reporting forms for suspicious transactions are appended as schedules to the *Suspicious Transaction Reporting Regulations*.[9]

---

[6] As an example, s. 23(1) of the Regulation requires every securities dealer to keep the following records:
(a) in respect of every account that the securities dealer opens, a signature card, an account operating agreement or an account application that
(i) bears the signature of the person who is authorized to give instructions in respect of the account, and
(ii) sets out the account number, where that person's identity was ascertained pursuant to subparagraph 64(1)(c)(ii);
(b) where the securities dealer opens an account in respect of a corporation, a copy of the part of official corporate records that contains any provision relating to the power to bind the corporation in respect of that account;
(c) where the securities dealer opens an account in the name of a person or of an entity other than a corporation, a record of the name and address and the nature of the principal business or occupation of the person or entity, as the case may be;
(d) every new account application, confirmation of purchase or sale, guarantee, trade authorization, power of attorney and joint account agreement, and all correspondence that pertains to the operation of accounts, that the securities dealer creates in the normal course of business; and
(e) a copy of every statement that the securities dealer sends to a client, if the information in the statement is not readily obtainable from other records that the securities dealer keeps and retains under these Regulations.
However, such reporting requirements with respect to paragraph (a) above "do not apply in respect of an account in the name of, or in respect of which instructions are authorized to be given by, a financial entity or securities dealer".
[7] Section 57 of the Regulation.
[8] Section 57(2) of the Regulation.
[9] SOR/2001-317.

To assure full compliance, the client records of a reporting entity should include all of the information required to be included in a report under each of the regulations. A specific question inquiring as to whether transactions have been, or will be, undertaken on behalf of third parties must be included. It does seem that written inquiry including all of the required information with a written and signed response by the customer, and a review of publicly issued identification, will suffice for satisfying the regulation's "know-your-client" rules and to have the necessary information to file the suspicious transaction or large cash transaction reports.

Note should be made that there are differences in the specifics for compliance dependent upon the industry sector, which is differentiated by the type of reporting entity.

There are exceptions to the requirement to obtain and maintain full client information for each transaction. The exceptions are identified on a reporting entity basis, such that specific reporting entities are excluded from the requirement to provide certain of the specified information. In addition, there are general exceptions included in the Regulation at section 50, as to the nature of the transaction and section 62 as to ascertaining identity of customers. They generally relate to transactions where the information would already be held, or where it would have been obtained and maintained, by another reporting entity. As an example, a securities dealer does not have to ascertain the identity of an individual who is authorized to give instructions in respect of an account that is opened for the sale of mutual funds where there are reasonable grounds to believe that that individual's identity has already been ascertained by another securities dealer in respect of the same transaction.[10] The same is true with respect to any individual who already has an account with the securities dealer or if there are reasonable grounds to believe that the account holder is a public body or a corporation with minimum net assets of $75,000,000 and whose shares are traded on a Canadian Stock Exchange, the New York Stock Exchange, the NASDAQ Market or the American Stock Exchange.[11]

An effective compliance regime will require that every employee who initiates a client relationship, or an individual transaction relationship, is aware of the requirement to obtain the necessary information for obtaining of information, maintenance of records and the filing of the reports under the 2000 Act. This will include the information required in the suspicious transaction reports, as well as those required for the large cash transaction reporting requirements. The required client and transaction information is clearly outlined in the schedules to the Regulation and the *Suspicious Transaction Reporting Regulations*. The most effective compliance regime will require that a transaction cannot be initiated unless the information has been obtained, recorded, and the back up verifications obtained. Instructions should specifically be given, together with an electronic or paper based information questionnaire, that the information must be obtained prior to undertaking a transaction which

---

[10] Section 56(5) of the Regulation.
[11] Section 62(2) of the Regulation.

could give rise to a need to report a suspicious transaction or a large cash transaction. The list of required information can be readily prepared from the information required to be obtained and reported in the regulations, which outlines both the required client information, third party information, and transaction information.

Requirements to ascertain identity of customers are included at section 53, but are subject to the exceptions at section 62 of the Regulation. Section 53 of the Regulation specifically provides that every person or entity that is required to keep and retain a large cash transaction record must ascertain the identity of the individual with whom they conduct a transaction. This supplements the requirements at section 8 of the Regulation which requires that those persons take reasonable measures to determine whether the individual is acting on behalf of a third party. Specific requirements are then included on a reporting entity basis, setting out the specifics applicable to each of the types of reporting entities. The *Suspicious Transaction Reporting Regulations* at section 13 lists the prescribed information as to the client, importer, exporter, and as to the financial transaction. Section 13(a)(vii) requires that the prescribed information include "the name and address of any person or entity on whose behalf the financial transaction, importation or exportation is conducted". Part E of the required suspicious transactions reporting form includes the information relating to a person on whose behalf a transaction is conducted, although Part E is not an asterisked portion of the report, that is, it is not a mandatory field to be completed, it will require that reasonable diligence be undertaken to obtain the necessary information. As a consequence, it is likely that a written inquiry, and response, as to whether the transaction is being undertaken on behalf of a third party will be needed to evidence the reasonable effort to obtain the information.

The *Proceeds of Crime (Money Laundering) and Terrorist Financing Regulations* also requires reporting entities to receive reliable evidence indicating whether or not an individual is acting on behalf of a third party. If the person is determined to be acting on behalf of a third party, the reporting entity must obtain and retain a statement, signed by the individual conducting the transaction, that sets out the third party's name, address and the nature of his, her or its principal business or occupation, and the nature of the relationship between the third party and the individual who signs the statement.[12] Where the reporting entity is advised that the individual is not acting on behalf of a third party, it should obtain a written statement from the individual stating that the individual is not acting on behalf of a third party.[13]

The identification of third parties is specifically required when a reporting entity is required to keep a signature card or an account operating agreement in respect of an account or a client information record.[14] It appears that, throughout the requirements for identification of third party participation, a direct question in writing to the person dealing with the reporting entity, and a written response by that person, will suffice for inquiry. Further investigation does not appear to

---

[12] Section 8(2) of the Regulation.
[13] Section 8(3) of the Regulation.
[14] Sections 9 and 10 of the Regulation, respectively.

be merited or required if the question is openly stated in the appropriate account opening or similar form and signed by the customer.

## B.    HOW ONE MUST ASCERTAIN IDENTITY

The Regulation prescribes not only when but also how a client's identity must be ascertained. This is initially to be done by referring to an individual's birth certificate, driver's licence, provincial health insurance card, passport or any similar record, other than the individual's social insurance card.[15] Where the individual is not physically present when the client information record is created, that person's identity may be ascertained by confirming that a cheque drawn by the individual on an account at a financial entity has been cleared or that the individual holds an account in the individual's name with a financial entity.[16] The Regulation also prescribes the information about an individual that must be recorded (*i.e.*, date of birth or account number of financial entity on which cheque was drawn).[17]

Specific information is required to be verified with regard to corporations and partnerships, this is outlined in detail in the Regulation. These generally require review of the publicly issued or registered information included in the appropriate public record in the jurisdiction of incorporation or formation. This information will vary dependent upon the jurisdiction, but will generally require the filing maintained in the public recording office for the recording of business names, partnerships, limited partnerships or corporations.

For corporations, the information can be verified from a public record which will permit confirmation of the incorporation, including the ability to obtain a copy of the incorporation documents, and the information filed with regard to the directors and officers.

Other entities may be registered under a public registry system, or in some instances can be formed without registration. Where an entity is formed without registration, such as a general partnership which does not require registration for the entity to be created, then the individual information as to each of the participants would appear to be required.

The legislation, even when read in the context of the Regulation and FINTRAC guidelines, does not provide an objective, statutorily dictated, level of diligence with regard to the review of presented identification and information. It would, however, appear that the standards to be followed by reporting entities must be considered in the context of the legislative intent, and the specific statements made that this is not intended to be criminal legislation. It has not been the stated intent of the legislation, or of FINTRAC in overseeing compliance with the legislation, that reporting entities are to become the equivalent to highly trained police investigators. The intention should be that reporting entities will have trained their employees, and have established their compliance systems, so as to be able to detect that a financial transaction is

---

[15]    Sections 64(1)(b) and 64(1)(c) of the Regulation.

[16]    *Ibid.*

[17]    Section 67 of the Regulation.

outside of the commercial norm, and that there is apparent reason for suspicion. This does not require that investigations be taken outside of the specific inquiries required to obtain the necessary filing information and the application of industry knowledge to identify that the transaction does not appear usual or normal.

The existence, name and address of a corporation and the name of its directors must be ascertained by referring to its certificate of corporate status and other required corporate public findings.[18] Similarly, the existence of a person that is neither an individual nor a corporation would be ascertained by referring to the partnership agreement, articles of association or other similar record that proves its existence.[19] In both cases, the records may be in paper or electronic form provided that they are obtained from a source that is accessible to the public. This will require that a record, electronic or paper, be made of the inquiry, and that inquiry be made, beyond the information provided by the customer, of the public records. It would appear that it is not advisable to simply accept a photocopy of a partnership agreement or articles of incorporation, unless they are received from a reliable source, such as legal counsel. It would appear that access to the public records should be made and a copy of the public recording obtained and compared to that provided.

The sources for client information that are considered to be accessible to the public are those where either personal attendance, written inquiry or computer access would provide information with regard to that entity from records maintained by public officials. These would include the corporate profile reports for Canadian corporations now available online for both federal and provincial corporations. Similar inquiries would be available for partnerships, limited liability partnerships and limited partnerships, although the information included in the public record is more limited. For entities where only a partial public recording is available, such as registration under the *Business Names Act* or *Partnerships Act*, further inquiries should be made in many instances beyond that of the public record. For example, in the case of partnerships, this would include a written statement as to the legal relationship and the full listing of the participants in the legal relationship.

---

[18] Section 65(1) of the Regulation.
[19] Section 66(1) of the Regulation.

# 6.

# RECORD KEEPING REQUIREMENTS

The *Proceeds of Crime (Money Laundering) and Terrorist Financing Regulations*[1] ("the Regulation") provides the detailed requirements for the reporting of financial transactions, and the record keeping required in connection with that record keeping. This generally requires the reporting of large cash transactions and the electronic transfer of funds over the amount of $10,000. It also sets out the requirements for ascertaining identity, the measures for ascertaining identity and the retention of records. Record keeping is also required to supplement the requirements for reporting as to suspicious transactions and the cross-border movement of currency; reference should be made to those regulations to ensure complete information is obtained to file required reports and necessary records are kept. In each instance where a report is required to be made, records must be maintained, including at least the information required to be included in the report, as well as the backup to that information.

The regulations, guidelines, and regulatory impact commentaries clearly recognize that different reporting entities will have different relationships with their clients and will engage in different types of transactions. As a consequence, slightly different requirements have been imposed for each of the different entities that are required to report. It will be necessary for reporting entities to review the regulations, and the guidelines, to ensure that the reporting requirements and the information required for their reporting requirements have been identified and made part of the reports and record keeping of the entity.[2]

The regulations set out the detailed contents of the various reports to be filed, by specifying the report form and content. These reports will require mandatory completion of several of the fields in the report. The balance will require at least reasonable diligence as to the requested information. Accordingly, it will be necessary to ensure that the reporting entities' client and transaction information records obtain and record the necessary information required. The guidelines include a more detailed description of the report contents by type of reporting entity.

The Regulation also includes technical provisions regarding *how* records should be kept. A record may be kept in machine-readable form or in an electronic form, provided that a paper copy can be readily produced from either source and, in the case of a copy in an electronic form, if an electronic signature of the individual who must sign the record is retained.[3] The detail as to

---

[1]   SOR/2002-184.

[2]   The reports have specific mandatory fields for reported information — the report is incomplete if that information is not provided. The mandatory verification information must also be in the reporting entity records.

[3]   Section 68 of the Regulation.

communication with FINTRAC, is set out in the guidelines, for ease of amendment by FINTRAC, as experience is gained with the reporting regime. Measures for ascertaining identity and for the retention of records are set out in the Regulation at sections 64 to 67. These will need to be reviewed, and the detailed requirements set out in that portion of the regulations incorporated into the inquiries and record keeping for the reporting entities.

Records must be retained for at least five years, except in certain cases of employment or other contractual relationships, and every record should be retained in such a way that it can be provided to an authorized person within 30 days after a request is made to examine it.[4] The authorized persons for the purposes of these sections are the representatives of FINTRAC, which has a right to demand access to the records without search warrant, under the provisions of the 2000 Act.[5] These rights of FINTRAC are explained later in this commentary under the heading Search and Seizure. For the purposes of record keeping, it is important to ensure that records, and record retention of the reporting entity not only comply with the strict requirements of the regulation, and preferably the guidelines, but are also accessible in the manner required.

Guideline 4,[6] outlining compliance regime, gives the general requirements for reporting and record keeping. Following the minimum requirements of Guideline 4 as to the compliance regime will provide the basics of the record keeping and retention. Record retention is also specifically dealt with in Part 6 of the Regulation, at sections 68 to 70. This portion of the Regulation specifies the manner in which a record must be kept, and specifically requires that it be available for examination as provided in the 2000 Act.

---

[4]  Section 69 of the Regulation.

[5]  S.C. 2000, c. 17.

[6]  FINTRAC, *Guideline 4: Implementation of a Compliance Regime* (November 2003), available online at http://www.fintrac.gc.ca/publications/guide/guide_e.asp.

# 7.

# SEARCH AND SEIZURE

## A.  CUSTOMS OFFICERS

Part 2 of the 2000 Act[1] gives "officers" broad search and seizure powers. An "officer", as defined in section 2(1) of the *Customs Act*, may search any person who has arrived in Canada, or who is about to leave Canada, if the officer suspects on reasonable grounds that the person has in his or her possession $10,000 or more in currency or monetary instruments that has not been reported.[2] He or she may also search any conveyance or baggage and even open any mail that weighs over 30 grams, if he or she reasonably suspects that there may be $10,000 or more in currency or monetary instruments contained therein.[3] In addition, an officer may request and receive from Canada Post any mail being sent from Canada to a foreign country, regardless of weight, that contains or is suspected to contain $10,000 or more in currency or monetary instruments, with no notice to the sender.[4] The 2000 Act deems mail while held by the officer as being mail in the course of the post, and deems currency or monetary instruments that are in excess of a prescribed amount to be unmailable material, under section 21(5). This appears to be an attempt to avoid the civil liberties issues as to interference with the mail; several commentators have raised constitutional questions about the effectiveness of this provision. To date, a constitutional challenge has not been launched on this issue.

The *Anti-terrorism Act*[5] amendments included as an additional suspected offence, which gives rise to these search and seizure powers, the financing of terrorist activity. Accordingly, all of the powers given to customs officers will be available regardless of whether the offence suspected is money laundering or terrorist activity financing.

In addition, the general search powers under section 62 of the 2000 Act grants similar powers with respect to other communications to FINTRAC for purposes of investigating and enforcing Part 1 obligations. FINTRAC has the power to demand, seize and review communications of all sorts where they have any grounds to believe that there may be failure to comply with Part 1. Officers and FINTRAC both have these search and seizure powers without the usual prior supervision of the courts. Only reasonable grounds to suspect are required on the part of officers or FINTRAC to exercise these rights. This is very considerably less, on its face, than the standards which would be required to obtain a search warrant. The checks and balance of search warrant procedures

---

[1]  S.C. 2000, c. 17.
[2]  Section 15(1) of the 2000 Act.
[3]  Sections 16(1) and 17(1) of the 2000 Act.
[4]  Section 21(1) of the 2000 Act.
[5]  S.C. 2000, c. 41.

are not required to be followed because the 2000 Act provides criminal investigative powers, and essentially criminal sanctions for breach of statute, without the counterbalancing of the criminal law protections that have evolved under the *Criminal Code*[6] and in legislation protecting civil rights.

The *Cross Border Currency and Monetary Instruments Reporting Regulations*,[7] set out reporting circumstances, reporting requirements, including the officer to whom the report is to be made and alternatives for delivery of the report where the office is closed. The officer must give notice in the prescribed manner before retaining the currency or monetary instruments.

Under the 2000 Act, an officer may retain any currency or monetary instruments for a prescribed period if a person or entity indicates that they have such currency or monetary instruments to report, but that the report has not yet been completed.[8] The officer may also retain currency or monetary instruments that are imported or exported by courier or in the mail, as long as he or she sends notice to the exporter, or if the exporter's address is not known, to the importer.[9] The currency or monetary instruments may no longer be retained once the officer is satisfied that they have been reported under the 2000 Act or if the importer or exporter advises the customs officer that they will not proceed with the importation or exportation.[10] The retained currency or monetary instruments are forfeited to the government at the end of the period for retention specified in the notice.[11] Section 14(5) of the 2000 Act provides that currency or monetary instruments that are retained by an officer are subject to forfeiture at the end of the period under subsection (1). Subsection (1) does not provide for a period of retention, it states that the officer may after giving notice in the prescribed manner retain the currency for the prescribed period, which requires reference to the then current regulation.

Officers have been given the power to seize and hold as forfeit any currency or monetary instruments, if they believe on reasonable grounds that the reporting requirements under Part 2 have been contravened.[12] Any currency or monetary instrument seized is forfeited to the government, and such forfeiture is final and not subject to review, except for the appeal procedures described in the 2000 Act.[13] Effectively, this means that the penalty is imposed, based upon the belief of an officer as to reasonable grounds, with an appeal right on unspecified grounds, with uncertain parameters as to the basis for decision, to the government agency to which currency or monetary instruments would be forfeited. There is no standard which indicates the basis upon which an appeal might be accepted, but, presumably, it would remain the reasonable grounds required for the officer's power to seize. This effectively means that penalties

---

[6]   R.S.C. 1985, c. C-46.
[7]   SOR/2002-412.
[8]   Section 14(1) of the 2000 Act.
[9]   Section 14(2) of the 2000 Act.
[10]  Section 14(3) of the 2000 Act.
[11]  Section 14(5) of the 2000 Act.
[12]  Section 18 of the 2000 Act.
[13]  Sections 23 and 24 of the 2000 Act.

usually imposed on criminals are being imposed without the protection of the usual criminal standards of proof or process.

The appeal process provides that a person from whom currency or monetary instruments are seized, or its lawful owner, may within 90 days after the date of the seizure request a decision of the Minister of Finance to determine whether reporting requirements were contravened.[14] The person making the request may furnish any evidence they consider relevant to the matter. If the Minister decides that reporting requirements were not contravened, the currency or monetary instruments along with any penalty that was paid or an amount of money equal to their value at the time of seizure shall be returned.[15] The requesting party may appeal any decision of the Minister, provided this step is taken within 90 days after being notified of the Minister's decision, to the Federal Court.[16] Section 30 of the 2000 Act says that a person who requested the decision of the Minister may within 90 days after being notified of the decision appeal the decision by way of action in the Federal Court. This appears to be the only judicial review for available seizure and forfeiture taken under the 2000 Act. The *Federal Courts Act* and the *Federal Court Rules* will apply to these actions, unless it is governed by special rules made in respect of such actions. No special rules have been announced or made to date. This again would mean that civil law level standards would be imposed to the determination of guilt or innocence, which would dictate forfeiture and nonforfeiture, rather than the criminal standards of proof beyond a reasonable doubt.

The 2000 Act also describes the procedures to be followed if a third party claims an interest, as owner, in any currency or monetary instruments that were seized. Any such third person may, within 90 days after the seizure, apply by notice in writing to the court for an order under section 33 of the 2000 Act.[17] Section 33 of the 2000 Act states that if a court, on hearing of an application, is satisfied that: (a) the applicant acquired the interests in good faith before the contravention; (b) the applicant is innocent of any complicity in the contravention; and (c) the applicant exercised all reasonable care to ensure that any person permitted to obtain possession of the currency or monetary instruments seized would report them in accordance with section 12(1) of the 2000 Act, then the applicant is entitled to an order declaring that their interest is not affected by the seizure and declaring the nature and extent of their interest at the time of the contravention. If an order is made under section 33 of the 2000 Act, the currency or monetary instruments are returned to the applicant.[18] Section 35 of the 2000 Act which dictates the return of the currency or monetary instruments to the applicant states that, upon a final order under section 33 or 34, the Minister of Public Works and Government Services must give the currency or monetary instruments to the person. It does not provide for the payment of

---

[14] Section 25 of the 2000 Act.
[15] Section 28 of the 2000 Act.
[16] Section 30 of the 2000 Act.
[17] Section 32(1) of the 2000 Act.
[18] Section 35(1) of the 2000 Act.

any interest, and does not provide for a time period for the return of the currency or instruments.

## B.    FINTRAC'S SEARCH POWERS

FINTRAC has broad search powers under the 2000 Act. Section 62(1) of the 2000 Act provides that a person authorized by the director of FINTRAC may, from time to time, examine the records and inquire into the business and affairs of a reporting entity for the purpose of insuring compliance with Part 1 of the 2000 Act. Additionally, FINTRAC has powers to enter any premises (other than a dwelling house) in which the authorized person believes, on reasonable grounds, that there are relevant records without a search warrant. That person authorized by FINTRAC may also use any computer system in the premises and print out any record for examination or copying. The owner or person in charge of the premises must provide all reasonable assistance and furnish any information that the authorized person may reasonably require.[19] An authorized person may also enter a dwelling house with the consent of the occupant or under the authority of a warrant.[20] Again, these search powers will be available to FINTRAC, regardless of whether the offence under consideration is a money laundering offence or the financing of terrorist activity.

The consequence of these provisions is that FINTRAC can demand review and can advise the criminal authorities regarding the existence of the records required to be kept under the 2000 Act. These records are accessible to FINTRAC without a search warrant, must be recoverable in form, and must be turned over upon request. FINTRAC will be providing only the "designated information" directly to law enforcement agencies and doing so outside of the protections of criminal law, and further access to information will require the police to obtain usual course search warrants. The amendments under the *Anti-terrorism Act* expand the ability of FINTRAC to release information to other agencies. Both the nature of the information which can be released, and the entities to which the information can be released appear to be broadened by the wording of the *Anti-terrorism Act* amendments and were further broadened by the *Public Safety Act*. *The Public Safety Act, 2002*[21] has specifically expanded FINTRAC's access to other government databases, and has expanded FINTRAC's requirement to provide reports to other law enforcement agencies with regard to compliance.

## C.    RELEASE OF INFORMATION

The Director reports to the Minister and shall keep him or her informed of any matter that could materially affect public policy or the strategic direction of FINTRAC, and any other matter that the Minister considers necessary. The Director is to disclose to the Minister any information that the Minister

---

[19]   Section 62(2) of the 2000 Act.
[20]   Section 63(1) of the 2000 Act.
[21]   Bill C-7 of the Third Session, 37th Parliament, 52-53 Elizabeth II, 2004.

considers relevant for the purpose of carrying out his or her duties under the 2000 Act.[22] However, the Director may not disclose any information that would directly or indirectly identify an individual who provided FINTRAC with a report or information, or a person or entity about whom a report or information was provided.[23] This is one of the few protections for the information gathered, and provides the only basic guideline as to what may or may not be disclosed by the Director to the Minister. The section 53 limitation on the disclosure of information regarding individuals is strictly with regard to the information to be provided to the Minister. There is no similar protection under section 55, which limits disclosure by FINTRAC to police and similar authorities, that goes on at section 55(3) to permit the disclosure of information where it is relevant to the investigation or prosecution of a money laundering offence, without such protection. There is a definition of the designated information which may be released in section 55(7), which includes the name of the client or importer or exporter, the name and address of the place of business where the transaction occurred, the amount and type of currency or monetary instruments, the transaction number and account number and similar information.

Section 100 of the *Public Safety Act, 2002* amends paragraph 54(b) of the 2000 Act by providing that FINTRAC may collect information considered relevant to money laundering activities or the financing of terrorist activities and that is publicly available, including from commercially available databases or from databases maintained by the federal or provincial governments for purposes related to law enforcement or national security. This access requires that an agreement has been entered into between the reporting agencies and FINTRAC. Section 65 of the 2000 Act has been amended by adding a statement that FINTRAC may disclose to or receive from any agency or body that regulates or supervises a reporting entity information relating to compliance. The restriction is that the information may only be used for purposes relating to compliance with the 2000 Act.

Subsection 55(1) of the 2000 Act was amended in the *Anti-Terrorism Act* by amending the references to the exceptions from the restrictions on FINTRAC as to disclosing information. Effectively, section 55(1) in its introductory language gives a specific list of exceptions to the restrictions on FINTRAC disclosing the information which has been gathered. The exceptions under the 2000 Act are now only in subsection 55(3). Under the amendment, only subsection (3) remain of the initial list, but this is only because of the movement of the disclosure to international organizations to section 56(1), from former sections 55(4) and (5). As a result, there is no practicable change, in the ability of FINTRAC to disclose the information to police forces and international institutions or agencies. Section 52 remains as an exception to the protection of confidentiality of information in that it gives FINTRAC the very broad requirement to disclose information to the Minister. The restrictions on disclosure by the Minister in section 53 are only that a director does not disclose

---

[22]  Section 52 of the 2000 Act.
[23]  Section 53 of the 2000 Act.

information that would directly or indirectly identify an individual who provided a report or a person or entity about whom a report was provided. All other information can be released by the Minister.

The remaining references to subsection 58(1), section 65, and subsection 12(1) of the *Privacy Act*[24] remain. Section 58(1) provides that FINTRAC can inform the persons who make a report about the steps or measures being taken as a consequence of that report. Section 65 permits FINTRAC to disclose to law enforcement agencies information under section 62 or 63. Sections 62 and 63 grant powers to FINTRAC to attend at premises, examine records, and inquire into the business and affairs of reporting entities, with a view to considering compliance. FINTRAC is therefore able to use its ability to search without warrant, obtain information about compliance, and report that to police authorities, who can then push forward criminal investigations, without usual criminal law protections as to the initial information released. Subsection 12(1) of the *Privacy Act* gives a person the right to access to their own personal information. The amendments made under the *Anti-terrorism Act* change only the references from subsections 52(4) and (5) to sections 55.1 and 56.1. Section 55.1 permits FINTRAC to release information to the Canadian Security Intelligence Service where it has reasonable grounds to suspect that the designated information will be relevant to threats to the security of Canada. Threats to the security of Canada are as defined under the *Canadian Security Intelligence Service Act*. Information which can be released is similar to the designated information which was permitted to be released under the provisions of section 55(7) in the 2000 Act. Section 55(1) permits the disclosure of the "designated information" to an institution or agency of a foreign state or international organization, effectively replacing section 55(4) and 55(5). The specific expansion is the ability to disclose to CSIS the matters of concern to the security of Canada, the remainder is simply a restatement of the prior included clauses.

Access to the records maintained by, and the requirement to provide information to, other regulatory entities in Canada has been imposed by the terms of the *Public Safety Act, 2002*. For the purpose of monitoring and ensuring compliance with the 2000 Act, FINTRAC may report to other regulatory bodies in Canada, and may access the databases maintained by those entities.

---

[24] R.S.C. 1985, c. P.21.

# 8.

# OFFENCES

Part 5 of the 2000 Act[1] contains a list of offences and the punishment for these offences. Those offences and punishment provisions are basically criminal in nature. The offences under the 2000 Act provide for both summary and indictable offence sanctions, involving both fines and imprisonment.[2] A summary conviction offence is a lesser offence and generally involves a fine or imprisonment which would be less than a two-year imprisonment in a higher security prison. An indictable offence is considered a more serious offence and has higher levels of fines and longer periods of imprisonment, as well as incarceration under the federal penal system.

Section 74 of the 2000 Act states that a person who knowingly contravenes, among other things, those provisions relating to the keeping and retaining of records and the truthful answering of questions that an officer asks in respect of currency or monetary instruments is guilty of an offence and liable:

> (a) on summary conviction to a fine of not more than $50,000 or to imprisonment for a term of not more than six months, or to both; or (b) on conviction on indictment, to a fine of not more than $500,000 or to imprisonment for a term of not more than five years, or to both.

These sanctions may be supplemented by the sanctions which could be imposed on reporting entities, and the employees of reporting entities, who are convicted under the 2000 Act if those persons operate in a regulated industry, as is the case with most reporting entities. Without the protection of criminal law standards for conviction, persons not only will face the fines and penalties of the 2000 Act, but also the possibility of losing their livelihood in regulated industries which may prevent the continued participation of a person who has been convicted of an indictable offence. Reporting entities, and the employees of reporting entities, will need to be concerned about the possibility of a recorded indictable offence which may prevent their continued participation in their industry.

Section 75(1) of the 2000 Act states that every person or entity that knowingly contravenes the reporting requirements under section 7 of the 2000 Act (suspicious transactions) is guilty of an offence and liable:

> (a) on summary conviction, (i) for a first offence, to a fine of not more than $500,000 or to imprisonment for a term of not more than six months, or to both, and (ii) for a subsequent offence to a fine of not more than $1,000,000 or to imprisonment for a term not more than 1 year, or to both; or (b) on conviction on indictment, to a fine of $2,000,000 or to imprisonment for a term of not more than five years, or to both.

Section 75(2) of the 2000 Act is a safe-harbour provision for employees, which prevents them from being convicted of an offence under section 75(1) of

---

[1] S.C. 2000, c. 17.
[2] See ss. 74 to 77 of the 2000 Act.

the 2000 Act for any transaction that they report to a superior. This section simply provides that no employee will be convicted of the offence of failing to provide a report under section 7, suspicious transactions reporting, if they reported the transaction to their superior.

Sections 74 and 75 of the 2000 Act both require knowing contravention for liability to attach. If general criminal law is applied to the 2000 Act for the interpretation of these sanctions and offences, then a knowing contravention will require a reasonably high standard of proof on the part of the prosecuting authorities. A knowing contravention would require, at the least, a blatant disregard for the duties or responsibilities amounting to negligence or wilful blindness.

Section 76 of the 2000 Act states that every person or entity that contravenes section 8 of the 2000 Act (prohibiting notification to the customer that a report has been made):[3]

> (a) is guilty of an offence punishable on summary conviction; or (b) is guilty of an indictable offence and liable to imprisonment for a term of not more than two years.

The offence under section 76 of disclosing that a report has been made or the contents of such a report does not require knowledge of the offence and it would appear that any disclosure could lead to conviction of the offence and the imposition of sanctions.

Section 77(1) of the 2000 Act states that every person or entity that contravenes subsection 9(1), the requirement to report prescribed financial transactions, those being the financial transactions which are prescribed in regulation or subsection 9(3), being the section requiring the maintenance of records regarding their clients and transactions where a report may not be required but only because of exceptions under the regulation,[4] "is guilty of an offence and liable on summary conviction to a fine of not more that $500,000 for a first offence and of not more than $1,000,000 for each subsequent offence". Sections 76 and 77 are two strict liability sections, which do not require knowledge of the offence for conviction.

Sections 76 and 77 have no required "knowingly" standard. As a result, any failure to comply with sections 8 and 9 will be an offence, whether known to the person committing the offence or not. This could be a problem to directors and officers of large corporations, who often may not know about a failure to report but who would still be liable under sections 76 and 77. A strict liability

---

[3]  Section 8 of the 2000 Act states "that no person or entity shall disclose that they have made a report under section 7, or disclose the contents of such a report, with the intent to prejudice a criminal investigation, whether or not a criminal investigation has begun."

[4]  Section 3(1) of the 2000 Act states that every person or entity shall report to FINTRAC, in the prescribed form and manner every financial transaction that occurs in the course of activities. Section 9(3) of the 2000 Act states:

> Every person or entity shall maintain a list, in prescribed form and manner, of their clients in respect of whom a report would have been required under subsection 1 were it not for subsection 2 [an exempting provision]. However, a person or an entity may choose to report a client's transactions under subsection (1) instead of maintaining the list in respect of that client.

offence is one where the person who is convicted need not have knowledge of
the commission of the offence, and may not have had any intent to contravene
the statute, that is, they can be convicted even if the contravention is wholly
innocent. A failure to be aware of the requirements of the 2000 Act, or failure to
recognize the application of the 2000 Act to the circumstances, will provide no
defence under these sections.

Section 78 of the 2000 Act provides that officers and directors who
directed, authorized, assented to, acquiesced in or participated in an offence are
liable even if the reporting entity of which they are an officer or director is not
prosecuted or convicted. The 2000 Act provides for these sanctions to ensure
that the directing minds of an entity are personally responsible. While it appears
that the extension to officers and directors primarily requires active participation
by them, wilful blindness or negligence will likely be sufficient for sanction
under this provision as amounting to assent or acquiescence. There is due
diligence defence available, which would require the director or officer to have
taken reasonable steps to ensure that a compliance program was implemented,
supervised and maintained, and that employees are made aware of both
corporate policy and the requirements of the compliance program. The specific
wording of section 78 would not appear to take away from the requirement that
directors and officers implement a compliance program or they may be
prosecuted under the individual responsibility for compliance. The section
makes it clear that it is not necessary for an action to be taken against the
reporting entity to convict an officer or director who was involved in the matter
giving rise to the offence. Direct prosecution can be started against a director or
officer even if they were involved only in permitting the act or omission to
continue once made aware of the breach of the 2000 Act.

If prosecuted under sections 75 or 77, a person will not be found guilty if
they establish that they exercised due diligence to prevent the commission of
those offences.[5] There is no guidance as of yet as to what will be sufficient due
diligence in the prevention of the commission of an offence. It would appear that
a properly developed compliance program, including, in particular, employee
education, would be a significant step towards providing evidence that due
diligence has been exercised. Enunciation and reasonable oversight of general
policies and establishing education programs causing employees to be alert to,
and to complete the required reporting and recording, would significantly assist
in establishing due diligence. The requirement to complete client information
forms which include a written inquiry of the matters necessary to complete
reports would be a necessary component of these procedures.

Proceedings under any of the above provisions may be instituted within,
but not after, one year after the time when the subject matter of the proceedings
arose.[6]

The consequences of an offence are significant. Prosecution under the
2000 Act, to a lower standard of proof as to guilt than that usual for criminal

---

[5]    Section 79(b) of the 2000 Act.
[6]    Section 81 of the 2000 Act.

offences, including the criminal offences in relation to which money laundering may relate, can result in conviction of a summary or indictable offence, with punishment by way of fine or jail sentence. In addition, for regulated entities and the employees, officers and directors of those regulated entities, where regulation may not permit continued participation in the industry if there is conviction on an indictable offence, it can mean loss of livelihood.

# 9.

# IMMUNITY FROM LEGAL ACTION ON COMPLIANCE

Section 10 of the 2000 Act[1] provides immunity from civil and criminal actions to reporting entities and their employees for making reports under the 2000 Act, stating that "no criminal or civil proceedings lie against a person or an entity for making a report in good faith under section 7, 7.1 or 9." However, there are concerns that this provision will not be effective, as a matter of law, for protection from civil proceedings. While, as a consequence of federal constitutional authority, the legislation can provide for criminal protection there is a lack of constitutional authority to provide the stated protection from civil liability. A federal criminal law statute should not be effective as to provincial jurisdiction, such as the regulation of professionals and the client rights which could lead to claims. Federal authorities appear to be attempting to piece their constitutional authority together from the federal authority over the postal system, criminal matters, certain of the regulated reporting entities, and matters of national security. If the federal authorities are properly occupying the field and if any of these is found to be extensive enough so as to permit the application of the 2000 Act to matters affecting civil rights, the federal authorities may be found to have properly exercised their constitutional authority. This issue has not been the subject matter of challenge.

Challenge was made by the Federation of Law Societies, on the basis of constitutional issues, focusing primarily on the issue of solicitor-client privilege and confidentiality. As a consequence of those challenges, amendments were made to the Regulation deleting legal counsel from the purview of the Regulation and legal counsel are no longer reporting entities at this time.

Although section 10 is intended to give statutory protection to the individuals responsible for filing the suspicious transaction reports, this section affords protection from civil liability only if they have acted in "good faith".[2] A clear legal definition of good faith will be difficult. "Good faith" has not been given an objective definition in law and there will be little surrounding law which will give assistance in determining what constitutes good faith in the circumstances. A sampling of legal dictionaries for the meaning of "good faith" focuses on a "bona fide" belief in a state of facts, and looks to reliance on statutory duty to support the determination made. It appears to require "honesty" but does not look to a test of negligence.

It would appear that the ordinary meaning which should be given to the phrase is that the report is made with an absence of malice or intention to harm the reputation of the person reported. However, this is not clearly enunciated in any statute, regulation or guidelines, and there is no similar concept included in criminal law statutes which most closely parallel the requirements of the

---

[1] S.C. 2000, c. 17.

[2] See *Chaput v. Rosmain* (1955), 1 D.L.R. (2d) 241 at 261; *R. v. Klimchuk* (1991), 67 C.C.C. (3d) 385 at 419, [1991] B.C.J. No. 2872 (C.A.).

statutes. The *Criminal Code*[3] protection at section 462.47 uses a concept of justifying the release of information.

There are some very real constitutional issues which could affect the availability of this liability protection. There is some very real doubt that the federal government has the constitutional authority to validly enact a provision which purports to deal with property and civil rights, as would be the effect of section 10 as to civil actions. The federal power over peace, order and good government is secondary to explicit provincial powers. Similarly, the federal jurisdiction over trade and commerce has generally given way to the provincial powers over property and civil rights in the province.

A potential solution to a portion of this shortcoming is to include a counterpart to the immunity provision in the *Criminal Code* and to provide for a good faith exception applicable to all offences prescribed in relation to criminal and civil proceedings. Moreover, the immunity should extend not merely to the making of reports but to the taking of any steps by a reporting entity in compliance with any requirement under the 2000 Act and regulations, such as permitting access to premises and records for search by FINTRAC. It is difficult to determine whether even this solution would be effective, particularly in a civil proceeding. It would, however, be a preferable step to that of providing simply for immunity from prosecution outside of the *Criminal Code*. Under criminal authority, the federal parliament clearly has the ability to provide immunity from criminal prosecution, at the least.

---

[3]   R.S.C. 1985, c. C-46.

# 10.

# COMPLIANCE REGIMES

## A.  GENERAL

The *Proceeds of Crime (Money Laundering) and Terrorist Financing Regulations* (the "Regulations")[1] requires reporting entities to implement written internal compliance regimes for compliance with the 2000 Act.[2] Internal compliance regimes for "financial entities" should be substantially similar to the regimes under the voluntary compliance, corporate governance and sound business practices requirements that they have been following under the 1991 Act, and for other regulatory purposes. The use of a compliance regime is far from novel and has been used in legislation dealing with corporate governance, securities law and the regulation of the financial services sector for several years. Government authorities have been effectively passing on the "first line" requirement to monitor and administer compliance with legislation to internal governance for some time. The compliance regime contemplated for money laundering terrorist financing is similar to that contemplated for many other regulated activities for the financial services sector.

Guideline 4,[3] relating to the implementation of compliance regimes went through extensive amendment following its initial release. These amendments primarily relate to the outline of reporting entities who have to implement a compliance regime and the specific requirements of those regimes. In addition, amendments were made to include specific requirements, under the compliance regime, as to financing of terrorist activity.

It is not enough for reporting entities to file reports and keep records, they must demonstrate audit and education programs to ensure there is a broad base of recognition of the policies, process and requirements for recording and reporting. The regulation requires reporting entities to set up internal compliance procedures to ensure that obligations of the Act are met. This requirement is expressed in section 71 of the Regulation which states that the compliance regime must include, as far as practicable:

(a)    the appointment of an individual who is to be responsible for the implementation of the regime;

(b)    the development and application of compliance policies and procedures;

(c)    a review as often as is necessary of those policies and procedures to test their effectiveness, to be conducted by an internal or external auditor or by the reporting entity itself, if it does not have an internal or external auditor; and

---

[1]    SOR/2002-184.

[2]    S.C. 2000, c. 17.

[3]    FINTRAC, *Guideline 4: Implementation of a Compliance Regime* (November 2003), online at http://www.fintrac.gc.ca/publications/guide/guide_e.asp.

(d)　where the Reporting Entity has employees, an ongoing employee compliance training program.

Section 71 of the Regulation states the requirement to implement formal compliance regimes for the purposes of assisting FINTRAC in carrying out the mandate of FINTRAC under section 40(e), ensuring compliance with Part 1 of the 2000 Act, and for the purposes of section 3(a) of the 2000 Act. It simply requires that every reporting entity shall implement a regime for complying with the 2000 Act and the regulations under the 2000 Act. Section 71(2) of the Regulation requires that the compliance regime include the appointment of an individual to be responsible for implementation, the development and application of compliance policies and procedures, a process for the review of the policies and procedures, and an on-going employee compliance-training program.

Specific reference should be made to Guideline 4 which provides a detailed outline of the requirements for an effective compliance regime.

## B.　COMPLIANCE OFFICER

FINTRAC Guideline 4 states that the appointed compliance officer should have the authority and the resources necessary to discharge his or her responsibility effectively.[4] Depending on the type of business, the compliance officer should report to the board of directors or senior management or to the owner or chief operator. Individuals who are subject to the 2000 Act may appoint themselves as their own compliance officer. When the reporting entity is a large business, the compliance officer should be from a senior level in order to have direct access to senior management and to the board of directors.[5] In smaller businesses, a senior manager or the owner or operator is the most appropriate person to be the compliance officer.[6]

There does not appear to be anything to prevent the use of an outsourced program for compliance. The specific requirement that there be a compliance program does not require that they be internal, merely that an "individual", which is an undefined term, be appointed. Accordingly, it would appear that provided the compliance program appropriately contemplates the requirements of the 2000 Act, and meets the requirements of section 71 of the Regulation, that outsourcing of the compliance officer and audit function may be permissible.

The reporting entity will be responsible for ensuring, to a high due diligence level, that any employee who is in a position to deal with the public, in a manner where they might identify a suspicious transaction or a prescribed transaction, is made fully aware of, and has the appropriate means, to permit the employee to complete the transaction reporting which is required. It also requires that the employees must be in a position where they have available, or are required to obtain, the information which is necessary to file a report. The

---

[4]　*Ibid.*, p. 5.
[5]　*Ibid.*
[6]　*Ibid.*

filing requirements provide for extensive information which is needed to complete the required information regarding the client or customer and the transaction. If the entity does not obtain and record the required information, it can't file the mandatory required information, and therefore fails to file the necessary report. Employee education and compliance policy must include mandatory recording and reporting requirements with mandatory collection of the required information or data. This must be required practice and must be brought to the attention of employees and senior officers as a compulsory requirement in the initiation and completion of financial transactions.

An employee can discharge the obligation to report under section 7 of the 2000 Act by making a report to a superior. The employee needs only to make a report to their superior and they will be protected from prosecution under the 2000 Act as to suspicious transaction reports. There is no similar protection for employees for other reports or requirements of the 2000 Act and regulations. Accordingly, in most instances, reporting under section 7 can be done on a centralized basis, with employees instructed to report internally to the appointed compliance officer. The reporting entity may be better served by having a consistent, fully informed report which is provided by a properly trained person who can screen, identify, and appropriately set out the requirements in the report. The issue which exists for partnerships is the failure of the section to extend the protections extended to employees to anyone other than an "employee". It would accordingly not extend to persons who participate in the relationship in a different manner, such as partners in a partnership, who remain directly responsible for reporting under section 7.

The reporting entity will need to have in place an adequate system for obtaining the required information to report, and a process for filing required reports with FINTRAC. The reporting entity must ensure that it has put into place an appropriate system to require and record the identification of information, and to complete any necessary filing of suspicious transactions reports, and to be doing so visibly, openly, and under official corporate policy.

Except that employees may comply by internal report for reports under section 7, the requirements to report under the 2000 Act are individual, that is, they lie with each individual who is in some manner involved with a reporting entity, and who identifies a transaction which would fall under the definition of a suspicious transaction and the other prescribed transactions (primarily large cash). Setting up the legislation in that manner means that the structure and design of the reporting and compliance arrangements are somewhat flexible and individual, depending on the structure of the reporting entity. It will be necessary to ensure that the compliance regime appropriately permits the centralization of the reporting function, to ensure consistency and accuracy of reporting, while recognizing the individual responsibility and liability, and permitting individuals to monitor the reporting process, and, in particular, compliance with regard to matters of which they become aware.

## C. COMPLIANCE POLICIES AND PROCEDURES

The degree of detail, specificity and formality of compliance policies and procedures to be implemented will vary according to the complexity of the legal structure of the reporting entity and the nature of the clients and transactions that the reporting entity is involved with, primarily as to the risk of exposure to money laundering.[7] The procedures should incorporate, at a minimum, the legislative and regulatory requirements, and should cover the following elements: (a) identifying reportable transactions; (b) completing and filing reports; (c) identifying exceptions; (d) record keeping, and (e) ascertaining identity.[8]

Section 71 of the Regulation merely states that there must be a compliance regime. The expected nature and standards for the compliance regime are not set out in the Regulation. It should, however, be clear to reporting entities that it must be to a standard that it would at least provide a due diligence defence under sections 77 and 79 of the 2000 Act. This should require, at the minimum, a program which alerts employees to the requirements to record and report, establish the necessary information to be obtained prior to accepting a new client or initiating a transaction, outline the nature of reports to be made and the responsibilities of the employees in making such reports. It is difficult to determine whether a detailed education program as to the specifics of what constitutes a money laundering offence, or the many elements of judgment which are required to be exercised in the making of a report, are necessary, or even suitable. An education program tailored to the types of transactions which would be dealt with by the employee will generally be sufficient.

The first step in developing a compliance regime is to determine how to educate those persons who will be dealing with the customers as to the need to report, the information required to report, and the types of transactions which must be reported. The first requirement for any employee is the proper basis for gathering of information. The compulsory reporting requirements will mean that certain information has to be obtained from a customer and maintained in customer files. If you do not have this information you cannot complete the mandatory fields on the transactions report and you will have an improper, or incomplete, report. The mandatory elements of the report are extensive, and require personal information, which must be verified, such as by review of a birth certificate, passport or similar photographic identification for individuals, and official, publicly filed corporate documentation for a corporation, with verification from the public records. Many of these enquiries would not be routinely obtained, particularly if there is only transactional involvement with the customer. Therefore, it is quite possible that the file or transaction opening information requirements must be expanded to include this additional information. It should be mandatory before a financial transaction is undertaken that the information required for reporting is obtained, whether the transaction is initially considered suspicious or not. You cannot always tell when initiating a

---

[7] *Ibid.*
[8] *Ibid.*

transaction whether it will turn out to be suspicious or not, and it is difficult to obtain the required information after the transaction is completed.

Therefore, the first step to an effective compliance regime would seem to be to ensure the client and transaction forms include the mandatory information, and to ensure that a transaction cannot be completed if this information is not obtained. This requirement is straightforward and the required information readily listed,[9] but is likely to cause some considerable additional cost and expense in either the paper or computer forms used to record a client transaction and in the time required to obtain and record the information. All of the employees who might deal with the initiation of a transaction will need to be trained to use the expanded forms, and will need to understand clearly that the transaction cannot be completed if the information is not obtained. Most of the compliance regimes suggested to date focus on the compulsory elements of the information required to be reported.

Once the reporting entity has the information recording requirements in place, if there is a need to report, the information that is needed to report will be available. The next step is to develop an education program to ensure that the individuals who deal with the customers are aware of their reporting responsibilities. As indicated previously, this education program should alert employees to the basic requirements of recording and reporting under the 2000 Act. It should include the compulsory obtaining of the necessary information for reports and recording, prior to initiating any client or transaction relationship, establish a reporting process for identified transactions which require reporting, to educate the employees as to the types of transactions which will necessarily require reporting. The most complex of the reporting requirements is the suspicious transaction reporting, and an employee should be educated as to what is a money laundering offence, a terrorist activity financing offence, and the need to report those financial transactions as suspicious transactions. There is clearly a need to educate on the reporting of other prescribed financial transactions and the importation and exportation of currency and monetary instruments.

## D.    REVIEW OF COMPLIANCE POLICIES AND PROCEDURES

A review of compliance policies and procedures must be conducted by internal or external auditors under regulation section 71(2)(c), or when a reporting entity does not have such auditors, he, she or it could conduct a "self-review".[10] When feasible, a self-review should be conducted by an individual who is independent of the reporting, record keeping and compliance monitoring functions. This individual could be an employee or an outside consultant.[11]

When the review is undertaken by internal or external auditors, it should include the following: (a) interviews with employees; (b) a sampling of large cash transactions followed by review of the reporting of such transactions; (c) a

---

[9]    The list is prepared simply by using the required information from the prescribed report form.

[10]    Guideline 4, p. 9.

[11]    *Ibid.*

review of the criteria and process for identifying and reporting suspicious transactions; (d) a test of the validity and reasonableness of exceptions that the reporting entity granted; and (e) a test of the record-keeping system for compliance with the legislation.[12] It is essential that the scope and the results of the review be documented. It should also identify weaknesses, corrective measures and follow-up actions.[13]

The failure to effectively implement, and monitor, the compliance regime can result in a breach of the 2000 Act through failure to properly comply with the reporting requirements and will reduce the ability to rely on the statutory due diligence defences. As a consequence, it will be necessary to ensure that there is a clear understanding among those responsible for compliance with the 2000 Act, and among all employees, of the nature of the sanctions and of the results of failure to appropriately comply with the recording and reporting requirements.

## E.  COMPLIANCE TRAINING FOR RELEVANT EMPLOYEES

Ongoing compliance training for employees is required, the concepts of the legislation require all personnel of a reporting entity to be generally familiar with the 2000 Act and the Regulation.[14] Section 71(1)(d) of the Regulation clearly establishes the requirement for employee compliance training. The object of this training should be to ensure employees are aware of the corporate policy, compliance program, and the legal obligations under the legislation. A training program must be implemented where there are employees and it must be monitored to ensure it is kept up to date and the relevant employees are regularly reminded of the requirements, both of law and corporate policy, as is implied by the requirement of the regulation that the training be "on-going".

The training program should cover the following elements: (a) an understanding of the legislative and regulatory requirements as well as the liabilities under the 2000 Act and the regulations; (b) an awareness of the internal policies and procedures for deterring and detecting money laundering that are associated with each employee's job; (c) an understanding of how the employee's institution, organization or profession is vulnerable to abuse by criminals laundering the proceeds of crime; and (d) background information on money laundering and terrorism financing to ensure that employees understand what it is.[15]

All employees, including senior management, who have contact with customers, who see customer transaction activity, or who handle cash in any way should receive training.[16] The training for employees of small businesses and for the individuals who are subject to Part 1 of the 2000 Act may be less formal and sophisticated.[17]

---

[12] *Ibid.*
[13] *Ibid.*, p. 10.
[14] *Ibid.*
[15] *Ibid.*, p. 11.
[16] *Ibid.*
[17] *Ibid.*, p. 12.

# PROCEEDS OF CRIME (MONEY LAUNDERING) AND TERRORIST FINANCING ACT

S.C. 2000, c. 17

**Amendments:** 2000, c. 24, s. 76.1 (in force October 23, 2000); 2001, c. 32, s. 70 (in force February 1, 2002); 2001, c. 41, s. 49 (in force December 24, 2001); 2001, c. 41, s. 47 (in force December 18, 2001); 2001, c. 41, s. 47 (in force on Royal Assent); 2001, c. 41, s. 48 (in force on Royal Assent); 2001, c. 41, s. 48 (in force December 18, 2001); 2001, c. 41, s. 50 (in force December 24, 2001); 2001, c. 41, s. 51 (in force December 24, 2001); 2001, c. 41, s. 52 (in force June 12, 2002); 2001, c. 41, s. 53 (in force December 24, 2001); 2001, c. 41, ss. 54-64 (in force January 6, 2003); 2001, c. 41, s. 65 (in force December 24, 2001); 2001, c. 12, s. 1 (in force June 14, 2001); 2001, c. 41, s. 66 (in force December 24, 2001); 2001, c. 41, s. 67(2) (in force June 12, 2002); 2001, c. 41, s. 67(3) (in force June 12, 2002); 2001, c. 41, s. 68 (in force December 24, 2001); 2001, c. 41, s. 69 (in force December 24, 2001); 2001, c. 41, s. 70 (in force December 24, 2001); 2001, c. 12, s. 3 (in force June 14, 2001); 2001, c. 32, s. 72 (in force February 1, 2002); 2001, c. 41, s. 71 (in force December 24, 2001); 2001, c. 41, s. 72 (in force December 24, 2001); 2001, c. 12, s. 4 (in force June 14, 2001); 2001, c. 41, s. 73 (in force December 24, 2001); 2001, c. 41, s. 74 (in force June 12, 2002).

An Act to facilitate combatting the laundering of proceeds of crime and combatting the financing of terrorist activities, to establish the Financial Transactions and Reports Analysis Centre of Canada and to amend and repeal certain Acts in consequence

[S.C. 2001, s. 47 (in force on royal assent).]

*Her Majesty, by and with the advice and consent of the Senate and House of Commons of Canada, enacts as follows:*

## SHORT TITLE

**1. Short title** — This Act may be cited as the *Proceeds of Crime (Money Laundering) and Terrorist Financing Act.*

[S.C. 2000, c. 17, s. 1, in force July 5, 2000 (SI/2000-55); S.C. 2001, c. 41, s. 48.]

## INTERPRETATION

**2. Definitions** — The definitions in this section apply in this Act.

"authorized person" means a person who is authorized under subsection 45(2).

"Centre" means the Financial Transactions and Reports Analysis Centre of Canada established by section 41.

"client" means a person or an entity that engages in a financial transaction or activity with a person or an entity referred to in section 5, and includes a person or an entity on whose behalf the person or the entity that engages in the transaction or activity is acting.

"Commissioner" has the same meaning as in section 2 of the *Canada Customs and Revenue Agency Act*.

"courier" means a courier as defined by regulation.

"customs office" has the same meaning as in subsection 2(1) of the *Customs Act*.

"entity" means a body corporate, a trust, a partnership, a fund or an unincorporated association or organization.

"legal counsel" means, in the Province of Quebec, an advocate or a notary and, in any other province, a barrister or solicitor.

"mail" has the same meaning as in subsection 2(1) of the *Canada Post Corporation Act*.

"Minister" means, in relation to sections 25 to 39, the Minister of National Revenue and, in relation to any other provision of this Act, the member of the Queen's Privy Council for Canada who is designated by the Governor in Council as the Minister for the purposes of that provision.

"money laundering offence" means an offence under subsection 462.31(1) of the *Criminal Code*.

"officer" has the same meaning as in subsection 2(1) of the *Customs Act*.

"person" means an individual.

"prescribed" means prescribed by regulations made by the Governor in Council.

"terrorist activity" has the same meaning as in subsection 83.01(1) of the *Criminal Code*.

"terrorist activity financing offence" means an offence under section 83.02, 83.03 or 83.04 of the *Criminal Code* or an offence under section 83.12 of the *Criminal Code* arising out of a contravention of section 83.08 of that Act.

"threats to the security of Canada" has the same meaning as in section 2 of the *Canadian Security Intelligence Service Act*.

[S.C. 2000, c. 17, s. 2, in force July 5, 2000 (SI/2000-55); S.C. 2000, c. 24, s. 76.1; S.C. 2001, c. 41, s. 49; S.C. 2001, c. 32, s. 70 (as amended by S.C. 2001, c. 41, s. 132).]

## OBJECT OF ACT

**3. Object** — The object of this Act is

(a)  to implement specific measures to detect and deter money laundering and the financing of terrorist activities and to facilitate the investigation and prosecution of money laundering offences and terrorist activity financing offences, including

   (i)  establishing record keeping and client identification requirements for financial services providers and other persons or entities that engage in businesses, professions or activities that are susceptible to being used for money laundering or the financing of terrorist activities,

   (ii)  requiring the reporting of suspicious financial transactions and of cross-border movements of currency and monetary instruments, and

(iii) establishing an agency that is responsible for dealing with reported and other information;

(b) to respond to the threat posed by organized crime by providing law enforcement officials with the information they need to deprive criminals of the proceeds of their criminal activities, while ensuring that appropriate safeguards are put in place to protect the privacy of persons with respect to personal information about themselves; and

(c) to assist in fulfilling Canada's international commitments to participate in the fight against transnational crime, particularly money laundering, and the fight against terrorist activity.

[S.C. 2000, c. 17, s. 3, in force July 5, 2000 (SI/2000-55); S.C. 2001, c. 41, s. 50.]

### HER MAJESTY

**4. Binding on Her Majesty** — This Act is binding on Her Majesty in right of Canada or a province.

[S.C. 2000, c. 17, s. 4, in force July 5, 2000 (SI/2000-55).]

# PART 1 RECORD KEEPING AND REPORTING OF SUSPICIOUS TRANSACTIONS

*Application*

**5. Application of Part** — This Part applies to the following persons and entities:

(a) authorized foreign banks within the meaning of section 2 of the *Bank Act* in respect of their business in Canada, or banks to which that Act applies;

(b) cooperative credit societies, savings and credit unions and caisses populaires regulated by a provincial Act and associations regulated by the *Cooperative Credit Associations Act*;

(c) life companies or foreign life companies to which the *Insurance Companies Act* applies or life insurance companies regulated by a provincial Act;

(d) companies to which the *Trust and Loan Companies Act* applies;

(e) trust companies regulated by a provincial Act;

(f) loan companies regulated by a provincial Act;

(g) persons and entities authorized under provincial legislation to engage in the business of dealing in securities, or to provide portfolio management or investment counselling services;

(h) persons and entities engaged in the business of foreign exchange dealing;

(i) persons and entities engaged in a business, profession or activity described in regulations made under paragraph 73(1)(a);

(j) persons and entities engaged in a business or profession described in regulations made under paragraph 73(1)(b), while carrying out the activities described in the regulations;

(k) casinos, as defined in the regulations, including those owned or controlled by Her Majesty;

(l) departments and agents of Her Majesty in right of Canada or of a province that are engaged in the business of accepting deposit liabilities or that sell money orders to the public, while carrying out the activities described in regulations made under paragraph 73(1)(c); and

(m) for the purposes of section 7, employees of a person or entity referred to in any of paragraphs (a) to (l).

[S.C. 2000, c. 17, s. 5, in force October 28, 2001 (SI/2001-88); S.C. 2001, c. 41, s. 51. ]

*Record Keeping*

**6. Duties** — Every person or entity shall keep and retain records that relate to financial activities in accordance with the regulations made under subsection 73(1).

[S.C. 2000, c. 17, s. 6, in force June 12, 2002 (SI/2002-84).]

*Reporting*

**7. Transactions if reasonable grounds to suspect** — In addition to the requirements of subsection 9(1), every person or entity shall report to the Centre, in the prescribed form and manner, every financial transaction that occurs in the course of their activities and in respect of which there are reasonable grounds to suspect that the transaction is related to the commission of a money laundering offence or a terrorist activity financing offence.

[S.C. 2000, c. 17, s. 7, in force October 28, 2001 (SI/2001-88); S.C. 2001, c. 41, s. 52. ]

**7.1 (1) Disclosure** — In addition to the requirements of section 7 and subsection 9(1), every person or entity that is required to make a disclosure under section 83.1 of the *Criminal Code* shall also make a report on it to the Centre, in the prescribed form and manner.

(2) **Limitation** — Subsection (1) does not apply to prescribed persons or entities, or prescribed classes of persons or entities, in respect of prescribed transactions or property, or classes of transactions or property, if the prescribed conditions are met.

[S.C. 2001, c. 41, s. 52.]

**8. No disclosure of reports** — No person or entity shall disclose that they have made a report under section 7, or disclose the contents of such a report, with the intent to prejudice a criminal investigation, whether or not a criminal investigation has begun.

[S.C. 2000, c. 17, s. 8, in force October 28, 2001 (SI/2001-88).]

**9. (1) Prescribed financial transactions** — Every person or entity shall report to the Centre, in the prescribed form and manner, every prescribed financial transaction that occurs in the course of their activities.

(2) **Limitation** — Subsection (1) does not apply to prescribed persons or entities, or prescribed classes of persons or entities, in respect of prescribed transactions, classes of transactions, clients or classes of clients, if the prescribed conditions are met.

(3) **List of persons** — Every person or entity shall maintain a list, in the prescribed form and manner, of their clients in respect of whom a report would have been required under subsection (1) were it not for subsection (2). However, a person or an entity may choose to report a client's transactions under subsection (1) instead of maintaining the list in respect of that client.

**9.1 Reports under other Acts** — Subject to section 9, every person or entity that is required to make a report to the Centre under an Act of Parliament or any regulations under it shall make it in the form and manner prescribed under this Act for a report under that Act.

[S.C. 2001, c. 41, s. 53.]

**10. Immunity** — No criminal or civil proceedings lie against a person or an entity for making a report in good faith under section 7, 7.1 or 9, or for providing the Centre with information about suspicions of money laundering or of the financing of terrorist activities.

[S.C. 2001, c. 41, s. 53.]

**11. Solicitor-client privilege** — Nothing in this Part requires a legal counsel to disclose any communication that is subject to solicitor-client privilege.

# PART 2 REPORTING OF CURRENCY AND MONETARY INSTRUMENTS

## *Reporting*

**12.** (1) **Currency and monetary instruments** — Every person or entity referred to in subsection (3) shall report to an officer, in accordance with the regulations, the importation or exportation of currency or monetary instruments of a value equal to or greater than the prescribed amount.

(2) **Limitation** — A person or entity is not required to make a report under subsection (1) in respect of an activity if the prescribed conditions are met in respect of the person, entity or activity, and if the person or entity satisfies an officer that those conditions have been met.

(3) **Who must report** — Currency or monetary instruments shall be reported under subsection (1)

(a) in the case of currency or monetary instruments in the actual possession of a person arriving in or departing from Canada, or that form part of their baggage if they and their baggage are being carried on board the same conveyance, by that person or, in prescribed circumstances, by the person in charge of the conveyance;

(b) in the case of currency or monetary instruments imported into Canada by courier or as mail, by the exporter of the currency or monetary instruments or, on receiving notice under subsection 14(2), by the importer;

(c) in the case of currency or monetary instruments exported from Canada by courier or as mail, by the exporter of the currency or monetary instruments;

(d) in the case of currency or monetary instruments, other than those referred to in paragraph (a) or imported or exported as mail, that are on board a conveyance arriving in or departing from Canada, by the person in charge of the conveyance; and

(e) in any other case, by the person on whose behalf the currency or monetary instruments are imported or exported.

(4) **Duty to answer and comply with the request of an officer** — If a report is made in respect of currency or monetary instruments, the person arriving in or departing from Canada with the currency or monetary instruments shall

(a) answer truthfully any questions that the officer asks with respect to the information required to be contained in the report; and

(b) on request of an officer, present the currency or monetary instruments that they are carrying or transporting, unload any conveyance or part of a conveyance or baggage and open or unpack any package or container that the officer wishes to examine.

(5) **Sending reports to Centre** — Officers shall send the reports they receive under subsection (1) to the Centre.

[S.C. 2001, c. 41, s. 54.]

**13. Decision not to proceed with importing or exporting** — A person or an entity that is required to report currency or monetary instruments may, at any time before they are retained under subsection 14(1) or forfeited as a result of a contravention of subsection 12(1), decide not to proceed further with importing or exporting them.

*Retention*

**14.** (1) **Temporary retention** — Subject to subsections (2) to (5), if a person or an entity indicates to an officer that they have currency or monetary instruments to report under subsection 12(1) but the report has not yet been completed, the officer may, after giving notice in the prescribed manner to the person or entity, retain the currency or monetary instruments for the prescribed period.

(2) **Importation or exportation by courier or as mail** — In the case of currency or monetary instruments imported or exported by courier or as mail, the officer shall, within the prescribed period, give the notice to the exporter if the exporter's address is known, or, if the exporter's address is not known, to the importer.

(3) **Limitation** — Currency or monetary instruments may no longer be retained under subsection (1) if, during the period referred to in that subsection,

(a) the officer is satisfied that the currency or monetary instruments have been reported under subsection 12(1); or

(b) the importer or exporter of the currency or monetary instruments advises the officer that they have decided not to proceed further with importing or exporting them.

(4) **Content of notice** — The notice referred to in subsection (1) must state

(a)  the period for which the currency or monetary instruments may be retained;

(b)  that if, within that period, the currency or monetary instruments are reported under subsection 12(1) or the importer or exporter decides not to proceed further with importing or exporting them, they may no longer be retained; and

(c)  that currency or monetary instruments retained at the end of that period are forfeited to Her Majesty in right of Canada at that time.

(5) **Forfeiture and report to Centre** — Currency or monetary instruments that are retained by an officer under subsection (1) are forfeited to Her Majesty in right of Canada at the end of the period referred to in that subsection, and the officer shall send any incomplete report in respect of the forfeited currency or monetary instruments made under subsection 12(1) to the Centre.

*Searches*

**15.** (1) **Search of the person** — An officer may search

(a)  any person who has arrived in Canada, within a reasonable time after their arrival in Canada,

(b)  any person who is about to leave Canada, at any time before their departure, or

(c)  any person who has had access to an area designated for use by persons about to leave Canada and who leaves the area but does not leave Canada, within a reasonable time after they leave the area,

if the officer suspects on reasonable grounds that the person has secreted on or about their person currency or monetary instruments that are of a value equal to or greater than the amount prescribed for the purpose of subsection 12(1) and that have not been reported in accordance with that subsection.

(2) **Person taken before senior officer** — An officer who is about to search a person under this section shall, on the person's request, without delay take the person before the senior officer at the place where the search is to take place.

(3) **Discharge or search** — A senior officer before whom a person is taken under subsection (2) shall, if the senior officer believes there are no reasonable grounds for suspicion under subsection (1), discharge the person or, if the senior officer believes otherwise, direct that the person be searched.

(4) **Search by same sex** — No person shall be searched under this section by a person who is not of the same sex, and if there is no officer of the same sex at the place where the search is to take place, an officer may authorize any suitable person of the same sex to perform the search.

[S.C. 2001, c. 41, s. 55.]

**16.** (1) **Search of conveyance** — If an officer suspects on reasonable grounds that there are, on or about a conveyance, currency or monetary instruments of a value equal to or greater than the amount prescribed for the purpose of subsection 12(1) and that have not been reported in accordance with that subsection, the officer may stop, board and search the conveyance, examine anything in or on it and open or cause to be opened any package or container in or on it and direct that the conveyance be moved to a customs office or other suitable place for the search, examination or opening.

(2) **Search of baggage** — If an officer suspects on reasonable grounds that there are, in baggage, currency or monetary instruments that are of a value equal to or greater than the amount prescribed for the purpose of subsection 12(1) and that have not been reported in accordance with that subsection, the officer may search the baggage, examine anything in it and open or cause to be opened any package or container in it and direct that the baggage be moved to a customs office or other suitable place for the search, examination or opening.

[S.C. 2001, c. 41, s. 56.]

**17.** (1) **Examination and opening of mail** — An officer may examine any mail that is being imported or exported and open or cause to be opened any such mail that the officer suspects on reasonable grounds contains currency or monetary instruments of a value equal to or greater than the amount prescribed for the purpose of subsection 12(1).

(2) **Exception** — An officer may not open or cause to be opened any mail that weighs 30 grams or less unless the person to whom it is addressed consents or the person who sent it consents or has completed and attached to the mail a label in accordance with article 116 of the *Detailed Regulations of the Universal Postal Convention.*

(3) **Opening of mail in officer's presence** — An officer may cause mail that weighs 30 grams or less to be opened in the officer's presence by the person to whom it is addressed, the person who sent it or a person authorized by either of those persons.

[S.C. 2001, c. 41, s. 57.]

*Seizures*

**18.** (1) **Seizure and forfeiture** — If an officer believes on reasonable grounds that subsection 12(1) has been contravened, the officer may seize as forfeit the currency or monetary instruments.

(2) **Return of seized currency or monetary instruments** — The officer shall, on payment of a penalty in the prescribed amount, return the seized currency or monetary instruments to the individual from whom they were seized or to the lawful owner unless the officer has reasonable grounds to suspect that the currency or monetary instruments are proceeds of crime within the meaning of subsection 462.3(1) of the *Criminal Code* or funds for use in the financing of terrorist activities.

(3) **Notice of seizure** — An officer who seizes currency or monetary instruments under subsection (1) shall

(a) if they were not imported or exported as mail, give the person from whom they were seized written notice of the seizure and of the right to review and appeal set out in sections 25 and 30;

(b) if they were imported or exported as mail and the address of the exporter is known, give the exporter written notice of the seizure and of the right to review and appeal set out in sections 25 and 30; and

(c) take the measures that are reasonable in the circumstances to give notice of the seizure to any person whom the officer believes on reasonable grounds is entitled to make an application under section 32 in respect of the currency or monetary instruments.

(4) **Service of notice** — The service of a notice under paragraph (3)(b) is sufficient if it is sent by registered mail addressed to the exporter.

[S.C. 2001, c. 41, s. 134.]

**19. Power to call in aid** — An officer may call on other persons to assist the officer in exercising any power of search, seizure or retention that the officer is authorized under this Part to exercise, and any person so called on is authorized to exercise the power.

**19.1 Recording of reasons for decision** — If an officer decides to exercise powers under subsection 18(1), the officer shall record in writing reasons for the decision.

**20. Report to Commissioner and the Centre** — If the currency or monetary instruments have been seized under section 18, the officer who seized them shall without delay report the circumstances of the seizure to the Commissioner and to the Centre.

*Exported Mail*

**21. (1) Mail to be made available to an officer** — On request of an officer, any mail that is being sent from a place in Canada to a place in a foreign country and that contains or is suspected to contain currency or monetary instruments that are of a value equal to or greater than the amount prescribed for the purpose of subsection 12(1) shall be submitted by the Canada Post Corporation to an officer.

(2) **Mail in the course of post** — All mail that is submitted to an officer under this section remains, for the purposes of the *Canada Post Corporation Act*, in the course of post unless it is retained or seized under this Part.

(3) **Notice of retention or seizure** — If mail is retained or seized under this Part, notice of the retention or seizure shall be given in writing to the Canada Post Corporation within 60 days after the retention or seizure unless the mail has, before the expiry of that period, been returned to the Corporation.

(4) **Mail subject to customs laws** — An officer shall deal with all mail submitted to the officer under this section in accordance with the laws relating to customs and this Part and, subject to those laws and this Part, shall return it to the Canada Post Corporation.

(5) **Non-mailable matter** — Any non-mailable matter found by an officer in mail made available to the officer under this section shall be dealt with in accordance with the regulations made under the *Canada Post Corporation Act*.

[S.C. 2000, c. 17, s. 21, in force January 6, 2003 (SI/ 2002-153); S.C. 2001, c. 41, s. 59.]

*Transfer to the Minister of Public Works and Government Services*

**22.** (1) **When forfeiture under s. 14(5)** — An officer who retains currency or monetary instruments forfeited under subsection 14(5) shall send the currency or monetary instruments to the Minister of Public Works and Government Services.

(2) **When seizure or payment of a penalty** — An officer who seizes currency or monetary instruments or is paid a penalty under subsection 18(2) shall send the currency or monetary instruments or the penalty, as the case may be, to the Minister of Public Works and Government Services.

[S.C. 2001, c. 41, s. 60.]

*Forfeiture*

**23. Time of forfeiture** — Subject to subsection 18(2) and sections 25 to 31, currency or monetary instruments seized as forfeit under subsection 18(1) are forfeited to Her Majesty in right of Canada from the time of the contravention of subsection 12(1) in respect of which they were seized, and no act or proceeding after the forfeiture is necessary to effect the forfeiture.

*Review and Appeal*

**24. Review of forfeiture** — The forfeiture of currency or monetary instruments seized under this Part is final and is not subject to review or to be set aside or otherwise dealt with except to the extent and in the manner provided by sections 25 to 30.

**25. Request for Minister's decision** — A person from whom currency or monetary instruments were seized under section 18, or the lawful owner of the currency or monetary instruments, may within 90 days after the date of the seizure request a decision of the Minister as to whether subsection 12(1) was contravened, by giving notice in writing to the officer who seized the currency or monetary instruments or to an officer at the customs office closest to the place where the seizure took place.

[S.C. 2001, c. 41, s. 61.]

**26.** (1) **Notice of Commissioner** — If a decision of the Minister is requested under section 25, the Commissioner shall without delay serve on the person who requested it written notice of the circumstances of the seizure in respect of which the decision is requested.

(2) **Evidence** — The person on whom a notice is served under subsection (1) may, within 30 days after the notice is served, furnish any evidence in the matter that they desire to furnish.

**27.** (1) **Decision of the Minister** — Within 90 days after the expiry of the period referred to in subsection 26(2), the Minister shall decide whether subsection 12(1) was contravened.

(2) **Deferral of decision** — If charges are laid with respect to a money laundering offence or a terrorist activity financing offence in respect of the currency or monetary instruments seized, the Minister may defer making a decision but shall

make it in any case no later than 30 days after the conclusion of all court proceedings in respect of those charges.

(3) **Notice of decision** — The Minister shall, without delay after making a decision, serve on the person who requested it a written notice of the decision together with the reasons for it.

[S.C. 2001, c. 41, s. 62.]

**28. If there is no contravention** — If the Minister decides that subsection 12(1) was not contravened, the Minister of Public Works and Government Services shall, on being informed of the Minister's decision, return the penalty that was paid, or the currency or monetary instruments or an amount of money equal to their value at the time of the seizure, as the case may be.

**29.** (1) **If there is a contravention** — If the Minister decides that subsection 12(1) was contravened, the Minister shall, subject to the terms and conditions that the Minister may determine,

> (a) decide that the currency or monetary instruments or, subject to subsection (2), an amount of money equal to their value on the day the Minister of Public Works and Government Services is informed of the decision, be returned, on payment of a penalty in the prescribed amount or without penalty;
>
> (b) decide that any penalty or portion of any penalty that was paid under subsection 18(2) be remitted; or
>
> (c) subject to any order made under section 33 or 34, confirm that the currency or monetary instruments are forfeited to Her Majesty in right of Canada.

The Minister of Public Works and Government Services shall give effect to a decision of the Minister under paragraph (a) or (b) on being informed of it.

(2) **Limit on amount paid** — The total amount paid under paragraph (1)(a) shall, if the currency or monetary instruments were sold or otherwise disposed of under the *Seized Property Management Act*, not exceed the proceeds of the sale or disposition, if any, less any costs incurred by Her Majesty in respect of the currency or monetary instruments.

**30.** (1) **Appeal to Federal Court** — A person who requests a decision of the Minister under section 25 may, within 90 days after being notified of the decision, appeal the decision by way of an action in the Federal Court in which the person is the plaintiff and the Minister is the defendant.

(2) **Ordinary action** — The *Federal Courts Act* and the rules made under that Act that apply to ordinary actions apply to actions instituted under subsection (1) except as varied by special rules made in respect of such actions.

(3) **Delivery after final order** — The Minister of Public Works and Government Services shall give effect to the decision of the Court on being informed of it.

(4) **Limit on amount paid** — If the currency or monetary instruments were sold or otherwise disposed of under the *Seized Property Management Act*, the total amount that can be paid under subsection (3) shall not exceed the proceeds

of the sale or disposition, if any, less any costs incurred by Her Majesty in respect of the currency or monetary instruments.

[S.C. 2000, c. 17, s. 30, in force January 6, 2003 (SI/2002-153); S.C. 2002, c. 8, s. 161 (as amended by S.C. 2001, c. 41, s. 139(1)).]

**31. Service of notices —** The service of the Commissioner's notice under section 26 or the notice of the Minister's decision under section 27 is sufficient if it is sent by registered mail addressed to the person on whom it is to be served at their latest known address.

[S.C. 2000, c. 17, s. 31, in force January 6, 2003 (SI/2002-153).]

## Third Party Claims

**32. (1) Interest as owner —** If currency or monetary instruments have been seized as forfeit under this Part, any person, other than the person in whose possession the currency or monetary instruments were when seized, who claims an interest in the currency or monetary instruments as owner may, within 90 days after the seizure, apply by notice in writing to the court for an order under section 33.

(2) **Date of hearing —** A judge of the court to which an application is made under this section shall fix a day, not less than 30 days after the date of the filing of the application, for the hearing.

(3) **Notice to Commissioner —** A person who makes an application under this section shall serve notice of the application and of the hearing on the Commissioner, or an officer designated by the Commissioner for the purpose of this section, not later than 15 days after a day is fixed under subsection (2) for the hearing of the application.

(4) **Service of notice —** The service of a notice under subsection (3) is sufficient if it is sent by registered mail addressed to the Commissioner.

(5) **Definition of "court" —** In this section and sections 33 and 34, "court" means

    (a)  in the Province of Ontario, the Superior Court of Justice;

    (b)  in the Province of Quebec, the Superior Court;

    (c)  in the Provinces of Nova Scotia and British Columbia, the Yukon Territory and the Northwest Territories, the Supreme Court;

    (d)  in the Provinces of New Brunswick, Manitoba, Saskatchewan and Alberta, the Court of Queen's Bench;

    (e)  in the Provinces of Prince Edward Island and Newfoundland, the Trial Division of the Supreme Court; and

    (f)  in Nunavut, the Nunavut Court of Justice.

[S.C. 2000, c. 17, s. 32, in force January 6, 2003 (SI/2002-153); S.C. 2001, c. 41, s. 63.]

**33. Order —** If, on the hearing of an application made under subsection 32(1), the court is satisfied

    (a)  that the applicant acquired the interest in good faith before the contravention in respect of which the seizure was made,

   (b) that the applicant is innocent of any complicity in the contravention of subsection 12(1) that resulted in the seizure and of any collusion in relation to that contravention, and

   (c) that the applicant exercised all reasonable care to ensure that any person permitted to obtain possession of the currency or monetary instruments seized would report them in accordance with subsection 12(1),

the applicant is entitled to an order declaring that their interest is not affected by the seizure and declaring the nature and extent of their interest at the time of the contravention.

[S.C. 2000, c. 17, s. 33, in force January 6, 2003 (SI/2002-153).]

**34.** (1) **Appeal** — A person who makes an application under section 32 or Her Majesty in right of Canada may appeal to the court of appeal from an order made under section 33 and the appeal shall be asserted, heard and decided according to the ordinary procedure governing appeals to the court of appeal from orders or judgments of a court.

(2) **Definition of "court of appeal"** — In this section, "court of appeal" means, in the province in which an order referred to in subsection (1) is made, the court of appeal for that province as defined in section 2 of the *Criminal Code*.

[S.C. 2000, c. 17, s. 34, in force January 6, 2003 (SI/2002-153).]

**35.** (1) **Delivery after final order** — The Minister of Public Works and Government Services shall, after the forfeiture of currency or monetary instruments has become final and on being informed by the Commissioner that a person has obtained a final order under section 33 or 34 in respect of the currency or monetary instruments, give to the person

   (a) the currency or monetary instruments; or

   (b) an amount calculated on the basis of the interest of the applicant in the currency or monetary instruments at the time of the contravention in respect of which they were seized, as declared in the order.

(2) **Limit on amount paid** — The total amount paid under paragraph (1)(b) shall, if the currency or monetary instruments were sold or otherwise disposed of under the *Seized Property Management Act*, not exceed the proceeds of the sale or disposition, if any, less any costs incurred by Her Majesty in respect of the currency or monetary instruments.

[S.C. 2000, c. 17, s. 35, in force January 6, 2003 (SI/2002-153).]

## *Disclosure of Information*

**36.** (1) **Prohibition** — Subject to this section and subsection 12(1) of the *Privacy Act*, no official shall disclose the following:

   (a) information set out in a report made under subsection 12(1), whether or not it is completed;

   (b) any other information obtained for the purposes of this Part; or

   (c) information prepared from information referred to in paragraph (a) or (b).

(2) **Disclosure of information to a police force** — An officer who has reasonable grounds to suspect that information referred to in subsection (1) would be relevant to investigating or prosecuting a money laundering offence or a terrorist activity financing offence may disclose the information to the appropriate police force.

(3) **Disclosure of information to the Centre** — An officer may disclose to the Centre information referred to in subsection (1) if the officer has reasonable grounds to suspect that it would be of assistance to the Centre in the detection, prevention or deterrence of money laundering or of the financing of terrorist activities.

(3.1) **Recording of reasons for decision** — If an officer decides to disclose information under subsection (2) or (3), the officer shall record in writing the reasons for the decision.

(4) **Powers, duties and functions** — An official may disclose information referred to in subsection (1) for the purpose of exercising powers or performing duties and functions under this Part.

(5) **Immunity from compulsory processes** — Subject to section 36 of the *Access to Information Act* and section 34 of the *Privacy Act*, an official is required to comply with a subpoena, an order for production of documents, a summons or any other compulsory process only if it is issued in the course of

(a) criminal proceedings under an Act of Parliament that have been commenced by the laying of an information or the preferring of an indictment; or

(b) any legal proceedings that relate to the administration or enforcement of this Part.

(6) **Definition of "official"** — In this section and section 37, "official" means a person who obtained or who has or had access to information referred to in subsection (1) in the course of exercising powers or performing duties and functions under this Part.

[S.C. 2000, c. 17, s. 36, in force January 6, 2003 (SI/2002-153); S.C. 2001, c. 41, s. 64.]

**37. Use of information** — No official shall use information referred to in subsection 36(1) for any purpose other than exercising powers or performing duties and functions under this Part.

[S.C. 2000, c. 17, s. 37, in force January 6, 2003 (SI/2002-153).]

*Agreements for Exchange of Information*

**38.** (1) **Agreements with foreign states** — The Minister, with the consent of the Minister designated for the purpose of section 42, may enter into an agreement or arrangement in writing with the government of a foreign state, or an institution or agency of that state, that has reporting requirements similar to those set out in this Part, whereby

(a) information set out in reports made under subsection 12(1) in respect of currency or monetary instruments imported into Canada from that state will be provided to a department, institution or agency of that state that has powers and duties similar to those of the Canada Customs and Revenue Agency; and

(b) information contained in reports in respect of currency or monetary instruments imported into that state from Canada will be provided to the Canada Customs and Revenue Agency.

(2) **Information sent under an agreement** — When an agreement or arrangement referred to in subsection (1) is in effect with a foreign state or an institution or agency of that state and a person fulfils the reporting requirements of that state in respect of currency or monetary instruments that are imported into that state from Canada, the person is deemed to have fulfilled the requirements set out in section 12 in respect of the exportation of the currency or monetary instruments.

(3) **Information received by the Centre** — The information received under an agreement or arrangement referred to in subsection (1) shall be sent to the Centre and, for the purposes of any provision of this Act dealing with the confidentiality of information or the collection or use of information by the Centre, is deemed to be information set out in a report made under section 12.

[S.C. 2000, c. 17, s. 38, in force July 5, 2000 (SI/2000-55).]

*Delegation*

**39.** (1) **Minister's duties** — The Minister may authorize an officer or a class of officers to exercise powers or perform duties of the Minister, including any judicial or quasi-judicial powers or duties of the Minister, under this Part.

(2) **Commissioner's duties** — The Commissioner may authorize an officer or a class of officers to exercise powers or perform duties of the Commissioner under this Part.

[S.C. 2000, c. 17, s. 39, in force January 6, 2003 (SI/2002-153).]

# PART 3 FINANCIAL TRANSACTIONS AND REPORTS ANALYSIS CENTRE OF CANADA

*Object*

**40. Object** — The object of this Part is to establish an independent agency that

(a) acts at arm's length from law enforcement agencies and other entities to which it is authorized to disclose information;

(b) collects, analyses, assesses and discloses information in order to assist in the detection, prevention and deterrence of money laundering and of the financing of terrorist activities;

(c) ensures that personal information under its control is protected from unauthorized disclosure;

(d) operates to enhance public awareness and understanding of matters related to money laundering; and

(e) ensures compliance with Part 1.

[S.C. 2000, c. 17, s. 40, in force July 5, 2000 (SI/2000-55); S.C. 2001, c. 41, s. 65.]

## *Establishment of the Centre*

**41.** (1) **Centre established** — There is hereby established the Financial Transactions and Reports Analysis Centre of Canada.

(2) **Powers of Centre** — The Centre may exercise powers only as an agent of Her Majesty in right of Canada.

[S.C. 2000, c. 17, s. 41, in force July 5, 2000 (SI/2000-55).]

**42.** (1) **Minister is responsible** — The Minister is responsible for the Centre.

(2) **Minister may direct** — The Minister may direct the Centre on any matter that, in the Minister's opinion, materially affects public policy or the strategic direction of the Centre.

(3) **Statutory instruments** — A direction under subsection (2) is not a statutory instrument for the purposes of the *Statutory Instruments Act*.

(4) **Advisor** — The Minister may from time to time engage the services of any person to advise and report to the Minister on any matter referred to in subsection (2).

[S.C. 2000, c. 17, s. 42, in force July 5, 2000 (SI/2000-55).]

## *Organization and Head Office*

**43.** (1) **Appointment of Director** — The Governor in Council shall appoint a Director to hold office during pleasure for a term of not more than five years.

(2) **Reappointment** — Subject to subsection (3), the Director is eligible to be reappointed on the expiry of a first or subsequent term of office.

(3) **Limitation** — No person shall hold office as Director for terms of more than ten years in the aggregate.

(4) **Absence or incapacity** — In the event of the absence or incapacity of the Director, or if the office of Director is vacant, the Governor in Council may appoint a qualified person to hold office instead of the Director for a term of not more than six months, and the person shall, while holding that office, have all of the powers, duties and functions of the Director under this Part.

(5) **Delegation by Director** — The Director may delegate to any person, subject to any terms and conditions that the Director may specify, any power, duty or function conferred on the Director under this Act.

[S.C. 2000, c. 17, s. 43, in force July 5, 2000 (SI/2000-55).]

**44. Accident compensation** — The Director and the employees of the Centre are deemed to be employees for the purposes of the *Government Employees Compensation Act* and to be employed in the public service of Canada for the purposes of any regulations made under section 9 of the *Aeronautics Act*.

[S.C. 2000, c. 17, s. 44, in force July 5, 2000 (SI/2000-55).]

**45.** (1) **Director's powers** — The Director is the chief executive officer of the Centre, has supervision over and direction of its work and employees and may exercise any power and perform any duty or function of the Centre. The Director has the rank and all the powers of a deputy head of a department.

(2) **Directions to authorized persons** — The Director may authorize any person to act, under the Director's direction, for the purposes of sections 62 to 64.

[S.C. 2000, c. 17, s. 45(1), in force July 5, 2000 (SI/2000-55), s. 45(2), in force June 12, 2002 (SI/2002-84).]

**46. Employees** — An employee of the Centre may exercise any power and perform any duty or function of the Centre if the employee is appointed to serve in the Centre in a capacity appropriate to the exercise of the power or the performance of the duty or function.

[S.C. 2000, c. 17, s. 46, in force July 5, 2000 (SI/2000-55).]

**47. Remuneration** — The Director shall be paid the remuneration fixed by the Governor in Council.

[S.C. 2000, c. 17, s. 47, in force July 5, 2000 (SI/2000-55).]

**48.** (1) **Head office** — The head office of the Centre is to be in the National Capital Region, as described in the schedule to the *National Capital Act*.

(2) **Other offices** — The Director may, with the approval of the Minister, establish other offices of the Centre elsewhere in Canada.

[S.C. 2000, c. 17, s. 48, in force July 5, 2000 (SI/2000-55).]

*Human Resources*

**49.** (1) **Personnel** — The Director has exclusive authority to

(a) appoint, lay off or terminate the employment of the employees of the Centre; and

(b) establish standards, procedures and processes governing staffing, including the appointment, lay-off or termination of the employment of employees otherwise than for cause.

(2) **Right of employer** — Nothing in the *Public Service Staff Relations Act* shall be construed so as to affect the right or authority of the Director to deal with the matters referred to in paragraph (1) (b).

(3) **Personnel management** — Subsection 11(2) of the *Financial Administration Act* does not apply to the Centre, and the Director may

(a) determine the organization of and classify the positions in the Centre;

(b) set the terms and conditions of employment for employees, including termination of employment for cause, and assign to them their duties;

(c) notwithstanding section 56 of the *Public Service Staff Relations Act*, in accordance with the mandate approved by the Treasury Board, fix the remuneration of the employees of the Centre; and

(d) provide for any other matters that the Director considers necessary for effective personnel management in the Centre.

[S.C. 2000, c. 17, s. 49, in force July 5, 2000 (SI/2000-55).]

**50. Political partisanship** — Sections 32 to 34 of the *Public Service Employment Act* apply to the Director and employees of the Centre. For the purposes of those sections, the Director is deemed to be a deputy head and the employees are deemed to be employees as defined in section 2 of that Act.

[S.C. 2000, c. 17, s. 50, in force July 5, 2000 (SI/2000-55).]

*Authority to Provide Services*

**51. Authority to provide services** — When a department or other portion of the public service of Canada specified in Schedule 1 to the *Public Service Staff Relations Act* is authorized to provide services to another department or portion of the public service of Canada specified in that Schedule, it may enter into an agreement to provide those services to the Centre if it considers it appropriate to do so.

[S.C. 2000, c. 17, s. 51, in force July 5, 2000 (SI/2000-55).]

*Disclosure of Information*

**52.** (1) **Director to report to Minister** — The Director shall report to the Minister from time to time on the exercise of the Director's powers and the performance of his or her duties and functions under this Act.

(2) **Director to keep Minister informed** — The Director shall keep the Minister informed of any matter that could materially affect public policy or the strategic direction of the Centre, and any other matter that the Minister considers necessary.

(3) **Director to disclose other information** — The Director shall, at the Minister's request, disclose to the Minister any information that the Minister considers relevant for the purpose of carrying out the Minister's powers and duties under this Act.

(4) **Disclosure of information to advisor** — The Director shall disclose to a person engaged under subsection 42(4) any information that the person considers relevant for the purpose of advising the Minister on any matter referred to in subsection 42(2).

[S.C. 2000, c. 17, s. 52, in force July 5, 2000 (SI/2000-55).]

**53. Limitation** — The Director may not disclose any information under section 52 that would directly or indirectly identify an individual who provided a report or information to the Centre, or a person or an entity about whom a report or information was provided under this Act.

[S.C. 2000, c. 17, s. 53, in force July 5, 2000 (SI/2000-55).]

*Reports and Information*

**54. Reports and information** — The Centre

(a) shall receive reports made under section 7, 7.1, 9, 12 or 20, incomplete reports sent under subsection 14(5), reports referred to in section 9.1, information provided to the Centre by any agency of another country that has powers and duties similar to those of the Centre, information provided to the Centre by law enforcement agencies or government institutions or agencies, and other information voluntarily provided to the Centre about suspicions of money laundering or of the financing of terrorist activities;

(b) may collect information that the Centre considers relevant to money laundering activities or the financing of terrorist activities and that is publicly available, including commercially available databases, or that is stored in databases maintained by the federal or provincial governments for purposes related to law enforcement or national security and in respect of which an agreement was entered into under subsection 66(1);

(c) shall analyse and assess the reports and information;

(d) subject to section 6 of the *Privacy Act*, shall retain each report and all information for five years after the date the report is received or the information is received or collected or, where information is disclosed under subsection 55(3), (4) or (5), shall retain the information and any report containing it for eight years after that date; and

(e) notwithstanding the *Library and Archives of Canada Act*, shall destroy each report received and all information received or collected on the expiry of the applicable period referred to in paragraph (d).

[S.C. 2000, c. 17, s. 54, partially in force July 5, 2000 (SI/ 2000-55), S.C. 2001, c. 17, s. 54, the portion before paragraph (b), in force October 28, 2001 (SI/2001-88); S.C. 2001, c. 12, s. 1; S.C. 2001, c. 41, s. 66; S.C. 2004, c. 11, s. 42; S.C. 2004, c. 15, s. 100.]

## Disclosure and Use of Information

**55.** (1) **Disclosure by Centre prohibited** — Subject to subsection (3), sections 52, 55.1 and 56.1, subsection 58(1) and section 65 and to subsection 12(1) of the *Privacy Act*, the Centre shall not disclose the following:

(a)   information set out in a report made under section 7;

(a.1) information set out in a report made under section 7.1;

(b)   information set out in a report made under section 9;

(b.1) information set out in a report referred to in section 9.1;

(c)   information set out in a report made under subsection 12(1), whether or not it is completed, or section 20;

(d)   information voluntarily provided to the Centre about suspicions of money laundering or of the financing of terrorist activities;

(e)   information prepared by the Centre from information referred to in paragraphs (a) to (d); or

(f)   any other information, other than publicly available information, obtained in the administration or enforcement of this Part.

(2) **Disclosure by others prohibited** — The prohibition in subsection (1) also applies to the following persons:

(a) any person who, in the course of exercising powers or performing duties or functions under this Part, obtained or has or had access to information referred to in subsection (1); and

(b) any person or an employee of any person with whom the Centre enters into a contract, memorandum of understanding or other agreement for the provision of goods or services.

(3) **Disclosure of designated information** — If the Centre, on the basis of its analysis and assessment under paragraph 54(c), has reasonable grounds to suspect that designated information would be relevant to investigating or prosecuting a money laundering offence or a terrorist activity financing offence, the Centre shall disclose the information to

(a)  the appropriate police force;

(b)  the Canada Customs and Revenue Agency, if the Centre also determines that the information is relevant to an offence of evading or attempting to evade paying taxes or duties imposed under an Act of Parliament administered by the Minister of National Revenue; and

(c)  [Repealed: S.C. 2001, c. 41, s. 67(6)]

(d)  the Department of Citizenship and Immigration, if the Centre also determines that the information would promote the objective set out in paragraph 3(1)(i) of the *Immigration and Refugee Protection Act* and is relevant to determining whether a person is a person described in sections 34 to 42 of that Act or to an offence under any of sections 117 to 119, 126 or 127 of that Act.

(4) [Repealed: S.C. 2001, c. 41, s. 67(7)]

(5) [Repealed: S.C. 2001, c. 41, s. 67(7)]

(5.1) **Recording of reasons for decision** — The Centre shall record in writing the reasons for all decisions to disclose information made under subsection (3).

(6) **Exception** — A person may disclose any information referred to in subsection (1) if the disclosure is necessary for the purpose of exercising powers or performing duties and functions under this Part.

(7) **Definition of "designated information"** — For the purposes of subsection (3), "designated information" means, in respect of a financial transaction or an importation or exportation of currency or monetary instruments,

(a)  the name of the client or of the importer or exporter, or any person acting on their behalf;

(b)  the name and address of the place of business where the transaction occurred or the address of the customs office where the importation or exportation occurred, and the date the transaction, importation or exportation occurred;

(c)  the amount and type of currency or monetary instruments involved or, in the case of a transaction, if no currency or monetary instruments are involved, the value of the transaction or the value of the funds that are the subject of the transaction;

(d)  in the case of a transaction, the transaction number and the account number, if any; and

(e)  any other similar identifying information that may be prescribed for the purposes of this section.

[S.C. 2000, c. 17, s. 55, partially in force July 5, 2000 (SI/ 2000-55); S.C. 2001, c. 17, s. 55(3) to (5.1) and (7), in force October 28, 2001 (SI/2001-88); S.C. 2001, c. 41, s. 67; S.C. 2001, c. 27, s. 270, as amended by S.C. 2001, c. 41, s. 123(1).]

**55.1** (1) **Disclosure of information to the Canadian Security Intelligence Service** — If the Centre, on the basis of its analysis and assessment under paragraph 54(c), has reasonable grounds to suspect that designated information would be relevant to threats to the security of Canada, the Centre shall disclose that information to the Canadian Security Intelligence Service.

(2) **Recording of reasons for decision** — The Centre shall record in writing the reasons for all decisions to disclose information made under subsection (1).

(3) **Definition of "designated information"** — For the purposes of subsection (1), "designated information" means, in respect of a financial transaction or an importation or exportation of currency or monetary instruments,

(a) the name of the client or of the importer or exporter, or any person or entity acting on their behalf;

(b) the name and address of the place of business where the transaction occurred or the address of the customs office where the importation or exportation occurred, and the date the transaction, importation or exportation occurred;

(c) the amount and type of currency or monetary instruments involved or, in the case of a transaction, if no currency or monetary instruments are involved, the value of the transaction or the value of the funds that are the subject of the transaction;

(d) in the case of a transaction, the transaction number and the account number, if any; and

(e) any other similar identifying information that may be prescribed for the purposes of this section.

[S.C. 2001, c. 41, s. 68.]

**56.** (1) **Agreements and arrangements** — The Minister may enter into an agreement or arrangement, in writing, with the government of a foreign state, or an international organization established by the governments of foreign states regarding the exchange, between the Centre and any institution or agency of that state or organization that has powers and duties similar to those of the Centre, of information that the Centre, institution or agency has reasonable grounds to suspect would be relevant to investigating or prosecuting a money laundering offence or a terrorist activity financing offence, or an offence that is substantially similar to either offence.

(2) **Agreements and arrangements - Centre** — The Centre may, with the approval of the Minister, enter into an agreement or arrangement, in writing, with an institution or agency of a foreign state that has powers and duties similar to those of the Centre, regarding the exchange, between the Centre and the institution or agency, of information that the Centre, institution or agency has reasonable grounds to suspect would be relevant to investigating or prosecuting a money laundering offence or a terrorist activity financing offence, or an offence that is substantially similar to either offence.

(3) **Purposes** — Agreements or arrangements entered into under subsection (1) or (2) must

(a) restrict the use of information to purposes relevant to investigating or prosecuting a money laundering offence or a terrorist activity financing offence, or an offence that is substantially similar to either offence; and

(b) stipulate that the information be treated in a confidential manner and not be further disclosed without the express consent of the Centre.

[S.C. 2000, c. 17, s. 56, in force July 5, 2000 (SI/2000-55); S.C. 2001, c. 41, s. 67.]

**56.1** (1) **Disclosure to foreign agencies** — The Centre may disclose designated information to an institution or agency of a foreign state or of an international organization established by the governments of foreign states that has powers and duties similar to those of the Centre, if

(a) the Centre has reasonable grounds to suspect that the information would be relevant to the investigation or prosecution of a money laundering offence or a terrorist activity financing offence, or an offence that is substantially similar to either offence; and

(b) the Minister has, in accordance with subsection 56(1), entered into an agreement or arrangement with that foreign state or international organization regarding the exchange of such information.

(2) **Disclosure to foreign agencies** — The Centre may disclose designated information to an institution or agency of a foreign state that has powers and duties similar to those of the Centre, if

(a) the Centre has reasonable grounds to suspect that the information would be relevant to the investigation or prosecution of a money laundering offence or a terrorist activity financing offence, or an offence that is substantially similar to either offence; and

(b) the Centre has, in accordance with subsection 56(2), entered into an agreement or arrangement with that institution or agency regarding the exchange of such information.

(2.1) **Request for information** — For greater certainty, designated information may be disclosed to an institution or agency under subsection (1) or (2) in response to a request made by the institution or agency.

(3) **Other disclosure** — In order to perform its functions under paragraph 54(c), the Centre may direct queries to an institution or agency in respect of which an agreement referred to in subsection (1) or (2) has been entered into, and in doing so it may disclose designated information.

(4) **Recording of reasons for decision** — The Centre shall record in writing the reasons for all decisions to disclose information made under paragraph (1)(a) or (2)(a).

(5) **Definition of "designated information"** — For the purposes of this section, "designated information" means, in respect of a financial transaction or an importation or exportation of currency or monetary instruments,

(a) the name of the client or of the importer or exporter, or any person or entity acting on their behalf;

(b) the name and address of the place of business where the transaction occurred or the address of the customs office where the importation or exportation occurred, and the date the transaction, importation or exportation occurred;

(c) the amount and type of currency or monetary instruments involved or, in the case of a transaction, if no currency or monetary instruments are involved, the value of the transaction or the value of the funds that are the subject of the transaction;

(d) in the case of a transaction, the transaction number and the account number, if any; and

(e) any other similar identifying information that may be prescribed for the purposes of this section.

[S.C. 2001, c. 41, s. 67.]

**57. Use of information** — No person who obtained or who has or had access to information referred to in subsection 55(1) in the course of exercising powers or performing duties and functions under this Part shall use the information for a purpose other than exercising those powers or performing those duties and functions.

[S.C. 2000, c. 17, s. 57, in force July 5, 2000 (SI/2000-55).]

**58.** (1) **Feedback, research and public education** — The Centre may

(a) inform persons and entities that have provided a report under section 7, 7.1 or 9, or a report referred to in section 9.1, about measures that have been taken with respect to reports under those sections;

(b) conduct research into trends and developments in the area of money laundering and the financing of terrorist activities and improved ways of detecting, preventing and deterring money laundering and the financing of terrorist activities; and

(c) undertake measures to inform the public, persons and entities referred to in section 5, authorities engaged in the investigation and prosecution of money laundering offences and terrorist activity financing offences, and others, with respect to

  (i) their obligations under this Act,

  (ii) the nature and extent of money laundering in Canada,

  (ii.1) the nature and extent of the financing of terrorist activities in Canada, and

  (iii) measures that have been or might be taken to detect, prevent and deter money laundering and the financing of terrorist activities in Canada, and the effectiveness of those measures.

(2) **Limitation** — The Centre may not disclose any information that would directly or indirectly identify an individual who provided a report or information to the Centre, or a person or an entity about whom a report or information was provided.

[S.C. 2000, c. 17, s. 58, in force July 5, 2000 (SI/2000-55); S.C. 2001, c. 41, s. 69.]

**59.** (1) **Immunity from compulsory processes** — Subject to section 36 of the *Access to Information Act* and section 34 of the *Privacy Act*, the Centre, and any person who has obtained or who has or had access to any information or documents in the course of exercising powers or performing duties and functions under this Act, other than Part 2, is required to comply with a subpoena, a summons, an order for production of documents, or any other compulsory process only if it is issued in the course of court proceedings in respect of a money laundering offence, a terrorist activity financing offence or an offence under this Act in respect of which an information has been laid or an indictment preferred or, in the case of an order for production of documents, if it is issued under section 60.1 for the purposes of an investigation in respect of a threat to the security of Canada.

(2) **Search warrants** — Despite any other Act, no search warrant may be issued in respect of the Centre.

[S.C. 2000, c. 17, s. 59, in force July 5, 2000 (SI/2000-55); S.C. 2001, c. 41, s. 70.]

**60.** (1) **Limitation on orders for disclosure of information** — Despite the provisions of any other Act, except sections 49 and 50 of the *Access to Information Act* and sections 48 and 49 of the *Privacy Act*, an order for disclosure of information may be issued in respect of the Centre only under subsection (4) or section 60.1.

(2) **Purpose of application** — The Attorney General may, for the purposes of an investigation in respect of a money laundering offence or a terrorist activity financing offence, make an application under subsection (3) for an order for disclosure of information.

(3) **Application** — An application shall be made *ex parte* in writing to a judge and be accompanied by an affidavit sworn on the information and belief of the Attorney General — or a person specially designated by the Attorney General for that purpose — deposing to the following matters:

(a)  the offence under investigation;

(b)  the person in relation to whom the information or documents referred to in paragraph (c) are required;

(c)  the type of information or documents — whether in written form, in the form of a report or record or in any other form — obtained by or on behalf of the Director in respect of which disclosure is sought;

(d)  the facts relied on to justify the belief, on reasonable grounds, that the person referred to in paragraph (b) has committed or benefited from the commission of a money laundering offence or a terrorist activity financing offence and that the information or documents referred to in paragraph (c) are likely to be of substantial value, whether alone or together with other material, to an investigation in respect of that offence;

(e)  a summary of any information already received from the Centre in respect of the offence; and

(f)  information respecting all previous applications brought under this section in respect of any person being investigated for the offence.

(4) **Order for disclosure of information** — Subject to the conditions that the judge considers advisable in the public interest, the judge to whom an application is made may order the Director — or any person specially designated in writing by the Director for the purposes of this section — to allow a police officer named in the order to have access to and examine all information and documents to which the application relates or, if the judge considers it necessary in the circumstances, to produce the information and documents to the police officer and allow the police officer to remove them, where the judge is satisfied

(a)  of the matters referred to in paragraph (3)(d); and

(b)  that there are reasonable grounds for believing that it is in the public interest to allow access to the information or documents, having regard to the benefit likely to accrue to the investigation if the access is obtained.

The order must be complied with within the period following the service of the order that the judge may specify.

(5) **Execution in another province** — A judge may, if the information or documents in respect of which disclosure is sought are in a province other than

the one in which the judge has jurisdiction, issue an order for disclosure and the order may be executed in the other province after it has been endorsed by a judge who has jurisdiction in that other province.

(6) **Service of order** — A copy of the order shall be served on the person to whom it is addressed in the manner that the judge directs or as may be prescribed by rules of court.

(7) **Extension of period for compliance with order** — A judge who makes an order under subsection (4) may, on application of the Director, extend the period within which it is to be complied with.

(8) **Objection to disclosure of information** — The Director — or any person specially designated in writing by the Director for the purposes of this section — may object to the disclosure of any information or document in respect of which an order under subsection (4) has been made by certifying orally or in writing that it should not be disclosed on the ground that

(a) the Director is prohibited from disclosing the information or document by any bilateral or international treaty, convention or other agreement to which the Government of Canada is a signatory respecting the sharing of information related to a money laundering offence or a terrorist activity financing offence, or an offence that is substantially similar to either offence;

(b) a privilege is attached by law to the information or document;

(c) the information or document has been placed in a sealed package pursuant to law or an order of a court of competent jurisdiction; or

(d) disclosure of the information or document would not, for any other reason, be in the public interest.

(9) **Determination of objection** — An objection made under subsection (8) may be determined, on application, in accordance with subsection (10), by the Chief Justice of the Federal Court, or by any other judge of that Court that the Chief Justice may designate to hear those applications.

(10) **Judge may examine information** — A judge who is to determine an objection may, if the judge considers it necessary to determine the objection, examine the information or document in relation to which the objection is made. The judge shall grant the objection and order that disclosure be refused if the judge is satisfied of any of the grounds mentioned in subsection (8).

(11) **Limitation period** — An application under subsection (9) shall be made within 10 days after the objection is made or within such greater or lesser period as the Chief Justice of the Federal Court, or any other judge of that Court that the Chief Justice may designate to hear those applications, considers appropriate in the circumstances.

(12) **Appeal to Federal Court of Appeal** — An appeal lies from a determination under subsection (9) to the Federal Court of Appeal.

(13) **Limitation period for appeal** — An appeal under subsection (12) shall be brought within 10 days after the date of the determination appealed from or within such further time as the Federal Court of Appeal considers appropriate in the circumstances.

(14) **Special rules for hearings** — An application under subsection (9) or an appeal brought in respect of that application shall be heard in private and, on the request of the person objecting to the disclosure of the information or documents, be heard and determined in the National Capital Region described in the schedule to the *National Capital Act*.

(15) **Ex parte representations** — During the hearing of an application under subsection (9) or an appeal brought in respect of that application, the person who made the objection in respect of which the application was made or the appeal was brought shall, on the request of that person, be given the opportunity to make representations *ex parte*.

(16) **Copies** — Where any information or document is examined or provided under subsection (4), the person by whom it is examined or to whom it is provided or any employee of the Centre may make, or cause to be made, one or more copies of it and any copy purporting to be certified by the Director or an authorized person to be a copy made under this subsection is evidence of the nature and content of the original information or document and has the same probative force as the original information or document would have had if it had been proved in the ordinary way.

(17) **Definitions** — The definitions in this subsection apply in this section.

"Attorney General" means the Attorney General as defined in section 2 of the *Criminal Code*.

"judge" means a provincial court judge as defined in section 2 of the *Criminal Code* or a judge as defined in subsection 462.3(1) of that Act.

"police officer" means any officer, constable or other person employed for the preservation and maintenance of the public peace.

[S.C. 2000, c. 17, s. 60, in force July 5, 2000 (SI/2000-55); S.C. 2001, c. 12, s. 3; S.C. 2001, c. 41, s. 71; S.C. 2001, c. 32, s. 72.]

**60.1** (1) **Application for production order** — The Director of the Canadian Security Intelligence Service, or any employee of the Canadian Security Intelligence Service, may, for the purposes of an investigation in respect of a threat to the security of Canada, after having obtained the approval of the Solicitor General of Canada, make an application under subsection (2) to a judge for an order for disclosure of information.

(2) **Matters to be specified in application for production order** — An application shall be made *ex parte* in writing and be accompanied by an affidavit of the applicant deposing to the following matters:

(a) the person or entity in relation to whom the information or documents referred to in paragraph (b) are required;

(b) the type of information or documents — whether in written form, in the form of a report or record or in any other form — obtained by or on behalf of the Director in respect of which disclosure is sought;

(c) the facts relied on to justify the belief, on reasonable grounds, that a production order under this section is required to enable the Canadian Security Intelligence Service to investigate a threat to the security of Canada;

(d) a summary of any information already received from the Centre in respect of the threat to the security of Canada; and

(e) information respecting all previous applications brought under this section in respect of any person or entity being investigated in relation to the threat to the security of Canada.

(3) **Order for disclosure of information** — Subject to the conditions that the judge considers advisable in the public interest, the judge to whom an application is made may order the Director — or any person specially designated in writing by the Director for the purpose of this section — to allow an employee of the Canadian Security Intelligence Service named in the order to have access to and examine all information and documents to which the application relates or, if the judge considers it necessary in the circumstances, to produce the information and documents to the employee and allow the employee to remove them, if the judge is satisfied

(a) of the matters referred to in subsection (2); and

(b) that there are reasonable grounds for believing that it is in the public interest to allow access to the information or documents, having regard to the benefit likely to accrue to the investigation if the access is obtained.

The order must be complied with within the period following the service of the order that the judge may specify.

(4) **Maximum duration of production order** — A production order shall not be issued under subsection (3) for a period exceeding sixty days.

(5) **Service of order** — A copy of the order shall be served on the person or entity to whom it is addressed in the manner that the judge directs or as may be prescribed by rules of court.

(6) **Extension of period for compliance with order** — A judge who makes an order under subsection (3) may, on application of the Director, extend the period within which it is to be complied with.

(7) **Objection to disclosure of information** — The Director — or any person specially designated in writing by the Director for the purposes of this section — may object to the disclosure of any information or document in respect of which an order under subsection (3) has been made by certifying orally or in writing that it should not be disclosed on the ground that

(a) the Director is prohibited from disclosing the information or document by any bilateral or international treaty, convention or other agreement to which the Government of Canada is a signatory respecting the sharing of information related to a money laundering offence or a terrorist activity financing offence, or an offence that is substantially similar to either offence;

(b) a privilege is attached by law to the information or document;

(c) the information or document has been placed in a sealed package pursuant to law or an order of a court of competent jurisdiction; or

(d) disclosure of the information or document would not, for any other reason, be in the public interest.

(8) **Determination of objection** — An objection made under subsection (7) may be determined, on application, in accordance with subsection (9), by the Chief Justice of the Federal Court, or by any other judge of that Court that the Chief Justice may designate to hear those applications.

(9) **Judge may examine information** — A judge who is to determine an objection may, if the judge considers it necessary to determine the objection, examine the information or document in relation to which the objection is made. The judge shall grant the objection and order that disclosure be refused if the judge is satisfied of any of the grounds mentioned in subsection (7).

(10) **Limitation period** — An application under subsection (8) shall be made within 10 days after the objection is made or within such greater or lesser period as the Chief Justice of the Federal Court, or any other judge of that Court that the Chief Justice may designate to hear those applications, considers appropriate in the circumstances.

(11) **Appeal to Federal Court of Appeal** — An appeal lies from a determination under subsection (8) to the Federal Court of Appeal.

(12) **Limitation period for appeal** — An appeal under subsection (11) shall be brought within 10 days after the date of the determination appealed from or within such further time as the Federal Court of Appeal considers appropriate in the circumstances.

(13) **Special rules for hearings** — An application under subsection (8) or an appeal brought in respect of that application shall be heard in private and, on the request of the person objecting to the disclosure of the information or documents, be heard and determined in the National Capital Region described in the schedule to the *National Capital Act*.

(14) **Ex parte representations** — During the hearing of an application under subsection (8) or an appeal brought in respect of that application, the person who made the objection in respect of which the application was made or the appeal was brought shall, on the request of that person, be given the opportunity to make representations *ex parte*.

(15) **Copies** — Where any information or document is examined or provided under subsection (3), the person by whom it is examined or to whom it is provided or any employee of the Centre may make, or cause to be made, one or more copies of it and any copy purporting to be certified by the Director or an authorized person to be a copy made under this subsection is evidence of the nature and content of the original information or document and has the same probative force as the original information or document would have had if it had been proved in the ordinary way.

(16) **Definition of "judge"** — In this section, "judge" means a judge of the Federal Court designated by the Chief Justice of the Federal Court for the purposes of the *Canadian Security Intelligence Service Act*.
[S.C. 2001, c. 41, s. 72.]

**60.2 Hearing of applications** — An application under subsection 60.1(2) to a judge for a production order, or an objection under subsection 60.1(7), shall be heard in private in accordance with regulations made under section 28 of the *Canadian Security Intelligence Service Act*.
[S.C. 2001, c. 41, s. 72.]

**61. Certain provisions not applicable** — Section 43 of the *Customs Act*, section 231.2 of the *Income Tax Act* and section 289 of the *Excise Tax Act* do not apply to the Centre or to its employees in their capacity as employees.

[S.C. 2000, c. 17, s. 61, in force July 5, 2000 (SI/2000-55).]

*Compliance Measures*

**62.** (1) **To ensure compliance** — An authorized person may, from time to time, examine the records and inquire into the business and affairs of any person or entity referred to in section 5 for the purpose of ensuring compliance with Part 1, and for that purpose may

(a)  at any reasonable time, enter any premises, other than a dwelling-house, in which the authorized person believes, on reasonable grounds, that there are records relevant to ensuring compliance with Part 1;

(b)  use or cause to be used any computer system or data processing system in the premises to examine any data contained in or available to the system;

(c)  reproduce any record, or cause it to be reproduced from the data, in the form of a printout or other intelligible output and remove the printout or other output for examination or copying; and

(d)  use or cause to be used any copying equipment in the premises to make copies of any record.

(2) **Assistance to Centre** — The owner or person in charge of premises referred to in subsection (1) and every person found there shall give the authorized person all reasonable assistance to enable them to carry out their responsibilities and shall furnish them with any information with respect to the administration of Part 1 or the regulations under it that they may reasonably require.

[S.C. 2000, c. 17, s. 62, in force June 12, 2002 (SI/2002-84).]

**63.** (1) **Warrant required to enter dwelling-house** — If the premises referred to in subsection 62(1) is a dwelling-house, the authorized person may not enter it without the consent of the occupant except under the authority of a warrant issued under subsection (2).

(2) **Authority to issue warrant** — A justice of the peace may issue a warrant authorizing the authorized person to enter a dwelling-house, subject to any conditions that may be specified in the warrant, if on *ex parte* application the justice is satisfied by information on oath that

(a)  there are reasonable grounds to believe that there are in the premises records relevant to ensuring compliance with Part 1;

(b)  entry to the dwelling-house is necessary for any purpose that relates to ensuring compliance with Part 1; and

(c)  entry to the dwelling-house has been refused or there are reasonable grounds for believing that entry will be refused.

(3) **Areas that may be entered** — For greater certainty, an authorized person who enters a dwelling-house under authority of a warrant may enter only a room or part of a room in which the person believes on reasonable grounds that a

person or an entity referred to in section 5 is carrying on its business, profession or activity.

[S.C. 2000, c. 17, s. 63, in force June 12, 2002 (SI/2002-84).]

**64. (1) Definition of "judge"** — In this section, "judge" means a judge of a superior court having jurisdiction in the province where the matter arises or a judge of the Federal Court.

**(2) No examination or copying of certain documents when privilege claimed** — If an authorized person acting under section 62 or 63 is about to examine or copy a document in the possession of a legal counsel who claims that a named client or former client of the legal counsel has a solicitor-client privilege in respect of the document, the authorized person shall not examine or make copies of the document.

**(3) Retention of documents** — A legal counsel who claims privilege under subsection (2) shall

(a) place the document, together with any other document in respect of which the legal counsel at the same time makes the same claim on behalf of the same client, in a package and suitably seal and identify the package or, if the authorized person and the legal counsel agree, allow the pages of the document to be initialled and numbered or otherwise suitably identified; and

(b) retain it and ensure that it is preserved until it is produced to a judge as required under this section and an order is issued under this section in respect of the document.

**(4) Application to judge** — If a document has been retained under subsection (3), the client or the legal counsel on behalf of the client may

(a) within 14 days after the day the document was begun to be so retained, apply, on three days notice of motion to the Deputy Attorney General of Canada, to a judge for an order
  (i) fixing a day, not later than 21 days after the date of the order, and a place for the determination of the question whether the client has solicitor-client privilege in respect of the document, and
  (ii) requiring the production of the document to the judge at that time and place;

(b) serve a copy of the order on the Deputy Attorney General of Canada; and

(c) if the client or legal counsel has served a copy of the order under paragraph (b), apply at the appointed time and place for an order determining the question.

**(5) Disposition of application** — An application under paragraph (4)(c) shall be heard in private and, on the application, the judge

(a) may, if the judge considers it necessary to determine the question, inspect the document and, if the judge does so, the judge shall ensure that it is repackaged and resealed;

(b) shall decide the question summarily and

      (i) if the judge is of the opinion that the client has a solicitor-client privilege in respect of the document, order the release of the document to the legal counsel, or

      (ii) if the judge is of the opinion that the client does not have a solicitor-client privilege in respect of the document, order that the legal counsel make the document available for examination or copying by the authorized person; and

  (c) at the same time as making an order under paragraph (b), deliver concise reasons that identify the document without divulging the details of it.

(6) **Order to deliver** — If a document is being retained under subsection (3) and a judge, on the application of the Attorney General of Canada, is satisfied that no application has been made under paragraph (4)(a) or that after having made that application no further application has been made under paragraph (4)(c), the judge shall order that the legal counsel make the document available for examination or copying by the authorized person.

(7) **Application to another judge** — If the judge to whom an application has been made under paragraph (4)(a) cannot act or continue to act in the application under paragraph (4)(c) for any reason, the application under paragraph (4)(c) may be made to another judge.

(8) **Costs** — No costs may be awarded on the disposition of an application under this section.

(9) **Prohibition** — The authorized person shall not examine or make copies of any document without giving a reasonable opportunity for a claim of solicitor-client privilege to be made under subsection (2).

(9.1) **Prohibition** — The authorized person shall not examine or make copies of a document in the possession of a person, not being a legal counsel, who contends that a claim of solicitor-client privilege may be made in respect of the document by a legal counsel, without giving that person a reasonable opportunity to contact that legal counsel to enable a claim of solicitor-client privilege to be made.

(10) **Waiver of claim of privilege** — If a legal counsel has made a claim that a named client or former client of the legal counsel has a solicitor-client privilege in respect of a document, the legal counsel shall at the same time communicate to the authorized person the client's latest known address so that the authorized person may endeavour to advise the client of the claim of privilege that has been made on their behalf and may by doing so give the client an opportunity, if it is practicable within the time limited by this section, to waive the privilege before the matter is to be decided by a judge.

[S.C. 2000, c. 17, s. 64, in force June 12, 2002 (SI/2002-84).]

**65.** (1) **Disclosure to law enforcement agencies** — The Centre may disclose to the appropriate law enforcement agencies any information of which it becomes aware under section 62 or 63 and that it suspects on reasonable grounds is evidence of a contravention of Part 1.

(2) **Compliance of persons or entities** — For the purpose of ensuring compliance with Part 1, the Centre may disclose to or receive from any agency or body

that regulates or supervises persons or entities to whom Part 1 applies information relating to the compliance of those persons or entities with that Part.

(3) **Limitation** — Any information disclosed by the Centre under subsection (2) may be used by an agency or body referred to in that subsection only for purposes relating to compliance with Part 1.

[S.C. 2000, c. 17, s. 65, in force June 12, 2002 (SI/2002-84); S.C. 2004, c. 15, s. 101.]

### Contracts and Agreements

**66.** (1) **Power to enter into** — The Centre may, for the purpose of exercising its powers or performing its duties and functions under this Part, enter into contracts, memoranda of understanding and other agreements with a department or an agency of the Government of Canada or the government of a province and with any other person or organization, whether inside or outside Canada, in its own name or in the name of Her Majesty in right of Canada.

(2) **Agreements re databases** — Agreements relating to the Centre's collection of information from databases referred to in paragraph 54(b) must specify the nature of and limits with respect to the information that the Centre may collect from those databases.

(3) **Limitation** — Despite subsection (1), only the Minister may enter into an agreement or arrangement referred to in subsection 56(1).

[S.C. 2000, c. 17, s. 66, in force July 5, 2000 (SI/2000-55).]

**67. Choice of service providers** — Despite section 9 of the *Department of Public Works and Government Services Act*, the Centre may, with the approval of the Governor in Council given on the recommendation of the Treasury Board, procure goods and services, including legal services, from outside the public service of Canada.

[S.C. 2000, c. 17, s. 67, in force July 5, 2000 (SI/2000-55).]

### Legal Proceedings

**68. Centre** — Actions, suits or other legal proceedings in respect of any right or obligation acquired or incurred by the Centre, whether in its own name or in the name of Her Majesty in right of Canada, may be brought or taken by or against the Centre in the name of the Centre in any court that would have jurisdiction if the Centre were a corporation that is not an agent of Her Majesty.

[S.C. 2000, c. 17, s. 68, in force July 5, 2000 (SI/2000-55).]

**69. No liability** — No action lies against Her Majesty, the Minister, the Director, any employee of the Centre or any person acting under the direction of the Director for anything done or omitted to be done in good faith in the administration or discharge of any powers, duties or functions that under this Act are intended or authorized to be exercised or performed.

[S.C. 2000, c. 17, s. 69, in force July 5, 2000 (SI/2000-55).]

*Audit*

**70.** (1) **Audit** — All receipts and expenditures of the Centre are subject to examination and audit by the Auditor General of Canada.

(2) **Use and disclosure** — The Auditor General of Canada and every person acting on behalf of or under the direction of the Auditor General of Canada shall not use or disclose any information referred to in subsection 55(1) that they have obtained, or to which they have had access, in the course of exercising powers or performing duties and functions under this Act or the *Auditor General Act*, except for the purposes of exercising those powers or performing those duties and functions.

[S.C. 2000, c. 17, s. 70, in force July 5, 2000 (SI/2000-55).]

*Reports*

**71.** (1) **Annual report** — The Director shall, on or before September 30 of each year following the Centre's first full year of operations, submit an annual report on the operations of the Centre for the preceding year to the Minister, and the Minister shall table a copy of the report in each House of Parliament on any of the first 30 days on which that House is sitting after the Minister receives the report.

(2) **Human rights and freedoms** — The report referred to in subsection (1) shall include a description of the management guidelines and policies of the Centre for the protection of human rights and freedoms.

[S.C. 2000, c. 17, s. 71, in force July 5, 2000 (SI/2000-55).]

**72. Review of Act by parliamentary committee** — Within five years after this section comes into force, the administration and operation of this Act shall be reviewed by the committee of Parliament that may be designated or established by Parliament for that purpose and the committee shall submit a report to Parliament that includes a statement of any changes to this Act or its administration that the committee recommends.

[S.C. 2000, c. 17, s. 72, in force July 5, 2000 (SI/2000-55).]

# PART 4 REGULATIONS

**73.** (1) **Regulations** — The Governor in Council may, on the recommendation of the Minister, make any regulations that the Governor in Council considers necessary for carrying out the purposes and provisions of this Act, including regulations

(a) describing businesses, professions and activities for the purpose of paragraph 5(i);

(b) describing businesses and professions for the purpose of paragraph 5(j), and the activities to which that paragraph applies;

(c) describing the activities to which paragraph 5(l) applies;

(d) specifying the types of records to be kept and retained under section 6 and the information to be included in them;

(e) specifying the period for which, and the methods by which, records re ferred to in paragraph (d) are to be retained;

(e.1) specifying the information to be contained in a report under section 7 or 7.1 or subsection 9(1);

(f) specifying measures that persons or entities are to take to identify any person or entity in respect of which a record is required to be kept or a report made;

(g) defining "casinos", "courier" and "monetary instruments";

(h) specifying the form and manner of reporting currency and monetary in- struments for the purpose of subsection 12(1), and the information to be contained in the form, and specifying the period within which the re- porting must be made; and

(i) prescribing anything else that by this Act is to be prescribed.

(2) [Repealed: S.C. 2001, c. 41, s. 73(2)]

(3) [Repealed: S.C. 2001, c. 41, s. 73(2)]

[S.C. 2000, c. 17, s. 73, in force July 5, 2000 (SI/2000-55); S.C. 2001, c. 41, s. 73.]

# PART 5 OFFENCES AND PUNISHMENT

**74. General offences** — Every person or entity that knowingly contravenes section 6, subsection 12(4) or 36(1), section 37, subsection 55(1) or (2), section 57 or subsection 62(2) or 64(3) or the regulations is guilty of an offence and liable

(a) on summary conviction, to a fine of not more than $50,000 or to impris- onment for a term of not more than six months, or to both; or

(b) on conviction on indictment, to a fine of not more than $500,000 or to im- prisonment for a term of not more than five years, or to both.

[S.C. 2000, c. 17, s. 74, in force July 5, 2000 (SI/2000-55).]

**75. (1) Reporting — sections 7 and 7.1** — Every person or entity that know- ingly contravenes section 7 or 7.1 is guilty of an offence and liable

(a) on summary conviction,

(i) for a first offence, to a fine of not more than $500,000 or to impris- onment for a term of not more than six months, or to both, and

(ii) for a subsequent offence, to a fine of not more than $1,000,000 or to imprisonment for a term of not more than one year, or to both; or

(b) on conviction on indictment, to a fine of not more than $2,000,000 or to imprisonment for a term of not more than five years, or to both.

(2) **Defence for employees** — No employee of a person or an entity shall be convicted of an offence under subsection (1) in respect of a transaction or pro- posed transaction that they reported to their superior or in respect of property whose existence they reported to their superior.

[S.C. 2000, c. 17, s. 75, in force July 5, 2000 (SI/2000-55); S.C. 2001, c. 41, s. 74.]

**76. Disclosure** — Every person or entity that contravenes section 8

(a) is guilty of an offence punishable on summary conviction; or

(b) is guilty of an indictable offence and liable to imprisonment for a term of not more than two years.

[S.C. 2000, c. 17, s. 76, in force July 5, 2000 (SI/2000-55).]

**77.** (1) **Reporting – section 9** — Every person or entity that contravenes subsection 9(1) or (3) is guilty of an offence and liable on summary conviction to a fine of not more than $500,000 for a first offence and of not more than $1,000,000 for each subsequent offence.

(2) **Due diligence defence** — No person or entity shall be convicted of an offence under subsection (1) if they exercised due diligence to prevent its commission.

[S.C. 2000, c. 17, s. 77, in force July 5, 2000 (SI/2000-55).]

**78. Liability of officers and directors** — If a person or an entity commits an offence under this Act, any officer, director or agent of the person or entity who directed, authorized, assented to, acquiesced in or participated in its commission is a party to and guilty of the offence and liable on conviction to the punishment provided for the offence, whether or not the person or entity has been prosecuted or convicted.

[S.C. 2000, c. 17, s. 78, in force July 5, 2000 (SI/2000-55).]

**79. Offence by employee or agent** — In a prosecution for an offence under section 75 or 77,

(a) it is sufficient proof of the offence to establish that it was committed by an employee or agent of the accused, whether or not the employee or agent is identified or has been prosecuted for the offence; and

(b) no person shall be found guilty of the offence if they establish that they exercised due diligence to prevent its commission.

[S.C. 2000, c. 17, s. 79, in force July 5, 2000 (SI/2000-55).]

**80. Exemption** — A peace officer or a person acting under the direction of a peace officer is not guilty of an offence under any of sections 74 to 77 if the peace officer or person does any of the things mentioned in those sections for the purpose of investigating a money laundering offence or a terrorist activity financing offence.

[S.C. 2000, c. 17, s. 80, in force July 5, 2000 (SI/2000-55; S.C. 2001, c. 41, s. 75.]

**81. Time limitation** — Proceedings under paragraph 74(a), 75(1)(a) or 76(a) or subsection 77(1) may be instituted within, but not after, one year after the time when the subject-matter of the proceedings arose.

[S.C. 2000, c. 17, s. 81, in force July 5, 2000 (SI/2000-55).]

**82. Venue** — A complaint or information in respect of an offence under this Act may be heard, tried or determined by a court if the accused is resident or carrying on business within the territorial jurisdiction of the court although the subject-matter of the complaint or information did not arise in that territorial jurisdiction.

[S.C. 2000, c. 17, s. 82, in force July 5, 2000 (SI/2000-55).]

# PART 6 TRANSITIONAL PROVISION, CONSEQUENTIAL AND CONDITIONAL AMENDMENTS, REPEAL AND COMING INTO FORCE

*Transitional Provision*

**83. Regulations remain in effect** — Every regulation made under the *Proceeds of Crime (Money Laundering) Act*, chapter 26 of the Statutes of Canada, 1991, that is in force immediately before the coming into force of this Act shall be deemed to have been made under this Act and shall remain in force until it is repealed or amended pursuant to this Act.

[S.C. 2000, c. 17, s. 83, in force June 12, 2002 (SI/2002-84).]

# PROCEEDS OF CRIME (MONEY LAUNDERING) AND TERRORIST FINANCING SUSPICIOUS TRANSACTION REPORTING REGULATIONS

## SOR/2001-317

**Amendments:** SOR/2002-185, ss. 1-4, in force May 9, 2002; SOR/2003-102, ss. 1-2, in force March 20, 2003; SOR/2003-358, ss. 1-3, in force November 6, 2003.

Whereas, pursuant to subsection 73(2) of the *Proceeds of Crime (Money Laundering) Act*, a copy of the proposed Proceeds of Crime (Money Laundering) Suspicious Transaction Reporting Regulations was published, substantially in the form set out in the annexed Regulations, as part of the Proceeds of Crime (Money Laundering) Regulations, 2000 in the Canada Gazette, Part I, on February 17, 2001 and a reasonable opportunity was thereby given to interested persons to make representations to the Minister of Finance with respect to the proposed Regulations;

Therefore, Her Excellency the Governor General in Council, on the recommendation of the Minister of Finance, pursuant to section 73 of the *Proceeds of Crime (Money Laundering) Act\**, hereby makes the annexed *Proceeds of Crime (Money Laundering) Suspicious Transaction Reporting Regulations*.

\* S.C. 2000, c. 17.

**1.** (1) **Interpretation** — For the purposes of the Act and in these Regulations, "casino" means a person or entity that is licensed, registered, permitted or otherwise authorized to do business under any of paragraphs 207(1)(a) to (g) of the *Criminal Code* and that conducts its business activities in a permanent establishment

(a) that the person or entity holds out to be a casino and in which roulette or card games are carried on; or

(b) where there is a slot machine, which, for the purposes of this definition, does not include a video lottery terminal.

It does not include a person or entity that is a registered charity as defined in subsection 248(1) of the *Income Tax Act* and is licensed, registered, permitted or otherwise authorized to carry on business temporarily for charitable purposes, if the business is carried out in the establishment of the casino for not more than two consecutive days at a time under the supervision of the casino.

(2) The definitions in this subsection apply in these Regulations.

"accountant" means a chartered accountant, a certified general accountant or a certified management accountant.

"accounting firm" means an entity that is engaged in the business of providing accounting services to the public and has at least one partner, employee or administrator that is an accountant.

"Act" means the *Proceeds of Crime (Money Laundering) and Terrorist Financing Act.*

"cash" means coins referred to in section 7 of the *Currency Act*, notes issued by the Bank of Canada pursuant to the *Bank of Canada Act* that are intended for circulation in Canada and coins or bank notes of countries other than Canada.

"cash" or "currency" [Repealed, SOR/2002-185, s. 2]

"CICA Handbook" means the handbook prepared and published by the Canadian Institute of Chartered Accountants, as amended from time to time.

"electronic funds transfer" means the transmission — through any electronic, magnetic or optical device, telephone instrument or computer — of instructions for the transfer of funds, including a SWIFT MT 100 or MT 103 message.

"financial entity" means an authorized foreign bank within the meaning of section 2 of the *Bank Act* in respect of its business in Canada or a bank to which that Act applies, a cooperative credit society, savings and credit union or caisse populaire that is regulated by a provincial Act, an association that is regulated by the *Cooperative Credit Associations Act*, a company to which the *Trust and Loan Companies Act* applies and a trust company and loan company regulated by a provincial Act. It includes a department or agent of Her Majesty in right of Canada or of a province where the department or agent is carrying out an activity referred to in section 8.

"funds" means cash, currency or securities, or negotiable instruments or other financial instruments, in any form, that indicate a person's or an entity's title or interest in them.

"legal firm" [Repealed, SOR/2003-102, s. 1]

"life insurance broker or agent" means a person or entity that is registered or licensed under provincial legislation to carry on the business of arranging contracts of life insurance.

"money services business" means a person or entity that is engaged in the business of remitting funds or transmitting funds by any means or through any person, entity or electronic funds transfer network, or of issuing or redeeming money orders, traveller's cheques or other similar negotiable instruments. It includes a financial entity when it carries out one of those activities with a person or entity that is not an account holder.

"real estate broker or sales representative" means a person or entity that is registered or licensed under provincial legislation in respect of the sale or purchase of real estate.

"SWIFT" means the Society for Worldwide Interbank Financial Telecommunication.

"trust company" means a company to which the *Trust and Loan Companies Act* applies or a trust company regulated by a provincial Act.

[SOR/2002-185, s. 2; SOR/2003-102, s. 1; SOR/2003-358, s. 1, in force November 6, 2003.]

**1.1** For the purposes of paragraph 5(i) of the Act, any business, temporarily conducted for charitable purposes in the establishment of a casino by a registered charity carried on for not more than two consecutive days at a time under the supervision of the casino, is considered to be an activity conducted by the supervising casino.

[SOR/2003-358, s. 2, in force November 6, 2003.]

**2.** For the purposes of these Regulations, a person acting on behalf of their employer is considered to be acting on behalf of another person or entity except when the person is depositing cash into the employer's account.

[SOR/2002-185, s. 3.]

## APPLICATION OF PART 1 OF THE ACT

**3.** Part 1 of the Act applies to life insurance brokers or agents.

[SOR/2002-185, s. 3.]

**4.** (1) Every money services business is subject to Part 1 of the Act when it engages in any of the following activities:

(a) remitting funds or transmitting funds by any means or through any person, entity or electronic funds transfer network; or

(b) issuing or redeeming money orders, traveller's cheques or other similar negotiable instruments.

(2) For greater certainty, paragraph (1)(b) does not apply in respect of the redemption of any cheque payable to a named person or entity.

[SOR/2002-185, s. 3.]

**5.** [Repealed, SOR/2003-102, s. 2]

**6.** (1) Subject to subsection (2), every accountant and every accounting firm is subject to Part 1 of the Act when they

(a) engage in any of the following activities on behalf of any person or entity, namely,

(i) receiving or paying funds,

(ii) purchasing or selling securities, real property or business assets or entities, or

(iii) transferring funds or securities by any means;

(b) give instructions on behalf of any person or entity in respect of any activity referred to in paragraph (a); or

(c) receive professional fees in respect of any activity referred to in paragraph (a) or in respect of any instructions referred to in paragraph (b).

(2) Subsection (1) does not apply in respect of an accountant when they engage in any of the activities referred to in paragraph (1)(a), (b) or (c) on behalf of their employer.

(3) For greater certainty, subsection (1) does not apply in respect of audit, review or compilation engagements carried out in accordance with the recommendations set out in the CICA Handbook.

[SOR/2002-185, s. 3.]

**7.** Every real estate broker or sales representative is subject to Part 1 of the Act when they engage in any of the following activities on behalf of any person or entity in the course of a real estate transaction:

(a)  receiving or paying funds;

(b)  depositing or withdrawing funds; and

(c)  transferring funds by any means.

**8.** Every department and agent of Her Majesty in right of Canada or of a province is subject to Part 1 of the Act when, in the course of providing financial services to the public, it

(a)  accepts deposit liabilities; or

(b)  sells or redeems money orders.

[SOR/2002-185, s. 4.]

**9.** (1) Subject to section 11, a report under section 7 of the Act concerning a financial transaction in respect of which there are reasonable grounds to suspect that the transaction is related to the commission of a money laundering offence or a terrorist activity financing offence shall contain the information set out in Schedule 1.

(2) The report shall be sent to the Centre within 30 days after the person or entity or any of its employees or officers first detects a fact respecting a transaction that constitutes reasonable grounds to suspect that the transaction is related to the commission of a money laundering offence or a terrorist activity financing offence.

[SOR/2002-185, s. 4.]

**10. Report made under Section 83.1 of the Criminal Code** — Subject to section 11, a report made under section 7.1 of the Act shall be sent without delay to the Centre and shall contain the information set out in Schedule 2.

[SOR/2002-185, s. 4.]

**11. Exemption** — The requirement to report information set out in Schedule 1 or 2 does not apply to a person or entity in respect of information set out in an item of that Schedule that is not marked with an asterisk if, after taking reasonable measures to do so, the person or entity is unable to obtain the information.

[SOR/2002-185, s. 4.]

**12.** (1) **Sending** — The report referred to in section 9 shall be sent electronically in accordance with guidelines for report submissions that are prepared by the Centre if the sender has the technical capabilities to do so.

(2) The report referred to in section 9 shall be sent in paper format in accordance with guidelines for report submissions that are prepared by the Centre if the sender does not have the technical capabilities to send the report electronically.

(3) The report referred to in section 10 shall be sent in paper format in accordance with guidelines for report submissions that are prepared by the Centre.

[SOR/2002-185, s. 4.]

**13. Prescribed Information** — The prescribed information for the purposes of paragraphs 55(7)(e), 55.1(3)(e) and 56.1(5)(e) of the Act is

  (a)  the following information concerning the client, importer or exporter, or any person acting on their behalf, namely,

      (i)    their alias, if any,

      (ii)   their date of birth,

      (iii)  their address,

      (iv)  their citizenship,

      (v)   their Record of Landing number, passport number or permanent resident card number, or all three numbers if applicable,

      (vi)  if the client, importer or exporter is a corporation, the date and jurisdiction of its incorporation and its incorporation number, and

      (vii) the name and address of any person or entity on whose behalf the financial transaction, importation or exportation is conducted; and

  (b)  in the case of a financial transaction, the following information, namely,

      (i)    the transit and account numbers,

      (ii)   the full name of every account holder,

      (iii)  the transaction number, if any,

      (iv)  the time of the transaction,

      (v)   the type of transaction, and

      (vi)  the names of the parties to the transaction.

[SOR/2002-185, s. 4; SOR/2003-358, s. 3, in force November 6, 2003.]

# PROCEEDS OF CRIME (MONEY LAUNDERING) AND TERRORIST FINANCING REGULATIONS

## SOR/2002-184

**Amendments:** SOR/2002-184, s. 72, in force November 30, 2002; SOR/2002-184, s. 73, in force November 30, 2002; SOR/2002-184, s. 74; SOR/2002-184, s. 75, in force November 30, 2002; SOR/2002-184, s. 76, in force November 30, 2002; SOR/2002-184, s. 78(2) in force November 30, 2002; SOR/2003-102, s. 3; SOR/2003-358, ss. 4(1) to (3), (4)(E), 5, in force November 6, 2003.

Her Excellency the Governor General in Council, on the recommendation of the Minister of Finance, pursuant to subsection 73(1)* of the *Proceeds of Crime (Money Laundering) and Terrorist Financing Act**, hereby makes the annexed *Proceeds of Crime (Money Laundering) and Terrorist Financing Regulations*.

\* [S.C. 2001, c. 41, s. 73 ** S.C. 2000, c. 17; 2001, c. 41, s. 48]

**1.** (1) **Interpretation** — For the purposes of the Act and in these Regulations, "casino" means a person or entity that is licensed, registered, permitted or otherwise authorized to do business under any of paragraphs 207(1)(a) to (g) of the *Criminal Code* and that conducts its business activities in a permanent establishment

(a) that the person or entity holds out to be a casino and in which roulette or card games are carried on; or

(b) where there is a slot machine, which, for the purposes of this definition, does not include a video lottery terminal.

It does not include a person or entity that is a registered charity as defined in subsection 248(1) of the *Income Tax Act* and is licensed, registered, permitted or otherwise authorized to carry on business temporarily for charitable purposes, if the business is carried out in the establishment of the casino for not more than two consecutive days at a time under the supervision of the casino.

(2) The following definitions apply in these Regulations.

"accountant" means a chartered accountant, a certified general accountant or a certified management accountant.

"accounting firm" means an entity that is engaged in the business of providing accounting services to the public and has at least one partner, employee or administrator that is an accountant.

"Act" means the *Proceeds of Crime (Money Laundering) and Terrorist Financing Act*.

"annuity" has the same meaning as in subsection 248(1) of the *Income Tax Act*.

"cash" means coins referred to in section 7 of the *Currency Act*, notes issued by the Bank of Canada pursuant to the *Bank of Canada Act* that are intended for circulation in Canada or coins or bank notes of countries other than Canada.

"CICA Handbook" means the handbook prepared and published by the Canadian Institute of Chartered Accountants, as amended from time to time.

"client credit file" means a record that relates to a credit arrangement with a client and includes the name, address and financial capacity of the client, the terms of the credit arrangement, the nature of the principal business or occupation of the client, the name of the business, if any, and the address of the client's business or place of work.

"client information record" means a record that sets out a client's name and address and the nature of the client's principal business or occupation.

"deferred profit sharing plan" has the same meaning as in subsection 248(1) of the *Income Tax Act*.

"deposit slip" means a record that sets out the date of a deposit, the holder of the account in whose name the deposit is made, the number of the account, the amount of the deposit and any part of the deposit that is made in cash.

"electronic funds transfer" means the transmission — through any electronic, magnetic or optical device, telephone instrument or computer — of instructions for the transfer of funds, other than the transfer of funds within Canada. In the case of SWIFT messages, only SWIFT MT 100 and SWIFT MT 103 messages are included.

"employees profit sharing plan" has the same meaning as in subsection 248(1) of the *Income Tax Act*.

"financial entity" means an authorized foreign bank within the meaning of section 2 of the *Bank Act* in respect of its business in Canada or a bank to which that Act applies, a cooperative credit society, savings and credit union or caisse populaire that is regulated by a provincial Act, an association that is regulated by the *Cooperative Credit Associations Act*, a company to which the *Trust and Loan Companies Act* applies and a trust company or loan company regulated by a provincial Act. It includes a department or agent of Her Majesty in right of Canada or of a province where the department or agent is carrying out an activity referred to in section 45.

"funds" means cash, currency or securities, or negotiable instruments or other financial instruments, in any form, that indicate a person's or an entity's title or interest in them.

"inter vivos trust" means a personal trust, other than a trust created by will.

"large cash transaction record" means a record that indicates the receipt of an amount of $10,000 or more in cash in the course of a single transaction and that contains the following information:

(a) as the case may be
    (i) if the amount is received for deposit by a financial entity, the name of each person or entity in whose account the amount is deposited, or
    (ii) in any other case, the name of the person from whom the amount is in fact received, their address and the nature of their principal business or occupation, if the information is not readily obtainable from other records that the recipient keeps and retains under these Regulations;

(b) the date of the transaction;

(c) where the transaction is a deposit that is made during normal business hours of the recipient, the time of the deposit or, where the transaction is a deposit that is made by means of a night deposit before or after those hours, an indication that the deposit was a night deposit;

(d) the number of any account that is affected by the transaction, and the type of that account, the full name of any person or entity that holds the account and the currency in which account transactions are conducted;

(e) the purpose and details of the transaction, including other persons or entities involved and the type of transaction (such as cash, electronic funds transfer, deposit, currency exchange or the purchase or cashing of a cheque, money order, traveller's cheque or banker's draft);

(f) whether the cash is received by armoured car, in person, by mail or in any other way; and

(g) the amount and currency of the cash received.

"legal firm" [Repealed, SOR/2003-102, s. 3]

"life insurance broker or agent" means a person or entity that is registered or licensed under provincial legislation to carry on the business of arranging contracts of life insurance.

"life insurance company" means a life company or foreign life company to which the *Insurance Companies Act* applies or a life insurance company regulated by a provincial Act.

"money services business" means a person or entity that is engaged in the business of remitting funds or transmitting funds by any means or through any person, entity or electronic funds transfer network, or of issuing or redeeming money orders, traveller's cheques or other similar negotiable instruments. It includes a financial entity when it carries out one of those activities with a person or entity that is not an account holder.

"public body" means

(a) any department or agent of Her Majesty in right of Canada or of a province;

(b) an incorporated city, town, village, metropolitan authority, township, district, county, rural municipality or other incorporated municipal body or an agent of any of them; and

(c) an organization that operates a public hospital and that is designated by the Minister of National Revenue as a hospital authority under the *Excise Tax Act*, or any agent of such an organization.

"real estate broker or sales representative" means a person or entity that is registered or licensed under provincial legislation in respect of the sale or purchase of real estate.

"registered pension plan" has the same meaning as in subsection 248(1) of the *Income Tax Act*.

"registered retirement income fund" has the same meaning as in subsection 248(1) of the *Income Tax Act*.

"securities dealer" means a person or entity that is authorized under provincial legislation to engage in the business of dealing in securities or to provide portfolio management or investment counselling services.

"senior officer", in respect of an entity, means, if applicable,

    (a)  a director of the entity who is one of its full-time employees;

    (b)  the entity's chief executive officer, chief operating officer, president, secretary, treasurer, controller, chief financial officer, chief accountant, chief auditor or chief actuary, or any person who performs any of those functions; or

    (c)  any other officer who reports directly to the entity's board of directors, chief executive officer or chief operating officer.

"signature" includes an electronic signature.

"signature card", in respect of an account, means any record that is signed by a person who is authorized to give instructions in respect of the account.

"SWIFT" means the Society for Worldwide Interbank Financial Telecommunication.

"transaction ticket" means a record respecting a foreign currency exchange transaction — which may take the form of an entry in a transaction register — that sets out

    (a)  the date, amount and currency of the purchase or sale;

    (b)  the method, amount and currency of the payment made or received; and

    (c)  in the case of a transaction of $3,000 or more that is carried out by a person, the name and address of that person.

"trust company" means a trust company to which the *Trust and Loan Companies Act* applies or a trust company regulated by a provincial Act.

[SOR/2002-184, s. 72; SOR/2003-102, s. 3; SOR/2003-358, ss. 4(1) to (3), (4)(E), (5), effective November 6, 2003 (Can. Gaz. Pt. II, Vol. 137, No. 24, p. 2755).]

## GENERAL

**2. Foreign Currency** — Where a transaction is carried out by a person or entity in a foreign currency, the amount of the transaction shall, for the purposes of these Regulations, be converted into Canadian dollars based on

    (a)  the official conversion rate of the Bank of Canada for that currency as published in the Bank of Canada's Daily Memorandum of Exchange Rates that is in effect at the time of the transaction; or

    (b)  if no official conversion rate is set out in that publication for that currency, the conversion rate that the person or entity would use for that currency in the normal course of business at the time of the transaction.

**3. Single Transactions** — In these Regulations, two or more cash transactions or electronic funds transfers of less than $10,000 each that are made within 24 consecutive hours and that total $10,000 or more are considered to be a single transaction of $10,000 or more if

(a)  where a person is required to keep a large cash transaction record or to report an electronic funds transfer in accordance with these Regulations, the person knows that the transactions or transfers are conducted by, or on behalf of, the same person or entity; and

(b)  where an entity is required to keep a large cash transaction record or to report an electronic funds transfer in accordance with these Regulations, an employee or a senior officer of the entity knows that the transactions or transfers are conducted by, or on behalf of, the same person or entity.

**4.** (1) **Sending Reports** — A report that is required to be made to the Centre shall be sent electronically in accordance with guidelines for report submissions that are prepared by the Centre, if the sender has the technical capabilities to do so.

(2) The report shall be sent in paper format, in accordance with guidelines for report submissions that are prepared by the Centre, if the sender does not have the technical capabilities to send the report electronically.

**5.** (1) **Reporting Time Limits** — A report that is required to be made under these Regulations in respect of an electronic funds transfer shall be sent to the Centre not later than five working days after the day of the transfer.

(2) A report in respect of a transaction for which a large cash transaction record must be kept and retained under these Regulations shall be sent to the Centre

(a)  within 30 days after the transaction, where the transaction occurs on the day on which this section comes into force or within 12 months after that day; or

(b)  in any other case, within 15 days after the transaction.

**6.** (1) **Transactions Conducted by Employees or Agents** — Where a person who is subject to the requirements of these Regulations is an employee of a person or entity referred to in any of paragraphs 5(a) to (l) of the Act, it is the employer rather than the employee who is responsible for meeting those requirements.

(2) Where a person or entity who is subject to the requirements of these Regulations, other than a life insurance broker or agent, is an agent of or is authorized to act on behalf of another person or entity referred to in any of paragraphs 5(a) to (l) of the Act, it is that other person or entity rather than the agent or the authorized person or entity, as the case may be, that is responsible for meeting those requirements.

**7.** For the purposes of these Regulations, a person acting on behalf of their employer is considered to be acting on behalf of a third party except when the person is depositing cash into the employer's account.

**8.** (1) **Third Party Determination** — Every person or entity that is required to keep a large cash transaction record under these Regulations shall take reasonable measures to determine whether the individual who in fact gives the cash in respect of which the record is kept is acting on behalf of a third party.

(2) Where the person or entity determines that the individual is acting on behalf of a third party, the person or entity shall keep a record that sets out

(a)  the third party's name and address and the nature of the principal business or occupation of the third party, if the third party is an individual;

(b) if the third party is an entity, the third party's name and address and the nature of the principal business of the third party, and, if the entity is a corporation, the entity's incorporation number and its place of issue; and

(c) the nature of the relationship between the third party and the individual who gives the cash.

(3) Where the person or entity is not able to determine whether the individual is acting on behalf of a third party but there are reasonable grounds to suspect that the individual is doing so, the person or entity shall keep a record that

(a) indicates whether, according to the individual, the transaction is being conducted on behalf of a third party; and

(b) describes the reasonable grounds to suspect that the individual is acting on behalf of a third party.

**9.** (1) Subject to subsection (4), every person or entity that is required to keep a signature card or an account operating agreement in respect of an account under these Regulations, or would be required to do so if not for subsection 23(2), shall, at the time that the account is opened, take reasonable measures to determine whether the account is to be used by or on behalf of a third party.

(2) Subject to subsections (5) and (6), where the person or entity determines that the account is to be used by or on behalf of a third party, the person or entity shall keep a record that sets out

(a) the third party's name and address and the nature of the principal business or occupation of the third party, if the third party is an individual;

(b) if the third party is an entity, the third party's name and address and the nature of the principal business of the third party, and, if the entity is a corporation, the entity's incorporation number and its place of issue; and

(c) the nature of the relationship between the third party and the account holder.

(3) Where the person or entity is not able to determine if the account is to be used by or on behalf of a third party but there are reasonable grounds to suspect that it will be so used, the person or entity shall keep a record that

(a) indicates whether, according to the individual who is authorized to act in respect of the account, the account is to be used by or on behalf of a third party; and

(b) describes the reasonable grounds to suspect that the individual is acting on behalf of a third party.

(4) Subsection (1) does not apply in respect of an account where the account holder is a financial entity or a securities dealer that is engaged in the business of dealing in securities in Canada.

(5) Subsection (2) does not apply where a securities dealer is required to keep an account operating agreement in respect of an account of a person or entity that is engaged in the business of dealing in securities only outside of Canada, or would be required to do so if not for subsection 23(2), and where

(a) the account is in a country that is a member of the Financial Action Task Force on Money Laundering;

(b)  the account is in a country that is not a member of the Task Force referred to in paragraph (a) but has implemented the recommendations of the Task Force relating to customer identification and, at the time that the account is opened, the securities dealer has obtained written assurance from the entity where the account is located that the country has implemented those recommendations; or

(c)  the account is in a country that is not a member of the Task Force referred to in paragraph (a) and has not implemented the recommendations of the Task Force relating to customer identification but, at the time that the account is opened, the securities dealer has ascertained the identity of all third parties relating to the account as described in paragraph 64(1)(c).

(6) Subsection (2) does not apply where

(a)  the account is opened by a legal counsel, an accountant or a real estate broker or sales representative; and

(b)  the person or entity has reasonable grounds to believe that the account is to be used only for clients of the legal counsel, accountant or real estate broker or sales representative, as the case may be.

**10.** (1) Every person or entity that is required to keep a client information record under these Regulations in respect of a client shall, at the time that the client information record is created, take reasonable measures to determine whether the client is acting on behalf of a third party.

(2) Where the person or entity determines that the client is acting on behalf of a third party, the person or entity shall keep a record that sets out

(a)  the third party's name and address and the nature of the principal business or occupation of the third party, if the third party is an individual;

(b)  if the third party is an entity, the third party's name and address and the nature of the principal business of the third party, and, if the entity is a corporation, the entity's incorporation number and its place of issue; and

(c)  the relationship between the third party and the client.

(3) Where the person or entity is not able to determine that the client in respect of whom the client information record is kept is acting on behalf of a third party but there are reasonable grounds to suspect that the client is so acting, the person or entity shall keep a record that

(a)  indicates whether, according to the client, the transaction is being conducted on behalf of a third party; and

(b)  describes the reasonable grounds to suspect that the client is acting on behalf of a third party.

**11.** A trust company that is required to keep a record in respect of an *inter vivos* trust in accordance with these Regulations shall keep a record that sets out the name and address and the nature of the principal business and occupation, of each of the beneficiaries that are known at the time that the trust company becomes a trustee for the trust.

## REPORTING OF FINANCIAL TRANSACTIONS AND RECORD KEEPING

**12.** (1) **Financial Entities** — Subject to subsection (5), section 50 and subsection 52(1), every financial entity shall report the following transactions and information to the Centre:

(a) the receipt from a client of an amount in cash of $10,000 or more in the course of a single transaction, together with the information referred to in Schedule 1, unless the cash is received from another financial entity or a public body;

(b) the sending out of Canada, at the request of a client, of an electronic funds transfer of $10,000 or more in the course of a single transaction, together with the information referred to in Schedule 2 or 5, as the case may be; and

(c) the receipt from outside Canada of an electronic funds transfer, sent at the request of a client, of $10,000 or more in the course of a single transaction, together with the information referred to in Schedule 3 or 6, as the case may be.

(2) For greater certainty, paragraph (1)(b) does not apply when the financial entity sends an electronic funds transfer to a person or entity in Canada, even if the final recipient is outside Canada.

(3) Paragraph (1)(b) applies in respect of a financial entity that orders a person or entity to which subsection (1), 24(1) or 28(1) applies to send an electronic funds transfer out of Canada, at the request of a client, unless it provides that person or entity with the name and address of that client.

(4) For greater certainty, paragraph (1)(c) does not apply when the financial entity receives an electronic funds transfer from a person or entity in Canada, even if the initial sender is outside Canada.

(5) [Repealed: SOR/2003-358, s. 5(2)]

[SOR/2002-184, s. 73; SOR/2003-358, s. 5, in force November 6, 2003.]

**13.** Subject to subsection 52(2), every financial entity shall keep a large cash transaction record in respect of every amount in cash of $10,000 or more that is received from a client in the course of a single transaction, unless the cash is received from another financial entity or a public body.

**14.** Every financial entity shall keep the following records:

(a) where it opens an account, a signature card in respect of each account holder for that account;

(b) where it opens an account in respect of a corporation, a copy of the part of official corporate records that contains any provision relating to the power to bind the corporation in respect of the account;

(c) where it opens an account in the name of a person or of an entity other than a corporation, a record of the name and address and the nature of the principal business or occupation of the person or entity, as the case may be;

(d) every account operating agreement that it creates in the normal course of business;

(e)  a deposit slip in respect of every deposit that is made to an account;

(f)  every debit and credit memo that it creates or receives in the normal course of business in respect of an account, except debit memos that relate to another account at the same branch of the financial entity that created the debit memo;

(g)  a copy of every account statement that it sends to a client, if the information in the statement is not readily obtainable from other records that are kept and retained by it under these Regulations;

(h)  every cleared cheque that is drawn on, and a copy of every cleared cheque that is deposited to, an account, unless

  (i)  the account on which the cheque is drawn and the account to which the cheque is deposited are at the same branch of the financial entity, or

  (ii)  the following conditions are met, namely,

    (A)  an image of the cheque has been recorded on microfilm or on an electronic medium,

    (B)  an image of the cheque can be readily reproduced from the microfilm or electronic medium,

    (C)  it is possible to readily ascertain where the image of any particular cheque is recorded, and

    (D)  the microfilm or electronic medium is retained for a period of at least five years;

(i)  every client credit file that it creates in the normal course of business; and

(j)  a transaction ticket in respect of every foreign currency exchange transaction.

**15.** (1) Every trust company shall, in addition to the records referred to in sections 13 and 14, keep the following records in respect of a trust for which it is trustee:

(a)  a copy of the trust deed;

(b)  a record of the settlor's name and address and the nature of the principal business or occupation of the settlor; and

(c)  where the trust is an institutional trust and the settlor is a corporation, a copy of the part of official corporate records that contains any provision relating to the power to bind the settlor in respect of the trust.

(2) In this section, "institutional trust" means a trust that is established by a corporation, partnership or other entity for a particular business purpose and includes pension plan trusts, pension master trusts, supplemental pension plan trusts, mutual fund trusts, pooled fund trusts, registered retirement savings plan trusts, registered retirement income fund trusts, registered education savings plan trusts, group registered retirement savings plan trusts, deferred profit sharing plan trusts, employee profit sharing plan trusts, retirement compensation arrangement trusts, employee savings plan trusts, health and welfare trusts, unemployment benefit plan trusts, foreign insurance company trusts, foreign reinsurance trusts, reinsurance trusts, real estate investment trusts, environmental trusts and trusts established in respect of endowments, foundations and registered charities.

**16. Life Insurance Companies and Life Insurance Brokers or Agents —** Part 1 of the Act applies to life insurance brokers or agents.

**17.** Subject to subsection 52(1), every life insurance company or life insurance broker or agent who receives from a client an amount in cash of $10,000 or more in the course of a single transaction shall report the transaction to the Centre, together with the information referred to in Schedule 1, except

(a) if the amount is received from a financial entity or a public body; or

(b) in respect of transactions referred to in subsection 62(1).

**18.** Subject to subsection 52(2), every life insurance company or life insurance broker or agent shall keep a large cash transaction record in respect of every amount in cash of $10,000 or more that is received from a client in the course of a single transaction, unless

(a) the cash is received from a financial entity or a public body; or

(b) the transaction is a transaction referred to in subsection 62(1).

**19.** (1) Subject to subsection (3), every life insurance company or life insurance broker or agent shall keep a client information record for every purchase from it of an immediate or deferred annuity or of a life insurance policy for which the client may pay $10,000 or more over the duration of the annuity or policy, irrespective of the means of payment.

(2) Subject to subsection (3), in the case of a life insurance policy that is a group life insurance policy or in the case of a group annuity, the client information record shall be kept in respect of the applicant for the policy or annuity.

(3) Subsections (1) and (2) do not apply to a purchase of

(a) an exempt policy as defined in subsection 306(1) of the Income Tax Regulations, as it read on May 1, 1992; or

(b) a group life insurance policy that does not provide for a cash surrender value or a savings component.

**20.** Every life insurance company or life insurance broker or agent who keeps a client information record in respect of a corporation in accordance with subsection 19(1) shall also keep a copy of the part of official corporate records that contains any provision relating to the power to bind the corporation in respect of the transaction with the life insurance company or life insurance broker or agent, if the copy of that part is obtained in the normal course of business.

**21. Securities Dealers —** Subject to subsection 52(1), every securities dealer who receives from a client an amount in cash of $10,000 or more in the course of a single transaction shall report the transaction to the Centre, together with the information set out in Schedule 1, unless the amount is received from a financial entity or a public body.

**22.** Subject to subsection 52(2), every securities dealer shall keep a large cash transaction record in respect of every amount in cash of $10,000 or more that is received from a client in the course of a single transaction, unless the cash is received from a financial entity or a public body.

**23.** (1) Subject to subsection (2), every securities dealer shall keep the following records:

(a) in respect of every account that the securities dealer opens, a signature card, an account operating agreement or an account application that

   (i) bears the signature of the person who is authorized to give instructions in respect of the account, and

   (ii) sets out the account number, where that person's identity was ascertained pursuant to subparagraph 64(1)(c)(ii);

(b) where the securities dealer opens an account in respect of a corporation, a copy of the part of official corporate records that contains any provision relating to the power to bind the corporation in respect of that account;

(c) where the securities dealer opens an account in the name of a person or of an entity other than a corporation, a record of the name and address and the nature of the principal business or occupation of the person or entity, as the case may be;

(d) every new account application, confirmation of purchase or sale, guarantee, trade authorization, power of attorney and joint account agreement, and all correspondence that pertains to the operation of accounts, that the securities dealer creates in the normal course of business; and

(e) a copy of every statement that the securities dealer sends to a client, if the information in the statement is not readily obtainable from other records that the securities dealer keeps and retains under these Regulations.

(2) Paragraph (1)(a) does not apply in respect of an account in the name of, or in respect of which instructions are authorized to be given by, a financial entity or another securities dealer.

[SOR/2003-358, s. 6, in force November 6, 2003.]

**24. (1) Persons or Entities Engaged in the Business of Foreign Exchange Dealing** — Subject to subsection 52(1), every person or entity engaged in the business of foreign exchange dealing shall report the following transactions and information to the Centre:

(a) the receipt from a client of an amount in cash of $10,000 or more in the course of a single transaction, together with the information referred to in Schedule 1, unless the cash is received from a financial entity or a public body;

(b) the sending out of Canada, at the request of a client, of an electronic funds transfer of $10,000 or more in the course of a single transaction, together with the information referred to in Schedule 2 or 5, as the case may be; and

(c) the receipt from outside Canada of an electronic funds transfer, sent at the request of a client, of $10,000 or more in the course of a single transaction, together with the information referred to in Schedule 3 or 6, as the case may be.

(2) For greater certainty, paragraph (1)(b) does not apply when the person or entity engaged in the business of foreign exchange dealing sends an electronic funds transfer to a person or an entity in Canada, even if the final recipient is outside Canada.

(3) Paragraph (1)(b) applies in respect of a person or entity engaged in the business of foreign exchange dealing that orders a person or entity to which subsection (1), 12(1) or 28(1) applies to send an electronic funds transfer out of Canada, at the request of a client, unless it provides that person or entity with the name and address of that client.

(4) For greater certainty, paragraph (1)(c) does not apply when the person or entity engaged in the business of foreign exchange dealing receives an electronic funds transfer from a person or an entity in Canada, even if the initial sender is outside Canada.

[SOR/2002-184, s. 74; SOR/2003-358, s. 7, in force November 6, 2003.]

**25.** Subject to subsection 52(2), every person or entity engaged in the business of foreign exchange dealing shall keep a large cash transaction record in respect of every amount in cash of $10,000 or more that is received from a client in the course of a single transaction, unless the amount is received from a financial entity or a public body.

**26.** Every person or entity engaged in the business of foreign exchange dealing shall keep the following records:

(a)  every client information record that is created for the purpose of an ongoing business relationship between the person or entity and a client;

(b)  where a client information record is created in respect of a client that is a corporation, a copy of the part of official corporate records that contains any provision relating to the power to bind the corporation in respect of transactions with the person or entity, if the copy of that part is obtained in the normal course of business;

(c)  a transaction ticket in respect of every foreign currency exchange transaction;

(d)  every client credit file that the person or entity creates in the normal course of business; and

(e)  every internal memorandum that the person or entity receives or creates in the normal course of business and that concerns account operations.

**27.** (1) **Money Services Businesses** — Every money services business is subject to Part 1 of the Act when it engages in any of the following activities:

(a)  remitting funds or transmitting funds by any means or through any person, entity or electronic funds transfer network; or

(b)  issuing or redeeming money orders, traveller's cheques or other similar negotiable instruments.

(2) For greater certainty, paragraph (1)(b) does not apply in respect of the redemption of any cheque payable to a named person or entity.

**28.** (1) Subject to subsection 52(1), every money services business shall report the following transactions and information to the Centre:

(a)  the receipt from a client of an amount in cash of $10,000 or more in the course of a single transaction, together with the information referred to in Schedule 1, unless the cash is received from a financial entity or a public body;

(b) the sending out of Canada, at the request of a client, of an electronic funds transfer of $10,000 or more in the course of a single transaction, together with the information referred to in Schedule 2 or 5, as the case may be; and

(c) the receipt from outside Canada of an electronic funds transfer, sent at the request of a client, of $10,000 or more in the course of a single transaction, together with the information referred to in Schedule 3 or 6, as the case may be.

(2) For greater certainty, paragraph (1)(b) does not apply when the money services business sends an electronic funds transfer to a person or an entity in Canada, even if the final recipient is outside Canada.

(3) Paragraph (1)(b) applies in respect of a money services business that orders a person or entity to which subsection (1), 12(1) or 24(1) applies to send an electronic funds transfer out of Canada, at the request of a client, unless it provides that person or entity with the name and address of that client.

(4) For greater certainty, paragraph (1)(c) does not apply when the money services business receives an electronic funds transfer from a person or an entity in Canada, even if the initial sender is outside Canada.

[SOR/2002-184, s. 75; SOR/2003-358, s. 8, in force November 6.]

**29.** Subject to subsection 52(2), every money services business shall keep a large cash transaction record in respect of every amount in cash of $10,000 or more that is received from a client in the course of a single transaction, unless the cash is received from a financial entity or a public body.

**30.** Every money services business shall keep the following records in respect of any of the activities referred to in section 27:

(a) every client information record that is created for the purpose of an ongoing business relationship between the money services business and a client;

(b) where a client information record is in respect of a client that is a corporation, a copy of the part of official corporate records that contains any provision relating to the power to bind the corporation in respect of transactions with the money services business, if the copy of that part is obtained in the normal course of business;

(c) where $3,000 or more is received in consideration of the issuance of traveller's cheques, money orders or other similar negotiable instruments, a record of the date, the amount received, the name and address of the person who in fact gives the amount and whether the amount received was in cash, cheques, traveller's cheques, money orders or other similar negotiable instruments;

(d) where money orders of $3,000 or more are cashed, a record of the name and address of the person cashing the money orders and the name of the issuer of the money orders; and

(e) where $3,000 or more is remitted or transmitted by any means or through any person, entity or electronic funds transfer network, a record of the name and address of the client who initiated the transaction.

**31. to 33.** [Repealed: SOR/2003-102, s. 4]

**34.** (1) **Accountants and Accounting Firms** — Subject to subsections (2) and (3), every accountant and every accounting firm is subject to Part 1 of the Act when they

(a) engage in any of the following activities on behalf of any person or entity, namely,

(i) receiving or paying funds,

(ii) purchasing or selling securities, real properties or business assets or entities, or

(iii) transferring funds or securities by any means;

(b) give instructions on behalf of any person or entity in respect of any activity referred to in paragraph (a); or

(c) receive professional fees in respect of any activity referred to in paragraph (a) or in respect of any instructions referred to in paragraph (b).

(2) Subsection (1) does not apply in respect of an accountant when they engage in any of the activities referred to in paragraph (1)(a), (b) or (c) on behalf of their employer.

(3) For greater certainty, subsection (1) does not apply in respect of audit, review or compilation engagements, carried out in accordance with the recommendations set out in the CICA Handbook.

**35.** Subject to subsection 52(1), every accountant and every accounting firm that, while engaging in an activity described in section 34, receives an amount in cash of $10,000 or more in the course of a single transaction shall report the transaction to the Centre, together with the information set out in Schedule 1, unless the cash is received from a financial entity or a public body.

**36.** Subject to subsection 52(2), every accountant and every accounting firm, while engaging in an activity described in section 34, shall keep a large cash transaction record in respect of every amount in cash of $10,000 or more that they receive in the course of a single transaction, unless the cash is received from a financial entity or a public body.

**37. Real Estate Brokers or Sales Representatives** — Every real estate broker or sales representative is subject to Part 1 of the Act when they engage in any of the following activities on behalf of any person or entity in the course of a real estate transaction:

(a) receiving or paying funds;

(b) depositing or withdrawing funds; or

(c) transferring funds by any means.

**38.** Subject to subsection 52(1), every real estate broker or sales representative who, while engaging in an activity described in section 37, receives an amount in cash of $10,000 or more in the course of a single transaction shall report the transaction to the Centre, together with the information set out in Schedule 1, unless the amount is received from a financial entity or a public body.

**39.** Subject to subsection 52(2), every real estate broker or sales representative, while engaging in an activity described in section 37, shall keep a large cash transaction record in respect of every amount in cash of $10,000 or more that they receive in the course of a single transaction, unless the cash is received from a financial entity or a public body.

**40. Casinos** — Subject to subsection 52(1), every casino shall report to the Centre the receipt of an amount in cash of $10,000 or more in the course of a single transaction, together with the information set out in Schedule 1, unless the amount is received from a financial entity.

**41.** (1) Subject to subsection 52(2), every casino shall keep a large cash transaction record in respect of every amount in cash of $10,000 or more that it receives in the course of a single transaction, unless the amount is received from a financial entity.

(2) For greater certainty, the transactions in respect of which a casino is required to keep large cash transaction records in accordance with subsection (1) include the following transactions involving an amount in cash of $10,000 or more:

(a)  the sale of chips, tokens or plaques;
(b)  front cash deposits;
(c)  safekeeping deposits;
(d)  the repayment of any form of credit, including repayment by markers or counter cheques;
(e)  bets of currency; and
(f)  sales of the casino's cheques.

**42.** (1) Subject to section 44, every casino shall keep a large cash disbursement record in respect of each of the following transactions in the course of which the total amount of cash disbursed is $10,000 or more:

(a)  the redemption of chips, tokens or plaques;
(b)  front cash withdrawals;
(c)  safekeeping withdrawals;
(d)  advances on any form of credit, including advances by markers or counter cheques;
(e)  payments on bets, including slot jackpots;
(f)  payments to a client of funds received for credit to that client or any other client;
(g)  the cashing of cheques or other negotiable instruments; and
(h)  reimbursements to clients of travel and entertainment expenses.

(2) For the purpose of subsection (1), the large cash disbursement record shall set out

(a)  the name of the person to whom the disbursement is made;
(b)  the person's address and the nature of their principal business or occupation; and
(c)  the date and nature of the disbursement.

**42.1** Any transaction described in section 40, 41 or 42 that occurs in the course of the business, temporarily conducted for charitable purposes in the establishment of a casino by a registered charity carried on for not more than two consecutive days at a time under the supervision of the casino, shall be reported by the supervising casino.

[SOR/2003-358, s. 9, in force November 6, 2003.]

**43.** Every casino shall keep the following records:

(a) with respect to every client account that it opens,

   (i) a signature card in respect of each account holder,

   (ii) every account operating agreement that is received or created in the normal course of business,

   (iii) a deposit slip in respect of every deposit that is made to the account, and

   (iv) every debit and credit memo that is received or created in the normal course of business;

(b) where it opens a client account in respect of a corporation, a copy of the part of the official corporate records that contains any provision relating to the power to bind the corporation in respect of the account;

(c) where it opens a client account in the name of a person or of an entity other than a corporation, a record of the name and address and the nature of the principal business or occupation of the person or entity, as the case may be;

(d) with respect to every extension of credit to a client of $3,000 or more, an extension of credit record that indicates

   (i) the client's name and address and the nature of the principal business or occupation of the client,

   (ii) the terms and conditions of the extension of credit, and

   (iii) the date and amount of the extension of credit; and

(e) with respect to every foreign currency exchange transaction of $3000 or more, a transaction ticket.

**44.** A casino is not required to keep a large cash disbursement record if the information that is required to be found in it is readily obtainable from other records that must be kept and retained by the casino under these Regulations.

*Departments and Agents of Her Majesty in Right of Canada or of a Province*

**45. Acceptance of Deposit Liabilities** — Every department and agent of Her Majesty in right of Canada or of a province is subject to Part 1 of the Act when it accepts deposit liabilities in the course of providing financial services to the public.

**46. Sale or Redemption of Money Orders** — Every department and agent of Her Majesty in right of Canada or of a province is subject to Part 1 of the Act when it sells or redeems money orders in the course of providing financial services to the public.

**47.** Subject to subsection 52(1), every department and agent of Her Majesty in right of Canada or of a province that, while engaging in an activity referred to in section 46, receives from a client an amount in cash of $10,000 or more in the course of a single transaction shall report the transaction to the Centre, together with the information set out in Schedule 1, unless the amount is received from a financial entity or a public body.

**48.** Subject to subsection 52(2), every department and agent of Her Majesty in right of Canada or of a province, while engaging in an activity referred to in section 46, shall keep a large cash transaction record in respect of every amount in cash of $10,000 or more that it receives from a client in the course of a single transaction, unless the amount is received from a financial entity or a public body.

**49.** Every department and agent of Her Majesty in right of Canada or of a province that engages in an activity referred to in section 46 shall keep the following records in respect of that activity:

(a) every client information record that is created for the purpose of an ongoing business relationship between the department or agent and a client;

(b) where the client information record is in respect of a corporation, a copy of the part of official corporate records that contains any provision relating to the power to bind the corporation in respect of transactions with the department or agent;

(c) where the department or agent receives $3,000 or more in consideration of the issuance of money orders or other similar negotiable instruments, a record of the date, the amount received, the name and address of the person who in fact gives the amount and whether the amount is in cash, cheques, traveller's cheques, money orders or other similar negotiable instruments; and

(d) where money orders of $3,000 or more are cashed, a record of the name and address of the person cashing the money orders and the name of the issuer of the money orders.

**50.** (1) **Exceptions** — A financial entity is not required to report transactions under paragraph 12(1)(a) in respect of a business of a client, if the following conditions are met:

(a) subject to subsection (2), the client is a corporation that carries on that business as an establishment described in sector 22, 44 (excluding codes 4411, 4412 and 44831) or 45 (excluding code 45392), or code 481, 482, 485 (excluding code 4853), 51322, 51331, 61121 or 61131 of the North American Industry Classification System as that sector or code read on January 31, 2003;

(b) the client has had
  (i) for the entire preceding 24-month period, an account in respect of that business with that financial entity, or
  (ii) an account in respect of that business with a financial entity other than the one referred to in subparagraph (i), for a continuous period of 24 months ending immediately before the client opened an account with that financial entity;

(c) the financial entity has records that indicate that the client has deposited $10,000 or more in cash into that account on an average of at least twice in every week for the preceding 12 months;

(d) the cash deposits made by the client are consistent with its usual practice in respect of the business;

(e) the financial entity has taken reasonable measures to determine the source of the cash for those deposits; and

(f) subject to subsection 52(1), the financial entity has provided to the Centre the information set out in Schedule 4.

(2) Paragraph (1)(a) does not apply to a corporation that carries on a business related to pawnbroking or a corporation whose principal business is the sale of vehicles, vessels, farm machinery, aircraft, mobile homes, jewellery, precious gems or metals, antiquities or art.

(3) A financial entity that, in accordance with subsection (1), chooses not to report transactions of more than $10,000 shall report to the Centre any change in the following information, within 15 days after the change is made:

(a) the name and address of the client;

(b) the nature of the client's business; and

(c) the client's incorporation number.

(4) A financial entity that, in accordance with subsection (1), chooses not to report transactions of more than $10,000 shall, at least once every 12 months,

(a) verify that the conditions referred to in subsection (1) are still met in respect of each client; and

(b) send a report to the Centre setting out the name and address of each client, together with the name of a senior officer of the financial entity who has confirmed that the conditions referred to in subsection (1) are still being met in respect of each client.

[SOR/2003-358, s. 10, in force November 6, 2003.]

**51.** Where a person or entity maintains a list of clients for the purposes of subsection 9(3) of the Act, the list must contain the name and address of each client and be kept in paper form or in a form referred to in section 68.

**52.** (1) The requirement to report information set out in Schedules 1 to 6 does not apply to a person or entity in respect of information set out in an item of any of those Schedules that is not marked with an asterisk if, after taking reasonable measures to do so, the person or entity is unable to obtain the information.

(2) The requirement that a person or entity keep or retain a large cash transaction record or include information in it does not apply if the information that must be found in the record is readily obtainable from other records that the person or entity is required to keep or retain under these Regulations.

(3) Despite subsection (1), for the application of section 3, the requirement to report information set out in Schedules 1 to 6 does not apply to a person or entity in respect of information set out in an item of any of those Schedules that is marked with an asterisk if, after taking reasonable measures to do so, the person or entity is unable to obtain the information.

(4) For greater certainty, Schedules 2 and 3 apply only to SWIFT members sending or receiving SWIFT messages.

[SOR/2003-358, s. 11, in force November 6, 2003.]

## ASCERTAINING IDENTITY

**53. Persons or Entities Required to Keep Large Cash Transaction Records** — Subject to subsection 63(1), every person or entity that is required to keep and retain a large cash transaction record under these Regulations shall ascertain, in accordance with paragraph 64(1)(d), the identity of every individual with whom the person or entity conducts a transaction in respect of which that record must be kept, other than a deposit to a business account or by means of an automated banking machine.

[SOR/2003-358, s. 12, in force November 6, 2003.]

**54.** (1) **Financial Entities** — Subject to subsections 62(2) and (4) and section 63, every financial entity shall

   (a) in accordance with paragraph 64(1)(a), ascertain the identity of every person who signs a signature card in respect of an account that the financial entity opens, except in the case of a business account the signature card of which is signed by more than three persons authorized to act with respect to the account, if the financial entity has ascertained the identity of at least three of those persons;

   (b) in accordance with paragraph 64(1)(a), ascertain the identity of every person who requests an electronic funds transfer of $3,000 or more, unless the person has signed a signature card in respect of an account held with the financial entity or is authorized to act with respect to such an account;

   (c) in accordance with paragraph 64(1)(a), ascertain the identity of every person who conducts a foreign currency exchange transaction of $3,000 or more with the financial entity, unless the person has signed a signature card in respect of an account held with it;

   (d) in accordance with section 65, confirm the existence of and ascertain the name and address of every corporation for which the financial entity opens an account and the names of the corporation's directors; and

   (e) in accordance with section 66, confirm the existence of every entity, other than a corporation, for which the financial entity opens an account.

(2) For the purpose of paragraph (1)(a), where the person who signs a signature card is under 12 years of age, the financial entity shall ascertain the identity of the father, mother or guardian of the person in accordance with paragraph 64(1)(a).

[SOR/2003-358, s. 13, in force November 6, 2003.]

**55.** Subject to subsection 62(4) and section 63, every trust company shall, in addition to complying with section 54,

   (a) in accordance with paragraph 64(1)(a), ascertain the identity of every person who is the settlor of an *inter vivos* trust in respect of which the company is required to keep records under section 15;

   (b) in accordance with section 65, confirm the existence of and ascertain the name and address of every corporation that is the settlor of an institutional trust in respect of which the company is required to keep records in accordance with section 15;

   (c) in accordance with section 66, confirm the existence of every entity, other than a corporation, that is the settlor of an institutional trust in respect of which the company is required to keep records in accordance with section 15;

(d) where an entity is authorized to act as a co-trustee of any trust

    (i) confirm the existence of the entity and ascertain its name and address in accordance with section 65 or confirm the existence of the entity in accordance with section 66, as the case may be, and

    (ii) in accordance with paragraph 64(1)(a), ascertain the identity of all persons — up to three — who are authorized to give instructions with respect to the entity's activities as co-trustee; and

(e) in accordance with paragraph 64(1)(a), ascertain the identity of each person who is authorized to act as co-trustee of any trust.

**56.** (1) **Life Insurance Companies and Life Insurance Brokers or Agents** — Subject to subsections (2), 62(1), (3) and (4) and 63(1), every life insurance company or life insurance broker or agent shall ascertain, in accordance with paragraph 64(1)(b), the identity of every person who conducts, on the person's own behalf or on behalf of a third party, a transaction with that life insurance company or life insurance broker or agent for which a client information record is required to be kept under section 19.

(2) A life insurance company or life insurance broker or agent is not required to ascertain the identity of a person where there are reasonable grounds to believe that the person's identity has been ascertained in accordance with paragraph 64(1)(b) by another life insurance company or life insurance broker or agent in respect of the same transaction or of a transaction that is part of a series of transactions that includes the original transaction.

(3) Subject to subsections 62(3) and (4) and 63(2), every life insurance company or life insurance broker or agent shall, in accordance with section 65, confirm the existence of and ascertain the name and address of every corporation in respect of which they are required to keep a client information record and the names of the corporation's directors.

(4) Subject to subsections 62(3) and (4) and 63(3), every life insurance company or life insurance broker or agent shall, in accordance with section 66, confirm the existence of every entity, other than a corporation, in respect of which they are required to keep a client information record.

**57.** (1) **Securities Dealers** — Subject to subsections (2) and (5), 62(2) and (4) and 63(1), every securities dealer shall ascertain, in accordance with paragraph 64(1)(c), the identity of every person who is authorized to give instructions in respect of an account for which a record must be kept by the securities dealer under subsection 23(1).

(2) Subsection (1) does not apply

(a) to business accounts in respect of which the securities dealer has already ascertained the identity of at least three persons who are authorized to give instructions in respect of the account;

(b) to accounts opened for the deposit and sale of shares from a corporate demutualization, an employee stock purchase plan or the privatization of a Crown corporation;

(c)  to registered plan accounts, including locked-in retirement plan accounts, registered retirement savings plan accounts and group registered retirement savings plan accounts;

(d)  to employees profit sharing plan accounts and deferred profit sharing plan accounts, unless the accounts are funded in whole or in part by contributions by a person or entity other than the employer;

(e)  to dividend reinvestment plan accounts sponsored by a corporation for its investors, unless the accounts are funded in whole or in part by a source other than the corporation; or

(f)  to accounts in the name of foreign affiliates of a financial entity.

(3) Subject to subsection 63(2), every securities dealer shall, in accordance with section 65, confirm the existence of and ascertain the name and address of every corporation for which it opens an account, and the names of the corporation's directors.

(4) Subject to subsection 63(3), every securities dealer shall, in accordance with section 66, confirm the existence of every entity, other than a corporation, for which it opens an account.

(5) A securities dealer is not required to ascertain the identity of a person who is authorized to give instructions in respect of an account that is opened for the sale of mutual funds where there are reasonable grounds to believe that the person's identity has been ascertained in accordance with paragraph 64(1)(c) by another securities dealer in respect of

(a)  the sale of the mutual funds for which the account has been opened; or

(b)  a transaction that is part of a series of transactions that includes that sale.

[SOR/2003-358, s. 14, in force November 6, 2003.]

**58.** (1) **Persons or Entities Engaged in the Business of Foreign Exchange Dealing** — Subject to subsection 63(1), every person or entity that is engaged in the business of foreign exchange dealing shall ascertain, in accordance with paragraph 64(1)(d), the identity of

(a)  every individual in respect of whom a client information record is required to be kept or who conducts a transaction on behalf of a person or entity in respect of which a client information record is required to be kept; and

(b)  every individual who conducts a transaction of $3,000 or more with that person or entity and in respect of whom no client information record is kept.

(2) Subject to subsection 63(2), every person or entity that is engaged in the business of foreign exchange dealing shall, in accordance with section 65, confirm the existence of and ascertain the name and address of every corporation in respect of which they keep a client information record and the names of the corporation's directors.

(3) Subject to subsection 63(3), every person or entity that is engaged in the business of foreign exchange dealing shall, in accordance with section 66, confirm the existence of every entity, other than a corporation, in respect of which they keep a client information record.

**59. Money Services Businesses** — Subject to section 63, every money services business shall

(a) in accordance with paragraph 64(1)(d), ascertain the identity of every person who conducts any of the following transactions, if the transaction is for $3,000 or more and no client information record is kept in respect of that person, namely,

    (i) the issuance or redemption of money orders, traveller's cheques or other similar negotiable instruments, and

    (ii) the remittance or transmission of $3,000 or more by any means through any person, entity or electronic funds transfer network;

(b) in accordance with paragraph 64(1)(d), ascertain the identity of every person in respect of whom a client information record is required to be kept, with respect to a transaction of $3,000 or more;

(c) in accordance with section 65, confirm the existence of and ascertain the name and address of every corporation in respect of which a client information record is required to be kept and the names of the corporation's directors; and

(d) in accordance with section 66, confirm the existence of every entity, other than a corporation, in respect of which a client information record is required to be kept.

**60. Casinos** — Subject to subsection 62(2) and section 63, every casino shall

(a) in accordance with paragraph 64(1)(a), ascertain the identity of every person who signs a signature card in respect of an account that the casino opens, except in the case of a business account whose signature card is signed by more than three persons authorized to act with respect to the account, if the casino has ascertained the identity of at least three of those persons;

(b) in accordance with paragraph 64(1)(d), ascertain the identity of every person who conducts a transaction with the casino for which a large cash disbursement record is required to be kept under subsection 42(1);

(c) in accordance with paragraph 64(1)(d), ascertain the identity of every person who conducts a transaction of $3,000 or more with the casino for which an extension of credit record is required to be kept under paragraph 43(d);

(d) in accordance with paragraph 64(1)(d), ascertain the identity of every person who conducts a foreign currency exchange transaction of $3,000 or more with the casino for which a transaction ticket is required to be kept under paragraph 43(e);

(e) in accordance with section 65, confirm the existence of and ascertain the name and address of every corporation for which the casino opens an account and the names of the corporation's directors; and

(f) in accordance with section 66, confirm the existence of every entity, other than a corporation, for which the casino opens an account.

[SOR/2003-358, s. 15, in force November 6, 2003.]

**61. Departments or Agents of Her Majesty in Right of Canada or of a Province that Sell or Redeem Money Orders** — Subject to section 63, a department or agent of Her Majesty in right of Canada or of a province that engages in an activity referred to in section 46 shall

(a)  in accordance with paragraph 64(1)(b), ascertain the identity of every person in respect of whom a client information record is kept under paragraph 49(a);

(b)  in accordance with paragraph 64(1)(d), ascertain the identity of every person in respect of whom no client information record is kept and who conducts a transaction that involves an amount of $3,000 or more for the issuance or redemption of money orders or other similar negotiable instruments;

(c)  in accordance with section 65, confirm the existence of and ascertain the name and address of every corporation in respect of which a client information record is kept under paragraph 49(a) and the names of the corporation's directors; and

(d)  in accordance with section 66, confirm the existence of every entity, other than a corporation, in respect of which a client information record is kept under paragraph 49(a).

**62.** (1) **Exceptions to Ascertaining Identity** — Subsection 56(1) does not apply in respect of any of the following transactions:

(a)  the purchase of an immediate or deferred annuity that is paid for entirely with funds that are directly transferred from a registered pension plan or from a pension plan that is required to be registered under the *Pension Benefits Standards Act, 1985*, or similar provincial legislation;

(b)  the purchase of a registered annuity policy in respect of an annuity referred to in subsection (5) or a registered retirement income fund;

(c)  the purchase of an immediate or deferred annuity that is paid for entirely with the proceeds of a group life insurance policy;

(d)  a transaction that is part of a reverse mortgage or of a structured settlement;

(e)  the opening of a registered plan account, including a locked-in retirement plan account, a registered retirement savings plan account and a group registered retirement savings plan account;

(f)  the opening of an employees profit sharing plan account or a deferred profit sharing plan account, unless the account is funded in whole or in part by contributions by a person or entity other than the employer; or

(g)  the opening of a dividend reinvestment plan account sponsored by a corporation for its investors, unless the account is funded in whole or in part by a source other than the corporation.

(2) Paragraph 54(1)(a), subsection 57(1) and paragraph 60(a) do not apply if

(a)  the person already has an account with the financial entity, the securities dealer or the casino, as the case may be; or

(b)  there are reasonable grounds to believe that the account holder is a public body or a corporation that has minimum net assets of $75 million on its last audited balance sheet and whose shares are traded on a Canadian stock exchange or a stock exchange that is prescribed by section 3201 of the Income Tax Regulations and operates in a country that is a member of the Financial Action Task Force on Money Laundering.

(3) Subsections 56(1), (3) and (4) do not apply if the entity in respect of which a client information record is required to be kept is a public body or a corporation referred to in paragraph (2)(b).

(4) Paragraphs 54(1)(a) and 55(b) and (c) and subsections 56(1), (3) and (4) and 57(1) do not apply if the account holder or settlor is a pension fund that is regulated by or under an Act of Parliament or of the legislature of a province.

(5) Subsection 54(1) does not apply in respect of

(a) employees profit sharing plan accounts and deferred profit sharing plan accounts, unless the accounts are funded in whole or in part by contributions by a person or entity other than the employer; or

(b) dividend reinvestment plan accounts sponsored by a corporation for its investors, unless the accounts are funded in whole or in part by a source other than the corporation.

[SOR/2003-358, s. 16, in force November 6, 2003.]

**63.** (1) Where a person has ascertained the identity of another person in accordance with section 64, the person is not required to subsequently ascertain that same identity again if they recognize that other person.

(2) Where a person has confirmed the existence of a corporation and ascertained its name and address and the names of its directors in accordance with section 65, the person is not required to subsequently confirm or ascertain that same information.

(3) Where a person has confirmed the existence of an entity other than a corporation in accordance with section 66, the person is not required to subsequently confirm that same information.

(4) Despite paragraphs 54(1)(d) and 55(b), subsections 56(3), 57(3) and 58(3) and paragraphs 59(c), 60(e) and 61(c), the name of a corporation's director need not be ascertained when the corporation is a securities dealer.

[SOR/2003-358, s. 17, in force November 6, 2003.]

## MEASURES FOR ASCERTAINING IDENTITY

**64.** (1) The identity of a person shall be ascertained, at the time referred to in subsection (2) and in accordance with subsection (3),

(a) in the cases referred to in paragraphs 54(1)(a) to (c), 55(a), (d) and (e) and 60(a),
   (i) by referring to the person's birth certificate, driver's licence, provincial health insurance card (if such use of the card is not prohibited by the applicable provincial law), passport or any similar record, or
   (ii) where the person is not physically present when the account is opened or when the trust is established, by confirming that a cheque drawn by the person on an account of a financial entity has been cleared;

(b) in the cases referred to in subsection 56(1) and paragraph 61(a),

       (i)  by referring to the person's birth certificate, driver's licence, provincial health insurance card (if such use of the card is not prohibited by the applicable provincial law), passport or any similar record, or

     (ii)  where the person is not physically present when the client information record is created, by confirming that

        (A)  a cheque drawn by the person on an account of a financial entity has been cleared, or

        (B)  the person holds an account in the person's name with a financial entity;

 (c)  in a case referred to in section 57,

       (i)  by referring to the person's birth certificate, driver's licence, provincial health insurance card (if such use of the card is not prohibited by the applicable provincial law), passport or any similar record, or

     (ii)  where the person is not physically present when the account is opened, by confirming that

        (A)  a cheque drawn by the person on an account of a financial entity has been cleared, or

        (B)  the person holds an account in the person's name with a financial entity; and

 (d)  in the cases referred to in section 53, subsection 58(1) and paragraphs 59(a) and (b), 60(b) to (d) and 61(b), by referring to the person's birth certificate, driver's licence, provincial health insurance card (if such use of the card is not prohibited by the applicable provincial law), passport or any similar record.

(2) The identity shall be ascertained

 (a)  in the cases referred to in paragraphs 54(1)(a) and 60(a), before any transaction other than an initial deposit is carried out on an account;

 (b)  in the cases referred to in section 53, paragraphs 54(1)(b) and (c), subsection 58(1) and paragraphs 59(a) and (b), 60(b) to (d) and 61(b), at the time of the transaction;

 (c)  in the cases referred to in paragraphs 55(a), (d) and (e), within 15 days after the trust company becomes the trustee;

 (d)  in the cases referred to in subsection 56(1) and paragraph 61(a), within six months after the client information record is created; and

 (e)  in the case referred to in section 57, within six months after the account is opened.

(3) A person who ascertains the identity of a person by referring to a document pursuant to subsection (1) shall refer to the original document and not a copy of it.

**65.** (1) The existence of a corporation shall be confirmed and its name and address and the names of its directors shall be ascertained as of the time referred to in subsection (2), by referring to its certificate of corporate status, a record that it is required to file annually under the applicable provincial securities legislation or any other record that ascertains its existence as a corporation. The record may be in paper form or in an electronic version that is obtained from a source that is accessible to the public.

(2) The information referred to in subsection (1) shall be ascertained,

(a) in the case referred to in paragraphs 54(1)(d) and 60(e), before any transaction other than the initial deposit is carried out on the account;

(b) in the cases referred to in paragraphs 55(b) and (d), within 15 days after the trust company becomes the trustee;

(c) in the cases referred to in subsections 56(3) and 58(2) and paragraphs 59(c) and 61(c), within six months after the client information record is created; and

(d) in the case referred to in subsection 57(3), within six months after the opening of the account.

(3) Where the information has been ascertained by referring to an electronic version of a record, the person or entity required to ascertain the information shall keep a record that sets out the corporation's registration number, the type of record referred to and the source of the electronic version of the record.

(4) Where the information has been ascertained by referring to a paper copy of a record, the person or entity required to ascertain the information shall retain the record or a copy of it.

**66.** (1) The existence of an entity, other than a corporation, shall be confirmed as of the time referred to in subsection (2), by referring to a partnership agreement, articles of association or other similar record that ascertains its existence. The record may be in paper form or in an electronic version that is obtained from a source that is accessible to the public.

(2) The existence of the entity shall be confirmed

(a) in the case referred to in paragraphs 54(1)(e) and 60(f), before any transaction other than the initial deposit is carried out on the account;

(b) in the cases referred to in paragraphs 55(c) and (d), within 15 days after the trust company becomes the trustee;

(c) in the cases referred to in subsections 56(4) and 58(3) and paragraphs 59(d) and 61(d), within six months after the client information record is created; and

(d) in the case referred to in subsection 57(4), within six months after the account is opened.

(3) Where the existence of the entity has been confirmed by referring to an electronic version of a record, the person or entity required to confirm that information shall keep a record that sets out the registration number of the entity whose existence is being confirmed, the type of record referred to and the source of the electronic version of the record.

(4) Where the existence of the entity has been confirmed by referring to a paper copy of a record, the person or entity required to confirm that information shall retain the record or a copy of it.

**67.** Every person or entity that is required to ascertain the identity of a person in accordance with any of sections 53 to 61 shall set out on the signature card, client information record, transaction ticket, large cash transaction record, large cash disbursement record, extension of credit record, account operating agreement or account application form, as the case may be,

(a) the date of birth of the person;

(b) the type and reference number of the record that is relied on to ascertain the identity of the person, where the record is a birth certificate, driver's licence, provincial health insurance card, passport or any similar record, and the place of issuance of that record;

(c) the financial entity and account number of the account on which the cheque was drawn, where the clearing of a cheque from a financial entity is relied on to ascertain the identity of the person; and

(d) the financial entity at which an account is held and the number of the account, where the identity of the person is ascertained by confirming that the person holds an account with a financial entity.

## RETENTION OF RECORDS

**68.** Where any record is required to be kept under these Regulations, a copy of it may be kept

(a) in a machine-readable form, if a paper copy can be readily produced from it; or

(b) in an electronic form, if a paper copy can be readily produced from it and an electronic signature of the person who must sign the record in accordance with these Regulations is retained.

**69.** (1) Subject to subsection (2), every person or entity that is required to obtain, keep or create records under these Regulations shall retain those records for a period of at least five years following

(a) in respect of signature cards, account operating agreements, client credit files and account application forms, the day of the closing of the account to which they relate;

(b) in respect of client information records, certificates of corporate status, records that are required to be filed annually under the applicable provincial securities legislation or other similar records that ascertain the existence of a corporation, and records that ascertain the existence of an entity, other than a corporation, including partnership agreements and articles of association, the day on which the last business transaction is conducted; and

(c) in respect of all other records, the day on which they were created.

(2) Where records that an individual keeps under these Regulations are the property of the individual's employer or a person or entity with which the individual is in a contractual relationship, the individual is not required to retain the records after the end of the individual's employment or contractual relationship.

**70.** Every record that is required to be kept under these Regulations shall be retained in such a way that it can be provided to an authorized person within 30 days after a request is made to examine it under section 62 of the Act.

## COMPLIANCE

**71.** (1) For the purposes of paragraph 3(a) of the Act, and to assist the Centre in carrying out its mandate under paragraph 40(e) of the Act, every person or entity to which any of paragraphs 5(a) to (l) of the Act applies shall implement a regime for complying with the Act and any Regulations made under the Act.

(2) The compliance regime shall include, as far as practicable,

(a) the appointment of a person — who may be the person referred to in subsection (1) — who is to be responsible for the implementation of the regime;

(b) the development and application of compliance policies and procedures;

(c) a review of those policies and procedures that is conducted as often as necessary to test their effectiveness by an internal or external auditor of the person or entity or, if it does not have such an auditor, by the person or entity itself; and

(d) where the person or entity has employees or agents or persons authorized to act on behalf of the person or entity, an ongoing compliance training program for those employees, agents or persons.

## AMENDMENTS TO THESE REGULATIONS

**72. to 76.** [Amendments]

## REPEAL

**77.** The *Proceeds of Crime (Money Laundering) Regulations\** are repealed.
*SOR/93-75

## COMING INTO FORCE

**78.** (1) Subject to subsection (2), these Regulations come into force on June 12, 2002.

(2) The following provisions come into force on the dates indicated:

(a) paragraph 12(1)(a), sections 17, 21, 24, 28, 32, 35, 38, 40, 47, 50 and 51 and Schedules 1 and 4 on January 31, 2003.

(b) sections 72 to 76 and Schedules 5 and 6 on March 31, 2003.

[SOR/2002-413, s. 1.]

# CROSS-BORDER CURRENCY AND MONETARY INSTRUMENTS REPORTING REGULATIONS

## SOR/2002-412

**Amendments:** SOR/2003-358, ss. 25-27, in force November 6, 2003.

Her Excellency the Governor General in Council, on the recommendation of the Minister of Finance, pursuant to subsection 73(1) (footnote a) of the *Proceeds of Crime (Money Laundering) and Terrorist Financing Act* (footnote b), hereby makes the annexed *Cross-border Currency and Monetary Instruments Reporting Regulations*.

a [S.C. 2001, c. 41, s. 73]

b [S.C. 2001, c. 17; S.C. 2001, c. 41, s. 48]

**1.** (1) **Interpretation** — The following definitions apply in the Act and these Regulations.

"courier" means a commercial carrier that is engaged in scheduled international transportation of shipments of goods other than goods imported or exported as mail.

"monetary instruments" means the following instruments in bearer form or in such other form as title to them passes on delivery, namely,

    (a) securities, including stocks, bonds, debentures and treasury bills; and

    (b) negotiable instruments, including bank drafts, cheques, promissory notes, travellers' cheques and money orders, other than warehouse receipts or bills of lading.

For greater certainty, this definition does not apply to securities or negotiable instruments that bear restrictive endorsements or a stamp for the purposes of clearing or are made payable to a named person and have not been endorsed.

(2) The following definitions apply in these Regulations.

"Act" means the *Proceeds of Crime (Money Laundering) and Terrorist Financing Act*.

"cargo ship" means a commercial vessel that is engaged in international transportation of shipments of goods other than goods imported or exported as mail.

"commercial passenger conveyance" means a conveyance that is used to carry passengers who have paid for passage.

"conveyance" means any vehicle, aircraft or water-borne craft, or other contrivance that is used to move persons, goods, currency or monetary instruments.

"cruise ship" means a commercial vessel that has sleeping facilities for over 70 persons who are not crew members but does not include a vessel engaged in passenger or cargo ferry service.

"emergency" means a medical emergency, fire, flood or other disaster that threatens life, property or the environment.

"non-commercial passenger conveyance" means a conveyance that does not have aboard any person who has paid for passage and includes corporate aircraft, private aircraft and marine pleasure craft.

"transfer agent" means a person or entity appointed by a corporation to maintain records of stock, debenture and bond owners, to cancel and issue certificates and to send out dividend cheques.

[SOR/2003-358, s. 25, in force November 6, 2003]

## REPORTING OF IMPORTATIONS AND EXPORTATIONS

**2.** (1) **Minimum Value of Currency or Monetary Instruments** — For the purposes of reporting the importation or exportation of currency or monetary instruments of a certain value under subsection 12(1) of the Act, the prescribed amount is $10,000.

(2) The prescribed amount is in Canadian dollars or its equivalent in a foreign currency, based on

(a) the official conversion rate of the Bank of Canada as published in the Bank of Canada's Daily Memorandum of Exchange Rates that is in effect at the time of importation or exportation; or

(b) if no official conversion rate is set out in that publication for that currency, the conversion rate that the person or entity would use for that currency in the normal course of business at the time of the importation or exportation.

**3. General Manner of Reporting** — Subject to subsections 4(3) and (3.1) and section 8, a report with respect to the importation or exportation of currency or monetary instruments shall

(a) be made in writing;

(b) contain the information referred to

    (i)   in Schedule 1, in the case of a report made by the person described in paragraph 12(3)(a) of the Act, if that person is not transporting on behalf of an entity or other person,

    (ii)  in Schedule 2, in the case of a report made by the person described in paragraph 12(3)(a) of the Act, if that person is transporting on behalf of an entity or other person,

    (iii) in Schedule 2, in the case of a report made by the person or entity described in paragraph 12(3)(6), (c) or (e) of the Act, and

    (iv) in Schedule 3, in the case of a report made by the person described in paragraph 12(3)(d) of the Act;

(c) contain a declaration that the statements made in the report are true, accurate and complete; and

(d) be signed and dated by the person or entity described in paragraph 12(3)(x), (b), (c), (d) or (e) of the Act, as applicable.

[SOR/2002-412, s. 19, in force September 25, 2003]

**4.** **(1) Importation Reporting** — Subject to subsections (2) to (5) and section 9, a report with respect to currency or monetary instruments transported by a person arriving in Canada shall be submitted without delay by the person at the customs office located at the place of importation or, if it is not open for business at the time of importation, at the nearest customs office that is open for business at that time.

(2) A report with respect to currency or monetary instruments transported by a person arriving in Canada on board a commercial passenger conveyance who has as their destination another place in Canada at which there is a customs office may be submitted without delay by the person at that customs office or, if it is not open for business at the time of importation, at the nearest customs office that is open for business at that time, on condition that

(a) the person does not disembark from the conveyance at the place of arrival in Canada and the currency or monetary instruments are not removed from the conveyance at that place, other than to be transferred under customs control directly to a commercial passenger conveyance for departure to the other place in Canada or directly to a holding area designated as such for the purposes of the Presentation of Persons (Customs) Regulations; and

(b) if the person and currency or monetary instruments are transferred under customs control directly to a designated holding area, the person does not leave and the currency or monetary instruments are not removed from that area, other than to board or to be loaded on board a commercial passenger conveyance for departure to the other place in Canada.

(3) A report with respect to currency or monetary instruments transported by a person arriving in Canada on board a non-commercial passenger conveyance at a customs office where, under the *Customs Act*, customs reporting may be done by radio or telephone may be submitted by radio or telephone to an officer by that person or the person in charge of the conveyance at that location, on condition that

(a) when the person informs the officer of their arrival for the purposes of section 11 of the *Customs Act*, they provide the information referred to in Schedule 1, 2 or 3, as applicable; and

(b) on the officer's request, they present themselves and make available for examination the currency or monetary instruments at the time and place specified by the officer.

(3.1) A report with respect to currency or monetary instruments transported by a person arriving in Canada on board a non-commercial passenger conveyance, at a customs office where the person is authorized in accordance with the Presentation of Persons (2003) Regulations to present in an alternative manner, may be submitted to an officer by telephone, by that person or the person in charge of the conveyance before arriving in Canada, on condition that

(a) when the person informs the officer of their arrival for the purposes of section 11 of the *Customs Act*, they provide the information referred to in Schedule 1, 2 or 3, as applicable; and

(b) on the officer's request, they present themselves and make available for examination the currency or monetary instruments on arrival in Canada at the time and place specified by the officer.

(4) A report with respect to currency or monetary instruments transported by a freight train crew member arriving in Canada on board the freight train shall be submitted without delay by the crew member at the customs office specified by the officer when the crew member presents himself or herself in accordance with section 11 of the *Customs Act*.

(5) A report with respect to currency or monetary instruments that are transported by courier into Canada on board an aircraft and that have as their destination another place in Canada at which there is a customs office, shall be submitted at the customs office located at the airport of destination shown on the air waybill, on condition that

(a) the currency or monetary instruments are not removed from the aircraft at the place of arrival, other than to be transferred under customs control directly to a holding area designated as such for the purposes of the Presentation of Persons (Customs) Regulations; and

(b) if the currency or monetary instruments are transferred under customs control directly to a designated holding area, they are not removed from that area, other than to be loaded on board an aircraft for departure to the other place in Canada.

[SOR/2002-412, s. 20, in force September 25, 2003]

**5.** Subject to section 10, a report made by an exporter with respect to the importation of currency or monetary instruments by mail shall be made by

(a) including inside the mail item an importation report with respect to the currency or monetary instruments; and

(b) affixing the customs declaration form required by the Universal Postal Convention, as amended from time to time, to the outside of the mail item and indicating that it contains currency or monetary instruments.

**6.** A report made with respect to the importation of currency or monetary instruments that have been retained under section 14 of the Act shall be submitted by the person or entity to whom the notice was given at the customs office indicated on the notice.

**7.** A report with respect to the importation of currency or monetary instruments, other than one referred to in sections 4 to 6, shall be submitted without delay at the customs office that is open for business at the time of the importation and that is nearest to the place of importation.

**8.** In an emergency, the person in charge of a conveyance who must unload currency or monetary instruments from the conveyance before being able to make or submit an importation report in accordance with these Regulations may submit the importation report by telephone or other expedient means and, as soon as possible after that, shall make or submit a report in accordance with these Regulations.

**9. (1) Exceptions to Importation Reporting** — Subject to subsections (2) and (3), currency or monetary instruments transported by a person arriving in Canada on board a commercial passenger conveyance who has as their destination a place outside Canada are not required to be reported under subsection 12(1) of the Act, on condition that

(a) the person does not disembark from the conveyance in Canada and the currency or monetary instruments are not removed from the conveyance in Canada other than to be transferred under customs control directly to a commercial passenger conveyance for departure to the place outside Canada or directly to a holding area designated as such for the purposes of the Presentation of Persons (Customs) Regulations; and

(b) if the person and currency or monetary instruments are transferred under customs control directly to a designated holding area, the person does not leave and the currency or monetary instruments are not removed from that area other than to board or be loaded on board a commercial passenger conveyance for departure to the place outside Canada.

(2) Subject to subsection (3), currency or monetary instruments that are transported by courier into Canada on board a conveyance and that have as their destination a place outside Canada are not required to be reported under subsection 12(1) of the Act, on condition that

(a) the currency or monetary instruments are not removed from the conveyance at the place of arrival, other than to be transferred under customs control directly to a holding area designated as such for the purposes of the Presentation of Persons (Customs) Regulations; and

(b) if the currency or monetary instruments are transferred under customs control directly to a designated holding area, they are not removed from that area, other than to be loaded on board a conveyance for departure to the place outside of Canada.

(3) Currency or monetary instruments that are transported into Canada on board a cruise ship or cargo ship and that have as their destination a place outside Canada are not required to be reported under subsection 12(1) of the Act, on condition that the currency or monetary instruments are not removed from the cruise ship or cargo ship while it is in Canada.

[SOR/2003-358, s. 26, in force November 6, 2003]

**10.** A person or entity is not required to make a report under subsection 12(1) of the Act with respect to the importation of currency or monetary instruments that are mailed from a location outside Canada to a destination outside Canada but that transit through Canada in the course of post, on condition that they will not leave the course of post until after they have left Canada.

**11. Exportation Reporting** — A report with respect to currency or monetary instruments transported by a person departing from Canada shall be submitted without delay by the person at the customs office located at the place of exportation or, if it is not open for business at the time of exportation, at the nearest customs office that is open for business at that time.

**12.** A report required to be made by an exporter with respect to the exportation by mail of currency or monetary instruments shall be made by

(a) including an exportation report inside the mail item; and

(b) mailing or submitting, at or before the time when the currency or monetary instruments are mailed, a copy of the exportation report to the customs office that is located nearest to the point at which the item was mailed.

**13.** A report made with respect to the exportation of currency or monetary instruments that have been retained under section 14 of the Act shall be submitted by the person or entity to whom the notice was given at the customs office indicated on the notice.

**14.** A report with respect to the exportation of currency or monetary instruments, other than one referred to in sections 11 to 13, shall be submitted without delay at the customs office that is open for business at the time of exportation and that is nearest to the place of exportation.

## EXCEPTION APPLICABLE TO THE BANK OF CANADA

**15.** A person or entity is not required to make a report under subsection 12(1) of the Act with respect to the importation or exportation of currency by or on behalf of the Bank of Canada for the purposes of the distribution, processing, or testing of banknotes intended for circulation in Canada.

## EXEMPTION APPLICABLE TO IMPORTED SHARES

**15.1** A person or entity is not required to make a report under subsection 12(1) of the Act with respect to stocks, bonds and debentures imported into Canada by courier or as mail if the importer is a financial entity or a securities dealer as defined in subsection 1(2) of the Proceeds of Crime (Money Laundering) and Terrorist Financing Regulations or a transfer agent.

[SOR/2003-358, s. 27, in force November 6, 2003]

## RETENTION

**16.** (1) For the purposes of subsection 14(1) of the Act, an officer shall give the person or entity written notice in person or, if the person is not present, shall send the notice by registered mail to the person's latest known address.

(2) For the purposes of subsection 14(2) of the Act, the notice is to be given within 60 days after the day on which the currency or monetary instruments are imported or exported, as the case may be.

**17.** The prescribed retention period, for the purposes of subsection 14(1) of the Act, is

(a) in the case of importation or exportation by courier or as mail, 30 days after the day on which the retention notice is given or sent; and

(b) in any other case, seven days after the day on which the retention notice is given or sent.

## PENALTIES

**18.** For the purposes of subsection 18(2) of the Act, the prescribed amount of the penalty is

(a) $250, in the case of a person or entity who
  (i) has not concealed the currency or monetary instruments,
  (ii) has made a full disclosure of the facts concerning the currency or monetary instruments on their discovery, and
  (iii) has no previous seizures under the Act;
(b) $2,500, in the case of a person or entity who
  (i) has concealed the currency or monetary instruments, other than by means of using a false compartment in a conveyance, or who has made a false statement with respect to the currency or monetary instruments, or
  (ii) has a previous seizure under the Act, other than in respect of any type of concealment or for making false statements with respect to the currency or monetary instruments; and
(c) $5,000, in the case of a person or entity who
  (i) has concealed the currency or monetary instruments by using a false compartment in a conveyance, or
  (ii) has a previous seizure under the Act for any type of concealment or for making a false statement with respect to the currency or monetary instruments.

## AMENDMENTS TO THESE REGULATIONS

**19. to 23.** Amendments have been incorporated into the relevant sections and Schedules of these regulations.

## COMING INTO FORCE

**24.** (1) Subject to subsection (2), these Regulations come into force on January 6, 2003.

(2) Sections 19 to 23 come into force on the day on which the Presentation of Persons (2003) Regulations come into force.

# UNITED NATIONS SUPPRESSION OF TERRORISM REGULATIONS

## SOR/2001-360

Whereas the Security Council of the United Nations, acting under section 41 of the Charter of the United Nations, adopted Security Council Resolution 1373 (2001) on September 28, 2001;

And whereas it appears to the Governor in Council to be necessary to make regulations for enabling the measures set out in that resolution to be effectively applied;

Therefore, Her Excellency the Governor General in Council, on the recommendation of the Minister of Foreign Affairs, pursuant to sections 2 and 3 of the *United Nations Act*, hereby makes the annexed United Nations Suppression of Terrorism Regulations.

**1. Interpretation** — The definitions in this section apply in these Regulations.

"Canadian" means an individual who is a citizen within the meaning of the *Citizenship Act*, or a body corporate incorporated or continued by or under the laws of Canada or a province.

"entity" means a body corporate, trust, partnership or fund or an unincorporated association or organization.

"listed person" means

(a) a person whose name appears on the list that the Committee of the Security Council of the United Nations, established by Resolution 1267 (1999) of October 15, 1999, establishes and maintains pursuant to that Resolution, Resolution 1333 (2000) of December 19, 2000 and Resolution 1390 (2002) of January 16, 2002; and

(b) a person whose name is listed in Schedule 1 in accordance with section 2.

"Minister" means the Minister of Foreign Affairs.

"person" means an individual or an entity.

"property" means real and personal property of every description and deeds and instruments relating to or evidencing the title or right to property, or giving a right to recover or receive money or goods, and includes any funds, financial assets or economic resources.

[SOR/2001-441, s. 1; SOR/2002-210, s. 1; SOR/2002-325, s. 1.]

**2.** (1) **List** — A person whose name is listed in Schedule 1 is a person who there are reasonable grounds to believe

(a) has carried out, attempted to carry out, participated in or facilitated the carrying out of a terrorist activity;

(b) is controlled directly or indirectly by any person conducting any of the activities set out in paragraph (a); or

(c) are acting on behalf of, or at the direction of, or in association with any person conducting any of the activities set out in paragraph (a).

(2) Any listed person may apply in writing to the Solicitor General to be removed from Schedule 1.

(3) After reviewing the application, the Solicitor General may recommend to the Governor in Council that the applicant be removed from Schedule 1, if there are reasonable grounds for doing so.

[SOR/2002-210, s. 5.]

**3. Providing or Collecting Funds** — No person in Canada and no Canadian outside Canada shall knowingly provide or collect by any means, directly or indirectly, funds with the intention that the funds be used, or in the knowledge that the funds are to be used, by a listed person.

**4. Freezing Property** — No person in Canada and no Canadian outside Canada shall knowingly

(a) deal directly or indirectly in any property of a listed person, including funds derived or generated from property owned or controlled directly or indirectly by that person;

(b) enter into or facilitate, directly or indirectly, any transaction related to a dealing referred to in paragraph (a);

(c) provide any financial or other related service in respect of the property referred to in paragraph (a); or

(d) make any property or any financial or other related service available, directly or indirectly, for the benefit of a listed person.

**5.** All secured and unsecured rights and interests held by a person, other than a listed person or their agent, in the frozen property are entitled to the same ranking as they would have been entitled to had the property not been frozen.

**6. Causing, Assisting Or Promoting** — No person in Canada and no Canadian outside Canada shall knowingly do anything that causes, assists or promotes, or is intended to cause, assist or promote, any activity prohibited by section 3 or 4, unless the person has a certificate issued by the Minister under section 11.

**7.** (1) **Duty to Determine** — Every Canadian financial institution within the meaning of section 2 of the *Bank Act* must determine on a continuing basis whether it is in possession or control of property owned or controlled by or on behalf of a listed person.

(2) Every financial institution referred to in subsection (1) must report monthly to the principal agency or body that supervises or regulates it under federal or provincial law

(a) that it is not in possession or control of any property referred to in subsection (1); or

(b) if it is in possession or control of such property, the number of persons, contracts or accounts involved and the total value of the property.

(3) This section also applies to an authorized foreign bank, within the meaning of section 2 of the *Bank Act*, in respect of their business in Canada and to a foreign

company, within the meaning of subsection 2(1) of the *Insurance Companies Act*, in respect of their business in Canada.

[SOR/2001-441, s. 2.]

**8. Disclosure** — Every person in Canada and every Canadian outside Canada shall disclose forthwith to the Commissioner of the Royal Canadian Mounted Police and to the Director of the Canadian Security Intelligence Service

(a) the existence of property in their possession or control that they have reason to believe is owned or controlled by or on behalf of a listed person; and

(b) information about a transaction or proposed transaction in respect of property referred to in paragraph (a).

**9. Offences and Punishment** — Any person who contravenes sections 3, 4, 6, 7 or 8 is guilty of an offence and liable,

(a) on summary conviction to the maximum fine or imprisonment, or both, as set out in the *United Nations Act*; or

(b) on conviction on indictment to the maximum fine or imprisonment, or both, as set out in the *United Nations Act*.

**10.** If a corporation commits an offence under these Regulations, any director, officer or agent of the corporation who directed, authorized, assented to, acquiesced in or participated in the commission of the offence is a party to and guilty of the offence and is liable on conviction to the punishment provided for the offence whether or not the corporation has been prosecuted.

**11. Certificate** — No offence is committed under section 9 for doing any act or thing that may be prohibited by these Regulations or omitting to do any act or thing that may be required by these Regulations if, before that person does or omits to do that act or thing, the Minister issues a certificate to the person stating that the Minister has reasonable grounds to believe that

(a) the Security Council of the United Nations Resolution 1373 adopted on September 28, 2001 does not intend that the act or thing be prohibited;

(b) the act or thing has been approved by the Security Council of the United Nations or by the Committee of the Security Council established by the Resolution referred to in paragraph (a); or

(c) the person named in the certificate is not a listed person.

[SOR/2001-441, s. 3.]

## COMING INTO FORCE

**12.** These Regulations come into force on the day on which they are registered.

# GUIDELINE 1: BACKGROUNDER

## March 24, 2003

TABLE OF CONTENTS

1.  **Introduction**

2.  **Money Laundering**

    2.1  What is Money Laundering?

    2.2  Methods of Money Laundering

    2.3  Importance of Combatting Money Laundering

    2.4  International Efforts to Combat Money Laundering

3.  **Terrorist Financing**

    3.1  What is Terrorist Financing?

    3.2  Methods of Terrorist Financing

    3.3  Laundering of Terrorist-Related Funds

    3.4  Importance of Combatting Terrorist Financing

    3.5  International Efforts to Combat Terrorist Financing

4.  **Canada's Legislation to Combat Money Laundering and Terrorist Financing**

    4.1  Anti-Money Laundering

    4.2  Anti-Terrorism

5.  **Canada's Legislation: The *Proceeds of Crime (Money Laundering) and Terrorist Financing Act***

    5.1  Objectives of the Act

    5.2  Who has to Report to FINTRAC?

    5.3  What has to be Reported to FINTRAC?

    5.4  Other Information about Reporting to FINTRAC

    5.5  Voluntary Information

6.  **The Financial Transactions and Reports Analysis Centre of Canada**

    6.1  What is FINTRAC?

    6.2  FINTRAC's Analysis

    6.3  Protection of Privacy

6.4   Disclosure by FINTRAC

6.5   Other Responsibilities of FINTRAC

**7.   Comments?**

**8.   How to Contact FINTRAC**


1 INTRODUCTION

The objective of the Canadian legislation called the *Proceeds of Crime (Money Laundering) and Terrorist Financing Act* is to help detect and deter money laundering and the financing of terrorist activities. It is also to facilitate investigations and prosecutions of money laundering and terrorist activity financing offences. This includes implementation of reporting and other requirements for financial service providers and those that engage in businesses, professions or activities susceptible to being used for money laundering or terrorist financing. The Act also established the Financial Transactions and Reports Analysis Centre of Canada (FINTRAC) as the agency responsible for the collection, analysis and disclosure of information to assist in the detection, prevention and deterrence of money laundering and terrorist financing in Canada and abroad.

This guideline has been prepared by FINTRAC to provide background information about money laundering and terrorist financing, including their international nature. It also provides an outline of the Canadian legislative requirements for a compliance regime, record keeping, client identification and sending reports to FINTRAC. In addition, it offers an overview of FINTRAC's mandate and responsibilities.

This guideline uses plain language to explain common reporting situations under the *Proceeds of Crime (Money Laundering) and Terrorist Financing Act* as well as the related Regulations. It is provided as general information only. It is not legal advice and is not intended to replace the Act and Regulations. For more information about money laundering, terrorist financing, or other reporting requirements under the Act and Regulations, see the guidelines in this series:

- *Guideline 1: Backgrounder* explains money laundering and terrorist financing and their international nature. It also provides an outline of the legislative requirements as well as an overview of FINTRAC's mandate and responsibilities.
- *Guideline 2: Suspicious Transactions* explains how to report a suspicious transaction. It also provides guidance on how to identify a suspicious transaction, including general and industry-specific indicators that may help when conducting or evaluating transactions.
- *Guideline 3: Submitting Suspicious Transaction Reports to FINTRAC* explains when and how to submit reports.
- *Guideline 4: Implementation of a Compliance Regime* explains the requirement for reporting persons and entities to implement a regime to

ensure compliance with their obligations under the *Proceeds of Crime (Money Laundering) and Terrorist Financing Act.*

- *Guideline 5: Submitting Terrorist Property Reports to FINTRAC* explains to reporting persons and entities when and how to submit a terrorist property report.
- *Guideline 6: Record Keeping and Client Identification* explains the requirement for reporting persons and entities to identify their clients and keep records. There are eight different versions of Guideline 6, by sector.
- *Guideline 7: Submitting Large Cash Transaction Reports to FINTRAC* explains when and how to submit large cash transaction reports.
- *Guideline 8: Submitting Electronic Funds Transfer Reports to FINTRAC* explains when and how to submit EFT reports.

If you need more help after you read this or other guidelines, call FINTRAC's national toll- free enquiries line at 1-866-346-8722.

Throughout these guidelines, several references are provided to additional information that may be available on external Web sites. FINTRAC is not responsible for the accuracy or reliability of the information contained on those external Web sites.

## 2 MONEY LAUNDERING

### 2.1 What is Money Laundering?

The United Nations defines money laundering as "any act or attempted act to disguise the source of money or assets derived from criminal activity." Essentially, money laundering is the process whereby "dirty money"— produced through criminal activity — is transformed into "clean money," the criminal origin of which is difficult to trace. There are three recognized stages in the money laundering process.

- **Placement** involves placing the proceeds of crime in the financial system.
- **Layering** involves converting the proceeds of crime into another form and creating complex layers of financial transactions to disguise the audit trail and the source and ownership of funds. This stage may involve transactions such as the buying and selling of stocks, commodities or property.
- **Integration** involves placing the laundered proceeds back in the economy to create the perception of legitimacy.

The money laundering process is continuous, with new dirty money constantly being introduced into the financial system.

Under Canadian law, a money laundering offence involves various acts committed with the intention to conceal or convert property or the proceeds of property (e.g. money) knowing or believing that these were derived from the commission of a designated offence. In this context, a designated offence means most serious offences under the *Criminal Code* or any other federal Act. It includes those relating to illegal drug trafficking, bribery, fraud, forgery, murder, robbery, counterfeit money, stock manipulation, etc. The few exceptions are for offences such as those related to tax evasion or breach of copyright, and some others that involve administrative and monetary penalty structure.

A money laundering offence may also extend to property or proceeds derived from illegal activities that took place outside Canada.

## 2.2 Methods of Money Laundering

There are as many methods to launder money as the imagination allows, and the schemes being used are becoming increasingly sophisticated and complicated as technology advances. The following are some examples of common money laundering methods.

- **Nominees**
  This is one of the most common methods of laundering and hiding assets. A launderer uses family members, friends or associates who are trusted within the community, and who will not attract attention, to conduct transactions on their behalf. The use of nominees facilitates the concealment of the source and ownership of the funds involved.

- **Structuring or "smurfing"**
  Many inconspicuous individuals deposit cash or buy bank drafts at various institutions, or one individual carries out transactions for amounts less than the amount that must be reported to the government, and the cash is subsequently transferred to a central account. These individuals, commonly referred to as "smurfs," normally do not attract attention as they deal in funds that are below reporting thresholds and they appear to be conducting ordinary transactions.

- **Asset purchases with bulk cash**
  Individuals purchase big-ticket items such as cars, boats and real estate. In many cases, launderers use the assets but distance themselves from them by having them registered in a friend's or relative's name. The assets may also be resold to further launder the proceeds.

- **Exchange transactions**
  Individuals often use proceeds of crime to buy foreign currency that can then be transferred to offshore bank accounts anywhere in the world.

- **Currency smuggling**
  Funds are moved across borders to disguise their source and ownership, and to avoid being exposed to the law and systems that record money entering into the financial system. Funds are smuggled in various ways (such as by mail, courier and body-packing) often to countries with strict bank secrecy laws.

- **Gambling in casinos**
  Individuals bring cash to a casino and buy gambling chips. After gaming and placing just a few bets, the gambler redeems the remainder of the chips and requests a casino cheque.

- **Black-market peso exchange**
  An underground network of currency brokers with offices in North America, the Caribbean and South America allows drug traffickers to exchange pesos for U.S. dollars. The dollars stay in the United States and are bought by South American (mainly Colombian) companies, which use them to buy American goods for sale back home (see information about financial investigations in the enforcement section of the U.S. Customs Web site at http://www.customs.ustreas.gov/xp/cgov/enforcement/investigations/financial_ investigations/ or http://www.customs.ustreas.gov/ImageCache/cgov/content/ publications/pesos_2epdf/v1/pesos.pdf).

## 2.3 Importance of Combatting Money Laundering

The vast majority of criminals would not be in the "business" of crime if it were not for the tremendous profits to be made. There is a direct relationship between the profitability of most types of crime and their prevalence. A major objective of the battle against crime in Canada and elsewhere is, therefore, to deprive criminals of the profits from their efforts. Only by effectively laundering illegal assets can criminals use them and thereby benefit from their crimes.

The sheer magnitude of money laundering activities demonstrates the importance of implementing strong anti-money laundering regimes in countries throughout the world. The International Monetary Fund has stated that the aggregate amount of money being laundered in the world could be somewhere between two and five percent of world gross domestic product, or between approximately C$900 billion and C$2.25 trillion. In Canada, money laundering is a multibillion-dollar problem. It is an integral element of organized criminal activity, and is the proven method by which organized crime groups seek to transform the proceeds of drug trafficking, contraband goods and people smuggling, extortion, fraud and other activities into apparently legitimately earned funds.

Laundered proceeds of crime provide seemingly legitimate financial support to drug dealers, terrorist organizations, arms dealers and other criminals to amass wealth and operate and expand their criminal empires. Investigations have revealed that those involved in money laundering attempts manipulate financial systems in Canada and abroad to foster a wide range of illicit activities. The economic and political influence of criminal organizations can potentially weaken the social fabric, collective ethical standards and, ultimately, the democratic institutions of society.

Money laundering activities have the potential to distort economic data and to cause economic growth to suffer. International Monetary Fund studies on the relationship between gross domestic product growth and money laundering in industrial countries have found evidence that significant reductions in annual gross domestic product growth rates were associated with increases in money laundering activities.

These are some of the reasons why Canada is serious in its commitment to combat money laundering. The increasingly international character of business and the often multinational nature of money laundering activities have resulted in stepped up international efforts and co-operation in the fight against money laundering.

## 2.4 International Efforts to Combat Money Laundering

An important objective of money laundering activities is to remove the proceeds of crime from the jurisdiction in which they were obtained to help disguise their origins. This frequently involves the international movement of those proceeds, which is facilitated by the increasingly international character of business, financial and criminal activity. Although money laundering has become a large global phenomenon that affects all countries in varying ways and degrees, jurisdictional boundaries have made international law enforcement difficult. International co-operation and co-ordination have become essential to the deterrence, detection and prosecution of money laundering, leading to the development of many international initiatives over the past decade to address this issue.

Perhaps the most well known of these initiatives is the Financial Action Task Force on Money Laundering (FATF), established by the G-7 countries in 1989. FATF is an intergovernmental body, comprising 29 countries and two international organizations, whose purpose is to develop and promote policies to combat money laundering. Canada has been a member of FATF since it was established. FATF has set out 40 recommendations that outline the basic framework for anti-money laundering efforts. These recommendations define international standards covering the criminal justice system and law enforcement, the financial system and its regulation, and international co-operation. More information about FATF and its 40 recommendations can be found at http://www.oecd.org/fatf.

Other international anti-money laundering initiatives include the following:

- Egmont Group of Financial Intelligence Units
- European Convention on Laundering, Search, Seizure and Confiscation of the Proceeds from Crime
- Asia Pacific Group on Money Laundering (APG)
- Caribbean Financial Action Task Force on Money Laundering (CFATF)
- United Nations Single Convention on Narcotic Drugs
- United Nations Convention on Psychotropic Substances
- United Nations Convention Against Illicit Traffic in Narcotic Drugs and Psychotropic Substances
- United Nations Convention Against Transnational Organized Crime

For more information about CFATF and APG, refer to http://www.cfatf.org and http://www.apgml.org/. For more information on United Nations Conventions refer to http://www.incb.org/e/conv/menu.htm.

As a member of FATF, a sponsoring country of the CFATF, and a signatory to the United Nations Conventions listed above, Canada is very active in the international fight against money laundering. The *Proceeds of Crime (Money Laundering) and Terrorist Financing Act* is a further demonstration of Canada's commitment to fighting money laundering. See Sections 4 and 5 (below) for more information about Canada's anti-money laundering efforts.

For more information on money laundering, you can also refer to the following web sites:

- Royal Canadian Mounted Police (http://www.rcmp-grc.gc.ca)
- Financial Crimes Enforcement Network (http://www.fincen.gov/)
- United Nations Office of Drug Control and Crime Prevention (http://www. odccp.org/money_laundering.html)
- Australian Transaction Reports Analysis Centre (http://www.austrac.gov.au)
- International Money Laundering Information Network (http://www.imolin. org/)
- Moneylaundering.com (http://moneylaundering.com).

## 3   TERRORIST FINANCING

### 3.1  What is Terrorist Financing?

Terrorist financing provides funds for terrorist activity. Terrorist activity has as its main objective to intimidate a population or compel a government to do something. This is done by intentionally killing, seriously harming or endangering a person, causing substantial property damage that is likely to seriously harm people or by seriously interfering with or disrupting essential services, facilities or systems.

Terrorist activity is undertaken for political, religious or ideological purposes. This does not mean that an expression of political, religious or ideological beliefs alone is a terrorist activity, unless it is part of a larger conduct that meets the definition explained above.

Terrorists need financial support to carry out terrorist activities and achieve their goals. In this respect, there is little difference between terrorists and other criminals in their use of the financial system. A successful terrorist group, much like a criminal organization, is one that is able to build and maintain an effective financial infrastructure. For this, it must develop sources of funding and means of obscuring the links between those sources and the activities the funds support. It needs to find a way to make sure that the funds are available and can be used to get whatever goods or services needed to commit terrorist acts.

The fundamental aim of terrorist financing is to obtain resources to support terrorist activities. The sums needed to mount terrorist attacks are not always large and the associated transactions are not necessarily complex.

## 3.2 Methods of Terrorist Financing

There are two primary sources of financing for terrorist activities. The first involves getting financial support from countries, organizations or individuals. The other involves revenue-generating activities. These are explained in further detail below.

### Financial Support

Terrorism could be sponsored by a country or government, although this is believed to have declined in recent years. State support may be replaced by support from other sources, such as individuals with sufficient financial means.

### Revenue-Generating Activities

The revenue-generating activities of terrorist groups may include criminal acts, and therefore may appear similar to other criminal organizations. Kidnapping and extortion can serve a dual purpose of providing needed financial resources while furthering the main terrorist objective of intimidating the target population. In addition, terrorist groups may use smuggling, fraud, theft, robbery, and narcotics trafficking to generate funds.

Financing for terrorist groups may also include legitimately earned income, which might include collection of membership dues and subscriptions, sale of publications, speaking tours, cultural and social events, as well as solicitation and appeals within the community. This fundraising might be in the name of organizations with charitable or relief status, so that donors are led to believe they are giving to a legitimate good cause.

Only a few non-profit organizations or supposedly charitable organizations have been implicated in terrorist financing networks in the past, worldwide. In these cases, the organizations may in fact have carried out some of the charitable or relief work. Members or donors may have had no idea that a portion of funds raised by the charity was being diverted to terrorist activities.

This type of "legitimately earned" financing might also include donations by terrorist group members of a portion of their personal earnings.

## 3.3 Laundering of Terrorist-Related Funds

As explained above, the methods used by terrorist groups to generate funds from illegal sources are often very similar to those used by "traditional" criminal organizations. Like criminal organizations, they have to find ways to launder these illicit funds to be able to use them without drawing the attention of the authorities.

For this reason, transactions related to terrorist financing may look a lot like those related to money laundering. Therefore, strong, comprehensive anti-money laundering regimes are key to also tracking terrorists' financial activities.

## 3.4 Importance of Combatting Terrorist Financing

Acts of terrorism pose a significant threat to the safety and security of people all around the world. Canada continues to work with other nations to confront terrorism and bring those who support, plan and carry out acts of terrorism to justice.

Business relationships with terrorist groups could expose financial institutions or financial intermediaries to significant reputational and operational risk, as well as legal repercussions. The risk is even more serious if the terrorist group is subsequently shown to have benefited from the lack of effective monitoring or wilful blindness of a particular institution or intermediary that enabled them to carry out terrorist activities.

## 3.5 International Efforts to Combat Terrorist Financing

Following the horrific events of September 11, 2001, the United Nations called on member states to freeze the assets of all groups or individuals involved in terrorist activities and to prohibit the provision and collection of funds for terrorist activities. The G-7 Finance Ministers and Central Bank Governors met on October 6, 2001, and released an action plan to combat the financing of terrorism. Shortly after, the Financial Action Task Force (FATF), of which Canada is a member, also issued *Special Recommendations on Terrorist Financing* that its members should apply to combat terrorist financing.

To be successful, the fight against terrorism has to be conducted on many fronts. Canada is committed to working with its international partners in confronting and stamping out terrorism around the world.

The Government of Canada's Anti-Terrorism Plan has four objectives:

- stop terrorists from getting into Canada and protect Canadians from terrorist acts;
- bring forward tools to identify, prosecute, convict and punish terrorists;
- prevent the Canada-U.S. border from being held hostage by terrorists and impacting upon the Canadian economy; and
- work with the international community to bring terrorists to justice and address the root causes of such hatred.

The measures flowing from this plan target people and activities that pose a threat to the security and well-being of Canadians or others throughout the world. This is a fight against terrorism, and not against any one community, group or faith.

For more information about international efforts to combat terrorism and terrorist activities, refer to the following Web sites:

- http://www. fin.gc.ca/activty/g7/g7102001e.html
- http://www1.oecd.org/fatf/TerFinance_en.htm
- http://www.cfatf.org/eng/
- http://www.un.org/terrorism/

More information about Canada's anti-terrorism efforts is included in Section 4.2 (below).

## 4 CANADA'S LEGISLATION TO COMBAT MONEY LAUNDERING AND TERRORIST FINANCING

### 4.1 Anti-Money Laundering

Money laundering became an offence in Canada several years ago, under amendments to the *Criminal Code*. These amendments also gave law enforcement the ability to search, seize and restrain property believed to be proceeds of crime.

The criminalization of the laundering of proceeds of crime (money laundering) led to many other legislative changes, such as amendments to the *Customs Act* and the *Excise Act,* among others. New legislation was introduced as part of these measures to create an anti-money laundering regime.

To assist in the detection and deterrence of money laundering, the first components of Canada's anti-money laundering regime consisted of certain record keeping and client identification requirements. These requirements applied to financial entities, such as banks, credit unions, caisses populaires, and trust and loan companies. They also applied to life insurance companies, securities dealers, casinos, foreign exchange dealers, and any person engaged in a business, profession or activity that received cash for payment or transfer to a third party. Although there were no reporting requirements at that time, these entities could provide information voluntarily about any suspicious transactions to law enforcement.

These measures were subsequently enhanced and additional components were introduced. These included reporting requirements, the first of which became effective in November 2001 for suspicious transactions. They also included other requirements, such as record keeping and client identification, that came into effect in 2002. Other reporting obligations are being phased-in over the course of 2002 and 2003. These are all explained in more detail in Section 5 (below) that covers Canada's *Proceeds of Crime (Money Laundering) and Terrorist Financing Ac*t.

### 4.2 Anti-Terrorism

The Government of Canada has taken steps to combat terrorist activities at home and abroad. These steps include signing and ratifying United Nations (UN) Conventions, such as the *International Convention for the Suppression of the Financing of Terrorism*, and implementing related UN resolutions through Regulations. They also include introducing tough new anti-terrorism measures in legislation called the *Anti-Terrorism Ac*t.

### *United Nations Suppression of Terrorism Regulations*

In early October 2001, Canada passed the *United Nations Suppression of Terrorism Regulation*s. These provide for a list of individuals or entities believed

to be involved in or associated with terrorist activity. They make it an offence for anyone in Canada, or any Canadian outside Canada, to provide or collect funds if they know these would be for use by anyone on the list.

These Regulations also make it an offence for anyone in Canada, or any Canadian outside Canada, to deal in any way with property if they know it is owned or controlled by anyone on the list. This includes any financial service or transaction relating to such property. It also includes making property available to anyone on the list.

In addition, these Regulations require that Canadian financial institutions determine on a continuing basis whether they are in possession or control of property owned or controlled by or on behalf of anyone on the list. Each Canadian financial institution must report monthly to their principal supervisory or regulatory body (for example, the Office of the Superintendent of Financial Institutions) concerning possession or control of any property described above. These financial institutions include banks, credit unions, caisses populaires, and trust and loan companies. They also include insurance companies, fraternal benefit societies, and entities that deal with securities.

Furthermore, these Regulations require anyone in Canada, as well as Canadians outside Canada, to disclose to the Royal Canadian Mounted Police (RCMP) and the Canadian Security Intelligence Service (CSIS) the existence of any property in their possession or control that they **believe** is owned or controlled by or on behalf of anyone on the list. This includes information about any transaction or proposed transaction relating to that property. Information is to be provided to them, without delay, as follows:

- RCMP, Financial Intelligence Branch unclassified fax: (613) 993-9474
- CSIS Security Screening Branch, Project Leader Government Operations, unclassified fax: (613) 842-1902

For more information about the requirements under these Regulations, including guidance regarding an individual or entity whose name is the same or resembles the name of a listed person, you can refer to the following Web sites:

- http://www.osfi-bsif.gc.ca/eng/publications/advisories/index_supervisory.asp?#Supter
- http://www.dfait-maeci.gc.ca/trade/sanctions-e.asp - terrorism
- http://www.dfait-maeci.gc.ca/trade/statement_of_guidance-e.asp
- http://canadagazette.gc.ca/partII/2002/20020111-x/html/sor42-e.html
- http://canadagazette.gc.ca/partII/tempPdf/g2-135x2.pdf
- http://www.sgc.gc.ca/national_security/counter_terrorism_e.asp

### *Anti-Terrorism Act*

Canada's *Anti-Terrorism Act* (ATA) created measures to deter, disable, identify, prosecute, convict and punish terrorist groups. It provides new investigative tools for law enforcement and national security agencies. It also ensures that Canadian values of respect and fairness are preserved and the root causes of hatred are addressed through stronger laws against hate crimes and propaganda. The package also includes rigorous safeguards to ensure that the fundamental rights and freedoms of Canadians are upheld.

The ATA includes significant additions to the *Criminal Code* to include offences relating to terrorist activities and the financing of terrorism. These changes make it a crime to do any of the following:

- knowingly collect or provide funds, either directly or indirectly, to carry out terrorist activities;
- knowingly participate in, contribute to or facilitate the activities of a terrorist group;
- instruct anyone to carry out a terrorist activity on behalf of a terrorist group; or
- knowingly harbour or conceal a terrorist.

These *Criminal Code* changes also include a requirement similar to the one described under the heading *United Nations Suppression of Terrorism Regulations* above. These changes to the *Criminal Code* require anyone in Canada, as well as Canadians outside Canada, to disclose to the RCMP and CSIS the existence of any property in their possession or control that they **know** is owned or controlled by or on behalf of a terrorist group. This includes information about any transaction or proposed transaction relating to that property. Information is to be provided to them, without delay, as follows:

- RCMP, Financial Intelligence Branch unclassified fax: (613) 993-9474
- CSIS Security Screening Branch, Project Leader Government Operations, unclassified fax: (613) 842-1902

A terrorist group includes anyone that has as one of their purposes or activities facilitating or carrying out any terrorist activity. This can be a person, a group, a trust, a partnership or a fund. It can also be an unincorporated association or organization. A list of terrorist groups is published in the *Regulations Establishing a List of Entities* made under the *Criminal Code.* More information about this is available from the following Web sites:

- http://www.osfi-bsif.gc.ca/eng/publications/advisories/index_supervisory.asp?#Supter
- http://www.sgc.gc.ca/national_security/counter_terrorism_e.asp

Many other legislative changes were included in the ATA. Among these are measures to revoke or deny an organization's charitable status if it is believed to support terrorist groups.

For more information about this, terrorist-related offences or other Government of Canada efforts to combat terrorism and terrorist activities, refer to the following Web sites:

- http://canada.justice.gc.ca/en/terrorism/
- http://canada.gc.ca/wire/2001/09/110901-US_e.html
- http://www.dfait-maeci.gc.ca/anti-terrorism/campaign-e.asp

The ATA also included expansion of the anti-money laundering legislation to include terrorist financing in its objectives. For more information about this, read the next section.

## 5 CANADA'S LEGISLATION: *THE PROCEEDS OF CRIME (MONEY LAUNDERING) AND TERRORIST FINANCING ACT*

### 5.1 Objectives of the Act

The *Proceeds of Crime (Money Laundering) and Terrorist Financing Act* has three key objectives:

- to implement specific measures to detect and deter money laundering and the financing of terrorist activities and to facilitate investigations and prosecution of the related offences;
- to respond to the threat posed by organized crime by providing law enforcement officials with the information they need to deprive criminals of the proceeds of their criminal activities, while protecting individual privacy; and
- to help fulfill Canada's international commitments to fight multinational crime.

The specific measures include the following:

- **Record keeping and reporting**
  Reporting persons and entities (see Section 5.2 below) have to implement a compliance regime, keep certain records and ascertain client identification. They also have to report suspicious transactions to FINTRAC. In addition, coming into effect over the course of 2002 and 2003, they will also have to report certain other financial transactions to FINTRAC (See Section 5.3 below).

- **Cross-border reporting**
  The import or export of currency or monetary instruments of or over $10,000 will have to be declared to the Canada Customs and Revenue Agency. This came into effect in early 2003.

- **Creation of FINTRAC**
  FINTRAC is an independent agency, at arm's length from law enforcement agencies, responsible for collecting, analyzing and, in appropriate circumstances, disclosing certain limited information to law enforcement agencies. FINTRAC is required to ensure that personal information under its control is protected from unauthorized disclosure, and is subject to the *Privacy Act*. For more information about FINTRAC, refer to Section 6 (below).

These measures, once fully implemented, will contribute to maintaining the integrity of Canada's financial infrastructure. They also represent sound business practices for reporting persons and entities to help them minimize their risk of being exposed to money laundering or terrorist financing and their negative consequences. Canada's regime is consistent with FATF's initiative to establish international standards aimed at improving national legal systems, enhancing the role of financial systems and strengthening international co-operation in the fight against money laundering and terrorist financing. The measures will help detect and deter organized criminal activities as well as terrorist activities in Canada and help ensure Canada is not used to facilitate money laundering or terrorist financing.

A link to the relevant legislation can be found on FINTRAC's Website at http://www.fintrac.gc.ca/act-loi/1_e.asp. A link to the Regulations can also be found on FINTRAC's Website at http://www.fintrac.gc.ca/reg/1_e.asp.

## 5.2 Who has to Report to FINTRAC?

The following persons and entities will have to report suspicious and certain other transactions to FINTRAC:

* financial entities (such as banks, credit unions, caisses populaires, trust and loan companies and agents of the Crown that accept deposit liabilities);
* life insurance companies, brokers and agents;
* securities dealers, portfolio managers and investment counsellors;
* persons engaged in the business of foreign exchange dealing;
* money services businesses (including alternative remittance systems, such as Hawala, Hundi, Chitti, etc.);
* Canada Post for money orders;
* accountants and accounting firms (when carrying out certain activities on behalf of their clients);
* real estate brokers or sales representatives (when carrying out certain activities on behalf of their clients); and
* casinos (including those authorized to do business in Canada, with a slot machine or roulette or card games, but excluding certain temporary charity casinos).

For purposes of suspicious transaction reporting, reporting persons include employees of the persons or entities described above. For more information about who has to report, see *Guideline 2: Suspicious Transactions*.

## 5.3 What has to be Reported to FINTRAC?

The first of the reporting requirements described below became effective in 2001. The rest of the reporting requirements will be phased in throughout 2002 and 2003. Other guidelines will be updated and new guidelines will be created to explain these reporting requirements in more detail. More information on sending reports to FINTRAC can be found in *Guideline 3: Submitting Suspicious Transaction Reports to FINTRAC*.

## Suspicious Transactions

Since November 8, 2001, reporting persons and entities (see Section 5.2 above) have to report transactions if there are reasonable grounds to suspect that the transactions are related to the commission of a money laundering offence. Since June 12, 2002, they also have to report transactions if there are reasonable grounds to suspect that the transactions are related to the commission of a terrorist activity financing offence. More information on reporting suspicious transactions can be found in *Guideline 2: Suspicious Transactions* and *Guideline 3: Submitting Suspicious Transaction Reports to FINTRAC*.

This does not prevent persons and entities from reporting suspicions of money laundering or terrorist financing directly to law enforcement, and FINTRAC encourages financial institutions and financial intermediaries to maintain established relationships with law enforcement.

## Other Financial Transactions

Depending on the type of activities they are involved in, these same reporting persons and entities will have to report the following financial transactions:

* as of June 12, 2002, the sending or receiving of international electronic funds transfers of $10,000 or more through the SWIFT network;
* as of January 31, 2003, large cash transactions involving amounts of $10,000 or more; and
* as of March 31, 2003, other international electronic funds transfers of $10,000 or more (through non-SWIFT networks).

## Terrorist Property

Since June 12, 2002, reporting persons and entities also have to report to FINTRAC if they have property in their possession or control that they know is owned or controlled by or on behalf of a terrorist group. As explained in Section 4.2, this information also has to be disclosed to the RCMP and CSIS.

## 5.4 Other Information about Reporting to FINTRAC

Reporting persons and entities are protected from criminal and civil legal proceedings when they submit suspicious transaction or other financial transaction reports in good faith to FINTRAC, as required. The same applies to terrorist property reports.

In addition to the reporting requirements, reporting persons and entities will also be required to keep certain records after conducting specified transactions. This will also include specific requirements about identifying individuals with whom a reporting person or entity conducts a transaction.

Failure to comply with reporting and record keeping requirements can lead to criminal charges against a reporting person or entity. There are some penalties that could apply in cases of failure to comply. More information about these can be found in *Guideline 4: Implementation of a Compliance Regime*.

## 5.5 Voluntary Information

Section 5.3 above explains reports that have to be sent to FINTRAC. In addition to those reports, anybody can voluntarily provide information about suspicions of money laundering or terrorist financing to FINTRAC. Anyone who does this is protected from criminal and civil legal proceedings when they do so in good faith.

To find out how to provide information voluntarily to FINTRAC about suspicions of money laundering or of the financing of terrorist activities, refer to FINTRAC's Web site at http://www.fintrac.gc.ca/reporting--declaration/vol/1_e.asp.

## 6 THE FINANCIAL TRANSACTIONS AND REPORTS ANALYSIS CENTRE OF CANADA

### 6.1 What is FINTRAC?

The Financial Transactions and Reports Analysis Centre of Canada (FINTRAC) is an independent government agency. It operates at arm's length from law enforcement agencies, and collects, analyzes and discloses information to help detect, prevent and deter money laundering and the financing of terrorist activities in Canada and abroad.

### 6.2 FINTRAC's Analysis

FINTRAC receives and analyzes reports from reporting persons and entities (see Section 5.2 above). It can also receive and analyze information from various other sources, such as similar agencies in other countries, law enforcement agencies, or government institutions and agencies. In addition, FINTRAC can receive and analyze any information about suspicions of money laundering or of the financing of terrorist activities that is provided voluntarily.

FINTRAC will also receive and analyze information that will be provided to the Canada Customs and Revenue Agency by exporters and importers of currency and monetary instruments. As explained in Section 5.1 above, this came into effect in early 2003.

FINTRAC relies on financial analysts and analytical technologies to produce high-quality analyses and assessments about suspicions of money laundering or terrorist financing. It participates in extensive research and international fora on the topics. In addition, FINTRAC uses a strategic approach to communicate information to stakeholders and to develop productive relationships with reporting entities, law enforcement and international agencies. FINTRAC is committed to being a centre of excellence on matters related to money laundering and terrorist financing.

### 6.3 Protection of Privacy

There are numerous safeguards to protect the privacy of individuals about whom information is sent to FINTRAC, including the following:

- the independence of FINTRAC from law enforcement and other agencies to which FINTRAC is authorized to disclose information;
- criminal penalties for any unauthorized use or disclosure of the personal information under FINTRAC's control;
- the requirement for police to get a court order to obtain further information from FINTRAC; and
- the application of the *Privacy Act* to FINTRAC.

## 6.4 Disclosure by FINTRAC

As explained above, FINTRAC is required to ensure that personal information under its control is protected from unauthorized disclosure. Information may only be disclosed to the appropriate law enforcement authorities when FINTRAC determines that there are reasonable grounds to suspect that the information would be relevant to investigating or prosecuting a money laundering offence or a terrorist activity financing offence.

When FINTRAC has made this determination, it discloses only designated information to law enforcement agencies. Designated information is limited to key identifying information, such as name and address, date of birth and citizenship. It also includes certain information about the transaction, such as the name and address of the place of business where it occurred, the date of the transaction, amount and type of currency or value of the funds, account number (if any), etc.

To obtain further information from FINTRAC, police must first get a court order.

When FINTRAC has made the determination relating to money laundering or terrorist financing, it also, under specified circumstances, discloses designated information to the following agencies and departments:

- Canada Customs and Revenue Agency, when FINTRAC also determines that the information is relevant to a tax or duty evasion offence;
- Department of Citizenship and Immigration, when FINTRAC also determines that the information would promote the objective set out in paragraph 3(j) of the *Immigration Act* — to promote international order and justice by denying the use of Canadian territory to persons who are likely to engage in criminal activity; and
- Foreign agencies with mandates similar to FINTRAC's and with which FINTRAC has entered into agreements to exchange information. Under such agreements, FINTRAC may provide designated information when it has reasonable grounds to suspect the information would be relevant to a money laundering or terrorist financing investigation or prosecution.

If FINTRAC determines that there are reasonable grounds to suspect that the information under its control would be relevant to threats to the security of Canada, designated information is disclosed to the Canadian Security Intelligence Service (CSIS). To obtain further information from FINTRAC, CSIS must first get a court order.

## 6.5 Other Responsibilities of FINTRAC

FINTRAC's mandate includes enhancing public awareness and understanding of matters related to money laundering. FINTRAC may issue periodic reports indicating in general terms the usefulness of the aggregate data it receives, without commenting specifically on individual cases or reports.

FINTRAC also has responsibility for ensuring compliance with the compliance regime, reporting, record-keeping and client identification requirements. *Guideline 4: Implementation of a Compliance Regime* contains more information about this.

## 7 COMMENTS?

These guidelines will be reviewed on a periodic basis. If you have any comments or suggestions to help improve them, please send your comments to the mailing address provided below, or by email to guidelines@fintrac.gc.ca.

## 8 HOW TO CONTACT FINTRAC

For further information on FINTRAC and its activities, and the guidelines, please go to FINTRAC's Web site (http://www.fintrac.gc.ca) or contact FINTRAC:
Financial Transactions and Reports Analysis Centre of Canada
234 Laurier Avenue West, 24th floor
Ottawa, Ontario
Canada K1P 1H7
Toll-free: 1-866-346-8722

# GUIDELINE 2: SUSPICIOUS TRANSACTIONS

## March 24, 2003

TABLE OF CONTENTS

**1.   General**

**2.   Suspicious Transaction Reporting**

    2.1   Who Must Report Suspicious Transactions?

    2.2   What are Suspicious Transactions

    2.3   Completed Transactions

    2.4   How to Make a Suspicious Transaction Report

    2.5   Additional Information Related to Reporting to FINTRAC

**3.   Identifying Suspicious Transactions**

    3.1   How to Identify a Suspicious Transaction

    3.2   Indicators Relating to Terrorist Activity Financing

    3.3   Indicators of Suspicious Transactions

**4.   Examples of Common Indicators**

    4.1   General

    4.2   Knowledge of Reporting or Record Keeping Requirements

    4.3   Identity Documents

    4.4   Cash Transactions

    4.5   Economic Purpose

    4.6   Transactions Involving Accounts

    4.7   Transactions Involving Areas Outside Canada

    4.8   Transactions Related to Offshore Business Activity

**5.   Examples of Industry-Specific Indicators**

    5.1   Industry-Specific Indicators

    5.2   Financial Entities

    5.3   Businesses who Send or Receive Electronic Funds Transfers

    5.4   Businesses who Provide Loans

    5.5   Life Insurance Companies, Brokers and Agents

5.6   Securities Dealers

5.7   Foreign Exchange Dealers and Money Services Businesses

5.8   Accountants

5.9   Real Estate Brokers or Sales Representatives

5.10  Casinos

**6.   Comments?**

**7.   How to Contact FINTRAC**

**1   GENERAL**

The *Proceeds of Crime (Money Laundering) and Terrorist Financing Act* requires reporting of suspicious transactions by the following persons and entities and their employees:

- financial entities (such as banks, credit unions, caisses populaires, trust and loan companies and agents of the Crown that accept deposit liabilities);
- life insurance companies, brokers and agents;
- securities dealers, portfolio managers and investment counsellors;
- persons engaged in the business of foreign exchange dealing;
- money services businesses (including alternative remittance systems, such as Hawala, Hundi, Chitti, etc.);
- Canada Post for money orders;
- accountants and accounting firms (when carrying out certain activities on behalf of their clients);
- real estate brokers or sales representatives (when carrying out certain activities on behalf of their clients); and
- casinos (including those authorized to do business in Canada, with a slot machine or roulette or card games, but excluding certain temporary charity casinos).

If you are one of these persons or entities, this guideline can help you meet your obligation to report suspicious transactions to the Financial Transactions and Reports Analysis Centre of Canada (FINTRAC). A suspicious transaction is one for which there are reasonable grounds to suspect that the transaction is related to a money laundering offence or a terrorist activity financing offence.

This guideline, which has been prepared by FINTRAC, contains indicators of suspicious transactions that might be useful in helping you assess whether a transaction is suspicious and should be reported. It is not intended as a substitute for your own assessment, based on your knowledge and experience as well as the specific circumstances of the financial transaction. This guideline uses plain language to explain common reporting situations under the *Proceeds of Crime (Money Laundering) and Terrorist Financing Act* as well as the related Regulations. It is provided as general information only. It is not legal advice and is not intended to replace the Act and Regulations. For more information about money laundering, terrorist activity financing or other reporting requirements under the Act and Regulations, see the guidelines in this series:

- *Guideline 1: Backgrounder* explains money laundering, terrorist financing, and their international nature. It also provides an outline of the legislative requirements as well as an overview of FINTRAC's mandate and responsibilities.
- *Guideline 2: Suspicious Transactions* explains how to report a suspicious transaction. It also provides guidance on how to identify a suspicious transaction, including general and industry-specific indicators that may help when conducting or evaluating transactions.
- *Guideline 3: Submitting Suspicious Transaction Reports to FINTRAC* explains when and how to submit reports.
- *Guideline 4: Implementation of a Compliance Regime* explains the requirement for reporting persons and entities to implement a regime to ensure compliance with their obligations under the *Proceeds of Crime (Money Laundering) and Terrorist Financing Act.*
- *Guideline 5: Submitting Terrorist Property Reports to FINTRAC* explains to reporting persons and entities when and how to submit a terrorist property report.
- *Guideline 6: Record Keeping and Client Identification* explains the requirement for reporting persons and entities to identify their clients and keep records. There are eight different versions of Guideline 6, by sector.
- *Guideline 7: Submitting Large Cash Transaction Reports to FINTRAC* explains when and how to submit large cash transaction reports.
- *Guideline 8: Submitting Electronic Funds Transfer Reports to FINTRAC* explains when and how to submit EFT reports.

If you need more help after you read this or other guidelines, call FINTRAC's national toll-free enquiries line at 1-866-346-8722.

Throughout these guidelines, several references are provided to additional information that may be available on external Web sites. FINTRAC is not responsible for the accuracy or reliability of the information contained on those external Web sites.

## 2 SUSPICIOUS TRANSACTION REPORTING

### 2.1 Who Must Report Suspicious Transactions?

If you are a **reporting person or entity** mentioned above, you must report suspicious transactions to FINTRAC.

If you are a money services business, a Crown agent, an accountant, a real estate broker or sales representative, or a casino, you are only subject to this when you engage in the following activities:

If you are a **money services business,** you are subject to this when you remit or transmit funds by any means through any person, entity or electronic funds transfer network. You are also subject to this when you issue or redeem money orders, traveller's cheques or other similar negotiable instruments, except when you redeem cheques payable to a named person or entity. Money services businesses include alternative money remittance systems, such as Hawala, Hundi, Chitti, etc. Money services businesses also include financial entities when they remit or transmit funds, issue or redeem money orders, traveller's cheques or other similar negotiable instruments for anyone who is not a client of theirs.

If you are an **agent of the Crown** (i.e., a Department or agent of her Majesty in right of Canada or of a province), you are subject to this when you sell or redeem money orders, such as Canada Post for example, or when you accept deposit liabilities in the course of providing financial services to the public.

If you are an **accountant or an accounting firm,** you are subject to this when you receive professional fees to engage in any of the following activities on behalf of any person or entity (other than your employer), or to give instructions in respect of those activities on behalf of any person or entity (other than your employer):

- receiving or paying funds;
- purchasing or selling securities, real property or business assets or entities; or
- transferring funds or securities by any means.

These accountant activities do not include audit, review or compilation work carried out according to the recommendations in the Canadian Institute of Chartered Accountants (CICA) Handbook.

If you are a **real estate broker or sales representative,** you are subject to this when you engage in any of the following activities on behalf of any person or entity in the course of a real estate transaction:

- receiving or paying funds;
- depositing or withdrawing funds; or
- transferring funds by any means.

If you are a **casino** authorized to do business in Canada, you are subject to this if roulette or card games are carried on in your establishment, or if your establishment has a slot machine. In this context, a slot machine does not include a video lottery terminal.

If you are a registered charity, you may be authorized to do business only temporarily as a casino for charitable purposes. If this is your situation, and you carry on business in the casino for two consecutive days or less under the supervision of an employee of the casino, you are not subject to this.

### 2.2 What are Suspicious Transactions?

Suspicious transactions are financial transactions that there are reasonable grounds to suspect are related to the commission of a **money laundering offence.** Since June 12, 2002, suspicious transactions also include financial transactions that there are reasonable grounds to suspect are related to the commission of a **terrorist activity financing offence.**

"Reasonable grounds to suspect" is determined by what is reasonable in your circumstances, including normal business practices and systems within your industry. While the Act and Regulations do not specifically require you to implement or use an automated system for detecting suspicious transactions, you may decide that such a system would be beneficial to your business.

More information about a money laundering offence and terrorist activity financing offences is provided below.

## Money Laundering Offence

Under Canadian law, a money laundering offence involves various acts committed with the intention to conceal or convert property or the proceeds of property (e.g. money) knowing or believing that these were derived from the commission of a designated offence. In this context, a designated offence means most serious offences under the *Criminal Code* or any other federal Act. It includes those relating to illegal drug trafficking, bribery, fraud, forgery, murder, robbery, counterfeit money, stock manipulation, etc. The few exceptions are for offences such as those related to tax evasion or breach of copyright, and some others that involve administrative and monetary penalty structure.

A money laundering offence may also extend to property or proceeds derived from illegal activities that took place outside Canada.

For information about money laundering methods, see *Guideline 1: Backgrounder.*

## Terrorist Activity Financing Offence

Under Canadian law, terrorist activity financing offences make it a crime to knowingly collect or provide property, such as funds, either directly or indirectly, to carry out terrorist crimes. This includes inviting someone else to provide property for this purpose. It also includes the use or possession of property to facilitate or carry out terrorist activities.

There are other offences associated with terrorist activities that are not specifically related to financing, such as participating in or facilitating terrorist activities, or instructing and harbouring terrorists. Only suspicion that a transaction is related to a terrorist activity financing offence triggers a requirement to report the suspicious transaction to FINTRAC as related to terrorist activity financing.

For more information about terrorist financing and other anti-terrorism measures, including other reporting requirements related to terrorist property, see *Guideline 1: Backgrounder.*

## 2.3 Completed Transactions

The requirement for you to report a suspicious transaction applies only when the financial transaction has occurred. For example, if you process a deposit from a client, a financial transaction has occurred, even if the final sale does not go through. In this example, the refund of the deposit would also be a financial transaction. If you decide or the client decides not to complete the transaction, there is no obligation to report it as a suspicious transaction to FINTRAC.

You could choose to report an uncompleted transaction and your suspicion about it to law enforcement. You could also choose to provide this information voluntarily to FINTRAC. To find out how to provide information voluntarily to FINTRAC about suspicions of money laundering or of the financing of terrorist activities, refer to FINTRAC's Web site at http://www.fintrac.gc.ca/reporting--declaration/vol/1_e.asp.

### Transactions Related to Terrorist Property

If you **know,** rather than suspect, that a transaction is related to property owned or controlled by or on behalf of a terrorist or a terrorist group, you should **not** complete the transaction. This is because terrorist property must be frozen under the *United Nations Suppression of Terrorism Regulations* as well as the *Criminal Code.*

This could occur, for example, if your concern about the transaction is because you know that the property in question is owned or controlled by or on behalf of a listed person or listed entity (that is, someone believed to be involved in terrorist activity). For more information about listed persons or entities, freezing of property, and the associated reporting requirement to FINTRAC, read Section 4.2 of *Guideline 1: Backgrounder.*

### 2.4  How to Make a Suspicious Transaction Report

Once you have detected a fact that leads you to have reasonable grounds to suspect that a transaction is related to the commission of a money laundering offence or to the commission of a terrorist activity financing offence, a suspicious transaction report must be sent to FINTRAC within 30 days.

Please refer to *Guideline 3: Submitting Suspicious Transaction Reports to FINTRAC* for more information about reporting timelines and for information on how to make a report.

Making a suspicious transaction report to FINTRAC does not prevent you from reporting suspicions of money laundering or terrorist financing directly to law enforcement. FINTRAC encourages you to maintain established relationships with law enforcement.

### 2.5  Additional Information Related to Reporting to FINTRAC

### Confidentiality

As a reporting person or entity, you are not allowed to inform anyone, including the client, about the contents of a suspicious transaction report or even that you have made such a report, if your intent is to harm or impair a criminal investigation. This applies whether or not such an investigation has begun.

Because it is important not to tip your client off that you are making a suspicious transaction report, you should not be requesting information that you

174

would not normally request during a transaction. The fields that are mandatory in the suspicious transaction report are for information without which you should not be able to complete a transaction. The rest of the fields are for you to provide information if it is available in your records or as a result of the transaction.

Since June 12, 2002, there are new client identification and record keeping requirements. More information about these is available in *Guideline 4: Implementation of a Compliance Regime* or *Guideline 6: Record Keeping and Client Identification.*

## Immunity

No criminal or civil proceedings may be brought against you for making a report in good faith concerning a suspicious transaction. This also applies if you are not required to submit a report to FINTRAC, but decide to provide information voluntarily to FINTRAC because of your suspicions of money laundering or financing of terrorist activity.

## Penalties

There are penalties if you fail to meet the suspicious transaction reporting obligations. Failure to report a suspicious transaction could lead to up to five years imprisonment, a fine of $2,000,000, or both. However, penalties for failure to report do not apply to employees who report suspicious transactions to their superior.

## Closing Accounts

There is no requirement under the *Proceeds of Crime (Money Laundering) and Terrorist Financing Act* to close a client's account when you have reported or are preparing to report a suspicious transaction. This is entirely up to you and your business practices.

## 3    IDENTIFYING SUSPICIOUS TRANSACTIONS

### 3.1  How to Identify a Suspicious Transaction

Transactions may give rise to reasonable grounds to **suspect** that they are related to money laundering or terrorist activity financing regardless of the sum of money involved. There is no monetary threshold for making a report on a suspicious transaction. A suspicious transaction may involve several factors that may on their own seem insignificant, but together may raise suspicion that the transaction is related to the commission of a money laundering offence, a terrorist activity financing offence, or both.

As a general guide, a transaction may be connected to money laundering or terrorist activity financing when you think that it (or a group of transactions) raises questions or gives rise to discomfort, apprehension or mistrust.

The context in which the transaction occurs is a significant factor in assessing suspicion. This will vary from business to business, and from one client to another. As a reporting person or entity, or an employee of a reporting person or entity, you should evaluate transactions in terms of what seems appropriate and is within normal practices in your particular line of business, and based on your knowledge of your client. The fact that transactions do not appear to be in keeping with normal industry practices may be a relevant factor for determining whether there are reasonable grounds to suspect that the transactions are related to money laundering or terrorist activity financing.

An assessment of suspicion should be based on a reasonable evaluation of relevant factors, including the knowledge of the customer's business, financial history, background and behaviour. Remember that **behaviour** is suspicious, not people. Also, it could be the consideration of many factors — not just one factor — that will lead you to a conclusion that there are reasonable grounds to suspect that a transaction is related to the commission of a money laundering offence, a terrorist activity financing offence, or both. All circumstances surrounding a transaction should be reviewed.

As the reporting person or entity with whom the transaction occurs, you have to assess whether there are reasonable grounds to suspect that a transaction is related to a money laundering offence or a terrorist activity financing offence. The following information concerning indicators is provided to help you with this.

### 3.2  Indicators Relating to Terrorist Activity Financing

Indicators to help establish suspicion that a transaction may be related to the commission of a terrorist activity financing offence mostly resemble those relating to money laundering. In fact, the indicators in this guideline are combined for both money laundering and terrorist financing. These are all intended to complement each other and reinforce already existing due diligence practices in dealing with financial transactions.

There are some small differences between money laundering and terrorist financing indicators. For example, amounts relating to terrorist financing generally may be smaller. However, there is no distinction made in the indicators included in Sections 4 and 5 below.

### Lists of persons and entities believed to be associated with terrorists

As part of international efforts to combat terrorism, the Government of Canada has published lists to prevent and suppress the financing of terrorist activities. Property of those whose names are published on any of these anti-terrorism lists are to be frozen. This means that transactions related to that property are prohibited.

A consolidated list for use by anyone in Canada and by Canadians outside Canada is published and maintained by the Office of the Superintendent of Financial Institutions (OSFI). You can find this list on OSFI's Web site: http://www.osfi-bsif.gc.ca/eng/publications/advisories/index_supervisory.asp?#Supter

If you determine that you are in control or possession of property that is owned by or on behalf of anyone on this list, you must report its existence, as well as any transactions or proposed transactions related to the property, to the Royal Canadian Mounted Police and the Canadian Security Intelligence Service. Please refer to *Guideline 1: Backgrounder* for more information about this.

Others outside Canada, such as the United States, the United Nations Security Council, among others, have also published lists. Some or all of the names on these foreign lists may also be added on the Canadian lists, if Canada has reasonable grounds to believe they are associated to terrorist activity.

### How to use lists as indicators of possible terrorist activity financing

If you know that the transaction is related to property owned or controlled by or on behalf of anyone whose name is on the lists, the property should be frozen. This means that any transactions relating to that property are prohibited. Therefore, such a transaction that would trigger suspicion about a terrorist activity financing offence should not be completed.

Because of this, and because the requirement to report a suspicious transaction only exists if a transaction is completed, it is expected that the number of transactions that could give rise to a suspicious transaction report related to terrorist activity financing will be limited. For more information about proposed transactions related to terrorist property, read Section 4.2 of *Guideline 1: Backgrounder*.

### Distinguishing between money laundering and terrorist activity financing suspicion

It may be difficult for you to distinguish between suspicion of money laundering and suspicion of terrorist activity financing. In fact, it is possible that a transaction could be related to both. For example, funds to be used for terrorist activity could be proceeds of criminal activity as well as from legitimate sources.

It is the information about the transaction and about what led to your suspicion that is important in a suspicious transaction report. Provide as many details as possible in your report about what led to your suspicion, including anything that made you suspect that it might be related to terrorist financing, money laundering, or both. If you cannot make the distinction based on the information available, remember that it is the information about your suspicion that is important, not the distinction between money laundering and terrorist activity offences.

### 3.3 Indicators of Suspicious Transactions

The indicators that follow are provided to help assess whether or not transactions might give rise to reasonable grounds for suspicion. They are examples of common and industry-specific indicators that may be helpful when evaluating transactions. They include indicators based on certain characteristics that have been linked to money laundering or terrorist activities in the past.

These indicators were compiled in consultation with reporting entities, law enforcement agencies and international financial intelligence organizations. They are not intended to cover every possible situation and are not to be viewed in isolation. A single indicator is not necessarily indicative of reasonable grounds to suspect money laundering or terrorist financing activity. However, if a number of indicators are present during a transaction or series of transactions, then you might want to take a closer look at other factors prior to making the determination as to whether the transaction must be reported.

The indicators have to be assessed in the context in which the transaction occurs. Each indicator may contribute to a conclusion that there are reasonable grounds to suspect that the transaction is related to the commission of a money laundering offence or a terrorist activity financing offence. However, it may also offer no indication of this in view of factors such as the client's occupation, business, financial history and past investment pattern. Taken together, the presence of one or more indicators as well as your knowledge of your client's business or financial affairs may help you identify suspicious transactions.

Some of the indicators provided could result in the transaction being aborted if the client requests a service that is prohibited by your business or by the anti-terrorism measures explained in Section 4.2 of *Guideline 1: Backgrounder*. Your policies, standards and procedures may already reflect these as inappropriate or questionable. As explained earlier, if a transaction is not completed, there is no requirement for you to make a suspicious transaction report to FINTRAC. However, the indicators detected during an aborted transaction should be considered, where possible, in subsequent dealings with the client if additional suspicious activity occurs.

In the case of a transaction aborted because you believe the property is owned or controlled by or on behalf of a terrorist or a terrorist group, this must be reported as explained in Section 3.2 above.

## 4 EXAMPLES OF COMMON INDICATORS

The following are examples of common indicators that may point to a suspicious transaction. Please read Section 3 (above) for general information about identifying suspicious transactions and how to use these indicators.

### 4.1 General

- Client admits or makes statements about involvement in criminal activities.
- Client does not want correspondence sent to home address.
- Client appears to have accounts with several financial institutions in one area for no apparent reason.
- Client repeatedly uses an address but frequently changes the names involved.
- Client is accompanied and watched.
- Client shows uncommon curiosity about internal systems, controls and policies.
- Client has only vague knowledge of the amount of a deposit.
- Client presents confusing details about the transaction.
- Client over justifies or explains the transaction.
- Client is secretive and reluctant to meet in person.
- Client is nervous, not in keeping with the transaction.

- Client is involved in transactions that are suspicious but seems blind to being involved in money laundering activities.
- Client's home or business telephone number has been disconnected or there is no such number when an attempt is made to contact client shortly after opening account.
- Client is involved in activity out-of-keeping for that individual or business.
- Client insists that a transaction be done quickly.
- Inconsistencies appear in the client's presentation of the transaction.
- Client appears to have recently established a series of new relationships with different financial entities.
- Client attempts to develop close rapport with staff.
- Client uses aliases and a variety of similar but different addresses.
- Client uses a post office box or General Delivery address, or other type of mail drop address, instead of a street address when this is not the norm for that area.
- Client offers you money, gratuities or unusual favours for the provision of services that may appear unusual or suspicious.
- You are aware that a client is the subject of a money laundering or terrorist financing investigation.

## 4.2 Knowledge of Reporting or Record Keeping Requirements

- Client attempts to convince employee not to complete any documentation required for the transaction.
- Client makes inquiries that would indicate a desire to avoid reporting.
- Client has unusual knowledge of the law in relation to suspicious transaction reporting.
- Client seems very conversant with money laundering or terrorist activity financing issues.
- Client is quick to volunteer that funds are "clean" or "not being laundered."

## 4.3 Identity Documents

- Client provides doubtful or vague information.
- Client produces seemingly false identification or identification that appears to be counterfeited, altered or inaccurate.
- Client refuses to produce personal identification documents.
- Client only submits copies of personal identification documents.
- Client wants to establish identity using something other than his or her personal identification documents.
- Client's supporting documentation lacks important details such as a phone number.
- Client inordinately delays presenting corporate documents.
- All identification presented is foreign or cannot be checked for some reason.
- All identification documents presented appear new or have recent issue dates.

179

## 4.4 Cash Transactions

- Client starts conducting frequent cash transactions in large amounts when this has not been a normal activity for the client in the past.
- Client frequently exchanges small bills for large ones.
- Client uses notes in denominations that are unusual for the client, when the norm in that business is much smaller or much larger denominations.
- Client presents notes that are packed or wrapped in a way that is uncommon for the client.
- Client deposits musty or extremely dirty bills.
- Client makes cash transactions of consistently rounded-off large amounts (e.g., $9,900, $8,500, etc.).
- Client consistently makes cash transactions that are just under the reporting threshold amount in an apparent attempt to avoid the reporting threshold.
- Client consistently makes cash transactions that are significantly below the reporting threshold amount in an apparent attempt to avoid triggering the identification and reporting requirements.
- Client presents uncounted funds for a transaction. Upon counting, the transaction is reduced to an amount just below that which could trigger reporting requirements.
- Client conducts a transaction for an amount that is unusual compared to amounts of past transactions.
- Client frequently purchases traveller's cheques, foreign currency drafts or other negotiable instruments with cash when this appears to be outside of normal activity for the client.
- Client asks you to hold or transmit large sums of money or other assets when this type of activity is unusual for the client.
- Shared address for individuals involved in cash transactions, particularly when the address is also for a business location, or does not seem to correspond to the stated occupation (for example, student, unemployed, self-employed, etc.).
- Stated occupation of the client is not in keeping with the level or type of activity (for example a student or an unemployed individual makes daily maximum cash withdrawals at multiple locations over a wide geographic area).

## 4.5 Economic Purpose

- Transaction seems to be inconsistent with the client's apparent financial standing or usual pattern of activities.
- Transaction appears to be out of the ordinary course for industry practice or does not appear to be economically viable for the client.
- Transaction is unnecessarily complex for its stated purpose.
- Activity is inconsistent with what would be expected from declared business.
- Transaction involves non-profit or charitable organization for which there appears to be no logical economic purpose or where there appears to be no

link between the stated activity of the organization and the other parties in the transaction.

## 4.6 Transactions Involving Accounts

- Opening accounts when the client's address is outside the local service area.
- Opening accounts in other people's names.
- Opening accounts with names very close to other established business entities.
- Attempting to open or operating accounts under a false name.
- Account with a large number of small cash deposits and a small number of large cash withdrawals.
- Funds are being deposited into several accounts, consolidated into one and transferred outside the country.
- Client frequently uses many deposit locations outside of the home branch location.
- Multiple transactions are carried out on the same day at the same branch but with an apparent attempt to use different tellers.
- Activity far exceeds activity projected at the time of opening of the account.
- Establishment of multiple accounts, some of which appear to remain dormant for extended periods.
- Account that was reactivated from inactive or dormant status suddenly sees significant activity.
- Reactivated dormant account containing a minimal sum suddenly receives a deposit or series of deposits followed by frequent cash withdrawals until the transferred sum has been removed.
- Unexplained transfers between the client's products and accounts.
- Multiple deposits are made to a client's account by third parties.
- Deposits or withdrawals of multiple monetary instruments, particularly if the instruments are sequentially numbered.
- Multiple personal and business accounts are used to collect and then funnel funds to a small number of foreign beneficiaries, particularly when they are in locations of concern, such as countries known or suspected to facilitate money laundering activities.

More information on which countries these characteristics may apply to can be found at the following Web sites:

http://www1.oecd.org/fatf/NCCT_en.htm (information from the Financial Action Task Force about non-cooperative countries and territories in the fight against money laundering and terrorist financing)

http://www.state.gov/www/global/narcotics_law/1999_narc_report/index.html (International Narcotics Control Strategy Report released by the Bureau for International Narcotics and Law Enforcement Affairs, U.S. Department of State, March 2000)

http://www.fintrac.gc.ca/publications/avs/2002-12-20_e.asp

## 4.7  Transactions Involving Areas Outside Canada

- Client and other parties to the transaction have no apparent ties to Canada.
- Transaction crosses many international lines.
- Use of a credit card issued by a foreign bank that does not operate in Canada by a client that does not live and work in the country of issue.
- Transactions involving countries deemed by the Financial Action Task Force as requiring enhanced surveillance, including the Republic of Nauru.
- Foreign currency exchanges that are associated with subsequent wire transfers to locations of concern, such as countries known or suspected to facilitate money laundering activities.
- Deposits followed within a short time by wire transfer of funds to or through locations of concern, such as countries known or suspected to facilitate money laundering activities.
- Transaction involves a country known for highly secretive banking and corporate law.
- Transaction involves a country where illicit drug production or exporting may be prevalent, or where there is no effective anti-money laundering system.
- Transaction involves a country known or suspected to facilitate money laundering activities.

More information on which countries these characteristics (i.e. those mentioned in the last two bullets) may apply to can be found at the following Web sites:

> http://www1.oecd.org/fatf/NCCT_en.htm (information from the Financial Action Task Force about non-cooperative countries and territories in the fight against money laundering and terrorist financing)
> http://www.state.gov/www/global/narcotics_law/1999_narc_report/index.html (International Narcotics Control Strategy Report released by the Bureau for International Narcotics and Law Enforcement Affairs, U.S. Department of State, March 2000)
> http://www.fintrac.gc.ca/publications/avs/2002-12-20_e.asp

## 4.8  Transactions Related to Offshore Business Activity

Any person or entity that conducts transactions internationally should consider the following indicators.

- Accumulation of large balances, inconsistent with the known turnover of the client's business, and subsequent transfers to overseas account(s).
- Frequent requests for traveller's cheques, foreign currency drafts or other negotiable instruments.
- Loans secured by obligations from offshore banks.
- Loans to or from offshore companies.
- Offers of multimillion-dollar deposits from a confidential source to be sent from an offshore bank or somehow guaranteed by an offshore bank.

- Transactions involving an offshore "shell" bank whose name may be very similar to the name of a major legitimate institution.
- Unexplained electronic funds transfers by client on an in-and-out basis.
- Use of letter-of-credit and other method of trade financing to move money between countries when such trade is inconsistent with the client's business.
- Use of a credit card issued by an offshore bank.

## 5 EXAMPLES OF INDUSTRY-SPECIFIC INDICATORS

### 5.1 Industry-Specific Indicators

In addition to the general indicators outlined above, the following industry-specific indicators may point to a suspicious transaction. Remember that **behaviour** is suspicious, not people. Also, it is the consideration of many factors — not any one factor — that will lead to a conclusion that there are reasonable grounds to suspect that a transaction is related to the commission of a money laundering or terrorist activity financing offence. All circumstances surrounding a transaction should be reviewed, within the context of your knowledge of your client.

Taken together, the general and industry-specific indicators that apply to your business may help you identify suspicious transactions. Depending on the services you provide, you may need information about indicators in more than one of the following sections. For example, if you are a financial advisor, you might sell life insurance products and securities. In this case, you would read the indicators in Section 5.5 (Life Insurance Companies, Brokers and Agents), as well as under Section 5.6 (Securities Dealers).

### 5.2 Financial Entities

### 5.3 Businesses who Send or Receive Electronic Funds Transfers

### 5.4 Businesses who Provide Loans

### 5.5 Life Insurance Companies, Brokers and Agents

### 5.6 Securities Dealers

### 5.7 Foreign Exchange Dealers and Money Services Businesses

### 5.8 Accountants

### 5.9 Real Estate Brokers or Sales Representatives

### 5.10 Casinos

## 6 Comments?

These guidelines will be reviewed on a periodic basis. If you have any comments or suggestions to help improve them, please send your comments to the mailing address provided below, or by email to guidelines@fintrac.gc.ca

## 7    How to Contact FINTRAC

For further information on FINTRAC and its activities, or about reporting suspicious transactions, please go to FINTRAC's Web site (http://www.fintrac.gc.ca) or contact FINTRAC:

Financial Transactions and Reports Analysis Centre of Canada
234 Laurier Avenue West, 24th floor
Ottawa, Ontario
Canada K1P 1H7
Toll-free: 1-866-346-8722

# GUIDELINE 3A: SUBMITTING SUSPICIOUS TRANSACTION REPORTS TO FINTRAC ELECTRONICALLY

## May 5, 2003

TABLE OF CONTENTS

1.  **General**

2.  **Suspicious Transaction Reporting Requirements**

    2.1  Suspicious Transaction Reporting Timelines

    2.2  Means of Reporting

    2.3  Information to be Contained in a Suspicious Transaction Report

3.  **Electronic Reporting**

    3.1  Options for Electronic Reporting

    3.2  How to Complete Electronic Reports

    3.3  Acknowledgement of Receipt of an Electronic Report

    3.4  Report Corrections

4.  **Instructions for Completing a Suspicious Transaction Report**

    4.1  General Instructions for Completing a Suspicious Transaction Report

    4.2  Instructions for Reporting Screens on FINTRAC's Web site

    4.3  Instructions for Submitting a New Report

    4.4  Instructions for Submitting a Change to a Previously Submitted Report

5.  **Comments?**

6.  **How to Contact FINTRAC**

Appendix 1 — Currency Codes

. . .

## 2   SUSPICIOUS TRANSACTION REPORTING REQUIREMENTS

### 2.1 Suspicious Transaction Reporting Timelines

If you are a reporting person or entity (see Section 1 above), you have to send a suspicious transaction report to FINTRAC when there are reasonable grounds to suspect that a transaction is related to the commission of a money laundering offence or a terrorist financing offence.

There is no minimum threshold amount for reporting a suspicious transaction. *Guideline 2: Suspicious Transactions* has more information on how to identify a suspicious transaction.

You have to submit suspicious transaction reports to FINTRAC, containing specific information (see Section 4 below). Once you have determined that there are reasonable grounds to suspect that the transaction is related to the commission of a money laundering or terrorist financing offence, your report, including all required and applicable information, must be sent within 30 calendar days.

This 30-day reporting time limit begins when you or any one of your employees first detects a fact about a transaction that constitutes reasonable grounds to suspect that it is related to the commission of a money laundering or terrorist financing offence. If such a fact is detected at the time of the transaction, the reporting timeline begins at the time of the transaction. However, if the fact is not detected at the time of the transaction, the 30-day time limit could begin at some time after. For example, if the fact were detected during a review by corporate security after the transaction took place, the 30-day time limit would begin when corporate security first detected the fact.

## Other Reports

Information about other reporting requirements under the *Proceeds of Crime (Money Laundering) and Terrorist Financing Act* that apply to reporting persons or entities can be found in the following guidelines:

*   *Guideline 5: Submitting Terrorist Property Reports to FINTRAC*
*   *Guideline 7: Submitting Large Cash Transaction Reports to FINTRAC*
*   *Guideline 8: Submitting Electronic Funds Transfer Reports to FINTRAC*

### 2.2 Means of Reporting

### Electronic Reporting

As a reporting person or entity, you have to submit all reports on suspicious transactions to FINTRAC **electronically** if you have the technical capabilities to do so. The minimum technical capabilities are as follows:

*   A personal computer with the following characteristics:
    *   32 MB memory
    *   640 x 480 VGA video display (800 x 600 or higher is preferable)
    *   any operating system running the following Web browsers: Internet Explorer version 5.x (Windows® 98/Me/NT/2000); and
    *   An Internet connection

The same electronic reporting requirements apply to reporting of large cash transactions and electronic funds transfers.

See Section 3 (below) for more information on submitting reports to FINTRAC electronically.

## Paper Reporting

If you do not have the technical capabilities to send reports electronically, you must submit reports on paper. See *Guideline 3B: Submitting Suspicious Transaction Reports to FINTRAC by Paper* for more information on submitting paper suspicious transaction reports to FINTRAC.

### 2.3 Information to be Contained in a Suspicious Transaction Report

Your suspicion about there being a relation to a money laundering or a terrorist financing offence may be as a result of more than one transaction. In this case, include all the transactions that contributed to your suspicion in the same report. See Section 4 (below) for more information about what has to be included in a suspicious transaction report.

## 3   ELECTRONIC REPORTING

### 3.1 Options for Electronic Reporting

As a reporting person or entity, you have to report electronically to FINTRAC if you have the technical capabilities (see Section 2.2 above).

There are three options for electronic reporting:

• FINTRAC's secure Web site for low volume and low frequency reporting
• FINTRAC's secure Web site with public key infrastructure (PKI) for low volume but high frequency reporting
• Batch file transfer for high volume and high frequency reporting.

For low volume reporting, FINTRAC is developing a stand-alone software application for you to capture, store, maintain and submit your electronic reports. More information about FINTRAC's Report Preparation Software is available from the Reporting section of FINTRAC's Web site (http://www.fintrac.gc.ca/reporting--declaration/1_e.asp), by selecting suspicious transaction report type and a reporting frequency of less than five reports per week.

In general, Web site reporting will likely be more appropriate for reporting persons and entities with low reporting volume and frequency. If you send on average less than one report per week to FINTRAC, you will not need to do anything before you start to report. Simply complete and send your reports from the reporting area of FINTRAC's Web site (http://www.fintrac.gc.ca/reporting--declaration/1_e.asp) (see Section 3.2 below).

If you send on average at least one report per week to FINTRAC over a 12-week period, you may apply for a public key infrastructure (PKI) certificate. Along with the PKI certificate you will require specialized software available from FINTRAC. For more information about PKI, see the reporting area of FINTRAC's Web site (http://www.fintrac.gc.ca/reporting--declaration/1_e.asp).

Batch file transfers will likely be more efficient for larger reporting entities with high reporting volume and frequency. If you send on average at least five reports per week to FINTRAC over a 12-week period, you can use the batch file reporting mechanism. To do so, you will require a PKI certificate and specialized software available from FINTRAC. Consult the following specifications documents for more information about batch reporting, available from the publications area of FINTRAC's Web site (see technical documentation at http://www.fintrac.gc.ca/publications/pub_e.asp):

- *Standard Batch Reporting Instructions and Specification*
- *SWIFT format EFT Transactions – Batch Reporting Instructions and Specification*

All these options provide for secure encrypted transmission to ensure data confidentiality and integrity. Reporting via batch, or through FINTRAC's secure Web site using PKI will require more advanced technical capability than explained in Section 2.2 (above).

### 3.2  How to Complete Electronic Reports

**Reporting via the Web**

FINTRAC's Web site contains forms for required reports. Senders will be able to select the appropriate one for the circumstances.

The suspicious transaction reporting screens contain completion instructions. Drop-down menus appear wherever a code or specific selection is required. In addition, details concerning formatting of a particular field may appear at the bottom of your screen.

See Section 4 (below) for additional completion instructions. It also includes details of what each field must contain for a suspicious transaction report.

**Reporting via Batch File Transfer**

As explained in Section 3.1(above), additional instructions are provided in separate publications if you want to send reports to FINTRAC via batch file transfer.

### 3.3  Acknowledgement of Receipt of an Electronic Report

FINTRAC will send you an acknowledgement message when your suspicious transaction report has been received electronically. This will include the date and time your report was received and a FINTRAC-generated identification number. Please keep this information for your records. For all reports submitted via the FINTRAC secure web site, please ensure you wait for the FINTRAC acknowledgement message, which can be printed from the browser window.

## 3.4 Report Corrections

If your suspicious transaction report contains incomplete information, FINTRAC may notify you. The notification will indicate the date and time your report was received, a FINTRAC-generated identification number, along with information on the fields that must be completed or corrected.

After receiving FINTRAC's notification, you should provide the necessary information to FINTRAC within the 30-calendar-day reporting deadline. In other words, this information should be sent to FINTRAC within 30 calendar days of the time the suspicion was first detected. Your obligation to report will not be fulfilled until you send the **complete** report to FINTRAC.

## 4   INSTRUCTIONS FOR COMPLETING A SUSPICIOUS TRANSACTION REPORT

### 4.1  General Instructions for Completing a Suspicious Transaction Report

The fields in this section refer to the numbered areas on the *Suspicious Transaction Report* screens. As explained in Section 2.2 (above), if you do not have the capability to report electronically, refer to *Guideline 3B: Submitting Suspicious Transactions to FINTRAC by Paper* for more information.

To make a suspicious transaction report, select this report from the drop-down menu of reports available from the reporting area of FINTRAC's Web site (http://www.fintrac.gc.ca/reporting--declaration/1_e.asp). Indicate your reporting frequency and click on "Proceed with the report". You will then be presented with the reporting mechanisms available to you.

The instructions that follow in Sections 4.2, 4.3 and 4.4 are based on the reporting screens through FINTRAC's secure Web site. However, the information about how to complete the fields can also be useful to those completing suspicious transactions through any electronic mechanism.

### 4.2  Instructions for Reporting Screens on FINTRAC's Web site

Before you get to the reporting screens, you will be asked if you are submitting a new report, or if this is a change to a previously submitted report. Section 4.3 (below) contains instructions for submitting a new report. Section 4.4 contains instructions for submitting a change to a previously submitted report.

You are also able to send a simulated report (for training purposes) by selecting the "Simulation" option.

### 4.3  Instructions for Submitting a New Report

There are eight parts on the *Suspicious Transaction Report* form, but some are only to be completed if applicable.

All fields of the report marked with an asterisk (*) **have to be completed.** Some fields have both an asterisk and "where applicable" next to them. These have to be completed if they are applicable to you or the transaction being reported. For all other fields, you have to make reasonable efforts to get the information. "Reasonable efforts" means that you tried to get the information requested on the report. If the information is available to you, you must provide it in the report. If the information was not available at the time of the transaction, and it is not contained in your files or records, the field may be left blank.

To report a suspicious transaction, follow the following five steps:

- Step 1 — Complete Part A to provide information about you as the reporting entity. Click on "next" at the bottom of Part A (under field 11) to go on to Step 2.

Throughout the report, if you have not completed any mandatory fields in any part, you will get a message to let you know which fields are missing. Click on "cancel" to go back and complete them. For fields that are mandatory where applicable, click on "cancel" to go back and complete them if those fields are applicable to you. If they are not applicable, click on "OK" to continue.

- Step 2 — Complete Part B1 to provide details about the transaction. If you have to include more than one transaction in this report, go through Steps 2, 3 and 4 for the first transaction, and then click on "next transaction" at the end of Step 4. Click on "next" at the bottom of Part B1 (under field 11) to go on to Step 3.
- Step 3 —Provide details about the transaction's disposition. To do this, complete Part B2. Depending on the disposition, you might also have to complete Part E or F, and Part C.

If the transaction's disposition was on behalf of the person who conducted the transaction, follow the instructions in Step 3A below. If the transaction's disposition was on behalf of anyone other than the person who conducted the transaction, follow the instructions in Step 3B below.

- Step 3A

    If the disposition was on behalf of the **person who conducted the transaction** (i.e., not on behalf of a business, other entity or another individual), click on "not applicable" at the top of Part B2. When you click on "next" at the bottom of Part B2 after completing the appropriate fields, you will go to Part C in case the disposition was related to an account.

    If the disposition was not related to an account, click on "next" at the bottom of Part C to go to Step 4. If the disposition was related to an account, Part C is applicable. Complete Part C before going on to Step 4.

    If you need to include more than one disposition for this transaction, click on "next disposition" instead of "next" at the end of Part C.

- Step 3B

    If the disposition was on behalf of someone **other than** the person who conducted the transaction, click on "business, corporation or other entity" or "another person" to indicate on whose behalf it was done. You will have to complete Part E (on behalf of a business, corporation or other entity) or Part F (on behalf of an individual).

Before you get to Part E or F, when you click on "next" at the bottom of Part B2, you will go to Part C in case the disposition was related to an account. If the disposition was related to an account, Part C is applicable. Complete Part C to provide details about the account before clicking on "next" to continue on to Part E or F. If the disposition was not related to an account, click on "next " under field 8 of Part C to get Part E or F, as required.

There are two screens to be completed for Part E, and three screens for Part F. Once you have completed each screen as required, click on "next". At the end of Part E or F, this will bring you to Step 4. If you need to include more than one disposition for this transaction, click on "next disposition" instead of "next" at the end of Part E or F.

- Step 4 — Complete Part D to provide information about the individual conducting the transaction.

There are three screens to be completed for Part D. Once you have completed each screen as required, click on "next". At the end of the third screen for Part D, clicking on "next" will bring you to Step 5. If you need to include more than one transaction in this report, click on "next transaction" instead of "next" at the end of Part D, and go through Steps 2, 3 and 4 for each transaction.

If you have to include more than one transaction in this report and information in Part D is the same from one transaction to another, you can indicate "same as previous" at the top of the first screen of Part D for the second or subsequent transactions to repeat the information from the previous transaction's Part D.

- Step 5 — Complete Part G to explain the reason for your suspicion. When you are finished with Part G, click on "next" at the bottom to get to Part H. Complete Part H to provide information about any action taken, if applicable.

Once you have gone through these five steps and all the required fields in each part are completed, you can click on "Continue" to send your report to FINTRAC. If there are any mandatory fields missing, you will get a message telling you which ones so that you can correct the report.

Before you finally submit it, you will be given the option to print the report.

When your report is received, FINTRAC will send you an acknowledgment message. This will include the date and time your report was received and a FINTRAC-generated identification number. Please keep this information for your records.

The rest of this section will cover each part of the *Suspicious Transaction Report* reporting screens.

**PART A: INFORMATION ABOUT WHERE THE TRANSACTION TOOK PLACE**

**Field 2\* Reporting person or entity's full name**

**Fields 3\* to 6\* Reporting person or entity's full address**

**Fields 7\*, 8\* and 9 Contact name**

**Field 10\* Contact telephone number**

**Field 11\* Which one of the following types of reporting entities best describes you?**

PART B1: INFORMATION ABOUT TRANSACTION(S)

**Fields 1\* to 3\* When the transaction took place**

**Field 4 Date of posting**

**Field 5\* Type of funds**

**Field 6\* Amount of transaction**

**Field 7\* Currency**

**Fields 8\* and 9\* Other institution, entity or person name, number and account number (where applicable)**

**Field 10\* How was the transaction conducted?**

**Field 11 ID number of the person initially identifying a suspicious transaction**

PART B2: INFORMATION ABOUT DISPOSITION(S)

**Field 12\*Disposition of funds**

**Field 13\* Amount of disposition**

**Field 14\* Currency**

**Fields 15\* and 16\* Other institution, entity or person name, number and account number (where applicable)**

PART C: ACCOUNT INFORMATION, IF THE TRANSACTION INVOLVED AN ACCOUNT

**Field 1\* Branch or transit number (if this Part is applicable)**

**Field 2\* Account number (if this Part is applicable)**

**Field 3\* Type of account (if this Part is applicable)**

**Field 4\* Type of Currency (if this Part is applicable)**

**Field 5\* Full name of each account holder (if this Part is applicable)**

**Field 6 Date opened**

**Field 7 Date closed**

**Field 8\* Status of the account at the time the transaction was initiated (if this Part is applicable)**

PART D: INFORMATION ABOUT INDIVIDUAL CONDUCTING TRANSACTION(S)

**Fields 1 to 3 Individual's full name**

**Field 4\* Entity client number (where applicable)**

**Fields 5 to 9 Individual's full address**

**Field 10 Country of residence**

**Field 10a Citizenship**

**Field 11 Home telephone number**

**Field 12 Individual's identifier**

**Field 13 ID Number**

**Fields 14 and 15 Place of issue**

**Field 16 Date of birth**

**Field 17 Individual's occupation**

**Field 18 Individual's business telephone number**

**Field 19 Individual's employer**

**Fields 20 to 24 Employer's business address**

**Field 25 Employer's business telephone number**

PART E: INFORMATION ABOUT THE ENTITY ON WHOSE BEHALF TRANSACTION WAS CONDUCTED (WHERE APPLICABLE)

**Field 1 Business, corporation or other entity name**

**Field 2 Type of business**

**Fields 3 to 7 Full address of business, corporation or other entity**

**Field 8 Business telephone number**

**Fields 9 to 11 Incorporation information**

**Field 12 Individual(s) authorized with respect to the account (up to three)**

PART F: INFORMATION ON PERSON ON WHOSE BEHALF TRANSACTION IS CONDUCTED (WHERE APPLICABLE)

**Fields 1 to 3 Individual's full name**

**Fields 4 to 8 Individual's full address**

**Field 9 Home phone number**

**Field 10 Office phone number**

**Field 11 Date of birth**

**Field 12 Individual's identifier**

**Field 13 ID number**

**Field 14 Country of residence**

**Field 14a Citizenship**

**Fields 15 and 16 Place of issue**

**Field 17 Individual's occupation**

**Field 18 Individual's employer**

**Fields 19 to 23 Employer's business address**

**Field 24 Employer's business phone number**

**Field 25 Relationship of the individual named in Part D to the individual named above**

PART G: DESCRIPTION OF SUSPICIOUS ACTIVITY

**Field 1\* Description of suspicious activity**

PART H: ACTION TAKEN (WHERE APPLICABLE)

**Field 1\* Action taken (if this Part is applicable)**

**4.4 INSTRUCTIONS FOR SUBMITTING A CHANGE TO A PREVIOUSLY SUBMITTED REPORT**

If you have to submit a change to a previously submitted report, there are two options: update or replace.

**Update**

This is to either modify or delete information on a report that you submitted previously.

Once you have selected the update option, you need to provide the date, time and FINTRAC-generated identification number for the previously submitted report, based on the acknowledgement you received from FINTRAC. Then, complete only the fields of the report that you need to correct.

If your correction involves removing information that was contained in a field, and you want that field to be left blank, you will have to put dashes in that field. If the field is under five characters, put dashes in each character space. If the field is over five characters, just enter 5 dashes.

If you need to add information to a field that was previously left blank or you need to change the information previously submitted, you have to provide the revised information in the applicable field. If you need to modify the text information previously submitted in Part G or H, make sure you enter all of the information you want the field to contain. This would include any of the information previously submitted that is not being revised.

If you want to notify FINTRAC that the entire report should not have been submitted, explain this, and the reason why it should not have been submitted, in Part G.

If you omitted to include a transaction or a disposition in a previous report, follow the replace instructions below.

## Replace

This is to identify an existing report that you want to replace with a new report.

Once you have selected the replace option, enter the report number, date and time of the report you want to replace, based on the acknowledgement you received from FINTRAC. Submit this information. You will then receive a new report with the same number as the original.

Next, you will have to re-enter all of the information from the original report and include any information that you want to add. In addition to explaining the reason for your suspicion in Part G, include an explanation of why you want to replace the original report.

## 5   COMMENTS?

These guidelines will be reviewed on a periodic basis. If you have any comments or suggestions to help improve them, please send your comments to the mailing address provided below, or by email to guidelines@fintrac.gc.ca.

## 6   HOW TO CONTACT FINTRAC

For further information on FINTRAC and its activities, and report submission, please go to FINTRAC's Web site (http://www.fintrac.gc.ca) or contact FINTRAC:

> Financial Transactions and Reports Analysis Centre of Canada
> 234 Laurier Avenue West, 24th floor
> Ottawa, Ontario
> Canada K1P 1H7
> Toll-free: 1-866-346-8722

# GUIDELINE 3B: SUBMITTING SUSPICIOUS TRANSACTION REPORTS TO FINTRAC BY PAPER

## May 5, 2003

TABLE OF CONTENTS

1. **General**

2. **Suspicious Transaction Reporting Requirements**

    2.1   Suspicious Transaction Reporting Timelines

    2.2   Means of Reporting

    2.3   Information to be Contained in a Suspicious Transaction Report

3. **Paper Reporting**

    3.1   How to Complete Paper Reports

    3.2   How to Send Paper Reports to FINTRAC

    3.3   Acknowledgement of Receipt of a Paper Report

4. **Instructions for Completing a Suspicious Transaction Report**

5. **Comments?**

6. **How to Contact FINTRAC**

**Appendix 1 — Currency Codes**

. . .

## 2 SUSPICIOUS TRANSACTION REPORTING REQUIREMENTS

### 2.1 Suspicious Transaction Reporting Timelines

If you are a reporting person or entity (see Section 1 above), you have to send a suspicious transaction report to FINTRAC when there are reasonable grounds to suspect that a transaction is related to the commission of a money laundering offence or a terrorist financing offence.

There is no minimum threshold amount for reporting a suspicious transaction. *Guideline 2: Suspicious Transactions* has more information on how to identify a suspicious transaction.

You have to submit suspicious transaction reports to FINTRAC, containing specific information (see Section 4 below). Once you have determined that there are reasonable grounds to suspect that the transaction is related to the commission of a money laundering or terrorist financing offence, your report, including all required and applicable information, must be sent within 30 calendar days.

This 30-day reporting time limit begins when you or any one of your employees first detects a fact about a transaction that constitutes reasonable grounds to suspect that it is related to the commission of a money laundering or terrorist financing offence. If such a fact is detected at the time of the transaction, the reporting timeline begins at the time of the transaction. However, if the fact is not detected at the time of the transaction, the 30-day time limit could begin at some time after. For example, if the fact were detected during a review by corporate security after the transaction took place, the 30-day time limit would begin when corporate security first detected the fact.

## Other Reports and Requirements

Information about other reporting requirements under the *Proceeds of Crime (Money Laundering) and Terrorist Financing Act* that apply to reporting persons or entities can be found in the following guidelines:

- *Guideline 5: Submitting Terrorist Property Reports to FINTRAC*
- *Guideline 7: Submitting Large Cash Transaction Reports to FINTRAC*
- *Guideline 8: Submitting Electronic Funds Transfer Reports to FINTRAC*

### 2.2 Means of Reporting

### Electronic Reporting

As a reporting person or entity, you have to submit all reports on suspicious transactions to FINTRAC **electronically** if you have the technical capabilities to do so. The minimum technical capabilities are as follows:
- A personal computer with the following characteristics:
  - 32 MB memory
  - 640 x 480 VGA video display (800 x 600 or higher is preferable)
  - any operating system running the following Web browsers: Internet Explorer version 5.x (Windows® 98/Me/NT/2000); and
  - An Internet connection

The same electronic reporting requirements apply to reporting of large cash transactions and electronic funds transfers.

See *Guideline 3 A: Submitting Suspicious Transaction Reports to FINTRAC Electronically* for more information on submitting reports to FINTRAC electronically.

### Paper Reporting

If you do not have the technical capabilities to send reports electronically, you must submit reports on paper. See Section 3 (below) for more information on submitting suspicious transaction reports to FINTRAC by paper.

## 2.3 Information to be Contained in a Suspicious Transaction Report

Your suspicion about there being a relation to a money laundering or a terrorist financing offence may be as a result of more than one transaction. In this case, include all the transactions that contributed to your suspicion in the same report. See Section 4 (below) for more information about what has to be included in a suspicious transaction report.

## 3 PAPER REPORTING

### 3.1 How to Complete Paper Reports

If you do **not** have the technical capability (see Section 2.2 above), you have to submit paper reports to FINTRAC. In this case, forms are available for paper filing as follows:

- A file can be accessed and printed from the Publications section of FINTRAC's Web site (choose "reporting forms" from http://www.fintrac.gc.ca/publications/pub_e.asp). If you do not have a computer or access to the Internet, you may be able to do this at your local library or any other public place with Internet access.
- Call 1-866-346-8722 for a copy to be faxed or mailed to you.

To ensure that the information provided is legible and to facilitate data entry, it would be preferable if the free-text areas of the paper reports (e.g., Part G) were completed using word-processing equipment or a typewriter. For reports completed by hand, the use of black ink and CAPITAL LETTERS is recommended.

See Section 4 (below) for completion instructions. It includes details of what each field must contain for a suspicious transaction report, and indicates which parts of the form you may need to make copies of before you complete your report.

### 3.2 How to Send Paper Reports to FINTRAC

There are two ways to send a paper report to FINTRAC:

- Fax: 1-866-226-2346; or

- Mail to the following address:
  Financial Transactions and Reports Analysis Centre of Canada
  Section A
  234 Laurier Avenue West, 24th floor
  Ottawa, ON
  Canada K1P 1H7

## 3.3 Acknowledgement of Receipt of a Paper Report

FINTRAC will not send you any acknowledgement when your paper report has been received.

## 4 INSTRUCTIONS FOR COMPLETING A SUSPICIOUS TRANSACTION REPORT

The fields in this section correspond with the *Suspicious Transaction Report*. As explained in Section 2.2 (above), completing a paper report is only permitted if you do not have the capability to report electronically.

All fields of the report marked with an asterisk (*) **have to be completed.** Some fields have both an asterisk and "where applicable" next to them. These have to be completed if they are applicable to you or the transaction being reported. For all other fields, you have to make reasonable efforts to get the information. "Reasonable efforts" means that you tried to get the information requested on the report. If the information is available to you, you must provide it in the report. If the information was not available at the time of the transaction, and it is not contained in your files or records, the field may be left blank.

When completing the paper form, enter the date and time when you begin completing it at the top of the form. If you have to file a correction to a report on paper, follow the instructions on the first page of the form. If you need to get a paper form, see Section 3 (above).

There are eight parts on the *Suspicious Transaction Report* form, but some are only to be completed if applicable. To report a suspicious transaction, follow the following five steps:

- Step 1 — Complete Part A to provide information about you as the reporting entity.
- Step 2 — Complete Part B1 to provide details about the transaction.
- Step 3 — Complete Part B2 to provide details about the transaction's disposition. If the transaction's disposition was related to an account, also complete Part C. If the transaction's disposition was on behalf of a business or corporation, also complete Part E, **or** if the transaction's disposition was on behalf of an individual, complete Part F.

    If there was more than one disposition for the transaction, repeat this step for each disposition.

- Step 4 — Complete Part D to provide information about the individual conducting the transaction.
- Step 5 — Complete Part G to explain the reason for your suspicion. Also, complete Part H to provide information about any action taken, if applicable.

    If you have to include more than one transaction in your report, repeat steps 2, 3 and 4 for each one. You may need to use extra copies of Parts B1, B2, C, D, E or F to complete your report.

    The rest of this section will cover each part of the *Suspicious Transaction Report* form.

**PART A: INFORMATION ABOUT WHERE THE TRANSACTION TOOK PLACE**

Field 1* Reporting person or entity's identifier number (where applicable)

Field 2* Reporting person or entity's full name

Fields 3* to 6* Reporting person or entity's full address

Fields 7*, 8* and 9 Contact name

Field 10* Contact telephone number

Field 11* Which one of the following types of reporting entities best describes you?

**PART B1: INFORMATION ABOUT TRANSACTION(S)**

Fields 1* to 3* When the transaction took place

Field 4 Date of posting

Field 5* Type of funds

Field 6* Amount of transaction

Field 7* Currency

Fields 8* and 9* Other institution, entity or person name, number and account number (where applicable)

Field 10* How was the transaction conducted?

Field 11 ID number of the person initially identifying a suspicious transaction

**PART B2: INFORMATION ABOUT DISPOSITION(S)**

Field 12* Disposition of funds

Field 13* Amount of disposition

Field 14* Currency code

Fields 15* and 16* Other institution, entity or person name, number and account number (where applicable)

**PART C: ACCOUNT INFORMATION, IF THE TRANSACTION INVOLVED AN ACCOUNT**

Field 1* Branch or transit number (if this Part is applicable)

Field 2* Account number (if this Part is applicable)

Field 3* Type of account (if this Part is applicable)

**Field 4\* Type of Currency (if this Part is applicable)**

**Field 5\* Full name of each account holder (if this Part is applicable)**

**Field 6 Date opened**

**Field 7 Date closed**

**Field 8\* Status of the account at the time the transaction was initiated (if this Part is applicable)**

**PART D: INFORMATION ABOUT INDIVIDUAL CONDUCTING TRANSACTION(S)**

**Fields 1 to 3 Individual's full name**

**Field 4\* Entity client number (where applicable)**

**Fields 5 to 9 Individual's full address**

**Field 10 Country of residence**

**Field 10a Citizenship**

**Field 11 Home telephone number**

**Field 12 Individual's identifier**

**Field 13 ID Number**

**Fields 14 and 15 Place of issue**

**Field 16 Date of birth**

**Field 17 Individual's occupation**

**Field 18 Individual's business telephone number**

**Field 19 Individual's employer**

**Fields 20 to 24 Employer's business address**

**Field 25 Employer's business telephone number**

**PART E: INFORMATION ABOUT THE ENTITY ON WHOSE BEHALF TRANSACTION WAS CONDUCTED (WHERE APPLICABLE)**

**Field 1 Business, corporation or other entity name**

**Field 2 Type of business**

**Fields 3 to 7 Full address of business or corporation**

**Field 8 Business telephone number**

**Fields 9 to 11 Incorporation information**

**Field 12 Individual(s) authorized with respect to the account (up to three)**

PART F: INFORMATION ON PERSON ON WHOSE BEHALF TRANSACTION IS CONDUCTED (WHERE APPLICABLE)

**Fields 1 to 3 Individual's full name**

**Fields 4 to 8 Individual's full address**

**Field 9 Home telephone number**

**Field 10 Office telephone number**

**Field 11 Date of birth**

**Field 12 Individual's identifier**

**Field 13 ID number**

**Field 14 Country of residence**

**Field 14a Citizenship**

**Fields 15 and 16 Place of issue**

**Field 17 Individual's occupation**

**Field 18 Individual's employer**

**Fields 19 to 23 Employer's business address**

**Field 24 Employer's business phone number**

**Field 25 Relationship of the individual named in Part D to the individual named above**

PART G: DESCRIPTION OF SUSPICIOUS ACTIVITY

**Field 1\* Description of suspicious activity**

PART H: ACTION TAKEN (WHERE APPLICABLE)

**Field 1\* Action taken (if this Part is applicable)**

## 5 COMMENTS?

These guidelines will be reviewed on a periodic basis. If you have any comments or suggestions to help improve them, please send your comments to the mailing address provided below, or by email to guidelines@fintrac.gc.ca.

## 6   HOW TO CONTACT **FINTRAC**

For further information on FINTRAC and its activities, and report submission, please go to FINTRAC's Web site (http://www.fintrac.gc.ca) or contact FINTRAC:

> Financial Transactions and Reports Analysis Centre of Canada
> 234 Laurier Avenue West, 24th floor
> Ottawa, Ontario
> Canada K1P 1H7
> Toll-free: 1-866-346-8722

# GUIDELINE 4: IMPLEMENTATION OF A COMPLIANCE REGIME

## November 2003

TABLE OF CONTENTS

1.  General

2.  Who Has to Implement a Compliance Regime?

    2.1  Financial Entities

    2.2  Life Insurance Companies, Brokers And Independent Agents

    2.3  Securities Dealers, Portfolio Managers and Investment Counsellors

    2.4  Casinos

    2.5  Real Estate Brokers or Sales Representatives

    2.6  Agents of the Crown that Sell or Redeem Money Orders

    2.7  Foreign Exchange Dealing

    2.8  Money Services Businesses

    2.9  Accountants and Accounting Firms

3.  What is a Compliance Regime?

4.  Basics of a Compliance Regime

    4.1  Appointment of the Compliance Officer

    4.2  Compliance Policies and Procedures

    4.3  Review of the Compliance Policies and Procedures

    4.4  Ongoing Compliance Training

5.  FINTRAC's Approach to Compliance Monitoring

6.  Penalties for Non-Compliance

7.  Comments?

8.  How to Contact FINTRAC

**APPENDIX 1 — Reporting, Record Keeping, Client Identification and Third Party Determination Requirements by Reporting Person or Reporting Entity Sector**

**Appendix 1 A — Financial Entities**

**Appendix 1 B — Life Insurance Companies, Brokers and Independent Agents**

**Appendix 1 C — Securities Dealers**

**Appendix 1 D — Casinos**

**Appendix 1 E — Real Estate Brokers or Sales Representatives**

**Appendix 1 F —Agents of the Crown That Sell or Redeem Money Orders**

**Appendix 1 G — Foreign Exchange Dealers**

**Appendix 1 H — Money Services Businesses**

**Appendix 1 I — Accountants and Accounting Firms**

. . .

## 2   WHO HAS TO IMPLEMENT A COMPLIANCE REGIME?

### 2.1  Financial Entities

If you are a financial entity, such as a bank, credit union, caisse populaire, trust company, loan company or an agent of the Crown that accepts deposit liabilities, you have to implement a compliance regime to comply with your reporting, record keeping and client identification requirements.

When you remit or transmit funds, issue or redeem money orders, traveller's cheques or other similar negotiable instruments for anyone who does not hold an account with you, you are considered to be a money services business. In this case, you have additional record keeping and client identification requirements.

### 2.2  Life Insurance Companies, Brokers And Independent Agents

If you are a life insurance company, broker or independent agent, you have to implement a compliance regime to comply with your reporting, record keeping and client identification requirements.

If you are an employee of a person or entity who is also subject to these requirements, your employer is responsible for the compliance regime. For example, when life insurance agents are employees of a life insurance company, the compliance regime requirement is the responsibility of the life insurance company.

If you are a life insurance broker or independent agent (i.e., you are not an employee), you are responsible for your own compliance regime.

## 2.3  Securities Dealers, Portfolio Managers and Investment Counsellors

If you are **provincially authorized** to engage in the business of dealing in securities, portfolio management or investment counselling, you have to implement a compliance regime to comply with your reporting, record keeping and client identification requirements.

If you are an employee of a person or entity who is also subject to these requirements, your employer is responsible for the compliance regime. For example, if you are an employee of an entity engaged in the business of dealing in securities, the compliance regime requirement is the responsibility of the entity.

Similarly, if you are an agent of (or you are authorized to act on behalf of) a person or entity who is also subject to these requirements, that other person or entity is responsible for the compliance regime.

## 2.4  Casinos

If you are a casino authorized to do business in Canada, you are required to implement a compliance regime if roulette or card games are carried on in your establishment, or if your establishment has a slot machine. In this context, a slot machine does not include a video lottery terminal.

If you are a registered charity, you may be authorized to do business only temporarily as a casino for charitable purposes. If this is your situation and you carry on business in the casino for two consecutive days or less under the supervision of the casino, you are not required to implement a compliance regime. If you are the supervising casino (i.e., the permanent establishment in which a charity casino operates), you remain responsible for the compliance regime, as well as the reporting and record keeping requirements under the Act and Regulations.

## 2.5  Real Estate Brokers or Sales Representatives

If you are a real estate broker or sales representative, you are required to implement a compliance regime if you engage in any of the following activities on behalf of any person or entity in the course of a real estate transaction:

- receiving or paying funds;
- depositing or withdrawing funds; or
- transferring funds by any means.

If you are an employee of a person or entity who is also subject to these requirements, your employer is responsible for the compliance regime. For example, if you are a sales representative who is an employee of a real estate broker, the compliance regime requirement is the responsibility of the broker.

Similarly, if you are an agent of (or you are authorized to act on behalf of) a person or entity who is also subject to these requirements, that other person or entity is responsible for the compliance regime.

## 2.6 Agents of the Crown that Sell or Redeem Money Orders

If you are a government department or an agent of the Crown (i.e., an agent of her Majesty in right of Canada or of a province), you are required to implement a compliance regime if you sell or redeem money orders.

If you accept deposit liabilities in the course of providing financial services to the public, such as a provincial savings office, you are considered a financial entity (see Section 2.1).

## 2.7 Foreign Exchange Dealing

If you are a person or entity engaged in the business of foreign exchange dealing, you have to implement a compliance regime to comply with your reporting, record keeping and client identification requirements.

If you are an employee of a foreign exchange dealer, it is your employer who is engaged in the business of foreign exchange dealing and therefore responsible for the compliance regime. If you are an agent of (or you are authorized to act on behalf of) a person or entity engaged in the business of foreign exchange dealing, that other person or entity is responsible for the compliance regime for the relevant activities.

## 2.8 Money Services Businesses

You are a money services business if you are a person or entity engaged in the following business activities:

- remitting or transmitting funds by any means through any person, entity or electronic funds transfer network; or
- issuing or redeeming money orders, traveller's cheques or other similar negotiable instruments.

This includes alternative money remittance systems, such as Hawala, Hundi, Chitti, etc. This also includes financial entities when they remit or transmit funds, issue or redeem money orders, traveller's cheques or other similar negotiable instruments for anyone who does not hold an account with them.

If you are a money services business, you have to implement a compliance regime to comply with your reporting, record keeping and client identification requirements when you engage any of the business activities described above. This does not include redeeming cheques payable to a named person or entity. In other words, if you are only involved in cashing cheques made out to a particular person or entity, you are not subject to this requirement.

If you are an employee of a money services business, it is your employer who is engaged in the business and therefore responsible for the compliance regime. If you are an agent of (or you are authorized to act on behalf of) another person or entity that is a money services business, that other person or entity is responsible for the compliance regime for the relevant activities that you perform on their behalf.

## 2.9 Accountants and Accounting Firms

If you are an accountant or an accounting firm, you are required to implement a compliance regime if you engage in any of the following activities on behalf of any person or entity (other than your employer) or give instructions in respect of those activities on behalf of any person or entity (other than your employer):

- receiving or paying funds;
- purchasing or selling securities, real property or business assets or entities; or
- transferring funds or securities by any means.

You are also subject to this if you receive professional fees to engage in any of these accountant activities.

These do not include audit, review or compilation work carried out according to the recommendations in the Canadian Institute of Chartered Accountants (CICA) Handbook.

If you are an employee of a person or entity who is also subject to these requirements, your employer is responsible for the compliance regime. For example, if you are an accountant who is an employee of an accounting firm, the compliance regime requirement is the responsibility of the firm.

Similarly, if you are an agent of (or you are authorized to act on behalf of) a person or entity who is also subject to these requirements, that other person or entity is responsible for the compliance regime.

## 3    WHAT IS A COMPLIANCE REGIME?

The implementation of a compliance regime is good business practice for anyone subject to the Act and its Regulations. A well-designed, applied and monitored regime will provide a solid foundation for compliance with the legislation. As not all persons and entities operate under the same circumstances, your compliance regime will have to be tailored to fit your individual needs. It should reflect the nature, size and complexity of your operations.

If you are a member of an association within your sector of activity, you may wish to check with them to find out if any information sharing about any aspect of compliance regime implementation is available. You may also check with any regulatory body covering your sector in this regard.

Your compliance regime should include the following, as far as practicable:

- the appointment of a compliance officer;
- the development and application of compliance policies and procedures;
- a review of your compliance policies and procedures to test their effectiveness; and
- if you have employees or agents or any other individuals authorized to act on your behalf, an on-going compliance training program for them.

These four elements are key to any effective system of internal controls and are expanded upon in Section 4.

## 4    BASICS OF A COMPLIANCE REGIME

### 4.1  Appointment of the Compliance Officer

The individual you appoint will be responsible for the implementation of your compliance regime. Your compliance officer should have the authority and the resources necessary to discharge his or her responsibilities effectively. Depending on your type of business, your compliance officer should report, on a regular basis, to the board of directors or senior management, or to the owner or chief operator.

If you are a small business, the appointed officer could be a senior manager or the owner or operator of the business. If you are an individual, you can appoint yourself as compliance officer or you may choose to appoint another individual to help you implement a compliance regime.

In the case of a large business, the compliance officer should be from a senior level and have direct access to senior management and the board of directors. Further, as a good governance practice, the appointed compliance officer in a large business should not be directly involved in the receipt, transfer or payment of funds.

For consistency and ongoing attention to the compliance regime, your appointed compliance officer may choose to delegate certain duties to other employees. For example, the officer may delegate an individual in a local office or branch to ensure that compliance procedures are properly implemented at that location.

### 4.2  Compliance Policies and Procedures

An effective compliance regime includes policies and procedures and shows your commitment to prevent, detect and address non-compliance.

The formality of these policies and procedures depends on your needs. Generally, the degree of detail, specificity and formality of the regime varies according to the complexity of the issues and transactions you are involved in. It will also depend on your risk of exposure to money laundering or terrorist financing. For example, the compliance policies and procedures of a small business may be less formal and simpler than those of a bank.

What is important for your compliance policies and procedures is that they are communicated, understood and adhered to by all within your business who deal with clients or any property owned or controlled on behalf of clients. This includes those who work in the areas relating to client identification, record keeping, and any of the types of transactions that have to be reported. They need enough information to process and complete a transaction properly as well as identify clients and keep records as required.

They also need to know when an enhanced level of caution is required in dealing with transactions, such as those involving countries or territories that have not yet established adequate anti-money laundering regimes consistent with international standards. Information about this, including updates to the list of non-cooperative countries and territories issued by the Financial Action Task

Force on Money Laundering is available from the "What's New?" section of FINTRAC's Web site or at the following link: http://www.fintrac.gc.ca/publications/avs/2003-11-07_e.asp.

Your compliance policies and procedures should incorporate, at a minimum, the reporting, record keeping, and client identification requirements applicable to you. For more information about these, see Appendix 1 of this guideline for each sector of activity that you are involved in. For example, in the case of your reporting obligations relating to terrorist property or suspicions of terrorist financing, your policies and procedures should reflect the verification of related lists published in Canada. These are available on the Office of the Superintendent of Financial Institutions' Web site at http://www.osfi-bsif.gc.ca, by referring to the "Suppression of Terrorism" link.

Although directors and senior officers may not be involved in day-to-day compliance, they need to understand the statutory duties placed upon them, their staff and the entity itself.

## 4.3 Review of the Compliance Policies and Procedures

Another component of a comprehensive compliance regime is a review of your compliance policies and procedures, as often as is necessary, to test their effectiveness. This will help evaluate the need to modify existing policies and procedures or to implement new ones.

Your appointed compliance officer will play a key role in assessing the need for a review. Several factors could trigger this need, such as changes in legislation, non-compliance issues, or new services or products. If you are in a sector that is regulated at the federal or provincial level, the need for review of your compliance policies and procedures could also be triggered by requirements administered by your regulator.

The review is to be conducted by an internal or external auditor, if you have one. The review by an internal or external auditor could include interviews, tests and samplings, such as the following:

- interviews with those handling transactions and with their supervisors to determine their knowledge of the legislative requirements and your policies and procedures.
- a review of the criteria and process for identifying and reporting suspicious transactions.
- a sampling of large cash transactions followed by a review of the reporting of such transactions.
- a sampling of international electronic funds transfers (if those are reportable by the reporting person or entity in question) followed by a review of the reporting of such transactions.
- a test of the validity and reasonableness of any exceptions to large cash transaction reports including the required annual report to FINTRAC (this is applicable only for financial entities who choose the alternative to large cash transactions for certain business clients).
- a test of the record keeping system for compliance with the legislation.

- a test of the client identification procedures for compliance with the legislation.

The scope and the results of the review should be documented. Any deficiencies should be identified and reported to senior management or the board of directors. This should also include a request for a response indicating corrective actions and a timeline for implementing such actions.

If you do not have an internal or external auditor, you can do a "self-review". If feasible, this self-review should be conducted by an individual who is independent of the reporting, record keeping and compliance-monitoring functions. This could be an employee or an outside consultant. The objective of a self-review is similar to the objectives of a review conducted by internal or external auditors. It should address whether policies and procedures are in place and are being adhered to, and whether procedures and practices comply with legislative and regulatory requirements.

The scope and details of the review will depend on the nature, size and complexity of your operations. The review process should be well documented and should identify and note weaknesses in policies and procedures, corrective measures and follow-up actions.

### 4.4 Ongoing Compliance Training

If you have employees, agents or other individuals authorized to act on your behalf, your compliance regime has to include training. This is to make sure that all those who have contact with customers, who see customer transaction activity, or who handle cash in any way understand the reporting, client identification and record keeping requirements. This includes those at the "front line" as well as senior management.

In addition others who have responsibilities under your compliance regime, such as information technology and other staff responsible for designing and implementing electronic or manual internal controls should receive training. This could also include the appointed compliance officer and internal auditors.

Standards for the frequency and method of training, such as formal, on-the-job or external, should be addressed. New people should be trained before they begin to deal with customers. All should be periodically informed of any changes in anti-money laundering or anti-terrorism legislation, policies and procedures, as well as current developments and changes in money laundering or terrorist activity financing schemes particular to their jobs. Those who change jobs within your organization should be given training as necessary to be up-to-date with the policies, procedures and risks of exposure to money laundering or terrorist financing that are associated with their new job.

The method of training may vary greatly depending on the size of your business and the complexity of the subject matter. The training program for a small business may be less sophisticated and not necessarily formalized in writing.

When assessing your training needs, consider the following elements:

- **Requirements and related liabilities**
  The training should give those who need it an understanding of the reporting, client identification and record keeping requirements as well as penalties for not meeting those requirements. For more information about this, see the other guidelines regarding each of those requirements applicable to you.

- **Policies and procedures**
  The training should make your employees, agents, or others who act on your behalf aware of the internal policies and procedures for deterring and detecting money laundering and terrorist financing that are associated with their jobs. It should also give each one a clear understanding of his or her responsibilities under these policies and procedures.

  They need to understand how their institution, organization or profession is vulnerable to abuse by criminals laundering the proceeds of crime or by terrorists financing their activities. Training should include examples of how your particular type of organization could be used to launder illicit funds or fund terrorist activity. This should help them to identify suspicious transactions and should give you some assurance that your services are not being abused for the purposes of money laundering or terrorist financing. For example, employees should also be made aware that they cannot disclose that they have made a Suspicious Transaction Report, or disclose the contents of such a report, with the intent to prejudice a criminal investigation, whether it has started or not. They should also understand that no criminal or civil proceedings may be brought against them for making a report in good faith.

- **Background information on money laundering and terrorist financing**
  Any training program should include some background information on money laundering so everyone who needs to can understand what money laundering is, why criminals choose to launder money and how the process usually works. They also need to understand what terrorist financing is and how that process usually works. For more information about this, see *Guideline 1: Backgrounder* and FINTRAC's website (http://www.fintrac.gc.ca).

  All businesses should consult, if possible, training material available through their associations. In addition, FINTRAC makes material available on its Web site that can provide help with training. For example, a simulation facility is available within the reporting section of FINTRAC's Web site that can be used for training. You can use this to complete simulated electronic reports.

## 5 FINTRAC'S APPROACH TO COMPLIANCE MONITORING

FINTRAC has a responsibility to ensure compliance with your legislative requirements under the *Proceeds of Crime (Money Laundering) and Terrorist Financing Act*. To do this, FINTRAC can examine your compliance regime and records. FINTRAC may also periodically provide you with feedback about the adequacy, completeness and timeliness of the information you have reported.

FINTRAC favours a co-operative approach to monitoring. The emphasis will be on working with you to achieve compliance. When compliance issues are identified, FINTRAC intends to work with you in a constructive manner to find reasonable solutions. If this is not successful, FINTRAC has the authority to refer non-compliance cases to the appropriate law enforcement agencies.

FINTRAC's compliance program will use risk management strategies to identify those most in need of improving compliance. Efforts will be focused on areas where there is greater risk of non-compliance and in which the failure to comply could have significant impact on the ability to detect and deter money laundering and terrorist financing.

Finally, FINTRAC will work with other regulators at the federal and provincial levels to identify areas of common interest and address the potential for overlap in some areas of its responsibilities. In that context, FINTRAC will explore avenues for cost efficiencies, consistency of approach and information sharing.

## 6   PENALTIES FOR NON-COMPLIANCE

As stated above, FINTRAC favours a co-operative approach to monitoring and to finding co-operative solutions. However, if this is not successful, FINTRAC has the authority to refer non-compliance cases to the appropriate law enforcement agencies.

Failure to comply with your legislative requirements can lead to criminal charges against you if you are a person or entity described in Section 2. The following are some of the penalties:

- failure to report a suspicious transaction or failure to make a terrorist property report — conviction of this could lead to up to five years imprisonment, to a fine of $2,000,000, or both.
- failure to report a large cash transaction or an electronic funds transfer — conviction of this could lead to a fine of $500,000 for a first offence and $1,000,000 for each subsequent offence.
- failure to retain records — conviction of this could lead to up to five years imprisonment, to a fine of $500,000, or both.
- failure to implement a compliance regime — conviction of this could lead to up to five years imprisonment, to a fine of $500,000, or both.

**APPENDIX 1: Reporting, Record Keeping, Client Identification and Third Party Determination Requirements by Reporting Person or Reporting Entity Sector**

The following appendices present summaries of reporting, record keeping, client identification and third party determination requirements under the *Proceeds of Crime (Money Laundering) and Terrorist Financing Act* (the Act) and associated Regulations.

- **Appendix 1 A: Financial Entities**
- **Appendix 1 B: Life Insurance Companies, Brokers and Independent Agents**
- **Appendix 1 C: Securities Dealers**
- **Appendix 1 D: Casinos**
- **Appendix 1 E: Real Estate Brokers or Sales Representatives**
- **Appendix 1 F: Agents of the Crown That Sell or Redeem Money Orders**
- **Appendix 1 G: Foreign Exchange Dealers**
- **Appendix 1 H: Money Services Businesses**
- **Appendix 1 I: Accountants and Accounting Firms**

APPENDIX 1 A: FINANCIAL ENTITIES

**Reporting**

- **Suspicious transactions**
- **Terrorist property**
- **Electronic funds transfers**
- **Large cash transactions**

**Record Keeping**

**Ascertaining Identity**

**Third-party Determination**


APPENDIX 1 B: LIFE INSURANCE COMPANIES, BROKERS AND INDEPENDENT AGENTS

**Reporting**

- **Suspicious transactions**
- **Terrorist property**
- **Large cash transactions**

**Record Keeping**

**Ascertaining Identity**

**Third-party Determination**

APPENDIX 1 C: SECURITIES DEALERS

### Reporting

- Suspicious transactions
- Terrorist property
- Large cash transactions

### Record Keeping

### Ascertaining Identity

### Third-party Determination

APPENDIX 1 D: CASINOS

### Reporting

- Suspicious transactions
- Terrorist property
- Large cash transactions

### Record Keeping

### Ascertaining Identity

### Third-party Determination

APPENDIX 1 E: REAL ESTATE BROKERS OR SALES REPRESENTATIVES

### Reporting

- Suspicious transactions
- Terrorist property
- Large cash transactions

### Record Keeping

### Ascertaining Identity

### Third-party Determination

APPENDIX 1 F: AGENTS OF THE CROWN THAT SELL OR REDEEM MONEY ORDERS

### Reporting

- Suspicious transactions
- Terrorist property
- Large cash transactions

**Record Keeping**

**Ascertaining Identity**

**Third-party Determination**


APPENDIX 1 G: FOREIGN EXCHANGE DEALERS

**Reporting**

- **Suspicious transactions**
- **Terrorist property**
- **Large cash transactions**
- **Electronic funds transfers**

**Record Keeping**

**Ascertaining Identity**

**Third-party Determination**


APPENDIX 1 H: MONEY SERVICES BUSINESSES

**Reporting**

- **Suspicious transactions**
- **Terrorist property**
- **Large cash transactions**
- **Electronic funds transfers**

**Record Keeping**

**Ascertaining Identity**

**Third-party Determination**


APPENDIX 1 I: ACCOUNTANTS AND ACCOUNTING FIRMS

**Reporting**

- **Suspicious transactions**
- **Terrorist property**
- **Large cash transactions**

**Record Keeping**

**Ascertaining Identity**

**Third-party Determination**

# GUIDELINE 5: SUBMITTING TERRORIST PROPERTY REPORTS TO FINTRAC

## December 24, 2003

TABLE OF CONTENTS

1.  **General**

2.  **Terrorist Property Reporting Requirements**

    2.1   When Does a Terrorist Property Report Have to be Made under the *Proceeds of Crime (Money Laundering) and Terrorist Financing Act*?

    2.2   Other *Criminal Code* Requirements

    2.3   Method of Reporting to FINTRAC

    2.4   Information to be Contained in a Terrorist Property Report

3.  **Sending Terrorist Property Reports to FINTRAC**

    3.1   How to Complete Paper Reports

    3.2   How to Send a Terrorist Property Report to FINTRAC

4.  **Instructions for Completing a Terrorist Property Report**

    *   **Part A:** Information about the person or entity filing this report

    *   **Part B:** Reason for filing this report

    *   **Part C:** Information about the property

    *   **Part D:** Account information (if the property involves an account)

    *   **Part E1:** Information about any transaction or proposed transaction (where applicable)

    *   **Part E2:** Information about the transaction or proposed transaction disposition(s) (where applicable)

    *   **Part F:** Information about the individual who conducted or proposed to conduct transaction(s) (where applicable)

    *   **Part G:** Information about the entity on whose behalf the transaction was conducted or proposed to be conducted (where applicable)

    *   **Part H:** Information about the individual on whose behalf the transaction was conducted or proposed to be conducted (where applicable)

5.  **Comments?**

6.  **How to Contact FINTRAC**

. . .

## 2 TERRORIST PROPERTY REPORTING REQUIREMENTS

### 2.1 When Does a Terrorist Property Report Have to be Made under the *Proceeds of Crime (Money Laundering) and Terrorist Financing Act*?

Since June 12, 2002, if you are a reporting person or entity (see Section 1), you have to send a terrorist property report to FINTRAC if you have property in **your possession or control** that you **know** is owned or controlled by or on behalf of a terrorist or a terrorist group. This includes information about any transaction or proposed transaction relating to that property.

In this context, property means any type of real or personal property in your possession or control. This includes any deed or instrument giving title or right to property, or giving right to money or goods. For example, cash, bank accounts, insurance policies, money orders, real estate, securities, and traveller's cheques, among other types of assets, are considered property.

A terrorist or a terrorist group includes anyone that has as one of their purposes or activities facilitating or carrying out any terrorist activity. This can be an individual, a group, a trust, a partnership or a fund. It can also be an unincorporated association or organization. A terrorist group will also include anyone on a list published in Regulations issued under the *Criminal Code*. More information about this list is available from the following Web sites:

- http://www.osfi-bsif.gc.ca/eng/publications/advisories/index-supervisory.asp?#Supter (This site contains a consolidated list of names subject to the *Regulations Establishing a List of Entities* made under the *Criminal Code* or the *United Nations Suppression of Terrorism Regulations*.)
- http://www.sgc.gc.ca/national-security/counter-terrorism-e.asp

Once you know that any property in your possession or control is owned or controlled by or on behalf of a terrorist or a terrorist group, or after any transaction is proposed for such a property, a terrorist property report must be sent to FINTRAC without delay.

If you do not know that you are dealing with a terrorist, but suspect that you might be, then a suspicious transaction report is required if a transaction was completed.

For more information about submitting reports to FINTRAC relating to suspicions of terrorist financing, terrorist-related offences or other Government of Canada efforts to combat terrorism and terrorist activities, refer to *Guideline 1: Backgrounder, Guideline 2: Suspicious Transactions* or the following Web sites:

- http://www.fintrac.gc.ca/reporting--declaration/1_e.asp
- http://canada.justice.gc.ca/en/terrorism/
- http://canada.gc.ca/wire/2001/09/110901-US_e.html
- http://www.dfait-maeci.gc.ca/anti-terrorism/campaign-e.asp

## 2.2 Other Criminal Code Requirements

The following section provides information with respect to other *Criminal Code* requirements for reporting terrorist property. Although these requirements do not form part of the PCMLTFA, it may be a useful reference as part of this guideline.

In addition to making a terrorist property report to FINTRAC about this type of property, there is also a requirement under the *Criminal Code* that applies to anyone in Canada and any Canadian outside Canada. Whether or not you are a reporting person or entity (as described in Section 1), you must disclose to the RCMP and CSIS, the existence of property in your possession or control that you know is owned or controlled by or on behalf of a terrorist or a terrorist group. This includes information about any transaction or proposed transaction relating to that property. Information is to be provided to them, without delay, as follows:

- RCMP, Financial Intelligence Task Force unclassified fax: (613) 993-9474 or RCMP Information Line 1-888-349-9963
- CSIS Security Screening Branch, Project Leader Government Operations: unclassified fax (613) 842-1902

It is an offence under the *Criminal Code* to deal with any property if you know that it is owned or controlled by or on behalf of a terrorist or a terrorist group. It is also an offence to be involved in any transactions in respect of such property.

## 2.3 Method of Reporting to FINTRAC

### Paper Reporting Only

Unlike other reports to FINTRAC, you must submit a terrorist property report on paper. You cannot send them electronically at this time. See Section 3 (below) for more information.

## 2.4 Information to be Contained in a Terrorist Property Report

The terrorist property report has to contain information that describes the property. The report also has to provide information about the terrorist or terrorist group and anyone who owns or controls the property on their behalf. In addition, if there were any transactions or proposed transactions related to the property, the report also has to contain information about them. In the case of a transaction or a proposed transaction, the information to be contained in the terrorist property report is very similar to a suspicious transaction report.

As explained in Section 2.2, it is an offence to deal with any property if you know that it is owned or controlled by or on behalf of a terrorist or a terrorist group. It is also an offence to be involved in any transactions in respect of such property.

See Section 4 for more information about what has to be included in a terrorist property report.

## 3 SENDING TERRORIST PROPERTY REPORTS TO FINTRAC

### 3.1 How to Complete Paper Reports

As explained above, you must submit paper terrorist property reports to FINTRAC. Forms are available as follows:

- A file can be accessed and printed from the Publications section of FINTRAC's Web site (choose "reporting forms" from http://www.fintrac.gc.ca/publications/pub_e.asp). If you do not have a computer or access to the Internet, you may be able to do this at your local library or any other public place with Internet access.
- Call 1-866-346-8722 for a copy to be faxed or mailed to you.

To ensure that the information provided is legible and to facilitate data entry, it would be preferable if the free-text areas of the paper report (such as, fields 1 and 2 of Part B) were completed using word-processing equipment or a typewriter. For the parts of the report that must be completed by hand, the use of black ink and CAPITAL LETTERS is recommended.

See Section 4 for completion instructions. It includes details of what each field must contain for a terrorist property report and indicates which parts of the form you may need to make copies of before you complete your report.

### 3.2 How to Send a Terrorist Property Report to FINTRAC

There are two ways to send a terrorist property report to FINTRAC in such a way as to obtain an acknowledgement of receipt of a paper report:

- Fax: 1-866-226-2346; or
- Registered mail to the following address:

  Financial Transactions and Reports Analysis Centre of Canada
  Section A
  234 Laurier Avenue West, 24th Floor
  Ottawa, ON
  Canada K1P 1H7

In addition, you may also send your report by mail to the FINTRAC address above. You should note that you will not receive any acknowledgement from FINTRAC when your paper report has been received.

## 4 INSTRUCTIONS FOR COMPLETING A TERRORIST PROPERTY REPORT

The fields in this section refer to the numbered areas on the *Terrorist Property Report* form. As explained in Section 2.3, these reports can only be completed and sent to FINTRAC on paper. There is no mechanism to report electronically.

All fields of the report marked with an asterisk (*) **must be completed.** Some fields have both an asterisk and "where applicable" next to them. These must be completed if they are applicable to you or to the property or the transaction being reported. For all other fields, you have to make reasonable efforts to get the information. "Reasonable efforts" means that you tried to get the information requested on the report. If the information is available to you, you must provide it in the report. In the case of a transaction or a proposed transaction, if the information is not contained in your files or records, and it was not available at the time of the transaction, the field may be left blank.

Enter the date and time when you begin completing the report at the top of the form. If you have to file a correction to a report on paper, follow the instructions on the first page of the form. If you need to get a paper form, see Section 3 (above).

There are eight parts on the *Terrorist Property Report* form, but some are only to be completed if applicable. To make a terrorist property report, follow the following four steps:

- Step 1 — Complete Part A to provide information about you as the reporting entity.
- Step 2 — Complete Part B to provide details about the terrorist or terrorist group, and anyone who owns or controls the property on their behalf. Part B is also for you to explain what led you to file the report, as well as how you came to know that the property is owned or controlled by or on behalf of a terrorist or terrorist group.
- Step 3 — Complete Part C to provide details about the property. If the property involves an account, also complete Part D. If there were no transactions or proposed transactions related to the property, do not complete the rest of the report.
- Step 4 — If there was a transaction relating to the property, complete Parts E1 and E2 to provide information about how the transaction was initiated and completed. Provide the same information if there was a proposed transaction relating to the property. Complete Part F to provide information about the individual who conducted or proposed to conduct the transaction. If the transaction or proposed transaction was on behalf of an entity (such as a corporation or trust), also complete Part G or, if it was on behalf of an individual, complete Part H.

The rest of this section will cover each part of the *Terrorist Property Report* form.

**PART A: INFORMATION ABOUT THE PERSON OR ENTITY FILING THIS REPORT**

**Field 1\* Reporting person or entity's identifier number (where applicable)**

**Field 2\* Reporting person or entity's full name**

**Fields 3\* to 6\* Reporting person or entity's full address**

**Fields 7\*, 8\* and 9\* Contact name**

**Field 10\* Contact telephone number**

**Field 11\* Type of reporting person or entity**

**PART B: REASON FOR FILING THIS REPORT**

**Field 1\* Reason for filing this report**

**Field 2 How you came to know that the property is terrorist property**

**Field 3 Full name of terrorist or terrorist group**

**Fields 4 to 8 Terrorist or terrorist group address**

**Field 9 Telephone number**

**Field 10 Name of individual or entity that owns or controls the property on behalf of the terrorist or terrorist group**

**Fields 11 to 15 Individual or entity address**

**Field 16 Telephone number**

**PART C: INFORMATION ABOUT THE PROPERTY**

**Field 1\* Type of property**

**Field 2 Property identifier**

**Field 3 Property identifier number**

**Field 4\* Actual or approximate value**

**Field 5 Description of property**

**PART D: ACCOUNT INFORMATION (IF THE PROPERTY INVOLVES AN ACCOUNT)**

**Field 1\* Branch or transit number (if this Part is applicable)**

**Field 2\* Account number (if this Part is applicable)**

**Field 3\* Type of account (if this Part is applicable)**

**Field 4\* Currency code (if this Part is applicable)**

**Field 5\* Full name(s) of account holder(s) (if this Part is applicable)**

**Field 6 Date opened**

**Field 7 Date closed**

**Field 8\* Status of the account (if this Part is applicable)**

**PART E1: INFORMATION ABOUT ANY TRANSACTION OR PROPOSED TRANSACTION (WHERE APPLICABLE)**

**Field 1\* Date of the transaction (if this Part is applicable)**

**Field 2 Time of transaction**

**Field 3\* Night deposit indicator (if this Part is applicable)**

**Field 4 Date of posting**

**Field 5\* Type of funds or other property involved in initiating transaction (if this Part is applicable)**

**Field 6\* Amount of transaction (if this Part is applicable)**

**Field 7\* Currency code (if this Part is applicable)**

**Fields 8\* and 9\* Other institution, entity or individual name, number and account number (if this Part is applicable)**

**Field 10\* How was the transaction conducted? (if this Part is applicable)**

**Field 11 ID number of the individual initially identifying a transaction for terrorist property**

**PART E2: INFORMATION ABOUT THE TRANSACTION OR PROPOSED TRANSACTION DISPOSITION(S) (WHERE APPLICABLE)**

**Field 12\* Disposition of funds (if this Part is applicable)**

**Field 13\* Amount of disposition (if this Part is applicable)**

**Field 14\* Currency code (if this Part is applicable)**

**Fields 15\* and 16\* Other institution, entity or individual name, number and account number (where applicable, if this Part is applicable)**

**PART F: INFORMATION ABOUT THE INDIVIDUAL WHO CONDUCTED OR PRO-POSED TO CONDUCT TRANSACTION(S) (WHERE APPLICABLE)**

**Fields 1 to 3 Individual's full name**

**Fields 1A to 3A Alias**

**Field 4 Entity client number (where applicable)**

**Fields 5 to 9 Individual's full address**

**Field 10 Country of residence**

**Field 11 Home telephone number**

**Field 12 Individual's identifier**

**Field 13 ID number**

**Field 13A Citizenship**

**Fields 14 and 15 Place of issue**

**Field 16 Date of birth**

**Field 17 Individual's occupation**

**Field 18 Individual's business telephone number**

**Field 19 Individual's employer**

**Fields 20 to 24 Employer's business address**

**Field 25 Employer's business telephone number**

**PART G: INFORMATION ABOUT THE ENTITY ON WHOSE BEHALF THE TRANSACTION WAS CONDUCTED OR PROPOSED TO BE CONDUCTED (WHERE APPLICABLE)**

**Field 1 Name of corporation, trust or other entity**

**Field 2 Type of business**

**Fields 3 to 7 Full address of entity**

**Field 8 Business telephone number**

**Fields 9 to 11 Incorporation information (where applicable)**

**Field 12 Signing authority names**

**PART H: INFORMATION ABOUT THE INDIVIDUAL ON WHOSE BEHALF THE TRANSACTION WAS CONDUCTED OR PROPOSED TO BE CONDUCTED (WHERE APPLICABLE)**

**Fields 1 to 3 Individual's full name**

**Fields 1A to 3A Individual's alias (where applicable)**

**Fields 4 to 8 Individual's full address**

**Field 9 Home telephone number**

**Field 10 Office telephone number**

**Field 11 Date of birth**

**Field 12 Individual's identifier**

**Field 13 ID number**

**Fields 14 and 15 ID place of issue**

**Field 16 Country of residence**

**Field 16A Citizenship**

**Field 17 Individual's occupation**

**Field 18 Individual's employer**

**Fields 19 to 23 Employer's business address**

**Field 24 Employer's business telephone number**

**Field 25 Relationship of the individual named in Part F to the individual named above (fields 1 to 3)**

## 5 COMMENTS?

These guidelines will be reviewed on a periodic basis. If you have any comments or suggestions to help improve them, please send your comments to the mailing address provided below, or by email to guidelines@fintrac.gc.ca.

## 6 HOW TO CONTACT FINTRAC

For further information on FINTRAC and its activities, and report submission, please go to FINTRAC's Web site (http://www.fintrac.gc.ca) or contact FINTRAC:

> Financial Transactions and Reports Analysis Centre of Canada
> 234 Laurier Avenue West, 24th floor
> Ottawa, Ontario
> Canada K1P 1H7
> Toll-free: 1-866-346-8722

**Note:** Guidelines for Record Keeping and Client Identification Obligations have been issued for the following industries: Life Insurance, Securities Dealers, Money Services Businesses, Agents of Her Majesty in Right of Canada or of a Province that sell or redeem money orders, Accountants and Accounting Firms, Real Estate Agents, Casinos, Financial Entities and Foreign Exchange Dealers. The Guideline for the Life Insurance Industry below is reproduced as a sample guideline.

# GUIDELINE 6: RECORD KEEPING AND CLIENT IDENTIFICATION FOR LIFE INSURANCE COMPANIES, BROKERS AND AGENTS

## June 11, 2002

TABLE OF CONTENTS

1.   **General**

2.   **Records To Be Kept**

    2.1   Large Cash Transaction Records

    2.2   Client Information Records

3.   **Client Identity**

    3.1   When and How Do You Have To Identify Clients?

    3.2   Client Identity for Large Cash Transactions

    3.3   Client Identity for Client Information Records: Individuals

    3.4   Client Identity for Client Information Records: Entities

    3.5   General Exceptions to Client Identification

4.   **Third Party Determination**

    4.1   When Does a Third Party Determination Have To Be Made?

    4.2   Third Party Determination for Large Cash Transactions

    4.3   Third Party Determination for Client Information Records

5.   **How Should Records Be Kept?**

6.   **Penalties for Non-Compliance**

7.   **Comments?**

8.   **How to Contact FINTRAC**

## 1. GENERAL

The objective of the *Proceeds of Crime (Money Laundering) and Terrorist Financing Act* is to help detect and deter money laundering and the financing of terrorist activities. It is also to facilitate investigations and prosecutions of money laundering and terrorist activity financing offences. This includes implementation of reporting, record keeping, client identification and compliance regime requirements for life insurance companies and life insurance brokers or agents (and others).

A life insurance company means one regulated by provincial legislation, or a life company or foreign life company under the *Insurance Companies Act*. A life insurance broker or agent means an individual or entity registered or licensed provincially to carry on the business of arranging contracts of life insurance.

If you are a life insurance company, broker or agent, this guideline has been prepared to help you meet your record keeping and client identification obligations. It uses plain language to explain the most common situations under the *Proceeds of Crime (Money Laundering) and Terrorist Financing Act* as well as the related Regulations. It is provided as general information only. It is not legal advice, and is not intended to replace the Act and Regulations.

Record keeping and client identification obligations for other types of reporting persons or entities are explained by sector in other versions of this guideline (financial entities, securities dealers, foreign exchange dealing, money services businesses, Canada Post, accountants, real estate, casinos and legal counsel).

The requirements in this guideline are general requirements for life insurance companies, brokers or agents however, it is important to note that other requirements may apply depending on the nature of the financial transaction that the life insurance companies, brokers or agents are involved in.

For more information about money laundering and terrorist financing, or other requirements under the Act and Regulations applicable to you, see the guidelines in this series:

- *Guideline 1: Backgrounder* explains money laundering, terrorist financing, and their international nature. It also provides an outline of the legislative requirements as well as an overview of FINTRAC's mandate and responsibilities.
- *Guideline 2: Suspicious Transactions* explains how to report a suspicious transaction. It also provides guidance on how to identify a suspicious transaction, including general and industry-specific indicators that may help when conducting or evaluating transactions.
- *Guideline 3: Submitting Suspicious Transaction Reports to FINTRAC* explains when and how to submit suspicious transaction reports electronically.
- *Guideline 4: Implementation of a Compliance Regime* explains the requirement for reporting persons and entities to implement a regime to ensure compliance with their obligations under the *Proceeds of Crime*

*(Money Laundering) and Terrorist Financing Act* and associated Regulations.

- *Guideline 5: Submitting Terrorist Property Reports to FINTRAC* explains when and how to submit terrorist property reports.
- *Guideline 6: Record Keeping and Client Identification* explains the requirement for reporting persons and entities to identify their clients and keep records. There are eight different versions of *Guideline 6,* by sector.
- *Guideline 7: Submitting Large Cash Transaction Reports to FINTRAC* explains when and how to submit large cash transaction reports.
- *Guideline 8:* Submitting Electronic Funds Transfer Reports to FINTRAC explains when and how to submit electronic funds transfer reports.

If you need more help after you read this or other guidelines, call FINTRAC's national toll-free enquiries line at 1-866-346-8722.

Throughout this guideline, several references are provided to additional information that may be available on external Web sites. FINTRAC is not responsible for the accuracy, reliability or currency of the information contained on those external Web sites.

## 2. RECORDS TO BE KEPT

As a life insurance company, broker or agent, you have to keep certain records under Canada's anti-money laundering and anti-terrorism legislation (i.e., the *Proceeds of Crime (Money Laundering) and Terrorist Financing Act)*. If you are a life insurance company, these record keeping obligations build on what you have been subject to for the past decade relating to Canada's previous anti-money laundering legislation. If you are a life insurance broker or agent, these record keeping obligations are new.

Effective June 12, 2002, as a life insurance company, broker or agent, you have to keep the following records:

- Large cash transaction records
- Client information records

Details about each of these types of records are provided in Sections 2.1 through 2.2 (below).

This guideline describes your record keeping obligations under Canada's *Proceeds of Crime (Money Laundering) and Terrorist Financing Act.* Your policies and procedures may cover situations other than the ones described in this guideline, and you may require additional records to be kept for purposes other than your requirements under this legislation. For example, the retention period for your records may vary for purposes other than what is described in this guideline.

### 2.1 Large Cash Transaction Records

This is a record for every amount of cash of $10,000 or more that you receive from a client in a single transaction. For example, if your client makes a deposit of $10,000 to purchase a life insurance policy, you have to keep a large cash transaction record. This type of transaction will also require a report to FINTRAC effective November 30, 2002, as explained in the new Large Cash Transaction Report Guideline.

If you know that two or more cash transactions of less than $10,000 each were made within a 24-hour period (i.e., 24 consecutive hours), by or on behalf of the same client, these are considered to be a single large cash transaction if they add up to $10,000 or more. In this case, you would have to keep a large cash transaction record, and report the transaction to FINTRAC as explained above.

You do **not** have to keep a large cash transaction record if the cash is received from a financial entity or a public body. In this context, a financial entity means a bank, credit union, caisse populaire, a trust and loan company or an agent of the Crown that accepts deposit liabilities.

Also in this context, a public body means any of the following or their agent:

- a provincial or federal department or Crown agency;
- an incorporated municipal body (including an incorporated city, town, village, metropolitan authority, district, county, etc.);
- a hospital authority. A hospital authority means an organization that operates a public hospital and that is designated to be a hospital authority for GST/HST purposes. For more information on the designation of hospital authorities, refer to GST/HST Memoranda Series, Chapter 25.2, *Designation of Hospital Authorities* available from the following Web site: http://www. ccra-adrc.gc.ca/E/pub/gm/25-2/25-2/README.html.

Likewise, you do **not** have to keep a large cash transaction record for any of the following transactions:

- the purchase of an annuity as a direct transfer from a registered pension plan;
- the purchase of a registered annuity policy or a registered retirement income fund;
- the purchase of an annuity paid for entirely with the proceeds of a group life insurance policy;
- a reverse mortgage or a structured settlement; or
- the opening of a registered plan account, including a locked-in retirement plan and an individual or group registered retirement savings plan.

## Contents of a large cash transaction record

For any large cash transaction, the information you have to keep in a large cash transaction record includes the following:

- the amount and currency of the cash received;
- the date and nature of the transaction;
- the purpose and details of the transaction;
- the type of transaction (for example, the cash was used to put a deposit on a purchase of a life insurance policy, etc.);

- whether any other individuals or entities were involved in the transaction; and
- how the cash was received (for example, in person, by mail, by armoured car, or any other way).
- the number and type of any account affected by the transaction;
- the full name of the client that holds the account; and
- the currency in which the account's transactions are conducted.

The large cash transaction record also has to include the name of the individual from whom you received the cash and that individual's address and principal business or occupation. If this information is readily available in other records that you have to keep (as described below), it does not have to be kept again as part of the large cash transaction record.

Unless an exception to the identification requirements applies (exceptions to identification requirements are also explained in Section 3.8), the large cash transaction record has to also contain the following information:

- the individual's date of birth; and
- the type of document used to confirm the individual's identity, the document's reference number and its place of issue.

## 2.2 Client Information Records

If your client pays you $10,000 or more for an annuity or a life insurance policy, over the duration of the annuity or policy, you have to keep a client information record. This has to be kept no matter how the client paid for the annuity or policy, whether or not it was in cash.

A client information record sets out your client's name, address and the nature of the client's principal business or occupation. In the case of a group life insurance policy or a group annuity, the client information record is about the applicant for the policy or annuity.

You do **not** have to keep a client information record for a policy that is an exempt policy (i.e., a policy issued mainly for insurance protection and not investment purposes as defined in Subsection 306(1) of the *Income Tax Regulations*). Likewise, you do **not** have to keep a client information record for a group life insurance policy that does not provide a cash surrender value or a savings component.

You are required to identify the individual purchasing the annuity or policy (as explained in Section 3.3 below). Unless an exception to the identification requirements applies (exceptions to identification requirements are also explained in Section 3.5), the client information record has to also contain the following information:

- the individual's date of birth;
- if the document used to confirm the individual's identity was a birth certificate, driver's licence, provincial health insurance card, passport or other similar record issued by the provincial, territorial, or the federal government, the type of document, its reference number and its place of issue; and

233

- if you used a cleared cheque to confirm the individual's identity, the name of the financial entity and the account number of the account on which the cheque was drawn; and
- if you confirmed the individual's identity by confirming that the individual holds an account with a financial entity, the name of the financial entity and the account number.

As explained in Section 2.1 (above), a financial entity means a bank, credit union, caisse populaire, a trust and loan company or an agent of the Crown that accepts deposit liabilities.

**Corporate purchases**

You have to keep a client information record for a corporation (as explained in Section 3.4 below). If, in the normal course of business, you get a copy of the part of the official corporate records showing the provisions that relate to the power to bind the corporation regarding the purchase, you have to keep a copy of it. This could be the articles of incorporation that set out those duly authorized to sign on behalf of the corporation, such as an officer, the comptroller, etc. If there were changes subsequent to the articles, then the board resolution stating the change would be included in this type of record.

## 3. CLIENT IDENTITY

### 3.1 When and How Do You Have To Identify Clients?

As a life insurance company, broker or agent, you have client identification obligations. You have to take the following measures to identify individuals or entities, subject to the general exceptions outlined in Section 3.5 (below). These identification requirements build on those in effect for the past decade for life insurance companies.

When you refer to a document to identify an individual, it has to be an original and not a copy of the document.

This guideline describes your client identification obligations, effective June 12, 2002, under Canada's *Proceeds of Crime (Money Laundering) and Terrorist Financing Act*. Your policies and procedures may cover requirements other than the ones described in this guideline, and you may need additional identification for purposes other than your requirements under this legislation. For example, you may have to request an individual's social insurance number for income tax purposes.

### 3.2 Client Identity for Large Cash Transactions

You have to identify any individual with whom you conduct a large cash transaction, at the time of the transaction, if it is one for which you have to keep a large cash transaction record, as described in Section 2.1 (above).

To identify an individual, refer to the individual's birth certificate, driver's licence, passport or other similar record issued by the provincial, territorial, or the federal government. You can refer to an individual's provincial health card, provided there is no provincial or territorial legislation preventing you from requesting or using it. For example, Ontario, Manitoba and Prince Edward Island prohibit health cards from being used for this purpose.

## 3.3 Client Identity for Client Information Records: Individuals

You have to identify any individual who purchases an annuity or a life insurance policy for whom you have to keep a client information record (as identified in Section 2.2 above), within six months of creating this record. This is true whether the transaction is conducted on the individual's own behalf, or on behalf of a third party. However, if you have reasonable grounds to believe that another life insurance company, broker or agent has confirmed the individual's identity as explained above for the same transaction, you do not have to confirm their identity again.

Furthermore, you do not have to identify an individual for whom you have to keep a client information record for any of the following transactions:

• the purchase of an annuity as a direct transfer from a registered pension plan;
• the purchase of a registered annuity policy or a registered retirement income fund;
• the purchase of an annuity paid for entirely with the proceeds of a group life insurance policy;
• a reverse mortgage or a structured settlement; or
• the opening of a registered plan account, including a locked-in retirement plan and an individual or group registered retirement savings plan.

You do not have to identify the individual if the client information record is about a federally or provincially regulated pension. Likewise, you do not have to identify the individual if the client information record is about a public body or a very large corporation. For more information about what is considered a public body in this context, see Section 2.1 (above). For information about what is considered a very large corporation, see Section 3.4 (below).

To identify an individual, refer to their birth certificate, driver's licence, passport or other similar record issued by the provincial, territorial, or the federal government. You can refer to an individual's provincial health card, unless it is from Ontario, Manitoba or Prince Edward Island where health cards cannot be used for this purpose.

If the individual is not physically present when the account is opened, you can confirm either of the following:

• that the individual holds an account (in the individual's name) with a financial entity; or
• that a cheque drawn on the individual's account with a financial entity has been cleared.

As explained in Section 2.1 (above), a financial entity means a bank, credit union, caisse populaire, a trust and loan company or an agent of the Crown that accepts deposit liabilities.

### 3.4 Client Identity for Client Information Records: Entities

You have to confirm the existence of any corporation or other entity that purchases an annuity or a life insurance policy and for which you have to keep a client information record, within six months of creating this record.

You do not have to confirm the existence of a corporation or other entity if the client information record is about a federally or provincially regulated pension. Likewise, you do not have to do this if the client information record is for a public body or a very large corporation.

In this context, a public body means any of the following or their agent:

- a provincial or federal department or Crown agency;
- an incorporated municipal body (including an incorporated city, town, village, metropolitan authority, district, county, etc.); and
- a hospital authority. A hospital authority means an organization that operates a public hospital and that is designated to be a hospital authority for GST/HST purposes. For more information on the designation of hospital authorities, refer to GST/HST Memoranda Series, Chapter 25.2, *Designation of Hospital Authorities* available from the following Web site: http://www.ccra-adrc.gc.ca/E/pub/gm/25-2/25-2-e.pdf.

Also in this context, a very large corporation is one that you believe has minimum net assets of $75 million on its last audited balance sheet. The corporation's shares have to be traded on a Canadian stock exchange or certain stock exchanges outside Canada, and the corporation also has to operate in a country that is a member of the Financial Action Task Force on Money Laundering.

For information about which stock exchanges outside Canada on which the stock of a large corporation could be traded, refer to section 3201 of the *Income Tax Regulations.* You can access this at the following Web site: http://laws.justice.gc.ca/en/I-3.3/C.R.C.-c.945/136876.html.

To find out which countries are members of the Financial Action Task Force, refer to the following Web site: http://www1.oecd.org/fatf/Members_en.htm.

### Corporations

To confirm the existence of a corporation, find out the corporation's name and address and the names of the corporation's directors. To do this, refer to the following documents:

- the corporation's certificate of corporate status;
- a record that has to be filed annually under provincial securities legislation; or
- any other record that confirms the corporation's existence.

The record you use to confirm a corporation's existence can be paper or an electronic version. If it is paper, you have to keep the record or a copy of it.

If the record is an electronic version, you have to keep a record of the corporation's registration number, the type and source of the record. An electronic version of a record has to be from a public source. For example, you can get information about a corporation's name and address and the names of its directors from Industry Canada's Strategis online corporations database at http://strategis.ic. gc.ca/cgi-bin/sc_mrksv/corpdir/dataOnline/corpns_se. As another example, you may also get this type of information if you subscribe to a corporate searching and registration service.

### Entities other than corporations

To confirm the existence of an entity other than a corporation, refer to a partnership agreement, articles of association or any other similar record that confirms the entity's existence. The record you use to confirm the existence of an entity can be paper or an electronic version. If it is paper, you have to keep the record or a copy of it.

If the record is an electronic version, you have to keep a record of the entity's registration number, the type and source of the record. An electronic version of a record has to be from a public source.

### 3.5  General Exceptions to Client Identification

Once you have confirmed the identity of an individual, you do not have to confirm their identity again if you recognize the individual in the future.

Once you have confirmed the existence of a corporation by confirming its name and address and the names of its directors (as explained above), you are not required to confirm that same information in the future.

Once you have confirmed the existence of an entity other than a corporation, you are not required to confirm that same information in the future.

### 4.  THIRD PARTY DETERMINATION

### 4.1  When Does a Third Party Determination Have To Be Made?

You have to make a third party determination when you have to keep a large cash transaction record or a client information record.

In making a third party determination when employees are acting on behalf of their employers, they are considered to be acting on behalf of a third party. The only exception to this is when an employee deposits cash to the employer's account. In that case, the employee is not considered to be acting on behalf of a third party.

## 4.2  Third Party Determination for Large Cash Transactions

Whenever you have to keep a large cash transaction record, you have to take reasonable measures to determine whether the individual who gives you the cash is acting on behalf of a third party. What constitutes reasonable measures will vary in accordance with the context in which they occur, and therefore could differ from one situation to the next. However, reasonable measures would include retrieving the information already contained in your files or elsewhere within your corporate environment, or obtaining the information directly from the client. With respect to Suspicious Transaction Reports, you cannot tip off the client that you are submitting a report. Therefore reasonable measures may not involve obtaining information from the client if you feel this would tip them off that a Suspicious Transaction Report is being submitted to FINTRAC.

If you determine that there is in fact a third party, you have to keep a record of the following information:

- the third party's name, address and principal business or occupation;
- the incorporation number and place of incorporation if the third party is a corporation; and
- the nature of the relationship between the third party and the individual who gives you the cash.

If you are not able to determine that there is in fact a third party, but you have reasonable grounds to suspect that the individual is acting on behalf of a third party, you have to keep a record to indicate whether, according to the individual giving the cash, the transaction is being conducted on behalf of a third party. This record must also indicate details of why you suspect the individual is acting on behalf of a third party.

## 4.3  Third Party Determination for Client Information Records

Whenever you are required to keep a client information record as explained in Section 2.2 (above), you have to take reasonable measures to determine whether the client is acting on behalf of a third party. What constitutes reasonable measures will vary in accordance with the context in which they occur, and therefore could differ from one situation to the next. However, reasonable measures would include retrieving the information already contained in your files or elsewhere within your corporate environment, or obtaining the information directly from the client. With respect to Suspicious Transaction Reports, you cannot tip off the client that you are submitting a report. Therefore reasonable measures may not involve obtaining information from the client if you feel this would tip them off that a Suspicious Transaction Report is being submitted to FINTRAC.

If you determine that the client is in fact acting on behalf of a third party, you have to keep a record of the following information:

- the third party's name, address and principal business or occupation;
- the incorporation number and place of incorporation if the third party is a corporation; and
- the nature of the relationship between the third party and the account holder.

If you are not able to determine that the client is in fact acting on behalf of a third party, but you have reasonable grounds to suspect that the client is so acting, you have to keep a record to indicate whether, according to the client, the transaction is being conducted on behalf of a third party. This record must also indicate details of why you suspect the client is acting on behalf of a third party.

## 5.  HOW SHOULD RECORDS BE KEPT?

You should maintain an effective record keeping system to enable FINTRAC to have access to the records in a timely fashion. Your records have to be kept in such a way that they can be provided to FINTRAC within 30 days of a request to examine them.

You can keep records in a machine-readable or electronic form, as long as a paper copy can be readily produced. Also, for records that are kept electronically, an electronic signature of the individual who must sign the record has to be retained.

### Timeframe for keeping records

In the case of client information records and records to confirm the existence of an entity (including a corporation), these records have to be kept for five years from the day the last business transaction was conducted. In the case of all other records, the records must be kept for a period of at least five years following the date they were created.

### Employees, contractors, or agents who keep records for you

Your employees who keep records (as described in Section 2 above) for you are not required to keep those records after the end of their employment with you. The same is true for individuals in a contractual relationship with you, after the end of that contractual relationship. This means that you have to get and keep the records that were kept for you by any employee or contractor before the end of that individual's employment or contract with you. If you are an independent life insurance agent or broker, you are deemed to be a reporting entity for the purposes of the *Proceeds of Crime (Money Laundering) and Terrorist Financing Act* and associated Regulations.

## 6.  PENALTIES FOR NON-COMPLIANCE

Failure to comply with your record keeping requirements can lead to criminal charges against you. Conviction of failure to retain records could lead to up to five years imprisonment, to a fine of $500,000, or both.

**B    Legal Counsel, Accountants and Real Estate Brokers or Sales Representatives**

**C    Money Services Businesses**

**D    Foreign Exchange Dealers**

**E    Securities Dealers**

**F    Casinos**

**G    Financial Entities**

**7.    COMMENTS?**

**8.    HOW TO CONTACT FINTRAC**

For further information on FINTRAC and its activities reporting and other obligations, please go to FINTRAC's Web site or contact FINTRAC:

Financial Transactions and Reports Analysis Centre of Canada
234 Laurier Avenue West, 24th floor
Ottawa, Ontario
Canada K1P 1H7
Toll-free: 1-866-346-8722

# GUIDELINE 7A: SUBMITTING LARGE CASH TRANSACTION REPORTS TO FINTRAC ELECTRONICALLY

### March 29, 2004

TABLE OF CONTENTS

1.  **General**

2.  **Large Cash Transaction Reporting Requirements**

    2.1   When Does a Large Cash Transaction Report Have to be Made?

    2.2   Cash Transactions in Foreign Currency

    2.3   Other Requirements Associated with Large Cash Transactions

    2.4    Means of Reporting to FINTRAC

3.  **Electronic Reporting**

    3.1   Options for Electronic Reporting

    3.2   How to Complete Electronic Reports

    3.3   Acknowledgement of Receipt of an Electronic Report

    3.4   Report Corrections

4.  **Instructions for Completing a Large Cash Transaction Report**

    4.1   General Instructions

    4.2   Instructions for Submitting a New Report

    4.3   Instructions for Submitting a Change to a Previously Submitted Report

    4.4   To Submit Changes Through FINTRAC's Secure Web Site

5.  **Comments?**

6.  **How to Contact FINTRAC**

**Appendix 1 — Field by Field Instructions for Large Cash Transaction Report**

**Appendix 2 —Navigation Through FINTRAC's Web Form**

**Appendix 2A —Reporting Screens (Web Form)**

. . .

## 2 LARGE CASH TRANSACTION REPORTING REQUIREMENTS

Throughout this guideline, any references to dollar amounts (such as $10,000) refer to the amount in Canadian dollars or its equivalent in foreign currency.

Furthermore, all references to cash mean money in circulation in any country (bank notes or coins). In this context, cash does not include cheques, money orders or other similar negotiable instruments.

### 2.1 When Does a Large Cash Transaction Report Have to be Made?

If you are a reporting person or entity (see Section 1), you have to send a large cash transaction report to FINTRAC in the following situations:

- You receive an amount of $10,000 or more in cash in the course of a single transaction; or
- You receive two or more cash amounts of less than $10,000 that total $10,000 or more. In this case, if you are an individual, you have to make a large cash transaction report if you know the transactions were made within 24 consecutive hours of each other by or on behalf of the same individual or entity. If you are an entity, you have to make a large cash transaction report if your employee or senior officer knows the transactions were made within 24 consecutive hours of each other by or on behalf of the same individual or entity.

You have to send large cash transaction reports to FINTRAC within 15 calendar days after the transaction.

If you are a reporting person and an employee of a reporting person or entity, your employer is responsible for meeting the large cash transaction reporting requirement associated to any of your activities as an employee.

Similarly, if you are a reporting person or entity and you are an agent of or you are authorized to act on behalf of a reporting person or entity, it is that reporting person or entity's responsibility to meet the large cash transaction reporting requirement associated to any of your activities on their behalf. However, if you are a life insurance broker or independent agent, you are responsible for reporting to FINTRAC (unless you are an employee as explained above).

You do **not** have to make a large cash transaction report to FINTRAC if the cash is received from a financial entity. In this context, a financial entity means a bank, credit union, caisse populaire, a trust and loan company or an agent of the Crown that accepts deposit liabilities.

If you are a reporting person or entity other than a casino, you do **not** have to make a large cash transaction report to FINTRAC if the cash is received from a public body. In this context, a public body means any of the following or their agent:

- a provincial or federal department or Crown agency;
- an incorporated municipal body (including an incorporated city, town, village, metropolitan authority, district, county, etc.);
- a hospital authority. A hospital authority means an organization that operates a public hospital and that is designated to be a hospital authority for GST/HST purposes. For more information on the designation of hospital authorities,

refer to GST/HST Memoranda Series, Chapter 25.2, *Designation of Hospital Authorities* available from the Canada Revenue Agency's Web site. At the time of publishing of this guideline, the document was available at the following link: http://www.ccra-adrc.gc.ca/E/pub/gm/25-2/README.html

Financial entities may choose, in certain specific circumstances, an alternative to making large cash transaction reports for certain clients that are corporations. If you are a financial entity, see *Guideline 9: Submitting Alternative to Large Cash Transaction Reports to FINTRAC* for more information about this.

## 2.2  Cash Transactions in Foreign Currency

If a cash transaction is in foreign currency, you will need to check whether it is the equivalent of 10,000 Canadian dollars or more to determine whether or not it is reportable as a large cash transaction. For this purpose only, use the last noon rate provided by the Bank of Canada available at the time of the transaction. This calculation is not based on the actual exchange rate used to process the transaction — this is only to check whether the $10,000 threshold is met for the transaction to be reportable as a large cash transaction.

For example, for a cash transaction in foreign currency that happened at 9:00 am on Tuesday following a holiday Monday, you would use the Bank of Canada noon rate from the previous Friday to determine whether it is a large cash transaction. You can find the noon rate applicable at the time of a transaction on the Bank of Canada Web site at http://www.bankofcanada.ca/en/exchange.htm. If there is no Bank of Canada noon rate published for the currency of the transaction, use the actual exchange rate applied when you processed the transaction to determine whether it is reportable.

Once you have determined that a cash transaction in foreign currency is in fact reportable based on the Bank of Canada noon rate, you will have to send a large cash transaction report to FINTRAC. On this report, you will indicate any amounts involved in the transaction in foreign currency, and indicate the appropriate currency code. The large cash transaction report does not require information about any exchange rate applicable to the transaction. The exchange rate is only relevant to determine whether or not the transaction is a large cash transaction.

## 2.3  Other Requirements Associated with Large Cash Transactions

In addition to the reporting requirements explained in this guideline, consider the following relating to a large cash transaction:

### Record keeping and client identification

Large cash transactions have associated record keeping and client identification requirements. These are explained in *Guideline 6: Record Keeping and Client Identification.*

## Electronic funds transfer report

If a large cash transaction results in an electronic funds transfer, you may have to make an electronic funds transfer report to FINTRAC about the same transaction in addition to the large cash transaction report.

For more information about making electronic funds transfer reports, consult *Guideline 8: Submitting Electronic Funds Transfer Reports to FINTRAC*.

## Suspicious transaction report

If anything about a large cash transaction gives you reasonable grounds to suspect that it could be related to a money laundering or a terrorist activity financing offence, you have to make a suspicious transaction report to FINTRAC. This would be in addition to making the large cash transaction report about the same transaction as required.

The suspicious transaction report has very similar fields to those of a large cash transaction report. There are some differences, such as a field in the suspicious transaction report for you to explain your suspicion about the transaction. There is also a field in that report for you to describe what action, if any, was taken by you as a result of the suspicious transaction. This would include stating that you have made a large cash transaction report for the same transaction (if that is the case).

For more information about suspicious transaction reports, consult the following:

- *Guideline 1: Backgrounder*
- *Guideline 2: Suspicious Transactions*
- *Guideline 3: Submitting Suspicious Transaction Reports to FINTRAC*

## Transactions related to terrorist property

If you know that any proposed transaction is related to property owned or controlled by or on behalf of a terrorist or a terrorist group, you cannot complete the transaction. This is because terrorist property must be frozen under the *United Nations Suppression of Terrorism Regulations* as well as the *Criminal Code*.

For more information about this and to find out what your obligations are regarding any terrorist property in your control or possession, consult the following:

- *Guideline 1: Backgrounder*
- *Guideline 5: Submitting Terrorist Property Reports to FINTRAC*

## 2.4  Means of Reporting to FINTRAC

### Electronic Reporting

As a reporting person or entity, you will have to submit all large cash transaction reports to FINTRAC **electronically** if you have the technical capabilities to do so. The minimum technical capabilities are as follows:

- A personal computer with the following characteristics:
  - 32 MB memory
  - 640 x 480 VGA video display (800 x 600 or higher is preferable)
  - any operating system running the following Web browsers: Internet Explorer version 5.x (Windows® 98/Me/NT/2000); and
- An Internet connection

See Section 3 for more information on submitting reports to FINTRAC electronically.

## Paper Reporting

If you do not have the technical capabilities to send reports electronically, you must submit reports on paper. See *Guideline 7B: Submitting Large Cash Transaction Reports to FINTRAC by Paper* for more information.

## 3 ELECTRONIC REPORTING

### 3.1 Options for Electronic Reporting

As a reporting person or entity, you will have to report large cash transactions electronically to FINTRAC if you have the technical capabilities (see Section 2.3).

There are several options for electronic reporting:

- FINTRAC's Report Preparation Software for low volume reporting;
- FINTRAC's secure Web site (Web form) for low volume and low frequency reporting;
- FINTRAC's secure Web site (Web form) with public key infrastructure (PKI) for low volume but high frequency reporting; and
- Batch file transfer for high volume and high frequency reporting.

All these options provide for secure encrypted transmission to ensure data confidentiality and integrity. Reporting via batch or through FINTRAC's secure Web site using PKI will require more advanced technical capability than explained in Section 2.3. For more information about which of these is more appropriate for you, please refer to the reporting area of FINTRAC's Web site (http://www.fintrac.gc.ca/reporting--declaration/1_e.asp).

### 3.2 How to Complete Electronic Reports

#### Reporting via FINTRAC's Report Preparation Software

FINTRAC's Report Preparation Software is a stand-alone software application for you to create, store, maintain and submit your electronic reports. More information about this is available from the Reporting section of FINTRAC's Web site (http://www.fintrac.gc.ca/reporting--declaration/1_e.asp), by selecting large cash transaction report type and a reporting frequency of less than five reports per week. The technical documentation, made up of a user guide and an administrator guide, explains how to use this software to submit reports. In addition, completion instructions for the fields of each report are built in to the application. You can also refer to Appendix 1 of this guideline for instructions regarding the content of fields in a large cash transaction report.

**Reporting via the Web**

FINTRAC's secure Web site contains large cash transaction reporting screens (i.e., Web form), with some completion instructions. Drop-down menus appear wherever a code or specific selection is required. In addition, details concerning formatting of a particular field may appear at the bottom of your screen.

See Section 4 for additional completion instructions. Also, Appendix 1 has details of what each field must contain for a large cash transaction report, and Appendix 2 explains how to navigate through the reporting screens.

**Reporting via Batch File Transfer**

If you send on average at least five reports per week to FINTRAC over a 12-week period, you can use the batch file reporting mechanism. To do so, you will require a PKI certificate and specialized software available from FINTRAC. Consult the specifications document called *Standard Batch Reporting Instructions and Specification* for more information about batch reporting, available from the publications area of FINTRAC's Web site (see technical documentation at http://www.fintrac.gc.ca/publications/pub_e.asp). You can also refer to Appendix 1 of this guideline for instructions regarding the content of fields in a large cash transaction report.

**3.3  Acknowledgement of Receipt of an Electronic Report**

FINTRAC will send you an acknowledgement message when your large cash transaction report has been received electronically. This will include the date and time your report was received and a FINTRAC-generated identification number. Please keep this information for your records.

For all reports submitted via the FINTRAC secure Web site, please ensure you wait for the FINTRAC acknowledgement message before closing any window after sending your report. This acknowledgement message can be printed from the browser window.

**3.4  Report Corrections**

If your large cash transaction report contains incomplete information, FINTRAC may notify you. The notification will indicate the date and time your report was received, a FINTRAC-generated identification number, along with information on the fields that must be completed or corrected.

After receiving FINTRAC's notification, you should provide the necessary information to FINTRAC within the reporting deadline. In other words, this information should be sent to FINTRAC within 15 calendar days after the transaction.

Your obligation to report will not be fulfilled until you send the **complete** report to FINTRAC.

## 4 INSTRUCTIONS FOR COMPLETING A LARGE CASH TRANSACTION REPORT

### 4.1 General Instructions

Instructions for each field of the *Large Cash Transaction Report* are contained in Appendix 1. Additional instructions in Appendix 2 relate to the reporting screens on FINTRAC's secure Web site.

If you report via batch or the FINTRAC Report Preparation Software, you need to refer to the appropriate technical documentation in addition to Appendix 1.

As explained in Section 2.3, if you do not have the technical capability to report electronically, refer to *Guideline 7 B: Submitting Large Cash Transaction Reports to FINTRAC by Paper* for more information.

Fields in reports are either mandatory, mandatory where applicable, or require "reasonable efforts" to complete, as follows:

- **Mandatory:** All fields of a report marked with an asterisk (*) **have to be completed.**
- **Mandatory where applicable:** The fields that have both an asterisk and "where applicable" next to them have to be completed if they are applicable to you or the transaction being reported.
- **Reasonable efforts:** For all other fields that do not have an asterisk, you have to make reasonable efforts to get the information. "Reasonable efforts" means that you tried to get the information requested on the report. If the information is available to you, you must provide it in the report. If the information was not available at the time of the transaction, and it is not contained in your files or records, the field may be left blank.

As explained in Section 2.1, a large cash transaction report can be about multiple transactions of less than $10,000 conducted within 24 consecutive hours of each other that add up to $10,000 or more. Because those individual transactions were under $10,000, the information for some mandatory fields in the report may not be available in your records or from the time of the transaction. In this case, "reasonable efforts" applies to those otherwise mandatory fields.

### 4.2 Instructions for Submitting a New Report

There are seven parts to the large cash transaction report, but some are only to be completed if applicable.

See Appendix 1 for instructions about each field in each part of the report. If you use FINTRAC's Web form, you should also refer to the instructions in Appendix 2 regarding the reporting screens. If you report via batch or the

FINTRAC Report Preparation Software, you should also refer to the appropriate technical documentation for specific instructions relating to that reporting mechanism.

## 4.3 Instructions for Submitting a Change to a Previously Submitted Report

If you have to submit a change to a previously submitted report, you must provide any required changes to FINTRAC within the reporting deadline for the report. In other words, this information should be sent to FINTRAC within 15 calendar days after the large cash transaction.

Situations where changes are required to a previously submitted report should be limited. This would include situations where information submitted was wrong and needs to be corrected or where required information was omitted when the report was filed. For example, if you submit a report without information in a "reasonable efforts" field and realize that the information was in fact available in your records, this information is required and must be submitted.

If you report via batch, you need to refer to the technical documentation called *Standard Batch Reporting Instructions and Specification* to find out how to submit corrections or replacements for previously submitted reports. If you report using FINTRAC's Report Preparation Software, refer to the information about "replace" in Chapter 5 of the technical documentation called *FINTRAC's Report Preparation Software User Guide*. Either of these documents can be accessed from the publications page of FINTRAC's Web site.

If you report using FINTRAC's secure Web site, read Section 4.4.

## 4.4 To Submit Changes Through FINTRAC's Secure Web Site

To make a change to a previously submitted large cash transaction report via FINTRAC's secure Web site, select this report from the drop-down menu of reports available from the reporting area (http://www.fintrac.gc.ca/reporting--declaration/1_e.asp). Indicate your reporting frequency and click on "Proceed with the report". You will then be presented with the reporting mechanisms available to you.

Select "FINTRAC's Web Form". If you have a PKI certificate, you will access the report you need to change using ViaSafe. Refer to the technical documentation called *PKI Reporting Guide* for more information about using ViaSafe to make a change to a report. This can be accessed from the publications page of FINTRAC's Web site.

If you do not have a PKI certificate, you can choose to send a simulated changed report (for training purposes) by selecting "Simulation" or send an actual change to a report by selecting "Click here to report". Before you get to the reporting screens, you will be asked if you are submitting a new report, or if you want to **update** or **replace** a previously submitted report. Each of these is explained below.

## Update

This is to either modify or delete information on a report that you submitted previously.

Once you have selected the update option, you need to provide the date, time and FINTRAC-generated identification number for the previously submitted report, based on the acknowledgement you received from FINTRAC. Then, complete only the fields of the report that you need to correct.

If your correction involves removing information that was contained in a field, and you want that field to be left blank, you will have to put dashes in that field. If the field is under five characters, put dashes in each character space. If the field is five or more characters, just enter five dashes.

If you need to add information to a field that was previously left blank or you need to change the information previously submitted, you have to provide the revised information in the applicable field.

If you omitted to include a transaction or a disposition in a previous report, follow the replace instructions.

## Replace

This is to identify an existing report that you want to replace with a new report.

Once you have selected the replace option, enter the date, time and FINTRAC-generated identification number for the previously submitted report that you want to replace, based on the acknowledgement you received from FINTRAC. Submit this information. You will then receive a new report with the same number as the original.

Next, you will have to re-enter all of the information from the original report and include any information that you want to add.

## 5  COMMENTS?

These guidelines will be reviewed on a periodic basis. If you have any comments or suggestions to help improve them, please send your comments to the mailing address provided below or by email to guidelines@fintrac.gc.ca.

## 6  HOW TO CONTACT FINTRAC

For further information on FINTRAC and its activities, and report submission, please go to FINTRAC's Web site (http://www.fintrac.gc.ca) or contact FINTRAC:

Financial Transactions and Reports Analysis Centre of Canada
234 Laurier Avenue West, 24th floor
Ottawa, Ontario
Canada K1P 1H7
Toll-free: 1-866-346-8722

**Appendix 1: Field by Field Instructions for Large Cash Transaction Report**

PART A: INFORMATION ABOUT WHERE THE TRANSACTION TOOK PLACE

**Field 1\* Reporting person or entity's identifier number**

**Field 2\* Reporting person or entity's full name**

**Fields 3\* to 6\* Reporting person or entity's full address**

**Fields 7\*, 8\* and 9 Contact name**

**Field 10\* Contact telephone number**

**Field 11\* Which one of the following types of reporting entities best describes you?**

PART B1: INFORMATION ABOUT TRANSACTION(S)

**Fields 1\* to 3\* When the transaction took place**

**Field 4 Date of posting**

**Field 5\* Amount of transaction**

**Field 6\* Currency**

**Field 7\* How was the transaction conducted?**

PART B2: INFORMATION ABOUT DISPOSITION(S)

**Field 8\* Disposition of funds**

**Field 9\* Amount of disposition**

**Field 10\* Currency**

**Fields 11\* and 12\* Other institution, entity or person name, number and account number (where applicable)**

PART C: ACCOUNT INFORMATION, IF THE TRANSACTION INVOLVED AN ACCOUNT

**Field 1\* Branch or transit number (if this Part is applicable)**

**Field 2\* Account number (if this Part is applicable)**

**Field 3\* Type of account (if this Part is applicable)**

**Field 4\* Type of currency (if this Part is applicable)**

**Field 5\* Full name of each account holder (if this Part is applicable)**

**PART D: INFORMATION ABOUT INDIVIDUAL CONDUCTING THE TRANSACTION THAT IS NOT A DEPOSIT INTO A BUSINESS ACCOUNT (IF APPLICABLE)**

**Fields 1\*, 2\* and 3 Individual's full name (if this Part is applicable)**

**Field 4\* Entity client number (where applicable and if this Part is applicable)**

**Fields 5\* to 9\* Individual's full address (if this Part is applicable)**

**Field 10 Country of residence**

**Field 11 Home telephone number**

**Field 12\* Individual's identifier (if this Part is applicable)**

**Field 13\* ID Number (if this Part is applicable)**

**Fields 14\* and 15\* Place of issue (if this Part is applicable)**

**Field 16\* Date of birth (if this Part is applicable)**

**Field 17\* Individual's occupation (if this Part is applicable)**

**Field 18 Individual's business telephone number**

**PART E: INFORMATION ABOUT INDIVIDUAL CONDUCTING THE TRANSACTION THAT IS A DEPOSIT INTO A BUSINESS ACCOUNT (OTHER THAN A QUICK DROP OR NIGHT DEPOSIT) (WHERE APPLICABLE)**

**Fields 1\*, 2\* and 3 Individual's full name (if this Part is applicable)**

**PART F: INFORMATION ABOUT THE BUSINESS, CORPORATION OR OTHER ENTITY ON WHOSE BEHALF TRANSACTION WAS CONDUCTED (WHERE APPLICABLE)**

**Field 1\* Corporation, trust or other entity name (if this Part is applicable)**

**Field 2\* Type of business (if this Part is applicable)**

**Fields 3\* to 7\* Full address of business, corporation or other entity (if this Part is applicable)**

**Field 8 Business telephone number**

**Fields 9\* to 11\* Incorporation information (where applicable if this Part is applicable)**

**Field 12 Individual(s) authorized with respect to the account (up to three)**

**PART G: INFORMATION ABOUT PERSON ON WHOSE BEHALF TRANSACTION WAS CONDUCTED (WHERE APPLICABLE)**

**Fields 1\*, 2\* and 3 Individual's full name (if this Part is applicable)**

**Fields 4\* to 8\* Individual's full address (if this Part is applicable)**

**Field 9 Home telephone number**

**Field 10 Office telephone number**

**Field 11 Date of birth**

**Field 12 Individual's identifier**

**Field 13 ID number**

**Field 14 Country of residence**

**Fields 15 and 16 Place of issue**

**Field 17 Individual's occupation**

**Field 18 Relationship of the individual named in Part D or Part E to the individual named above**

# GUIDELINE 7B: SUBMITTING LARGE CASH TRANSACTION REPORTS TO FINTRAC BY PAPER

## March 29, 2004

TABLE OF CONTENTS

1.   **General**

2.   **Large Cash Transaction Reporting Requirements**

    2.1   When Does a Large Cash Transaction Report Have to be Made?

    2.2   Cash Transactions in Foreign Currency

    2.3   Other Requirements Associated with Large Cash Transactions

    2.4   Means of Reporting to FINTRAC

3.   **Paper Reporting**

    3.1   How to Complete Paper Reports

    3.2   How to Send Paper Reports to FINTRAC

    3.3   Acknowledgement of Receipt of a Paper Report

4.   **Instructions for Completing a Large Cash Transaction Report**

5.   **Comments?**

6.   **How to Contact FINTRAC**

. . .

## 2   LARGE CASH TRANSACTION REPORTING REQUIREMENTS

Throughout this guideline, any references to dollar amounts (such as $10,000) refer to the amount in Canadian dollars or its equivalent in foreign currency.

Furthermore, all references to cash mean money in circulation in any country (bank notes or coins). In this context, cash does not include cheques, money orders or other similar negotiable instruments.

### 2.1 When Does a Large Cash Transaction Report Have to be Made?

If you are a reporting person or entity (see Section 1), you have to send a large cash transaction report to FINTRAC in the following situations:

*   You receive an amount of $10,000 or more in cash in the course of a single
*   transaction; or
*   You receive two or more cash amounts of less than $10,000 that total $10,000 or more. In this case, if you are an individual, you have to make a large cash transaction report if you know the transactions were made within

24 consecutive hours of each other by or on behalf of the same individual or entity. If you are an entity, you have to make a large cash transaction report if your employee or senior officer knows the transactions were made within 24 consecutive hours of each other by or on behalf of the same individual or entity.

- You have to send large cash transaction reports to FINTRAC within 15 calendar days after the transaction.

If you are a reporting person and an employee of a reporting person or entity, your employer is responsible for meeting the large cash transaction reporting requirement associated to any of your activities as an employee.

Similarly, if you are a reporting person or entity and you are an agent of or you are authorized to act on behalf of a reporting person or entity, it is that reporting person or entity's responsibility to meet the large cash transaction reporting requirement associated to any of your activities on their behalf. However, if you are a life insurance broker or independent agent, you are responsible for reporting to FINTRAC (unless you are an employee as explained above).

You do **not** have to make a large cash transaction report to FINTRAC if the cash is received from a financial entity. In this context, a financial entity means a bank, credit union, caisse populaire, a trust and loan company or an agent of the Crown that accepts deposit liabilities.

If you are a reporting person or entity other than a casino, you do **not** have to make a large cash transaction report to FINTRAC if the cash is received from a public body. In this context, a public body means any of the following or their agent:

- a provincial or federal department or Crown agency;
- an incorporated municipal body (including an incorporated city, town, village, metropolitan authority, district, county, etc.);
- a hospital authority. A hospital authority means an organization that operates a public hospital and that is designated to be a hospital authority for GST/HST purposes. For more information on the designation of hospital authorities, refer to GST/HST Memoranda Series, Chapter 25.2, *Designation of Hospital Authorities* available from the Canada Revenue Agency's Web site. At the time of publishing of this guideline, the document was available at the following link: http://www.ccra-adrc.gc.ca/E/pub/gm/25-2/README.html

Financial entities may choose, in certain specific circumstances, an alternative to making large cash transaction reports for certain clients that are corporations. If you are a financial entity, see *Guideline 9: Submitting Alternative to Large Cash Transaction Reports to FINTRAC* for more information about this.

## 2.2 Cash Transactions in Foreign Currency

If a cash transaction is in foreign currency, you will need to check whether it is the equivalent of $10,000 Canadian dollars or more to determine whether or not it is reportable as a large cash transaction. For this purpose only, use the last noon rate provided by the Bank of Canada available at the time of the transaction. This calculation is not based on the actual exchange rate used to process the transaction — this is only to check whether the $10,000 threshold is met for the transaction to be reportable as a large cash transaction.

For example, for a cash transaction in foreign currency that happened at 9:00 am on Tuesday following a holiday Monday, you would use the Bank of Canada noon rate from the previous Friday to determine whether it is a large cash transaction. You can find the noon rate applicable at the time of a transaction on the Bank of Canada Web site at http://www.bankofcanada.ca/en/exchange.htm. If there is no Bank of Canada noon rate published for the currency of the transaction, use the actual exchange rate applied when you processed the transaction to determine whether it is reportable.

Once you have determined that a cash transaction in foreign currency is in fact reportable based on the Bank of Canada noon rate, you will have to send a large cash transaction report to FINTRAC. On this report, you will indicate any amounts involved in the transaction in foreign currency, and indicate the appropriate currency code. The large cash transaction report does not require information about any exchange rate applicable to the transaction. The exchange rate is only relevant to determine whether or not the transaction is a large cash transaction.

## 2.3  Other Requirements Associated with Large Cash Transactions

In addition to the reporting requirements explained in this guideline, consider the following relating to a large cash transaction:

### Record keeping and client identification

Large cash transactions have associated record keeping and client identification requirements. These are explained in *Guideline 6: Record Keeping and Client Identification.*

### Electronic funds transfer report

If a large cash transaction results in an electronic funds transfer, you may have to make an electronic funds transfer report to FINTRAC about the same transaction in addition to the large cash transaction report.

For more information about making electronic funds transfer reports, consult *Guideline 8: Submitting Electronic Funds Transfer Reports to FINTRAC.*

### Suspicious transaction report

If anything about a large cash transaction gives you reasonable grounds to suspect that it could be related to a money laundering or a terrorist activity financing offence, you have to make a suspicious transaction report to FINTRAC. This would be in addition to making the large cash transaction report about the same transaction as required.

The suspicious transaction report has very similar fields to those of a large cash transaction report. There are some differences, such as a field in the suspicious transaction report for you to explain your suspicion about the transaction. There is also a field in that report for you to describe what action, if any, was taken by you as a result of the suspicious transaction. This would include stating that you have made a large cash transaction report for the same transaction (if that is the case).

For more information about suspicious transaction reports, consult the following:

- *Guideline 1: Backgrounder*
- *Guideline 2: Suspicious Transactions*
- *Guideline 3: Submitting Suspicious Transaction Reports to FINTRAC*

**Transactions related to terrorist property**

If you know that any proposed transaction is related to property owned or controlled by or on behalf of a terrorist or a terrorist group, you cannot complete the transaction. This is because terrorist property must be frozen under the *United Nations Suppression of Terrorism Regulations* as well as the *Criminal Code*.

For more information about this and to find out what your obligations are regarding any terrorist property in your control or possession, consult the following:

- *Guideline 1: Backgrounder*
- *Guideline 5: Submitting Terrorist Property Reports to FINTRAC*

**2.4  Means of Reporting to FINTRAC**

**Electronic Reporting**

As a reporting person or entity, you will have to submit all large cash transaction reports to FINTRAC **electronically** if you have the technical capabilities to do so. The minimum technical capabilities are as follows:

- A personal computer with the following characteristics:
  - 32 MB memory
  - 640 x 480 VGA video display (800 x 600 or higher is preferable)
  - any operating system running the following Web browsers: Internet Explorer version 5.x (Windows® 98/Me/NT/2000); and
- An Internet connection

See *Guideline 7A: Submitting Large Cash Transactions to FINTRAC Electronically* for more information.

**Paper Reporting**

If you do not have the technical capabilities to send reports electronically, you must submit reports on paper. See Section 4 for more information on submitting paper large cash transaction reports to FINTRAC.

## 3  PAPER REPORTING

### 3.1  How to Complete Paper Reports

If you do **not** have the technical capability (see Section 2.3), you will have to submit paper large cash transaction reports to FINTRAC. In this case, forms will be available for paper filing as follows:

- A file is accessible from the reporting forms area of the publications section of FINTRAC's Web site (http://www.fintrac.gc.ca/publications/pub_e.asp) to be printed at your local library or any other place with Internet access.
- Call 1-866-346-8722 for a copy to be faxed or mailed to you.

See Section 4 for completion instructions. It includes details of what each field must contain for a large cash transaction report.

### 3.2  How to Send Paper Reports to FINTRAC

There are two ways to send a paper report to FINTRAC:

- Fax: 1-866-226-2346; or
- Mail to the following address:

  Financial Transactions and Reports Analysis Centre of Canada
  Section A
  234 Laurier Avenue West, 24th floor
  Ottawa, ON
  Canada K1P 1H7

### 3.3  Acknowledgement of Receipt of a Paper Report

FINTRAC will not send you any acknowledgement when your paper large cash transaction report has been received.

## 4  INSTRUCTIONS FOR COMPLETING A LARGE CASH TRANSACTION REPORT

The fields in this section refer to those on the paper report form. As explained in Section 2.3, completing a paper report is only permitted if you do not have the capability to report electronically.

Fields in reports are either mandatory, mandatory where applicable, or require "reasonable efforts" to complete, as follows:

- **Mandatory:** All fields of a report marked with an asterisk (*) **have to be completed.**

- **Mandatory where applicable:** The fields that have both an asterisk and "where applicable" next to them have to be completed if they are applicable to you or the transaction being reported.
- **Reasonable efforts:** For all other fields that do not have an asterisk, you have to make reasonable efforts to get the information. "Reasonable efforts" means that you tried to get the information requested on the report. If the information is available to you, you must provide it in the report. If the information was not available at the time of the transaction, and it is not contained in your files or records, the field may be left blank.

As explained in Section 2.1, a large cash transaction report can be about multiple transactions of less than $10,000 conducted within 24 consecutive hours of each other that add up to $10,000 or more. Because those individual transactions were under $10,000, the information for some mandatory fields in the report may not be available in your records or from the time of the transaction. In this case, "reasonable efforts" applies to those otherwise mandatory fields.

There are seven parts to the large cash transaction report, but some are only to be completed if applicable. To report a large cash transaction follow the following four steps:

- Step 1 — Complete Part A to provide information about you as the reporting entity or reporting person.
- Step 2 — Complete Part B1 to provide details about the transaction. If you have to include more than one transaction in your report (for cash transactions of less than $10,000 made within 24 consecutive hours of each other that total $10,000 or more), repeat steps 2, 3 and 4 for each one.

If the transaction was a night deposit or a quick drop to a business account, make sure to indicate this in field B3.

- Step 3 — Complete Part B2 to provide details about the transaction's disposition. If the transaction's disposition was related to an account, also complete Part C. If the transaction's disposition was on behalf of a corporation or other entity (other than an employee depositing cash into his or her employer's account), also complete Part F. If the transaction's disposition was on behalf of an individual (other than an employee depositing cash into his or her employer's account), complete Part G.

If there was more than one disposition for the transaction, repeat this step for each disposition.

- Step 4 — Complete Part D or E to provide information about the individual conducting the transaction, depending on whether or not the transaction's disposition was a deposit to a business account. If the transaction had no other dispositions than deposits to a business account, complete Part E. If the transaction involved a disposition that was **not** a deposit to a business account, complete Part D. However, if the transaction was a night deposit or a quick drop to a business account, neither Part D nor Part E is required.

The rest of this section will cover each part of the large cash transaction report form.

PART A: INFORMATION ABOUT WHERE THE TRANSACTION TOOK PLACE

**Field 1\* Reporting person or entity's identifier number**

**Field 2\* Reporting person or entity's full name**

**Fields 3\* to 6\* Reporting person or entity's full address**

**Fields 7\*, 8\* and 9 Contact name**

**Field 10\* Contact telephone number**

**Field 11\* Which one of the following types of reporting entities best describes you?**

PART B1: INFORMATION ABOUT THE TRANSACTION(S)

**Fields 1\* to 3\* When the transaction took place**

**Field 4 Date of posting**

**Field 5\* Amount of transaction**

**Field 6\* Currency**

**Field 7\* How was the transaction conducted?**

PART B2: INFORMATION ABOUT THE TRANSACTION DISPOSITION(S)

**Field 8\* Disposition of funds**

**Field 9\* Amount of disposition**

**Field 10\* Currency**

**Fields 11\* and 12\* Other institution, entity or person name, number and account number (where applicable)**

PART C: ACCOUNT INFORMATION, IF THE TRANSACTION INVOLVED AN ACCOUNT

**Field 1\* Branch or transit number (if this Part is applicable)**

**Field 2\* Account number (if this Part is applicable)**

**Field 3\* Type of account (if this Part is applicable)**

**Field 4\* Type of currency (if this Part is applicable)**

**Field 5\* Full name of each account holder (if this Part is applicable)**

**PART D: INFORMATION ABOUT THE INDIVIDUAL CONDUCTING THE TRANSACTION IF IT IS NOT A DEPOSIT INTO A BUSINESS ACCOUNT (WHERE APPLICABLE)**

Fields 1*, 2* and 3 Individual's full name (if this Part is applicable)

Field 4* Entity client number (where applicable and if this Part is applicable)

Fields 5* to 9* Individual's full address (if this Part is applicable)

Field 10 Country of residence

Field 11 Home telephone number

Field 12* Individual's identifier (if this Part is applicable)

Field 13* ID Number (if this Part is applicable)

Fields 14* and 15* Place of issue (if this Part is applicable)

Field 16* Date of birth (if this Part is applicable)

Field 17* Individual's occupation (if this Part is applicable)

Field 18 Individual's business telephone number

**PART E: INFORMATION ABOUT THE INDIVIDUAL CONDUCTING THE TRANSACTION IF IT IS A DEPOSIT INTO A BUSINESS ACCOUNT (OTHER THAN A QUICK DROP OR NIGHT DEPOSIT) (WHERE APPLICABLE)**

Fields 1*, 2* and 3 Individual's full name (if this Part is applicable)

**PART F: INFORMATION ABOUT THE ENTITY ON WHOSE BEHALF TRANSACTION WAS CONDUCTED (WHERE APPLICABLE)**

Field 1* Corporation, trust or other entity name (if this Part is applicable)

Field 2* Type of business (if this Part is applicable)

Fields 3* to 7* Full address of business, corporation or other entity (if this Part is applicable)

Field 8 Business telephone number

Fields 9* to 11* Incorporation information (if this Part is applicable)

Field 12 Individual(s) authorized with respect to the account (up to three)

**PART G: INFORMATION ABOUT THE INDIVIDUAL ON WHOSE BEHALF TRANSACTION WAS CONDUCTED (WHERE APPLICABLE)**

Fields 1*, 2* and 3 Individual's full name (if this Part is applicable)

**Fields 4\* to 8\* Individual's full address (if this Part is applicable)**

**Field 9 Home telephone number**

**Field 10 Office telephone number**

**Field 11 Date of birth**

**Field 12 Individual's identifier**

**Field 13 ID number**

**Field 14 Country of residence**

**Fields 15 and 16 Place of issue**

**Field 17 Individual's occupation**

**Field 18 Relationship of the individual named in Part D or Part E to the individual named above**

## 5   COMMENTS?

These guidelines will be reviewed on a periodic basis. If you have any comments or suggestions to help improve them, please send your comments to the mailing address provided below or by email to guidelines@fintrac.gc.ca.

## 6   HOW TO CONTACT FINTRAC

For further information on FINTRAC and its activities, and report submission, please go to FINTRAC's Web site (http://www.fintrac.gc.ca) or contact FINTRAC:
Financial Transactions and Reports Analysis Centre of Canada
234 Laurier Avenue West, 24th floor
Ottawa, Ontario
Canada K1P 1H7
Toll-free: 1-866-346-8722

# GUIDELINE 8: SUBMITTING ELECTRONIC FUNDS TRANSFER REPORTS TO FINTRAC

### February 3, 2003

TABLE OF CONTENTS

1. **General**

2. **Electronic Funds Transfer Reporting Requirements**

   2.1 When Do You Have to Report Electronic Funds Transfers?

   2.2 SWIFT Electronic Funds Transfers

   2.3 All Electronic Funds Transfers

   2.4 Financial Entities

   2.5 Money Services Businesses or Foreign Exchange Dealers

   2.6 Electronic Funds Transfers in Foreign Currency

   2.7 Other Requirements Associated with Electronic Funds Transfers

   2.8 Reporting Timeframes for Electronic Funds Transfer Reports

   2.9 Means of Reporting Electronic Funds Transfers to FINTRAC

3. **Electronic Reporting**

   3.1 Options for Electronic Reporting

   3.2 How to Complete Electronic Reports

   3.3 Acknowledgement of Receipt of an Electronic Report

   3.4 Report Corrections

4. **Paper Reporting**

   4.1 How to Complete Paper Reports

   4.2 How to Send Paper Reports to FINTRAC

   4.3 Acknowledgement of Receipt of a Paper Report

5. **Contents of an Electronic Funds Transfer Report**

6. **Comments?**

7. **How to Contact FINTRAC**

## Appendix 1 — Contents of Electronic Funds Transfer Reports

Appendix 1A — Contents of an Outgoing SWIFT Messages Report

Appendix 1B — Contents of an Incoming SWIFT Messages Report

Appendix 1C — Contents of an Outgoing International non-SWIFT Electronic Funds Transfer Report (from March 31, 2003 to November 30, 2003)

Appendix 1D — Contents of an Incoming International non-SWIFT Electronic Funds Transfer Report (effective March 31, 2003)

Appendix 1E — Contents of an Outgoing International non-SWIFT Electronic Funds Transfer Report (effective November 30, 2003)

## Appendix 2 — Instructions for Completing the *International Electronic Funds Transfer Report* (Non-SWIFT)

. . .

## 2   ELECTRONIC FUNDS TRANSFER REPORTING REQUIREMENTS

Throughout this guideline, any references to dollar amounts (such as $10,000) refer to the amount in Canadian dollars or its equivalent in foreign currency.

### 2.1  When Do You Have to Report Electronic Funds Transfers?

If you are a financial entity, a money services business or a foreign exchange dealer, you will have to report certain EFTs to FINTRAC. These reporting requirements are being phased-in over the course of 2002 and 2003.

When you have to start reporting EFTs depends on whether or not your EFT transmissions are SWIFT messages. Reportable SWIFT EFTs are explained in Section 2.2 (below). The other types of reportable EFTs are explained in Section 2.3. Reporting timeframes are explained in Section 2.8.

### 2.2  SWIFT Electronic Funds Transfers

The first reporting requirement for EFTs came into effect June 12, 2002. This is only applicable to you if you are a **financial entity** and you send EFTs by transmission of a **SWIFT MT 100** or **MT 103 message**, as a SWIFT member, through the SWIFT network. SWIFT means the Society for Worldwide Interbank Financial Telecommunication. It is a co-operative owned by the international banking community that operates a global data processing system for the transmission of financial messages.

If you are a financial entity you have to report the following transactions to FINTRAC as of June 12, 2002:

- You send an outgoing SWIFT MT 100 or MT 103 message for $10,000 or more outside Canada at the request of a client in the following manner:
  - in a single transaction; or

- in two or more transfers of less than $10,000 (that total $10,000 or more) if your employee or senior officer knows they were made within 24 consecutive hours of each other by or on behalf of the same individual or entity.
- You receive an incoming SWIFT MT 100 or MT 103 message for $10,000 or more sent from outside Canada at the request of a client in the following manner:
  - in a single transaction; or
  - in two or more transfers of less than $10,000 (that total $10,000 or more) if your employee or senior officer knows they were made within 24 consecutive hours of each other by or on behalf of the same individual or entity.

These reports can only be made electronically using the batch file reporting mechanism, as explained in Section 3 below.

You do not have to make an EFT report if you send a transfer to an individual or an entity in Canada, even if the final recipient is outside Canada. Similarly, you do not have to make an EFT report if you receive a transfer from an individual or an entity in Canada, even if the original sender was outside Canada.

Effective March 31, 2003, as a financial entity, your reporting obligations regarding EFTs will expand to include sending or receiving EFTs by any means, as explained below.

## 2.3  All Electronic Funds Transfers

The other reporting requirement for EFTs comes into effect March 31, 2003 and applies to you if you are a financial entity, a money services business or a foreign exchange dealer.

This reporting covers EFTs that are the transmission of instructions for a transfer of funds through any electronic, magnetic or optical device, telephone instrument or computer. This includes SWIFT MT 100 or MT 103 messages described above.

Effective March 31, 2003, if you are a financial entity, a money services business or a foreign exchange dealer, you have to send a report to FINTRAC for the following transactions:

- You send outgoing EFTs. These are instructions sent electronically for the transfer of $10,000 or more outside Canada at the request of a client in the following manner:
  - in a single transaction;
  - in two or more transfers of less than $10,000 (that total $10,000 or more) in the following situations:
    - if you are an entity, your employee or senior officer knows the transfers were made within 24 consecutive hours of each other by or on behalf of the same individual or entity; or

- • if you are an individual, you know the transfers were made within 24 consecutive hours of each other by or on behalf of the same individual or entity.
- • You receive incoming EFTs. These are instructions sent electronically for transfer of $10,000 or more from outside Canada at the request of a client in the following manner:
  - • in a single transaction;
  - • in two or more transfers of less than $10,000 (that total $10,000 or more) in the following situations:
    - • if you are an entity, your employee or senior officer knows the transfers were made within 24 consecutive hours of each other by or on behalf of the same individual or entity; or
    - • if you are an individual, you know the transfers were made within 24 consecutive hours of each other by or on behalf of the same individual or entity.

The following provides additional information, according to your sector of activity, about when an EFT report has to be made as of March 31, 2003.

## 2.4 Financial Entities

If you are a financial entity, you do not have to make an EFT report if you receive instructions for a transfer from an individual or an entity in Canada, even if the original sender was outside Canada.

If a client requests a transfer of funds and, instead of sending the EFT yourself, you order another financial entity to send it, you have to make the related EFT report to FINTRAC if you do not provide that other financial entity with the client's name and address. In cases where you send the EFT yourself, you do not have to make an EFT report if you send the instructions for transfer of funds to an individual or an entity in Canada, even if the final recipient is outside Canada.

You do not have to make an EFT report for a transfer of funds between two accounts that are both held within your entity. For example, you do not have to report an EFT transaction between an account in one of your branches inside Canada to another account in one of your branches outside Canada, but you would have to report if the EFT transaction was to an account with a subsidiary outside Canada.

## 2.5 Money Services Businesses or Foreign Exchange Dealers

If you are a money services business or a foreign exchange dealer, you do not have to make an EFT report if you receive instructions for a transfer of funds from an individual or an entity in Canada, even if the original sender was outside Canada.

If a client requests a transfer of funds and, instead of sending the EFT yourself, you order a financial entity to send it, you would have to make the related EFT report to FINTRAC if you do not provide the financial entity with the client's name and address. In cases where you send the EFT yourself, you do not have to make an EFT report if you send the instructions for transfer of funds to an individual or an entity in Canada, even if the final recipient is outside Canada. For example, if you order a financial entity to send an EFT at the request of the client, and you provide the name and address of the client, you do not have to make a report to FINTRAC.

## 2.6 Electronic Funds Transfers in Foreign Currency

If you send an EFT in a foreign currency, you will need to check whether it is the equivalent of 10,000 Canadian dollars or more to determine whether or not it is reportable to FINTRAC. For this purpose only, use the last noon rate provided by the Bank of Canada available at the time of the transaction, instead of the actual exchange rate used to process the transaction. This calculation is only to check whether the $10,000 threshold is met for the transaction to be reportable as an EFT transaction.

For example, for an EFT that happened at 9:00 am on Tuesday following a holiday Monday, you would use the Bank of Canada noon rate from the previous working day (in this case, Friday) to determine whether the transaction is reportable. You can find the noon rate on the Bank of Canada Web site at http://www.bankofcanada.ca/en/exchange.htm.

If there is no Bank of Canada noon rate published for the currency of the transaction, use the actual exchange rate applied when you processed the transaction to determine whether it is reportable.

Once you have determined that an EFT in a foreign currency is reportable based on the Bank of Canada noon rate, you will have to send an EFT report to FINTRAC. On the EFT report in Part A, enter the amount of the transaction in the foreign currency. If you converted this amount to or from Canadian dollars when you processed the transaction (other than using the Bank of Canada noon rate to determine whether or not it was reportable), enter the actual exchange rate you used to process the EFT in Part A of the report.

## 2.7 Other Requirements Associated with Electronic Funds Transfers

In addition to the reporting requirements explained in this guideline, consider the following relating to an EFT transaction:

### Record keeping and client identification

EFTs have associated record keeping and client identification requirements. These are explained in *Guideline 6: Record Keeping and Client Identification.*

### Large cash transaction report

If an EFT transaction is initiated in cash (in the amount of $10,000 or more), you may have to make a large cash transaction report to FINTRAC in addition to making the EFT report about the transaction as required.

For more information about making large cash transaction reports, consult *Guideline 7: Submitting Large Cash Transaction Reports to FINTRAC.*

## Suspicious transaction report

If anything about an EFT transaction gives you reasonable grounds to suspect that it could be related to a money laundering or a terrorist activity financing offence, you have to make a suspicious transaction report to FINTRAC about the same transaction. This would be in addition to making the EFT report about the transaction as required.

The suspicious transaction report has many fields that are different from those of an EFT report. For example, there is a field in the suspicious transaction report for you to explain your suspicion about the transaction. There is also a field in that report for you to describe what action, if any, was taken by you, as a result of the suspicious transaction. This would include stating that you have made an EFT report for the same transaction (if that is the case). For more information about making suspicious transaction reports, consult the following guidelines:

- *Guideline 1: Backgrounder*
- *Guideline 2: Suspicious Transactions*
- *Guideline 3: Submitting Suspicious Transaction Reports to FINTRAC*

## Transactions related to terrorist property

If you know that any proposed transaction is related to property owned or controlled by or on behalf of a terrorist or a terrorist group, you should not complete the transaction. This is because terrorist property must be frozen under the *United Nations Suppression of Terrorism Regulations* as well as the *Criminal Code.*

For more information about this and to find out what your obligations are regarding any terrorist property in your control or possession, consult the following guidelines:

- *Guideline 1: Backgrounder*
- *Guideline 5: Submitting Terrorist Property Reports to FINTRAC*

## 2.8 Reporting Timeframes for Electronic Funds Transfer Reports

You have to send EFT reports to FINTRAC no later than five working days after the day of the transfer.

## 2.9 Means of Reporting Electronic Funds Transfers to FINTRAC

### Electronic reporting

As a reporting person or entity, you will have to submit all EFT reports to FINTRAC **electronically** if you have the technical capabilities to do so. The minimum technical capabilities are as follows:

- A personal computer with the following characteristics:
  - 32 MB memory
  - 640 x 480 VGA video display (800 x 600 or higher is preferable)
  - any operating system running the following Web browsers: Internet Explorer version 5.x (Windows® 98/Me/NT/2000); and
- An Internet connection

See Section 3 (below) for more information on submitting reports to FINTRAC electronically.

## Paper reporting

If you do not have the technical capabilities to send reports electronically, you must submit reports on paper. See Section 4 (below) for more information on submitting paper EFT reports to FINTRAC.

SWIFT EFT reports (as described in Section 2.2 above) cannot be made on paper. They can only be made electronically, using the batch file reporting mechanism, as explained in Section 3 below.

## 3   ELECTRONIC REPORTING

### 3.1  Options for Electronic Reporting

As a reporting person or entity, you have to report EFTs electronically to FINTRAC if you have the technical capabilities (see Section 2.9 above).

### SWIFT EFT Reporting

SWIFT EFT reports (as described in Section 2.2 above) can only be submitted electronically. These have to be reported using the batch file reporting mechanism. To do so, you need a public key infrastructure (PKI) certificate and specialized software available from FINTRAC. This specialized software can be installed on a workstation or a network server with the necessary operating system and browser characteristics. For more information about batch reporting for SWIFT EFTs, consult the specifications document *SWIFT format EFT Transactions – Batch Reporting Instructions and Specification*, available from the publications area of FINTRAC's Web site (see technical documentation at http://www.fintrac.gc.ca/publications/pub_e.asp).

### Other EFT Reporting

Other "non-SWIFT" EFTs (i.e., those that you do not transmit as a SWIFT member through the SWIFT network) will have to be reported using one of the following:

- FINTRAC's secure Web site for low volume reporting; or
- Batch file transfer for high volume and high frequency reporting.

For low volume reporting, you have to use a stand-alone software application that FINTRAC is developing for you to capture, store, maintain and submit your electronic reports. More information about FINTRAC's Report Preparation Software (FRPS) is available in the "What's New?" section of FINTRAC's Web site (http://www.fintrac.gc.ca/new-neuf/1_e.asp). Only "non-SWIFT" EFT reports can be completed using FRPS, and these cannot be sent to FINTRAC until March 31, 2003.

For the batch file reporting mechanism, you need a PKI certificate and specialized software available from FINTRAC. For more information about batch reporting for non-SWIFT EFTs, consult the specifications document *Standard Batch Reporting Instructions and Specification*, available from the publications area of FINTRAC's Web site (see technical documentation at http://www.fintrac.gc.ca/publications/pub_e.asp).

**More information about electronic reporting**

All the options described above for EFT reporting provide for secure encrypted transmission to ensure data confidentiality and integrity. Reporting via batch using PKI will require more advanced technical capability than explained in Section 2.9 (above).

For more information about reporting, including how to get a PKI certificate and the specialized software required, refer to the reporting area of FINTRAC's Web site (http://www.fintrac.gc.ca/reporting--declaration/1_e.asp). Select the type of report and reporting frequency to get the information applicable to your situation.

**3.2 How to Complete Electronic Reports**

See Section 5 (below) and Appendix 1 for details of what each field must contain for each type of EFT report.

**Reporting via Batch File Transfer**

As explained in Section 3.1 (above), additional instructions are provided in separate publications for reports to FINTRAC via batch file transfer.

**3.3 Acknowledgement of Receipt of an Electronic Report**

FINTRAC will send you an acknowledgement message when your EFT report has been received electronically. This will include the date and time your report was received and a FINTRAC-generated identification number. Please keep this information for your records.

If you send your reports by batch, you will receive two acknowledgements. The first will confirm that your batch has been received by FINTRAC. The second will confirm that it has been processed.

## 3.4 Report Corrections

If your EFT report contains incomplete information, FINTRAC may notify you. The notification will indicate the date and time your report was received, the FINTRAC-generated identification number, along with information on the fields that must be completed.

After receiving FINTRAC's notification, you should provide the necessary information to FINTRAC within the five-working-day reporting deadline. In other words, this information should be sent to FINTRAC within five working days of the transaction. Your obligation to report will not be fulfilled until you send the **complete** report to FINTRAC.

## 4  PAPER REPORTING

### 4.1 How to Complete Paper Reports

If you do **not** have the technical capability to submit reports electronically (see Section 2.9 above), you will have to submit paper EFT reports to FINTRAC. In this case, forms will be available for paper filing as follows:

- A file will be accessible from the publications area of FINTRAC's Web site (http://www.fintrac.gc.ca/publications/pub_e.asp) to be printed at your local library or any other place with Internet access.
- Call 1-866-346-8722 for a copy to be faxed or mailed to you.

See Section 5 (below) and Appendix 1 for details of what each field must contain for each type of EFT report.

If you have to submit SWIFT EFT reports, these cannot be made on paper. They can only be made electronically, using the batch file reporting mechanism, as explained in Section 3 above.

### 4.2  How to Send Paper Reports to FINTRAC

There are two ways to send a paper report to FINTRAC:

- Fax: 1-866-226-2346; or
- Mail to the following address:

  Financial Transactions and Reports Analysis Centre of Canada
  Section A
  234 Laurier Avenue West, 24th floor
  Ottawa, ON
  Canada K1P 1H7

### 4.3  Acknowledgement of Receipt of a Paper Report

FINTRAC will not send you any acknowledgement when your paper EFT report has been received.

## 5    CONTENTS OF AN ELECTRONIC FUNDS TRANSFER REPORT

The contents of an EFT report depend on whether the report is about a SWIFT message (i.e., a SWIFT MT 100 or MT 103 message) or a non-SWIFT EFT and whether it is an outgoing or incoming transfer. There are four different types of EFT reports as follows:

- Outgoing SWIFT Messages Report    (effective June 12, 2002)
- Incoming SWIFT Messages Report    (effective June 12, 2002)
- Outgoing non-SWIFT EFT Report     (effective March 31, 2003)
- Incoming non-SWIFT EFT Report     (effective March 31, 2003)

The fields for each type of report are listed in Appendix 1. Fields are either mandatory, mandatory where applicable, or require reasonable efforts to complete, as follows:

- **Mandatory:** All fields of a report marked with an asterisk (*) **have to be completed.**
- **Mandatory where applicable:** The fields that have both an asterisk and "where applicable" next to them have to be completed if they are applicable to you or the transaction being reported.
- **Reasonable efforts:** For all other fields that do not have an asterisk, you have to make reasonable efforts to get the information. "Reasonable efforts" means that you tried to get the information requested on the report. If the information is available to you, you must provide it in the report. If the information was not available at the time of the transaction, and it is not contained in your files or records, the field may be left blank.

As explained in Section 2.2 (above), reporting SWIFT messages only applies to financial entities.

The outgoing and incoming non-SWIFT EFT reports will have the same mandatory, mandatory where applicable and reasonable efforts fields in effect from March 31, 2003 until November 30, 2003. These are listed in Appendix 1C and 1D, and further explained in Appendix 2. As of November 30, 2003, some of the reasonable efforts fields on the outgoing non-SWIFT EFT report will become mandatory. The revised fields are reflected in Appendix 1E.

### APPENDIX 1 — CONTENTS OF ELECTRONIC FUNDS TRANSFER REPORTS

**Appendix 1A:**
Contents of an Outgoing SWIFT Messages Report
(Effective June 12, 2002)

**Appendix 1B:**
Contents of an Incoming SWIFT Messages Report
(Effective June 12, 2002)

**Appendix 1C:**
Contents of an Outgoing International non-SWIFT Electronic Funds Transfer Report
(Effective from March 31, 2003 to November 30, 2003)

**Appendix 1D:**
Contents of an Incoming International non-SWIFT Electronic Funds Transfer Report
(Effective March 31, 2003)

**Appendix 1E:**
Contents of an Outgoing International non-SWIFT Electronic Funds Transfer Report
(Effective November 30, 2003).

# GUIDELINE 9: SUBMITTING ALTERNATIVE TO LARGE CASH TRANSACTION REPORTS TO FINTRAC

## February 2004

TABLE OF CONTENTS

1.   General

2.   Can You Choose the Alternative to Large Cash Transaction Reports?

    2.1   Which Clients Can You Consider?

    2.2   How to Choose the Alternative to Large Cash Transaction Reports

3.   Report to FINTRAC About the Business Client

    3.1   If You Use Batch Transmission Software

    3.2   If You Do Not Use Batch Transmission Software

    3.3   Report Certain Changes About the Business Client

    3.4   Annual Verification

4.   List to be maintained

5.   Comments?

6.   How to Contact FINTRAC

Appendix 1 — Financial Entity Alternative To Large Cash Transaction Reports — Types of Businesses for Clients that are Corporations

    Appendix 1A — NAICS Sector Code 22 Utilities

    Appendix 1B — NAICS Sector Codes 44-45 Retail Trade

    Appendix 1C — NAICS Subsector Code 481 Air Transportation

    Appendix 1D — NAICS Subsector Code 482 Rail Transportation

    Appendix 1E — NAICS Subsector Code 485 Transit and Ground Passenger Transportation

    Appendix 1F — NAICS Industry Code 51322 Cable and Other Program Distribution

    Appendix 1G — NAICS Industry Code 51331 Wired Telecommunications Carriers

    Appendix 1H — Colleges and Universities (NAICS Industry Codes 61121 and 61131)

**Appendix 2 — Contents of the *Financial Entity Business Client Report***

**Appendix 3 — Can Your Client be Considered for the Alternative to Large Cash Transaction Reports?**

**Appendix 4 — Examples of How to Apply the Conditions in Considering the Alternative to Large Cash Transaction Reports**

. . .

## 2 CAN YOU CHOOSE THE ALTERNATIVE TO LARGE CASH TRANSACTION REPORTS?

### 2.1 Which Clients Can You Consider?

If you are a financial entity you can choose the alternative to large cash transaction reports regarding a client's **business** transactions that would otherwise require such a report if all of the following conditions are met:

- your client is a **corporation** that carries on business within those types of businesses that can be considered for purposes of the alternative to large cash transaction reports, as described in Appendix 1. You cannot choose the alternative to large cash transaction reports for any client carrying on a pawnbroking business, or for any client whose principal business is the sale of vehicles, vessels, farm machinery, aircraft, mobile homes, jewellery, precious gems or metals, antiquities or art. There are some other exclusions, and these are noted in Appendix 1;
- your client has had an account with you for at least 24 months **or**, immediately before opening an account with you, your client has had an account with another financial entity for at least 24 months. This means that a client who had an account for 12 months with you and 12 months with another financial entity would not meet this condition;
- you have records to show that your client deposited $10,000 or more in cash into that account at least twice weekly, on average, for the preceding 12 months. This means your client has to have made at least 104 such deposits over the preceding 12 months;
- your client's cash deposits are consistent with the usual practice of this business; and
- you have taken reasonable measures to determine the source of the cash for those deposits.

Once you have determined that all of the conditions outlined above are met for any one of the corporation's business accounts, you can choose the alternative to large cash transaction reports for that business. This would apply to all the accounts of that business.

If your client is a corporation with more than one business for income tax purposes, the alternative to large cash transaction reports has to be considered separately for each distinct business. As explained above, you cannot choose the alternative to large cash transaction reports if any of the corporation's businesses relate to pawnbroking, or if the corporation's principal business is the sale of vehicles, vessels, farm machinery, aircraft, mobile homes, jewellery, precious gems or metals, antiquities or art.

If several corporations operate the same businesses, each corporation has to be considered separately. For example, if you have accounts with a corporation that operates a retail store and you also have accounts with other corporations who have bought franchises of that retail store, you would have to consider each corporation separately for purposes of the alternative to large cash transactions reports.

For additional information to help you determine whether you can choose the alternative to large cash transaction reports for a client, see the following appendices:

- Appendix 3 presents the conditions in a question-based flow.
- Appendix 4 outlines examples of situations for clients for whom you could or could not consider the alternative to large cash transaction reports.

## 2.2 How to Choose the Alternative to Large Cash Transaction Reports

If all the conditions listed in Section 2.1 are met and you choose the alternative to large cash transaction reports for a client, you have to do the following:

- send a report to FINTRAC about the business client for whom you are making this choice (see Section 3);
- report certain changes about the business client to FINTRAC (see Section 3);
- verify annually that conditions are met for each client and report this to FINTRAC (see Section 3); and
- maintain a list with the name and address of each client for whom you have chosen not to report large cash transactions (see Section 4).

Once you become aware that any of the conditions are no longer being met for a client for whom you had chosen the alternative to large cash transaction reports, as of the time you become aware, you must resume reporting large cash transactions conducted for that client.

## 3    REPORT TO FINTRAC ABOUT THE BUSINESS CLIENT

If all the conditions listed in Section 2.1 are met and you choose the alternative to large cash transaction reports for a client, you have to send a report to FINTRAC with information about the business client for whom you are choosing this. This is to provide information about the client, including name and address, nature of the client's business, incorporation number and incorporation jurisdiction, as well as the total monetary value and number of cash deposits for the client's business over the preceding 12 months.

Until this report, called the *Financial Entity Business Client Report*, is sent to FINTRAC, you have to report any large cash transactions for the client as explained in *Guideline 7: Submitting Large Cash Transaction Reports to FINTRAC*.

If you use the batch file transfer mechanism for sending reports to FINTRAC, read Section 3.1 to find out how to make this report. If you do not use the batch file transfer mechanism read section 3.2.

## 3.1 If You Use Batch Transmission Software

If you use the batch file transfer reporting mechanism, use your batch transmission software (ViaSafe) to submit your *Financial Entity Business Client Report* to FINTRAC. You will have to notify FINTRAC that you will use your batch transmission software to send this type of report. If you do not already transmit reports this way, see Section 3.2.

For your **first** *Financial Entity Business Client Report*, follow these steps:

- **Step 1** — From the reporting section of FINTRAC's website, download and save a copy of the *Financial Entity Business Client Report* spreadsheet **for batch transmission.**
- **Step 2** — Complete the *Financial Entity Business Client Report* spreadsheet. Indicate that you are completing an original report by entering "O" in the area above Part A. For more information on how to fill out the fields, refer to Appendix 2. Do not complete Part D, as this is only applicable to the annual verification explained in Section 3.4.
- **Step 3** — Once you have completed the spreadsheet, save it in its default format (i.e., xls, qpw or wk4) for future reference and updating.
- **Step 4** — Before you submit the file to FINTRAC, save it again in a comma separated value format. Only **this** copy is to be sent to FINTRAC.

To save your file in a comma separated value format, open the completed *Financial Entity Business Client Report* spreadsheet. Go to the **File** menu and select **Save As**. In the **File name** : section, follow the format **PKIUSERID_YYYYMMDD_##.csv**, and substitute each element as follows:

- PKIUSERID is your 10-digit PKI User ID number issued by FINTRAC.
- YYYYMMDD is the date the file is sent to FINTRAC (i.e., the current date).
- ## is a two-digit number to differentiate between reports. Use "01" unless you send more than one *Financial Entity Business Client Report* within the same day. If you do send more than one report in the same day, then increment "##" accordingly (i.e., 01, 02, etc.).
- csv is the file extension of the spreadsheet to be submitted (i.e., for a comma separated value or comma delimited format, the extension is "csv").

When selecting which file type to save as, choose one of the following:

- In Microsoft Excel, select **CSV (comma delimited) (*.csv)**.

- In Quattro Pro, select **CSV (Comma delimited)**.
- In Lotus 1-2-3, select **Comma Separated Value (CSV)**.

- **Step 5** — Once the file has been saved in a comma separated value format, submit it to FINTRAC with your batch transmission software provided to you by FINTRAC. Remember that you have to first notify FINTRAC that you will be sending this type of report by batch.

Use the batch report channel called **Alt to LCTR** (alternative to large cash transaction reports) to drop the spreadsheet for transmission. Please refer to the *PKI Reporting Guide* for more information about the transmission of files. This is available in the reporting section of FINTRAC's Web site at http://www.fintrac.gc.ca/reporting--declaration/docs/PKI/training_guide_2002_eng.pdf.

You will be notified if the transmission of the file was successful. However, you will not receive a secondary acknowledgement about processing results.

If you have sent a *Financial Entity Business Client Report* before and you need to add new business clients, start with the spreadsheet you saved in its default format, as explained in Step 3 above. Indicate that this is an update to a previously submitted report in the area of the report above Part A. Also, enter "A" in the "Update indicator" column to the left of field B1 for each business client to be added. Once you have finished adding the clients to your spreadsheet, follow Steps 3 to 5 above to submit the updated report.

### 3.2 If You Do Not Use Batch Transmission Software

If you do **not** use the batch file transfer reporting mechanism, you can submit your *Financial Entity Business Client Report* to FINTRAC by fax. Once you have completed the spreadsheet, you should save it for future reference and updating.

For your **first** *Financial Entity Business Client Report*, follow these steps:

- **Step 1** — From the reporting section of FINTRAC's website download and save a copy of the *Financial Entity Business Client Report* spreadsheet **for non-batch transmission.**
- **Step 2** — Complete the *Financial Entity Business Client Report* spreadsheet. For more information on how to fill out the fields, refer to Appendix 2. Do not complete Part D, as this is only applicable to the annual verification explained in Section 3.4.
- **Step 3** — Once you have completed the spreadsheet, save it for future reference and updating. As this file is for your own records, the file naming convention is up to you.
- **Step 4** — Print the file and send to FINTRAC by fax at 1-866-226-2346.

If you have sent a *Financial Entity Business Client Report* before and you need to add new business clients, start with the spreadsheet you saved, as explained in Step 3 above. Indicate that this is an update to a previously submitted report in the area above Part A. Also, enter "A" in the "Update indicator" column to the left of field B1 for each new business client to be added. Once you have finished adding the information for each one to your spreadsheet, follow Steps 3 and 4 above to submit the updated report.

### 3.3 Report Certain Changes About the Business Client

Once the information about business clients described above has been sent to FINTRAC, if there are any changes to the client's name or address, the nature of the client's business or the business incorporation number, you have to report the change to FINTRAC. This has to be done within 15 calendar days after the change is made.

In this context, a change in the nature of the client's business includes anything that would cause you to revise the description of the nature of the business or the *North American Industry Classification System* (NAICS) code indicated for the client in your financial entity business client report. For more information about NAICS, refer to Appendix 1.

If there is a change to the nature of the business, you need to ensure the business is still within those types of businesses described as eligible in Appendix 1.

To report these types of changes to FINTRAC, make the change required to your "saved spreadsheet" described in Step 3 of Section 3.1 or 3.2. Indicate that this is an update to a previously submitted report by entering "U" in the area above Part A. Also, enter "C" in the "Update Indicator" column to the left of field B1 for each business whose information is being changed. Do not complete Part D, as this is only applicable to the annual verification explained in Section 3.4.

Re-save the spreadsheet and submit it in its entirety to FINTRAC, according to the batch transmission or fax instructions that apply to you. Repeat this process any time you have to report a change.

For more information about this report, see Appendix 2.

If you discover that a client no longer meets the criteria described in Section 2.1, you must remove them from your alternative to large cash reports list. You do not have to report to FINTRAC that you have removed a client from your list. However, you must resume reporting any large cash transactions conducted for that client after you discovered that the criteria are no longer met. Delete the information about any removed clients from the spreadsheet before you send your next update or your next annual verification to FINTRAC.

### 3.4 Annual Verification

Once you have chosen the alternative to large cash transaction reports, you have to verify **at least once every 12 months** that all the conditions listed in Section 2.1 are still met for each client. Once this is done, you have to complete Part D of your *Financial Entity Business Client Report* and send it to FINTRAC to provide the name of your senior officer who has confirmed that the conditions are still being met for a particular client.

To do this, you will need to start with your latest "saved copy" of your spreadsheet (as described in Step 3 of Section 3.1 or 3.2 or in Section 3.3).

Indicate that this is an annual verification by entering a "V" in the area above Part A. Also, enter "V" in the "Update indicator" column to the left of field B1 for each business whose information is being verified and complete Part D for each one.

Please do **not** include any new business clients and do **not** make any changes to information in Parts A, B or C on the report at the time of your annual verification. If you need to add new business clients or make changes, do so by submitting the related information as an update as described in Section 3.3.

Re-save the spreadsheet and submit it in its entirety to FINTRAC, according to the batch transmission or fax instructions that apply to you. Repeat this process any time you have to report annual verification for a business client.

While conducting your annual verification for a particular client, if you discover that the client no longer meets the criteria described in Section 2.1, delete the information about that client from the spreadsheet before you send your annual verification to FINTRAC. As explained above, once you become aware that the criteria are no longer met for a client, you must resume reporting any large cash transactions conducted for that client as of that time.

## 4   LIST TO BE MAINTAINED

In addition to the information you send to FINTRAC in the reports described in Section 3, you must maintain a list with the name and address of each client for whom you have chosen this alternative to large cash transaction report.

You can keep this list in paper form, or in a machine-readable or electronic form, as long as a paper copy can be readily produced. You can use your copy of the spreadsheet for this purpose.

The reports that you send to FINTRAC are not to seek approval for the clients on your alternative to large cash transaction list. You are responsible for making sure that each client meets the criteria described in Section 2.1. If you discover that any clients on your list no longer meet these criteria, you must remove them from your list immediately and report large cash transactions for those clients.

## APPENDIX 1: FINANCIAL ENTITY ALTERNATIVE TO LARGE CASH TRANSACTION REPORTS — TYPES OF BUSINESSES FOR CLIENTS THAT ARE CORPORATIONS

As explained in Section 2 of this guideline, you cannot choose the alternative to large cash transaction reports if any of the corporation's businesses relate to pawnbroking, or if the corporation's principal business is the sale of vehicles, vessels, farm machinery, aircraft, mobile homes, jewellery, precious gems or metals, antiquities or art. If this is your client's situation, you will not need this appendix to determine anything further about the type of business for that client.

In all other cases, the following provides information about the types of businesses in which a client that is a corporation can be engaged for you to choose the alternative to large cash transaction reports for the business. For more information about this and the other conditions to be met, see Section 2 of this guideline.

The descriptions below are for eligible business types for purposes of the alternative to large cash transaction reports, described in the codes of the *North American Industry Classification System* (NAICS) 1997, as described in the following appendices:

> Appendix 1A — **NAICS Sector Code 22 Utilities**
> Appendix 1B — **NAICS Sector Codes 44-45 Retail Trade**
> Appendix 1C — **NAICS Subsector Code 481 Air Transportation**
> Appendix 1D — **NAICS Subsector Code 482 Rail Transportation**
> Appendix 1E — **NAICS Subsector Code 485 Transit and Ground Passenger Transportation**
> Appendix 1F — **NAICS Industry Code 51322 Cable and Other Program Distribution**
> Appendix 1G — **NAICS Industry Code 51331 Wired Telecommunications Carriers**
> Appendix 1H — **Colleges and Universities (NAICS Industry Codes 61121 and 61131)**

Only the specific industries described in those NAICS codes are eligible business types for purposes of the alternative to large cash transaction reports. The descriptions are as they read on January 31, 2003. Any differences between these and the codes of NAICS 2002 published in May 2003 are noted.

For more information about NAICS, refer to the information in the section about standard industry classifications on the Statistics Canada Web site. At the time of publishing this guideline, this information can be accessed at http://www.statcan.ca/english/concepts/industry.htm. To convert NAICS 2002 codes to or from NAICS 1997 codes, or to convert NAICS 1997 codes to or from the *Standard Industrial Classification System* (SIC), refer to the concordance tables, also available on the Statistics Canada Web site.

If the client's business is described in NAICS codes other than those included in Appendices 1A to 1H, you cannot choose the alternative to large cash transaction reports for that business. For example, businesses described in the following NAICS sector codes are **excluded** for purposes of the alternative to large cash transaction reports:

- Sector 11 Agriculture, Forestry, Fishing and Hunting
- Sector 21 Mining and Oil and Gas Extraction
- Sector 23 Construction
- Sector 31-33 Manufacturing
- Sector 41 Wholesale Trade
- Sector 52 Finance and Insurance
- Sector 53 Real Estate and Rental and Leasing
- Sector 54 Professional, Scientific and Technical Services
- Sector 55 Management of Companies and Enterprises

- Sector 56 Administrative and Support, Waste Management and Remediation Services
- Sector 62 Health Care and Social Assistance
- Sector 71 Arts, Entertainment and Recreation
- Sector 72 Accommodation and Food Services
- Sector 81 Other Services (except Public Administration)
- Sector 91 Public Administration.

**APPENDIX 3: CAN YOUR CLIENT BE CONSIDERED FOR THE ALTERNATIVE TO LARGE CASH TRANSACTION REPORTS?**

The following nine questions, if answered in order, will help you determine whether or not a particular business of a corporation can be considered for the alternative to large cash transaction reports. The first three questions are about the corporation, and the rest are about the business. If you get to question 4 for a corporation that has more than one business, go through questions 4 to 9 to get a distinct answer for each business that you wish to consider.

For more information about the conditions, see Section 2 of this guideline.

1. Is the client a corporation?
   - If the answer is yes, continue to question 2.
   - If the answer is no, the client cannot be considered for the alternative to large cash transaction reports.

2. Is any of the corporation's business related to pawnbroking?
   - If the answer is yes, the client cannot be considered for the alternative to large cash transaction reports.
   - If the answer is no, continue to question 3.

3. Is the corporation's **principal** business the sale of vehicles, vessels, farm machinery, aircraft, mobile homes, jewellery, precious gems or metals, antiquities or art?
   - If the answer is yes, the client cannot be considered for the alternative to large cash transaction reports.
   - If the answer is no, continue to question 4.

4. Is the corporation's business a business type that can be considered for purposes of the alternative to large cash transaction reports (see Appendix 1)?
   - If the answer is yes, continue to question 5.
   - If the answer is no, the client cannot be considered for the alternative to large cash transaction reports.

5. Has the client had an account with you for the business for at least 24 months?
   - If the answer is yes, skip question 6 and continue to question 7.
   - If the answer is no, continue to question 6.

6. Did the client have an account for the business with another financial entity for at least 24 months immediately before opening an account with you? (Answer this question only if you answered **no** to question 5.)
   • If the answer is yes, continue to question 7.
   • If the answer is no, the client cannot be considered for the alternative to large cash transaction reports.

7. Do you have records that show that, in the preceding 12 months, the client deposited $10,000 or more in cash, on an annual average of at least twice a week, into the account referred to in question 5 or question 6?

- If the answer is yes, continue to question 8.
- If the answer is no, the client cannot be considered for the alternative to large cash transaction reports.

8.  Were the cash deposits of this business consistent with the business' usual practices?
    - If the answer is yes, continue to question 9.
    - If the answer is no, the client cannot be considered for the alternative to large cash transaction reports.

9.  Have you taken reasonable measures to determine the source of cash for those deposits?
    - If yes, you may choose the alternative to large cash transaction reports for this business.
    - If no, the client's business cannot be considered for the alternative to large cash transaction reports.

# DRAFT REVISED GUIDELINE

Reference: **Guideline for Banks/FBBs/T&L/ Co-ops/Life**

File P2200-22

July 12, 2004

**TO:**  Banks
Foreign Bank Branches
Federally Regulated Trust and Loan Companies
Federally Regulated Cooperative Credit Associations
Federally Regulated Life Insurance Companies

**Subject:  Draft Revised Guideline B-8 on Deterring and Detecting Money Laundering and Terrorist Financing**

This Guideline sets out OSFI's expectations for federally regulated financial institutions (FRFIs) with respect to the establishment of policies and procedures to combat money laundering and terrorist financing. For the purposes of this Guideline, FRFI includes banks, authorized foreign banks in respect of their business in Canada (foreign bank branches), cooperative credit associations, trust and loan companies, and federally incorporated or regulated life insurance companies.

This Guideline has been modified to reflect developments that have taken place since it was issued in April 2003, including:

- OSFI's experience in conducting anti-money laundering and anti-terrorist financing assessments; and
- The Revised Forty Recommendations issued by the Financial Action Task Force on Money Laundering (FATF) in June 2003 (further information can be obtained from the FATF Web site at http://wwwl.oecd.org/fatf/.

A Guideline Impact Analysis Statement (GIAS) accompanies this letter. The GIAS outlines the principal changes to the Guideline in more detail. The focus of this Guideline continues to be the identification and mitigation of risks related to money laundering, to which is added the risks associated with terrorist financing.

Institutions are invited to provide comments regarding the Guideline by August 16, 2004 through their industry associations. Questions concerning the Guideline should be addressed to Nicolas Burbidge, Senior Director, Compliance Division, at (416) 973-6177, or by facsimile at (416) 954-3169.

Julie Dickson
Assistant Superintendent
Regulation Sector

# DRAFT GUIDELINE

**Subject:** **Deterring and Detecting Money Laundering and Terrorist Financing**

**Category:** **Sound Business and Financial Practices**

| | | | |
|---|---|---|---|
| **No:** | **B-8** | **Date:** | **April 2003** |
| | | **Revised:** | **July 2004** |

Money laundering and terrorist financing activities (MLTFA) continue to be a serious international problem that is receiving increasing attention as nations attempt to deal with issues such as organized crime and terrorism. Financial institutions, in particular, are at risk of being used by criminal organisations to launder money and by terrorist groups to facilitate the financing of their activities.

When necessary, this Guideline references the work of the Financial Action Task Force on Money Laundering (FATF), the international body, of which Canada is a member, that develops and monitors international anti-money laundering and terrorist financing standards.

This guideline is intended to identify some of the steps that federally regulated financial institutions (FRFIs) should take to assist their compliance with the various legal requirements related to deterring and detecting money laundering and terrorist financing and, more generally, to minimize the possibility that they could become a party to MLTFA. Effective policies and procedures are essential to reducing the risk that facilitating MLTFA poses to FRFIs' reputations and operations. Both management and the boards of directors of FRFIs are responsible for the development of specific policies and procedures for deterring and detecting MLTFA as well as for ensuring that FRFIs adhere to those policies and procedures. OSFI also expects that institutions will be able to demonstrate, on request, that they have developed and implemented policies and procedures consistent with this guideline, and that staff are applying them as intended.

OSFI will work closely with the Financial Transactions and Reports Analysis Centre of Canada (FINTRAC) concerning the policies and procedures that FRFIs have in place for complying with Part I of the *Proceeds of Crime (Money Laundering) and Terrorist Financing Act* (PCMLTFA). Recently adopted provisions of the PCMLTFA and the *Criminal Code* give FINTRAC and OSFI responsibility for dealing with issues related to the financing of terrorist activities. FINTRAC's objectives now include the detection, prevention and deterrence of the financing of terrorist activities, while OSFI has assumed the role of a central reporting point for the aggregate reporting requirements outlined in subsection 83.11(2) of the *Criminal Code.*

With respect to FRFIs' reporting requirements to OSFI related to terrorist assets, OSFI posts on its Web site (www.osfi-bsif.gc.ca) lists of terrorist individuals and organizations, and will continue to receive reports from FRFIs as required by the *United Nations Suppression of Terrorism Regulations* or by subsection 83.11(1) of the *Criminal Code* in respect of entities listed in the

*Regulations Establishing a List of Entities* made under subsection 83.05(1) of the *Criminal Code*. In addition, FINTRAC and a number of international organisations have published information related to terrorist financing activities FINTRAC has also issued a guideline on Submitting Terrorist Property Reports. FRFIs should keep in mind that the financing of terrorist activities is sometimes linked to money laundering. In addition, actual or suspected FRFI involvement in facilitating the financing of terrorist activities may expose FRFIs to risks similar to those related to the facilitation of money laundering.

TABLE OF CONTENTS

I.   **Introduction and Background**

II.  **Programs to Combat MLTFA**

  a.   MLTFA Risks

  b.   Board and Management Oversight

  c.   Policies and Procedures

  d.   Customer Identification

## I. INTRODUCTION AND BACKGROUND

This guideline applies to banks, authorized foreign banks in respect of their business in Canada (foreign bank branches or FBBs), companies to which the *Trust and Loan Companies Act* applies, cooperative credit associations subject to the *Cooperative Credit Associations Act*, and life companies or foreign life company branches to which the *Insurance Companies Act* applies. For the purposes of this guideline, they will be referred to as federally regulated financial institutions (FRFIs). FRFIs should also ensure that subsidiaries having potential exposure to money laundering or terrorist financing activities follow the guideline.

This guideline reflects actions taken both nationally and internationally to deal with money laundering and terrorist financing. Key among the actions taken in Canada was the enactment of the *Proceeds of Crime (Money Laundering) and Terrorist Financing Act* (PCMLTFA), the creation of the Financial Transactions and Reports Analysis Centre of Canada (FINTRAC) and the development of the current transaction reporting regime. FRFIs should be aware of the specific requirements related to customer identification set out in the PCMLTFA and the Regulations.[1] Both the PCMLTFA and the Regulations are available from the Department of Justice Web site (http://www.canada.justice.gc.ca/) and from the FINTRAC Web site (http://www.fintrac.gc.ca).

FINTRAC, an agency of the federal government, is Canada's financial intelligence unit and has a mandate to collect, analyze and assess information related

---

[1]   *Proceeds of Crime (Money Laundering) and Terrorist Financing Regulations* (PCMLTFR) *and Proceeds of Crime (Money Laundering) and Terrorist Financing Suspicious Transactions Regulations* (PCMLTFSTR).

to money laundering and terrorist financing activities, and to disclose certain information to law enforcement and intelligence authorities to assist in the detection, prevention and deterrence of these criminal activities. FINTRAC is also responsible for ensuring that FRFIs comply with the record keeping, reporting, and customer identification requirements set out in Part 1 of the PCMLTFA and the accompanying Regulations. More information on FINTRAC is available on its Web site, noted above.

Specific requirements related to the reporting of various transactions are outlined in the Regulations and in FINTRAC guidelines. The Regulations set out reporting and record keeping requirements for suspicious transactions (including terrorist property reporting), large cash transactions and international electronic funds transfers. Among other things, the Regulations also outline requirements for client identification, retention of records, and the implementation of a compliance regime, including staff training. Please refer to the FINTRAC Web site for copies of the PCMLTFA, Regulations, and FINTRAC guidelines, as well as for general information related to money laundering and terrorist financing.

## II. PROGRAMS TO COMBAT MLTFA

### (a) MLTFA Risks

Financial regulators and international organizations recognize that MLTFA is a serious problem that can pose a number of risks to financial institutions. The failure of a financial institution to implement policies and procedures to deter and detect MLTFA can have a negative impact on its reputation and, consequently, on its ability to carry on business.

FRFIs that fail to implement adequate measures in relation to the prevention of money laundering and the reporting of terrorist financing activities are exposed to potentially serious regulatory intervention initiatives, both domestically and internationally.

Consistent with the duty of care imposed by FRFI legislation on boards of directors and on officers of FRFIs, standards of sound business and financial practices, and OSFI's Supervisory Framework, which focuses on identifying and mitigating risks, FRFIs should have policies and procedures related to deterring and detecting MLTFA that are adapted to their individual situations. Where appropriate, these policies and procedures should articulate a group- or enterprise-wide standard, applicable to the FRFI itself, all domestic or foreign subsidiaries and all foreign branches. FRFIs should design these policies and procedures to ensure compliance with legal requirements related to deterring and detecting MLTFA. As appropriate, such policies and procedures should go beyond specific legal requirements to take into account the business environment and activities specific to the institution. Policies and procedures should be formally documented. Not only will this assist OSFI and FINTRAC, it will also enhance a FRFI's internal compliance function and the overall effectiveness of its policies and procedures.

The policies and procedures should include measures to permit the FRFI to identify and report Large Cash Transactions as required by the PCMLTFA and the Regulations. The policies and procedures should also include measures to monitor transactions. These measures will help FRFIs to identify potentially suspicious transactions by using criteria that will enable them to detect unusual or abnormal activity. Where appropriate (for example, where the volume of transactions is high), FRFIs should consider whether monitoring activity could be strengthened by information technology solutions.

To identify their level of exposure to potential MLTFA and the associated risks, FRFIs must understand the nature of the risks associated with the different parts of their operations:

### *Products and Services*

Although MLTFA are frequently associated with deposit accounts, other financial products, such as loans, mortgages and other credit products, may also be used to hide the proceeds of crime or terrorist funds. For life insurers, attention should be paid to products and services that permit a customer to make substantial funds withdrawals and/or large single-premium payments.

### *Customers*

Both the FATF and the Basel Committee believe that it is vital that financial institutions adequately identify those who beneficially own corporate customers who do business with them. This goes further than merely ascertaining that an entity exists. The FATF recommends that financial institutions "understand the ownership and control structure" of their customers. OSFI suggests that this principle is particularly important when dealing with privately owned companies, trusts and customers with more complex legal structures. In addition, certain customers may merit additional due diligence. Examples could include businesses that handle large amounts of cash, or that deal in luxury or high-end consumer goods. Finally, customers that hold important public positions (often referred to as "politically exposed persons") may require special attention.

### *Reliance on Others*

FRFIs that outsource record keeping or other functions that form part of their PCMLTFA compliance regime, or that utilize introducers to gather new business (such as deposit brokers, mortgage brokers, correspondents, law firms, accounting firms, etc., including those outside Canada) are reminded that they retain full accountability for having customer identification and verification processes, and for obtaining customer records with respect to accounts opened through such sources.

With respect to introduced business, FRFIs must obtain the necessary customer information for their records prior to, at, or at a reasonable time after, the time that the business is accepted. OSFI recommends that relationships with introducers be documented to ensure that the responsibility for collecting and verifying customer identification information is clearly understood. FRFIs should consider terminating relationships with introducers that cannot, or fail to, provide the FRFI with the requisite customer identification and verification data that the FRFI is required to obtain under the PCMLTFA and the Regulations.

## *Geography*

FRFIs with operations that conduct business in offshore jurisdictions, or that have customers that operate in those jurisdictions, need to be especially vigilant. The FATF and the IMF/World Bank have highlighted the risks of doing business internationally, and issue reports identifying jurisdictions that have deficiencies in their anti-money laundering regimes, or that are Non-Cooperating Countries and Territories.[2] FRFIs should note that the Regulations do not permit the same degree of reliance on the acceptance of cheques drawn on banks outside Canada as they do for cheques drawn on Canadian institutions. Therefore, it is suggested that FRFIs ensure that if they accept foreign cheques, they are satisfied with the reputation and standing of the foreign institution upon which such cheques are drawn. Likewise, attention should be paid to wire transfers (particularly those from outside Canada, non-customers or non-correspondent banks), or pass-through accounts at FRFIs that are opened by foreign institutions to allow their customers to conduct business in Canada.

The degree of potential exposure to MLTFA should be understood, and the implementation of measures to deter and detect these activities should be flexible in order to reflect the features of different products and service locations, as well as changes in legal requirements.

## *(b) Board and Management Oversight*

Given their ultimate responsibility for the success of a FRFI's programs to deter and detect MLTFA, the board of directors and senior management must be strongly committed to ensuring that measures designed to address risks associated with money laundering are effective. It is essential that both the board of directors and senior management support these programs through all stages — design, approval, imple-mentation, and review. The board and senior management should be directly involved in the approval and review stages, principally throughout the receipt and review of the FRFI's self-assessment discussed under (c)(v) below.

## *(c) Policies and Procedures*

Senior management is responsible for the development of risk management programs and for keeping the board of directors adequately informed about these programs and their effectiveness. Policies and procedures to combat MLTFA should form an integral part of a FRFI's overall compliance function. The

---

[2] The FATF provides updates on the progress being made by jurisdictions named in its report and conducts reviews of additional countries and jurisdictions. Jurisdictions making sufficient progress in strengthening their anti-money laundering regimes are de-listed, while others may face various countermeasures if progress is insufficient. To obtain additional information on this report or on other FATF activities, FRFIs should refer to the FATF Web site located at http://www.oecd.org/fatf.

following steps would form a sound basis for a comprehensive set of policies and procedures to deter and detect these activities.

i)   Ensure that the FRFI has sufficient qualified resources to comply with all legal requirements.

ii)  Name a "designated officer" to be responsible for corporate-wide measures to combat MLTFA and who will report directly to senior management and the board of directors. The designated officer should ensure that each operating division of the FRFI having potential exposure to MLTFA appoints an officer to ensure that these divisions carry out policies and procedures as required. These officers should report regularly on compliance issues and the need for any revisions to policies and procedures. At each branch or unit that deals directly with the public, FRFIs should designate an employee(s) (who need not be full time compliance officers) to be accountable for ensuring that anti-MLTFA policies and procedures intended for these branches or units are applied.

iii) Ensure that managers are aware of their overall compliance responsibilities, and, in particular, those linked to areas such as MLTFA where non-compliance has the potential to cause damage to the FRFI's reputation.

iv)  Establish internal compliance reporting processes[3] capable of demonstrating, at a minimum, conformity with *all* anti-MLTFA legal requirements. Further, the internal compliance reporting system should provide for regular reviews of compliance issues, for the documentation of such reviews, and for a process to address instances of non-compliance or any general areas of weakness identified. Where a FRFI believes the review has identified significant issues, it should review such issues with OSFI. Policies and procedures should be adequately documented to permit independent testing (referred to below) and OSFI to understand the processes described.

v)   Establish an annual self-assessment program designed to 1) evaluate, on a group-wide basis, the effectiveness of the FRFI's anti-MLTFA procedures for identifying areas and types of risk, and 2) suggest corrective measures to address any weaknesses or gaps identified in the risk management systems. The annual self-assessment should include a report for senior management and the board of directors that summarizes the assessment's findings, including the scope of the review, the main elements of anti-MLTFA policies and procedures, the level of adherence to them, and evidence that the policies and procedures comply with the PCMLTFA and the Regulations, and with applicable FINTRAC and OSFI guidelines.

vi)  Establish a system of independent procedures testing to be conducted at least annually by the internal audit department, compliance department, or by an outside party such as the FRFI's external auditor. The scope of the testing and results should be documented, with deficiencies in anti-MLTFA

---

[3]   It should be noted that OSFI has issued guidance on legislative compliance management and that it refers to compliance requirements in both FRFI governing statutes (e.g., *Bank Act*) and in other egislation that affects FRFIs, such as the PCMLTFA.

systems being reported to senior management and to the board of directors, and with a summary of steps taken (or to be taken) to address any deficiencies. The report should address areas such as: employee knowledge of legal requirements and the FRFI's policies and procedures; the FRFI's systems for client identification and for suspicious and large cash transaction identification and reporting; and the associated record-keeping system.

vii) Ensure that appropriate employees are given sufficient training. This should include knowledge of the FRFI's anti-MLTFA policies and procedures, the techniques[4] used by criminals to launder funds through financial institutions, and the current anti-MLTFA legislation and regulations. Front-line staff plays an essential role in implementing anti-MLTFA measures and, therefore, must receive appropriate training to understand problems associated with MLTFA, the financial institution's anti-MLTFA policies, and the proper application of procedures.

### (d) Customer Identification

Comprehensive customer identification policies and procedures can greatly reduce the risk of exposure to money laundering and terrorist financing activities, and should form a key part of an anti-MLTFA program. The importance of customer identification is recognized by international bodies such as the FATF and the Basel Committee on Banking Supervision (Basel Committee). The International Association of Insurance Supervisors (IAIS) has also issued anti-money laundering guidance that highlights the importance of customer identification issues.

In October 2001, the Basel Committee released a final version of its paper entitled *Customer Due Diligence for Banks*. The paper sets out minimum standards for the development of appropriate practices in this area. OSFI believes that the customer due diligence standards identified in this paper represent a sound basis for ensuring that FRFIs have adequate "know your customer" controls and procedures in place. OSFI encourages FRFIs to familiarize themselves with the standards outlined in the paper and to implement these standards in a manner appropriate to the size, complexity, and nature of the institution's business activities. The paper is available on the BIS Web site (http://www. bis.org/publ/bcbs85.pdf).

More recently, the FATF has made substantial revisions to its Forty Recommendations, which can be referenced at the FATF Web site (http://www. fatf-gafi.org/40Recs_en.htm). The FATF has also released a number of Special Recommendations on Terrorist Financing, some dealing more specifically with roles and responsibilities of financial institutions for combating terrorist financing activities (http://www.fatf-gafi.org/TerFinance_en.htm).

---

[4]   The three stages of money laundering (placement, layering and integration) should be covered by appropriate training material, ideally geared to the FRFI's own products and services.

The IAIS approved the final draft of its *Anti-Money Laundering Guidance Notes for Insurance Supervisors and Insurance Entities* (http://www.iaisweb.org/02money.pdf) at its January 2002 Continued General Meeting. Life insurance entities should familiarize themselves with this document, as it provides a strong summary of key elements of an anti-money laundering program from an insurance entity perspective. The guidance notes, and especially those related to customer verification procedures and know your customer standards, can be used by life insurers to assist in the development of their anti-money laundering programs. In 2003 the IAIS commenced a review of the guidance notes with the aim of making it consistent with the revised FATF Forty Recommendations, but also to give specific guidance with respect to customer due diligence.

## III. Review by the Office of the Superintendent of Financial Institutions

As part of its risk-based supervisory framework, OSFI reviews the adequacy of FRFIs' enterprise-wide anti-MLTFA policies and procedures, and their implementation, to determine whether FRFIs are taking appropriate steps to address MLTFA and associated risks. OSFI may share results of these reviews with FINTRAC,[5] as they relate to compliance with Part 1 of the PCMLTFA. FRFIs should be prepared to provide information or material on MLTFA deterrence and detection procedures to OSFI personnel when they are conducting an on-site review and, upon request, at any other time. (Note: additional information related to the items below can be found in Section II(c).) Material that may be examined would include, but would not necessarily be limited to:

i) Board-approved policies on anti-MLTFA and related procedures;
ii) The self-assessment referred to in *(c)* (v) above;
iii) Documented evidence of tests undertaken to confirm the appropriate functioning of the entity's anti-MLTFA policies and procedures;
iv) The name of the officer designated as responsible for the institution's overall MLTFA deterrence and detection procedures, usually referred to by OSFI as the Chief Anti-Money Laundering Officer (CAMLO);
v) A description of the frequency and type of reporting to the CAMLO and by the CAMLO to senior management and the board;
vi) Electronic or paper evidence (could include FINTRAC confirmation of report filings) of all suspicious transaction, large cash transaction, electronic funds transfer, and other reports made by the FRFI pursuant to its reporting obligations; and
vii) Evidence of a summary report to senior management in respect of suspicious transactions reports, large cash transaction reports, and cross border currency reports that were made to FINTRAC.

---

[5]  In accordance with section 97 of Bill C-7 (the *Public Safety Act, 2002*).

# GUIDELINE IMPACT ANALYSIS STATEMENT — DRAFT REVISED GUIDELINE B-8: DETERRING AND DETECTING MONEY LAUNDERING AND TERRORIST FINANCING

## 1. BACKGROUND

OSFI's Guideline B-8, Deterring and Detecting Money Laundering, was originally released in 1996 and was revised in April 2003 to reflect significant changes to Canadian legislation resulting from the introduction of the *Proceeds of Crime (Money Laundering) and Terrorist Financing Act* (Act).

The Guideline highlights the need for federally regulated financial institutions (FRFIs) (except property and casualty insurance companies) to develop and operate anti-money laundering programs. This would reduce the susceptibility of FRFIs to being used by individuals or organizations in respect of money laundering, thereby reducing the risk of sustaining damage to their reputation, which is a key component to success in the financial services industry.

In addition to issuing the Guideline, OSFI has been assessing the anti-money laundering and terrorist financing activities (MLTFA) programs operated by FRFIs.

## II. PROBLEM IDENTIFICATION

Although most of OSFI's anti-MLTFA assessment program findings to date relate to matters that have been addressed by the current Guideline, the passage of time, combined with recent experience, has identified additional issues that should be addressed, including:

1. The use of introducers. FRFIs that use introducers (e.g. mortgage or deposit brokers, correspondent banks, lawyers, etc.) may not always obtain the requisite customer identification and verification information from these parties. As a result, a FRFI could inadvertently be dealing with parties who are conducting or facilitating money laundering or financing terrorist activities, thereby exposing itself to possible criminal sanction. The FRFI may also be exposed to increased risk of reputational damage, whether or not it was criminally responsible. FRFIs with weak systems for combating MLTFA may also face increased levels of regulatory scrutiny and, if warranted, intervention.

2. The need for OSFI and FRFIs to remain current with international standards. The Financial Action Task Force (FATF) issued a revised version of its Forty Recommendations in June 2003, which have increased customer due diligence standards applicable to FRFIs (especially for higher risk customers such as dealers in cash, precious metals or gems, and for corporate customers and complex corporate structures where determination of beneficial ownership may be difficult). Failure by OSFI to ensure that guidance remains up-to-date and meets international minimums could lead to the perception that the Canadian regulatory regime is not dealing with

these issues effectively. Similarly, failure of FRFIs to adopt certain of the FATF recommendations can increase the potential for reputation risk associated with facilitating money laundering or terrorist financing activities.

## III. OBJECTIVES

The objective of revising Guideline B-8 is to remind all FRFIs that:

1. Outsourcing, including the use of introducers, does not obviate the FRFI's full accountability for having customer identification and verification processes, and for obtaining customer records with respect to accounts opened through such sources.
2. Higher risk customers, including those that deal in cash, gems or other high-end items, may require additional due diligence and monitoring.
3. A substantial amount of international guidance is available, and in particular, that significant revisions have been made to the FATF's Forty Recommendations, which now also address anti-terrorist financing (ATF) issues.

Consequential objectives of this revision include updating the Guideline to further clarify that FRFIs are expected to develop and implement robust ATF policies and procedures.

## IV. IDENTIFICATION AND ASSESSMENT OF OPTIONS

*Option 1 — Revise Guideline E-8 to address the objectives in this Analysis Statement.*

Under this option, Section II(a) of Guideline B-8 would be revised to more clearly identify different parts of a FRFI's operations that might give rise to MLTFA risks including certain products and services, types of customers, reliance on others (the use of introducers by FRFIs), and geography (dealings with off-shore clients). The Guideline would also be adjusted to more clearly indicate that FRFIs are expected to develop and implement ATF programs in concert with anti-money laundering programs, and to include an updated reference to the FATF's Revised Forty Recommendations.

OSFI will incur some costs related to revising Guideline B-8, including the consultative process, but on balance this option represents a more efficient means of communicating information than Option 3. Institutions will also face somewhat higher compliance costs, as more FRFIs will likely be required to revise their policies and procedures on a shorter time frame.

However, these costs are outweighed by the benefits. This option demonstrates that OSFI is proactively ensuring its guidance remains relevant and on a par with international standards. In addition, it would result in a more "level playing field", as **all** FRFIs would simultaneously be made aware of OSFI's new expectations and their new responsibilities with respect to their anti-MLTFA policies and procedures.

*Option 2 — Status Quo — Do not revise Guideline B-8 or take other steps to achieve the objectives outlined in this Analysis Statement.*

This option presents no incremental financial costs to either OSFI or FRFIs, and could be seen as limiting regulatory burden.

However, FRFIs that do not appropriately address the issues in the revised Guideline may be exposed to legal or regulatory sanction and increased reputational risks. OSFI may also be exposed to reputational risks if it were determined that a lack of regulatory vigilance contributed to FRFIs potentially facilitating inappropriate or illegal activities.

*Option 3 — Leave Guideline B-8 unchanged but communicate additional information and expectations to individual FRFIs when anti-MLTFA assessments are conducted.*

Under this option, the Guideline would remain unchanged, but OSFI would communicate, as part of its anti-MLTFA assessments, the additional information and expectations that would otherwise be included in a revised guideline.

For OSFI, this would be inefficient. Further, OSFI could be criticised for adopting the new higher international standards too slowly and applying them inconsistently. Some FRFIs would also face higher costs (versus status quo) but may benefit from a reduction in their potential exposure to legal and reputational risks. The biggest drawback of this option is that FRFIs would not be subject to consistent and transparent expectations.

## V. CONSULTATIONS

As part of its anti-MLTFA assessment program, OSFI told various FRFIs that it would likely provide additional guidance in certain areas (i.e. those that have been addressed in the revisions to the Guideline). OSFI has also made reference at various industry conferences to the fact that it would provide additional guidance in a number of areas. In general, feedback has been positive because FRFIs recognize their anti-MLTFA responsibilities and therefore welcome guidance that assists them in complying with these responsibilities.

OSFI is posting on its Internet Web site a draft copy of the revised Guideline for comment by members of the financial services industry and other interested parties. Given the nature of some revisions, OSFI has also informed the Canadian Institute of Mortgage Brokers and Lenders (CIMBL) and invites their comment.

## VI. RECOMMENDATION

The most appropriate method of disseminating additional information and expectations regarding anti-MLTFA systems would be through targeted revisions to the current Guideline (i.e. Option 1).

# GLOSSARY

Sources: FINTRAC Annual Report, March 31, 2003 and Finance Canada web site

**Bank for International Settlements (BIS)**

A central banking institution owned and controlled by central banks, with a board comprising the governors of the central banks of the Group of Ten countries. The BIS has become an important forum for international monetary and financial co-operation between central bankers and, increasingly, other regulators and supervisors. For more information, visit the Bank for International Settlements Web site.

**CCRA**

Canada Customs and Revenue Agency — an agency of the Government of Canada that administers tax laws for the Government of Canada and for most of the provinces and territories, and that provides all customer services.

**Cross-Border Currency Report (CBCR)**

A report that must be filed by a person entering or leaving Canada advising that the person is carrying large sums of currency or monetary instruments ($10,000 or more), or by a person mailing or sending such large sums into or out of Canada.

**CSIS**

Canadian Security Intelligence Service — Canada's national security agency that has the mandate to investigate and report on threats to the security of Canada.

**Customs Seizure Report**

A report filed with FINTRAC by a CCRA officer who seizes cash or monetary instruments for which a Cross-Border Currency Report should have been filed but was not. The report indicates the circumstances of the seizure.

**Department of Finance**

The federal department primarily responsible for providing the government with analysis and advice on the broad economic and financial affairs of Canada. Its responsibilities include preparing the federal budget, preparing tax and tariff legislation, managing federal borrowing on financial markets and representing Canada within international financial institutions. To fulfil the department's role, finance officials monitor and research the performance of the Canadian economy in all important aspects: output and growth, employment and income, price stability and monetary policy, and long-term structural change. The department is also vitally concerned with trade, monetary affairs and other aspects of the global economy that bear on Canada's domestic performance.

### Electronic Funds Transfer (EFT) Report
A report that a reporting entity must file with FINTRAC in respect of a transmission of instructions for the transfer of a sum of $10,000 or more out of or into Canada, through any electronic, magnetic or optical device, telephone instrument or computer.

### Financial Action Task Force (FATF)
An inter-governmental body, established by the G-7 Summit in 1989, whose purpose is the development and promotion of policies, both at national and international levels, to combat money laundering. At a special plenary meeting held in October 2001, FATF's mandate was expanded to include the combating of terrorist financing.

### Financial Action Task Force on Money Laundering (FATF)
Established in 1989 at the G-7 Economic Summit, the FATF addresses the international problem of money laundering. In 1990 the Task Force proposed 40 recommendations to improve national legal systems, enhance the role of financial systems and strengthen international co-operation against money laundering. The recommendations are not a binding international convention, but each of the FATF members has made a firm political commitment to combat money laundering. In 1996, the recommendations were modified to take into account recent money laundering trends and potential future threats. Visit the FATF Web site for more information.

### Group of Seven (G-7)
The G-7 consists of the world's seven largest industrial market economies: the United States, Japan, Germany, France, Britain, Italy and Canada. The leaders of these countries meet annually to discuss political and economic issues of mutual concern. In addition, G-7 finance ministers meet several times a year to discuss economic policy. Their work is supported by regular, functional meetings of officials, including the G-7 Finance Deputies.

### Large Cash Transaction Report (LCTR)
A report that a reporting entity must file with FINTRAC when it receives $10,000 or more in cash in the course of a single transaction; or when it receives two or more cash amounts totaling $10,000 or more that it knows were made within 24 consecutive hours of each other by or on behalf of the same individual or entity.

### Office of the Superintendent of Financial Institutions (OSFI)
A federal agency established under the *Financial Institutions and Deposit Insurance System Amendment Act* to supervise all federally regulated financial institutions. These include all banks, all federally-incorporated or registered insurance, trust, and loan companies, co-operative credit associations, and fraternal benefit societies. OSFI is also responsible for

monitoring federally regulated pension plans. For more information, visit the Office of the Superintendent of Financial Institutions Web site.

**Suspicious Transaction Report (STR)**

A report that a reporting entity must file with FINTRAC in respect of a financial transaction that occurs in the course of its activities and for which there are reasonable grounds to suspect that the transaction is related to the commission of a money laundering or terrorist activity financing offence.

**SWIFT**

The Society for Worldwide Financial Telecommunication, a cooperative owned by the international banking community that operates a global data processing system for the transmission of financial messages

**Terrorist Property Report (TPR)**

A report that a reporting entity must file with FINTRAC when it has in its possession or control property that it knows is owned or controlled by or on behalf of a terrorist group. This includes information about any transaction or proposed transaction relating to that property. This report is triggered by a requirement in the *Criminal Code* that mandates the reporting of such situations to the RCMP and CSIS.

# REFERENCE WEB SITES

The following is a list of organizations and their web sites where additional information may be obtained regarding the prevention of money laundering. Many of the sites provide search engines that can be of assistance in obtaining helpful documentation.

## Domestic Organizations

Office of the Superintendent of Financial Institutions (OSFI)
http://www.osfi-bsif.gc.ca/

Financial Transactions and Report Analysis Centre of Canada (FINTRAC)
http://www.fintrac.gc.ca/

Department of Justice (Canada)
http://Canada.justice.gc.ca

For reference to legislation including the *United Nations Act* and regulations
laws.justice.gc.ca

Ontario Securities Commission
www.osc.gov.on.ca

Canada Customs and Revenue Agency
http://www.cra-arc.gc.ca

## International Organizations

Bank for International Settlements (BIS) (Basel Committee)
http://www.bis.org/

Financial Action Task Force on Money Laundering (FATF)
http://www1.oecd.org/fatf/ or
http://www.fatf-gafi.org

International Association of Insurance Supervisors (IAIS)
http://www.iaisweb.org/

Board of Governors of the Federal Reserve System (Federal Reserve)
http://www.federalreserve.gov/

Office of the Comptroller of the Currency (OCC)
http://www.occ.treas.gov/

Financial Crimes Enforcement Network (FinCEN)
http://www.fincen.gov/wn_main.html

U.K. Financial Services Authority (FSA)
http://www.fsa.gov.uk/ or
http://www.hm-treasury.gov.uk

Australian Transaction and Reports Analysis Centre (AUSTRAC)
http://www.austrac.gov.au/

# WRITTEN MATERIALS USEFUL FOR REVIEW

*Anti-Money Laundering Guidance Notes for Insurance Supervisors and Insurance Entities*, January 2002, Guidance Paper No. 5: International Association of Insurance Supervisors

*Criminal Code*, R.S.C. 1985, c. C-46, s. 83.11(1)

*Cross-Border Currency and Monetary Instruments Reporting Regulations*, SOR/2002-412

Customer Due Diligence For Banks: Basel Committee Publications No. 85, October 2001 (Bank for International Settlements (BIS))

Directive 2001/97/EC of the European Parliament and Council amending the directive on money laundering, and the creation of the FATF Special Recommendations on Terrorist Financing

Financial Action Task Force on Anti-Money Laundering, *Review of the FATF Forty Recommendations: Consultation Paper* (May 30, 2002)

FINTRAC Guidelines: Refer to Department of Justice website http://canada-justice.gc.ca

Guidance: Reference Guidelines for Banks, File P2200-22, April 7, 2003 Subject: Revised Guideline 8 on Deterring and Detecting Money Laundering http://www.osfi-bsif.gc.ca/documents

*Proceeds of Crime Act, 2002* (United Kingdom)

*Proceeds of Crime (Money Laundering) and Terrorist Financing Suspicious Transaction Reporting Regulations*: Refer to FINTRAC website http://www.fintrac.gc.ca or Department of Justice website http://Canada.justice.gc.ca

*Public Safety Act*, Bill C-17 (37th Parliament, Second Session, reintroduced as Bill C-7, 37th Parliament, Third Session)

U.N. Convention on Transnational Organized Crime

*United Nations Act*, R.S. 1985, c. U-2 and the *United Nations Suppression of Terrorism Regulations*, SOR/2001-360

*USA Patriot Act*, including the *International Money Laundering Abatement Act and Anti-Terrorist Financing Act of 2001*

# INDEX

## A

Access to information, 3
Access to mail provisions, 51
Accountants, 124, 172, 183, 209, 217
Accounting firm, 209, 217
Accounts, 181
Acknowledgment of receipt, 188, 200
Agent of the Crown, 126–28, 133, 172, 208, 216–17
Agents, *see also* Life insurance industry
  • life insurance, 239
  • regulations, 115
Agreements for exchange of information, 82–83
Airports, 142
Alternative money remittance systems, 208
Alternative to large cash transaction reports, 254
Annual verification, 280–81
*Anti-Money Laundering Guidance Notes for Insurance Supervisors and Insurance Entities*, 296
Anti-money laundering initiatives, 156–57
Anti-money laundering regime, 160
Anti-terrorism, 160–63
*Anti-Terrorism Act*
  • amendments, 20
  • financing of terrorist activities, reporting of, 21
  • funding sources to terrorist linked groups, 3
  • Guidelines summary of, 161–63
  • immunity section, 40
  • money laundering amendments, 39
  • overview, 37–40
  • reporting requirements, 39
  • suspected terrorist organizations, 7
  • terrorist activities, 38
  • terrorist activity financing offence, 28–29
  • terrorist activity financing offences, 4, 38, 51
  • terrorist groups, 38–39
  • terrorist property, freezing of, 174
Appeal process, 36, 52–53, 78–80, 93–94
Areas outside of Canada, 182
Asset purchases with bulk cash, 154
Audit, 209, 294–95
Auditor, 211

## B

*Bank Act*, 24, 148
Bank of Canada exception, 144
Bank of International Settlements (BIS), 301
Banks, 287–98. *See also* Financial entities

Basel Committee, 292
Batch file transfer, 188, 246, 248, 270
Batch transmission software, 278–79
Behaviour, suspicious nature of, 183
Black-market peso exchange, 155
Board and management oversight, 293–94
Brokers. *See* Life insurance industry
Bulk cash purchases, 154
*Business Names Act*, 48
Business transactions, as indicators, 183
Businesses providing loans, as indicator, 183

## C

Canada Customs and Revenue Agency (CCRA), 163, 167, 301
Canadian, 147
Canadian Security Intelligence Service, 56, 88, 149, 161, 177, 221, 301
*Canadian Security Intelligence Service Act*, 56
Cash, 33, 242, 253
Cash deposits, 276
Casinos, 125–26, 132, 155, 172, 183, 207, 216–17
Charitable organizations, 172, 207
Chitti, 208
Client identification
  • agent of the Crown, 133
  • casinos, 132
  • compliance program, 45–46
  • compliance regime, 206, 208
  • corporations, 47, 48, 236–37
  • electronic funds transfers, 267
  • electronic submission of large cash transaction reports, 243–44
  • entities other than corporations, 237
  • exceptions, 45, 133–34
  • financial entities, 129–30
  • foreign exchange dealers, 131
  • general exceptions, 237
  • individuals, 235–36
  • "know your client" rules, 43–47
  • large cash transactions, 46, 235
  • life insurance industry, 130, 235
  • measures for, 134–37
  • money services businesses, 132
  • partnerships, 47, 48
  • presented identification, 47
  • procedure for ascertaining identity, 47–48
  • regulations, 129–34
  • requirements, 32, 49
  • securities dealers, 130–31
  • sources for client information, 48
  • Suspicious Transaction Reporting Regulation, 44

Index

**Client identification** — *cont'd*
- third parties, 46–47
- under the Regulation, 43–44

**Client information records**
- entities, and client identifications, 236–37
- individuals, and client identification, 235–36
- life insurance industry, 233–34, 238–39
- third-party determination, 238–39

**Closing accounts,** 175

**Commercial passenger conveyance,** 139

**Common indicators.** *See* **Indicators**

**Completion of transactions,** 173–74

**Compliance costs,** 298

**Compliance monitoring,** 213–14

**Compliance officer,** 64–65, 209, 210

**Compliance policies and procedures,** 209, 210–12, 292, 293–95

**Compliance recommendations of guidelines,** 7–8

**Compliance regime,** *see also* **Guideline 4 (compliance regimes)**
- basics, 13, 210–13
- client identification, 206, 208
- communication, 13
- compliance officer, 64–65
- compliance training program, 212–13
- described, 209
- directors' liability, 59
- electronic funds transfers, 34
- elements of, 209
- employees' reporting obligations, 64–65
- employers' responsibility, 206
- failure to implement and monitor, 68
- general requirements, 63–64
- identity of client, 45–46
- individual requirements, 64–65
- internal compliance reporting process, 294
- internal controls, 209
- officers' liability, 59
- periodic reviews, 13
- policies and procedures, 67–68
- record-keeping requirements, 206, 208
- reporting requirements, 208
- requirement for, 9
- requirements, 7–8, 11–14, 63–64
- review of policies and procedures, 67–68, 211–12
- training, 68

**Compliance training program,** 11, 13, 212–13, 295

**Confidentiality of client information,** 174–75

**Constitutional issues,** 62

**Contractors,** 239

**Control of property,** 148

**Conversion rate,** 140

**Conveyance,** 139

**Cooperative credit association,** 287–98

**Cooperative Credit Associations Act,** 290

**Corporate transactions, as indicators,** 183

**Corporations,** 47, 48, 277, 281–83. *See also* **Client identification**

**Courier,** 139, 143

**"Course of their activities",** 21–22

**Criminal charges,** 214. *See also* **Offences and punishment**

*Criminal Code*
- aggregate reporting requirements, 289
- aiding suspected criminal activity, 30
- broad definitions in, 39
- compliance requirements, 7
- designated offence, 173
- money laundering, 3–4, 28
- *Public Safety Act, 2002* amendments to, 4
- terrorist activities financing offences, 6–7, 28–29
- terrorist activity, 29
- terrorist group, definition of, 39
- terrorist property, 221, 256

**Criminal investigations,** 56

*Cross-Border Currency and Monetary Instruments Reporting Regulations.* See **Cross-Border Reporting Regulation**

**Cross-Border Currency Report (CBCR),** 301

**Cross-Border Reporting Regulation**
- amendments to, 145
- Bank of Canada exception, 144
- coming into force, 145
- exceptions to importation reporting, 143
- export of currency, 10, 140–44
- exportation reporting, 143–44
- import of currency, 10, 140–44
- importation report, 142
- importation reporting, 141–42
- imported shares exemption, 144
- interpretation, 139–40
- monetary instruments, 10
- overview, 9–10
- penalties, 145
- prescribed amounts, 140
- prescribed retention period, 144
- retention, 144
- retention notice, 144

**Cross-border transfer of funds,** 35–36

**Crown agent.** *See* **Agent of the Crown**

**Currency,** *see also* **Cross-Border Reporting Regulation**
- cash transactions in foreign currency, 243, 255
- electronic funds transfers in foreign currency, 267
- equivalents, 8
- import and export of, 10, 36, 140–44
- smuggling, 154

**Customer identification processes,** 292, 295–96, 297

# Index

*Customs Act*, 35, 51, 141
**Customs control,** 141
**Customs officers,** 35, 51–54, 141
**Customs seizure report,** 301

## D

**Department of Citizenship and Immigration,** 167
**Department of Finance,** 301
**Designated information,** 87, 88, 90
**Designated offence,** 173
**Designated officer,** 294
**Destination of funds,** 7
**Director of FINTRAC,** 15, 54–55
**Directors**
- liability, 59, 149
- oversight, and OSFI draft guideline, 293–94
- statutory duties, 211
**Disclosure of information**
- agreements for exchange of information, 82–83
- by Director of FINTRAC, 54–56
- by FINTRAC, 54, 86, 167–68
- designated information, 87, 88, 90
- exceptions to restrictions, 55
- generally, 17
- immunity, 166
- international organizations, 55–56
- legislation, 81–82
- limitation on, 55
- of report, 58
- order for, 92–93
- suspicious transaction report, 29–30
- *United Nations Suppression of Terrorism Regulations*, 160–61
**Due diligence,** 26, 59
**Duty of care,** 291

## E

**Economic purpose, as indicator,** 180–81
**EFTs.** *See* **Electronic funds transfers**
**Electronic filing.** *See* **Electronic reporting**
**Electronic funds transfer network,** 208
**Electronic funds transfer reports,** 244, 255, 302. *See also* **Guideline 8 (electronic funds transfer reports)**
**Electronic funds transfers,** 19, 31, 33, 34, 49, 183
**Electronic reporting,** *see also* **Guideline 3A** (electronic reporting)
- acknowledgment of receipt, 188, 246, 270–71
- batch file transfer, 188
- completion instructions, 189–95, 270
- completion of electronic reports, 188, 245–46
- corrections, 189

- described, 186–87, 244–45
- electronic funds transfers, 269–70
- large cash transaction reports. *See* **Guideline 7A (electronic submission of large cash transaction reports)**
- options, 187–88, 245
- public key infrastructure, 187
- report corrections, 246–47, 271
- Report Preparation Software, 245–46
- requirements, 43, 49–50, 245, 256
- technical filing requirements, 41
- Web site reporting, 187
**Electronic reporting system,** 25
**Electronic wire transfer,** 8
**Eligible business types,** 281–83
**Employees**
- compliance regime and, 206
- compliance training, 68
- individual responsibility, 23
- large cash transaction reporting requirements, 242
- life insurance industry, 239
- obligation to report, 64–65
- regulations, 115
- reporting requirements, 8
- safe harbour provision, 57–58
- training, 295
**Employers,** 23, 206
**Entity,** 147, 242. *See also* **Financial entities**
**Exceptions**
- alternatives to large cash transaction reports, 276–77. *See also* **Guideline 9 (alternative to large cash transaction reports)**
- client identification, 45, 133–34, 237
- disclosure of information restrictions, 55
- electronic funds transfer reports, 266
- large cash transaction reports, 242–43, 254
- to importation reporting, 143
- to reporting requirements, 31–32, 34–35
**Exchange rate,** 243
**Exchange transactions,** 154
**Export of currency,** 10, 36, 140–44
**Exportation reporting,** 143–44
**Exported mail,** 77
**Exporter's report,** 142

## F

**FATF Forty Recommendations,** 295, 297
*Federal Court Act,* 53
*Federal Court Rules,* 53
**Federally regulated financial institutions (FRFIs),** 286–98. *See also* **Financial institutions; OSFI draft guideline**
**Federation of Law Societies challenge,** 61
**Filing requirements,** 41
**Financial Action Task Force,** 302

**Financial Action Task Force on Money Laundering (FATF),** 156, 159, 289, 292, 295, 297, 302

**Financial entities,** 31–32, 118–19, 129–30, 183, 206, 215, 242–43, 254–55, 264–65, 266. *See also* **Guideline 9 (alternative to large cash transaction reports)**

**Financial institutions,** 24, 33, 148, 286–98

**Financial Intelligence Task Force,** 221

**Financial intermediary,** 6, 23–24

**Financial transactions,** 6–7, 20, 165

**Financial Transactions and Reports Analysis Centre of Canada (FINTRAC).** *See* **FINTRAC**

**Financing of terrorist activities.** *See* **Terrorist financing**

**FINTRAC,** 3, 5
- analysis by, 166
- collection of information, 31–32
- compliance, responsibility for, 13
- compliance measures, 97–100
- compliance monitoring, 213–14
- confidentiality, 174–75
- contact information, 168, 184, 227, 240, 249, 261
- creation of, 163
- criminal investigations, 56
- described, 166, 290–91
- Director of, 15, 54–55
- disclosure of information, 30, 31–32, 54, 86, 167–68
- electronic reporting system, 25
- establishment, 83–84
- guidelines, 7
- Guidelines summary, 166–68
- head office, 84–85
- human resources, 85
- immunity, 91
- large cash transactions, 35
- legal proceedings, 100
- mandate, 40
- organization, 84–85
- organization of information, 17
- other responsibilities, 168
- powers, 16
- privacy protection, 167
- privacy protocols, 25
- purpose, 15
- reasonable grounds, 22
- release of information, 54–56
- Report Preparation Software, 245–46
- reporting to. *See* **Reporting requirements**
- reports of, 101
- responsibilities, 15–16
- search powers, 54, 56
- technical filing requirements, 41
- voluntary information, 166
- Web site, 188, 246, 248–49

**FINTRAC Guidelines,** *see also* **specific Guidelines**
- described, 40
- general indicators, 27–28
- reporting requirements, 7–8
- reports, 40

*FINTRAC's Report Preparation Software User Guide,* 248

**Foreign agencies,** 167

**Foreign authorities, disclosure to,** 82–83, 89–90

**Foreign bank branches,** 286–98, 290

**Foreign banks,** 148–49

**Foreign cheques,** 293

**Foreign currency,** 114, 243, 253, 255, 267

**Foreign exchange dealers,** 121–22, 131, 183, 208, 217, 265, 266–67

**Forfeiture,** 78

**Freight trains,** 142

**Funding of terrorist activities.** *See* **Terrorist financing**

**Funds,** 33

**G**

**Gambling,** 155

**General indicators,** 27–28
  *see also* **Indicators**

**Glossary,** 301–03

**Good faith,** 61

**Good faith standard,** 27

**Group of Seven (G-7),** 302

**Guideline 1 (backgrounder)**
- anti-money laundering, 160
- anti-terrorism, 160–63
- *Anti-Terrorism Act,* 161–63
- Canadian legislation, 160–68
- comments, 168
- described, 40
- FINTRAC, 166–68
- introduction, 152–53
- money laundering, 153–57
- *Proceeds of Crime (Money Laundering) and Terrorist Financing Act,* 163–66
- terrorist financing, 157–60
- *United Nations Suppression of Terrorism Regulations,* 160–61
- United Nations (UN) Conventions, 160–61

**Guideline 2 (suspicious transactions)**
- comments, 183
- common indicators, 178–83
- described, 27, 40
- general, 170–71
- identification of suspicious transactions, 175–76
- industry-specific indicators, 183
- suspicious transactions reporting, 171–75
- terrorist financing indicators, 176–77

Index

**Guideline 3A (electronic reporting)**
- account information, 192
- acknowledgment of receipt, 188
- action taken, 194
- change, submission of, 194–95
- completion instructions, 189–95
- completion of electronic reports, 188
- contents of report, 187
- corrections, 189
- description of suspicious activity, 194
- disposition information, 192
- electronic reporting options, 187–88
- individual information, 193
- location of transaction, 191–92
- means of reporting, 187–88
- new report, submission of, 189–91
- reporting screens, 189
- suspicious transactions reporting requirements, 185–87
- suspicious transactions reporting timelines, 185–86
- third party information, 193–94
- transaction information, 192

**Guideline 3B (paper reporting)**
- account information, 201–202
- acknowledgment of receipt, 200
- action taken, 203
- comments, 203
- completion instructions, 200–203
- completion of paper reports, 199
- contents of report, 199
- delivery of paper reports, 199
- description of suspicious activity, 203
- disposition information, 201
- electronic reporting, 198
- individual information, 202
- location of transaction, 201
- means of reporting, 198–99
- paper reporting, 199–200
- suspicious transactions reporting requirements, 197–99
- suspicious transactions reporting timelines, 197–98
- third party information, 202–203
- transaction information, 201

**Guideline 4 (compliance regimes)**
- accountants, 209, 217
- accounting firm, 209, 217
- agent of the Crown, 208, 216–17
- basics of compliance regime, 210–13
- casinos, 207, 216–17
- charitable organizations, 207
- compliance monitoring, and FINTRAC, 213–14
- compliance officer, 210
- compliance policies, 210–11
- compliance regime, described, 209
- compliance training program, 212–13
- described, 12–14, 40, 50
- financial entities, 206, 215
- foreign exchange dealers, 208, 217
- implementation of compliance regime, 206–209
- internal controls, 209
- investment counsellors, 207
- life insurance industry, 206, 215
- money services business, 208, 217
- non-compliance penalties, 214
- portfolio managers, 207
- real estate brokers, 207, 216
- review of policies and procedures, 211–12
- sales representatives, 207, 216
- securities dealers, 207, 216

**Guideline 5 (terrorist property reports)**
- account information, 224
- comments, 227
- completion instructions, 222–27
- contents of report, 221
- *Criminal Code* terrorist property requirements, 221
- disposition information, 225
- filer, information about, 223–24
- how to complete report, 222
- individual information, 225–26
- property, information about, 224
- reasons for filing report, 224
- reporting methods, 221
- sending report to FINTRAC, 222
- terrorist property reporting requirements, 220–21
- third parties, 226
- transaction/proposed transaction information, 225
- when report must be made, 220

**Guideline 6 (life insurance industry)**
- client identification, 235
- client information records, 233–34
- comments, 240
- corporate purchases, 234
- general, 230–31
- large cash transaction records, 231–32
- non-compliance penalties, 239–40
- record keeping methods, 239
- record keeping requirements, 231–34
- third-party determination, 237–39

**Guideline 7A (electronic submission of large cash transaction reports)**
- account information, 250
- acknowledgment of receipt, 246
- batch file transfer, 246
- cash, references to, 242
- cash transactions in foreign currency, 243
- change to previously submitted report, 248
- changes through FINTRAC's Web site, 248–49
- client identification, 243–44

# Index

**Guideline 7A (electronic submission of large cash transaction reports)**—*cont'd.*
- comments, 249
- completion of electronic reports, 245–46
- disposition information, 250
- dollar amounts, references to, 242
- electronic funds transfer reports, 244
- entity information, 251
- exceptions, 242–43
- field-by-field instructions, 250–52
- FINTRAC Report Preparation Software, 245–46
- FINTRAC's secure Web site, 246
- individual information, 251
- instructions for completing report, 247–49
- large cash transactions reporting requirements, 242–45
- means of reporting, 244–45
- new report submission, 247–48
- options for electronic reporting, 245
- other requirements, 243–44
- reasonable efforts, 247
- record keeping, 243–44
- report corrections, 246–47
- single transaction, 242
- suspicious transaction reports, 244
- terrorist property, 244
- third parties, 251–52
- transaction, location of, 250
- transaction information, 250
  when to report, 242–43

**Guideline 7B (paper reporting for large cash transactions)**
- account information, 259
- acknowledgment of receipt, 257
- cash, references to, 253
- cash transactions in foreign currency, 255
- comments, 261
- completion instructions, 257–58
- completion of paper reports, 257
- delivery of paper reports, 257
- disposition information, 259
- dollar amounts, references to, 253
- electronic funds transfer reports, 255
- entity information, 260
- exceptions, 254
- field-by-field instructions, 259–61
- individual information, 260
- large cash transaction reporting requirements, 253–56
- other requirements, 255–56
- paper reporting requirements, 257
- reasonable efforts, 258
- suspicious transaction report, 255–56
- terrorist property transactions, 256
- third parties, 260–61
- transaction, location of, 259

- transaction information, 259
- when to make report, 253–54

**Guideline 8 (electronic funds transfer reports)**
- acknowledgment of receipt, 270–71, 272
- all electronic funds transfers, 265–66
- batch file transfer, 270
- client identification, 267
- completion of electronic reports, 270
- contents, 272–73
- electronic funds transfer reporting requirements, 264–69
- electronic reporting, 269–70
- exception, 266
- financial entities, 264–65
- foreign currency, 267
- foreign exchange dealers, 265, 266–67
- high frequency reporting, 269
- large cash transaction reports, 268
- low volume reporting, 269
- means of reporting, 269
- money services business, 265, 266–67
- other requirements, 267–68
- paper reporting, 269, 271–72
- reasonable efforts, 272
- record keeping, 267
- report corrections, 271
- reporting timeframes, 268
- suspicious transaction report, 268
- SWIFT electronic funds transfers, 264–65, 269
- terrorist property, 268

**Guideline 9 (alternative to large cash transaction reports)**
- annual verification, 280–81
- batch transmission software, 278–79
- cash deposits, 276
- certain changes, reporting of, 280
- conditions for, 276–77, 284–85
- corporations, 277
- criteria, no longer meeting, 280
- eligible business types, 281–83
- excluded NAICS sector codes, 282–83
- how to choose, 277
- list to be maintained, 281
- no batch file transfer report mechanism, 279–80
- *North American Industry Classification System (NAICS)*, 280, 282
- pawnbroking business, 276, 282
- report to FINTRAC about business client, 277–78
- retail trade, 282
- types of businesses for corporate clients, 281–83
- when to make report, 276–77

**Guideline indicators,** 26

# H

Hawala, 208
High frequency reporting, 269
Higher risk customers, 298
Hundi, 208

# I

Identification information, 26
Identity, ascertaining. *See* Client
 identification
Identity documents, as indicator, 179–80
Identity of clients. *See* Client identification
*Immigration Act*, 167
Immunity
 • from action, 61–62
 • *Anti-terrorism Act,* 40
 • disclosure of information, 166
 • FINTRAC, 91
 • suspicious transactions reporting, 175
Import of currency, 10, 36, 140–44
Importation report, 142
Importation reporting, 141–42
Imported shares exemption, 144
Indicators
 • accountants, 183
 • businesses providing loans, 183
 • cash transactions, 180
 • casinos, 183
 • common, 178–83
 • corporate and business transactions, 183
 • economic purpose, 180–81
 • electronic funds transfers, 183
 • foreign exchange dealers, 183
 • general, 178–79
 • identity documents, 179–80
 • knowledge of reporting or record keeping
   requirements, 179
 • life insurance industry, 183
 • list of terrorist-related persons and entities,
   177
 • money services business, 183
 • offshore business activity, 182–83
 • real estate brokers, 183
 • securities dealers, 183
 • suspicious transactions, 177–78
 • terrorist activity financing, 176–77
 • transactions involving accounts, 181
 • transactions involving areas outside of
   Canada, 182
Individual responsibility, 23
Industry-specific indicators. *See* Indicators
Institutional responsibility, 23
*Insurance Companies Act*, 290
Insurance industry. *See* Life insurance
 industry
Integration, 4, 153
Internal compliance reporting process, 294

Internal controls, 209
*International Convention for the Suppression
 of the Financing of Terrorism*, 160
International efforts, 155–57, 156–57, 159–60
International organizations, 55–56
Investment counsellors, 207

# K

"Know your client" rules, 47–48

# L

Large cash transaction records
 • client identification requirements, 46
 • exception, 34
 • life insurance industry, 231–32
Large cash transaction reports, *see also*
 Guideline 7A (electronic submission of
 large cash transaction reports); Guideline
 7B (paper reporting for large cash
 transactions)
 • defined, 302
 • electronic funds transfers, 268
 • electronic report field-by-field instructions,
   250–52
 • electronic reporting instructions, 247–49
 • federally regulated financial institutions,
   292
 • paper report field-by-field instructions,
   259–61
 • paper reporting instructions, 257–58
Large cash transactions, 8, 30–35, 49, 180,
 235, 238. *See also* Guideline 7A (electronic
 submission of large cash transaction
 reports); Guideline 7B (paper reporting for
 large cash transactions)
Layering, 4, 153
Legal counsel, 61
Life insurance companies. *See* Life insurance
 industry
Life insurance industry, 120, 130, 183, 206,
 215, 286–98. *See also* Guideline 6 (life
 insurance industry)
List of terrorist-related persons and entities,
 177
Listed person, 147, 148
Low volume reporting, 269

# M

Mail, 51, 77
Minister of Finance, 15, 17, 54–56
Minister of Foreign Affairs, 147
Monetary instruments, 10, 139
Money laundering
 • Canadian legislation, 160–63. *See also*
   *Proceeds of Crime (Money Laundering)
   and Terrorist Financing Act*
 • criminalization of, 160

**Money laundering** — *cont'd*
- definitions of, 3–4, 153
- financing of terrorist activities, inclusion of, 25
- Guideline 1, 151–68
- importance of fighting against, 158
- international efforts against, 155–57
- legal claims, protection from, 27
- methods of, 154–55
- offence, 172–73
- OSFI draft guideline, 286–98
- schemes, 21
- stages of, 3–4
- *vs.* terrorist activity financing, 177

**Money orders,** 206, 208. *See also* **Agent of the Crown**

**Money services businesses,** 122–23, 132, 171, 183, 208, 217, 265, 266–67

**Monitoring,** 213–14

### N

**Negotiable instruments,** 206

**Nominees,** 154

**Non-compliance penalties,** 214, 239–40

***North American Industry Classification System (NAICS),*** 280, 282–83

### O

**Offences and punishment**
- and compliance training, 213
- consequences of offence, 59–60
- Cross-Border Reporting Regulation, 145
- directors, 59
- disclosure of report, 58
- due diligence, 59
- knowing contravention, 57–58
- list of, 57
- non-compliance penalties, 214
- officers, 59
- provisions, 102–103
- reporting requirement, contravention of, 58–59
- safe-harbour provision, 57–58
- *United Nations Suppression of Terrorism Regulations,* 149

**Office of the Superintendent of Financial Institutions (OSFI),** 176, 302–03. *See also* **OSFI draft guideline**

**Officers**
- liability, 59, 149
- statutory duties, 211

**Offshore business activity,** 182–83

**Offshore jurisdictions,** 293

**OSFI,** 176, 292, 302–03. *See also* **OSFI draft guideline**

**OSFI draft guideline**
- application of, 290

- audit, 294–95
- background, 290–91, 297
- board and management oversight, 293–94
- compliance costs, 298
- compliance policies and procedures, 292
- customer identification processes, 292, 295–96, 297
- customers, 292
- designated officer, 294
- duty of care, 291
- employee training, 295
- geography, 293
- guideline impact analysis statement, 297–98
- higher risk customers, 298
- internal compliance reporting process, 294
- introduction, 290–91
- lists of terrorists, 289–90
- objectives, 298
- OSFI, role of, 289
- OSFI reviews, 296
- outsourcing record keeping, 292–93, 298
- policies and procedures, 293–95
- problem identification, 297–98
- products and services, 292
- programs to combat money laundering and terrorist financing activities, 291–96
- purpose of, 289
- regulatory intervention initiatives, 291
- release of, 297
- reliance on others, 292–93
- risk management, 293–95
- risks of money laundering and terrorist financing activities, 291–93
- verification, 292, 297

**OSFI Web site,** 289

**Outsourcing record keeping,** 292–93, 298

### P

**Paper reporting**
- acknowledgment of receipt, 200, 257, 272
- completion of paper reports, 199–200, 257
- delivery of reports, 199, 257
- described, 245
- electronic funds transfers, 269, 271–72
- large cash transactions. *See* **Guideline 7B (paper reporting for large cash transactions)**
- requirements, 257
- terrorist property reports, 221

**Partnerships,** 47, 48

***Partnerships Act,*** 48

**Pawnbroking business,** 276, 282

**Penalties.** *See* **Offences and punishment**

**Personal information, access to,** 56

**Peso exchange, black market,** 155

**Placement,** 4, 153

**Portfolio managers,** 207
**Possession of property,** 148
**Prescribed retention period,** 144
**Prescribed transactions,** 30–35
*Privacy Act,* 56
**Privacy protection,** 167
**Privacy protocols,** 25
*Proceeds of Crime (Money Laundering) Act*
(**1991**), 2
*Proceeds of Crime (Money Laundering) and
Terrorist Financing Act*
- access to mail provisions, 51
- agreements for exchange of information,
  82–83
- appeal process, 78–80, 93–94
- binding on Her Majesty, 71
- closing accounts, no requirement for, 175
- compliance measures, 97–100
- cross-border reporting, 163
- currency and monetary instruments, 73–83
- definitions, 69–70
- designated information, 87, 88, 90
- disclosure of information, 81–82, 86
- establishment of FINTRAC, 83–84
- exported mail, 77
- failure to comply, 165–66
- financial transactions, 165
- Financial Transactions and Reports
  Analysis Centre of Canada. *See*
  **FINTRAC**
- foreign authorities, disclosure to, 89–90
- forfeiture, 78
- Guidelines summary, 163–66
- head office of FINTRAC, 84–85
- human resources, and FINTRAC, 85
- immunity, 61–62, 91
- interpretation, 69–70
- legal proceedings, 100
- liability in relation to reporting, 166
- money laundering offences, defined, 3
- objectives, 3, 70–71, 163–64
- offences and punishment, 57–60, 102–103
- organization of FINTRAC, 84–85
- origins and status, 1–3
- overview, 5–8
- production order, 94–95
- regulations, provisions for, 101–102
- reporting and record keeping provisions,
  5–6, 71–73, 163, 170
- reporting entities, 164
- reports from FINTRAC, 101
- retention, 74–75
- search and seizure, 75–77
- short title, 69
- suspicious transactions, 165
- terrorist property reports, 165–66, 220
- third parties, 80–81
- transfer to government official, 78

- transitional provision, 104
- voluntary information, 166
*Proceeds of Crime (Money Laundering) and
Terrorist Financing Regulations. See*
**Regulation, the**
*Proceeds of Crime (Money Laundering) and
Terrorist Financing Suspicious Transaction
Reporting Regulations. See* **Suspicious
Transaction Reporting Regulation**
**Production order,** 94–95
**Public body,** 242–43
**Public key infrastructure,** 187
*Public Safety Act, 2002,* 3, 4, 37–40, 55, 56
**Punishment.** *See* **Offences and punishment**

**R**

**Real estate brokers,** 124–25, 172, 183, 207, 216
**Real estate sales representative.** *See* **Real
estate brokers**
**Reasonable efforts,** 247, 258, 272
**Reasonable grounds,** 21, 22–23, 24, 172–73
**Receipt, acknowledgment of,** 188
**Record keeping requirements**
- compliance regime, 206, 208
- content of reports, 49
- described, 49–50
- electronic funds transfers, 267
- electronic submission of large cash
  transaction reports, 243–44
- Guidelines summary, 163
- knowledge of, as indicator, 179
- large cash transactions, 33–34
- life insurance industry, 231–234, 239
- methods of record keeping. *See* specific
  Guideline 6
- non-compliance penalties, 239–40
- outsourcing, 292–93
- provisions in Act, 71–73
- regulation, 118–128
- retention of records, 49, 137
- technical provisions, 49–50
- test of record-keeping system, 211
- timeframe for keeping records, 239
**Registered charities.** *See* **Charitable
organizations**
**Regulation, the**
- accountants, 124
- agents of the Crown, 126–28, 133
- casinos, 125–26, 132
- client identification, 67–68, 129–34
- client identification requirements, 43–44
- coming into force, 138
- compliance, 137–38
- compliance program, 7
- compliance regime, 9, 11
- cross-border reporting. *See* **Cross-Border
  Reporting Regulation**

Index

**Regulation, the** — *cont'd*
- definitions, 111–14
- exceptions to reporting requirements, 31–32, 34–35
- financial entities, 118–119, 129–30
- financial transactions, reporting of, 49
- foreign currency, 114
- foreign exchange dealers, 121–22, 131
- general provisions, 8–9, 115–17
- identity of clients, 32
- interpretation, 111–14
- know your client rules, 43–44
- large cash disbursement record, 34
- large cash transaction section, 30–35
- legal counsel, deletion as reporting entities, 61
- life insurance industry, 120, 130
- money services businesses, 122–23, 132
- overview, 8–9, 8–10
- provisions for, 101–02
- real estate brokers, 124–25
- record keeping, 118–28
- record keeping requirements, 49
- repeal of former regulation, 138
- reporting entities, 8
- reporting of financial transactions, 118–28
- reporting procedures, 40–41
- retention of records, 137
- securities dealers, 120–21, 130–31
- single transaction, 9
- single transactions, 114–15
- suspicious transaction reporting. *See* **Suspicious Transaction Reporting Regulation**
- SWIFT, 31
- third-party determination, 115–16

**Regulators,** 214
**Regulatory intervention initiatives,** 291
**Release of information,** 54–56
**Reporting entities,** 8, 164
- different reporting requirements, 30, 33, 49
- list of, 170
- new, 23–24
- segregation by type, 31–32
- suspicious transactions reporting, 170–71

**Reporting person,** 244
**Reporting procedures,** 40–41. *See also* **Electronic reporting; Paper reporting**
**Reporting requirements**
- compliance regime, 208
- cross-border transfer of funds, 35–36, 163. *See also* **Cross-Border Reporting Regulation**
- differences in reporting requirements, 30, 33, 49
- employees, 8, 64–65
- exceptions, 31–32, 34–35
- immunity from action, 61–62

- knowledge of, as indicator, 179
- large cash transactions, 8–9, 30–35. *See also* **Guideline 7A (electronic submission of large cash transaction reports); Guideline 7B (paper reporting for large cash transactions)**
- offences and punishments, 58–59
- overview, 5–6
- prescribed transactions, 30–35
- procedures. *See* **Reporting procedures**
- provisions in Act, 71–73
- regulations, 7–8, 118–28
- responsibility for reporting, 8
- suspicious transactions reporting. *See* **Suspicious transactions reporting**
- terrorist activity financing offences, 170

**Reports, generally,** 40
**Responsibility for reporting,** 8
**Retail trade,** 282
**Retailers,** 32
**Retention,** 74–75, 144
**Retention notice,** 144
**Retention of records,** 137
**Review of policies and procedures,** 67–68, 211–12
**Risk management,** 214, 293–95
**Royal Canadian Mounted Police,** 149, 161, 177, 221

**S**

**Safe-harbour provision,** 57–58
**Sales representatives,** 207, 216
**Search and seizure**
- access to mail provisions, 51
- appeal process, 52–53
- communications to FINTRAC, 51
- currency or monetary instruments, 52, 75–77
- customs officers, 51–54
- Financial Transactions and Reports Analysis Centre of Canada, 91
- FINTRAC, 54
- general search powers, 51–52
- third parties, 53, 80–81

**Securities dealers,** 120–121, 130–31, 183, 207, 216
**Securities industry,** 45
**Security threats,** 56
**Seizure,** 36
**Self-review,** 67
**Ships,** 143
**Single transactions,** 9, 114–15, 242
**"Smurfing,"** 154
**Society for Worldwide Interbank Financial Telecommunication.** *See* **SWIFT**
**Solicitor-client privilege,** 61
**Sound business and financial practices,** 289

# Index

*Special Recommendations on Terrorist Financing*, 159
*Standard Batch Reporting Instructions and Specification*, 248
**Structuring,** 154
**Suspicious transaction report,** 29–30, 244, 255–56, 268, 303
**Suspicious Transaction Reporting Regulation**
- application of Part 1 of Act, 107–109
- breach of statute, 26
- client identification requirements, 44
- complexity of reporting requirements, 67
- details of reporting of suspicious transactions, 20
- due diligence, 26
- employment, course of, 23
- filing of reports, 45
- financial institutions, 24
- financing of terrorist activity, 20
- good faith standard, 27
- identification information, 26
- individual responsibility, 23
- institutional responsibility, 23
- interpretation, 105–106
- legal claims arising from reporting, 27
- listed person, funds used by, 24
- overview, 9
- prescribed information, 26, 108–109
- reporting information required, 25
- reports, 9
- required information, 45–46
- required report form and contents, 21
- suspicion, reasonable grounds of, 21
- terrorist activity financing offence, reporting of, 39
- terrorist financing, suspicions of, 24
- third party, transaction on behalf of, 19–20
**Suspicious transactions**
- completed transactions, 173–74
- definitions of, 172–73
- guideline indicators, 26
- identification of, 175–76, 292
- indicators, 177–78
- money laundering offence, 172–73
- reasonable grounds to suspect, 172–73
- reporting of, 20
- terrorist activity financing offence, 172, 173
**Suspicious transactions reporting,** *see also* **Guideline 2 (suspicious transactions); Suspicious Transaction Reporting Regulation**
- accountants, 172
- agent of the Crown, 172
- casinos, 172
- charitable organizations, 172
- closing accounts, 175
- completed transactions, 173–74
- confidentiality of client information, 174–75
- contents of report, 187, 199
- "course of their activities," 21–22
- definitions, 20
- electronic filing. *See* **Guideline 3A (electronic reporting)**
- employees' reporting obligations, 64–65
- financial transactions, 20
- Guidelines summary, 171–75
- identification of reporting situations, 27
- identity of client, 45–46
- immunity, 175
- industry-specific indicators, 28
- making a report, 174
- means of reporting, 187–188, 198–99
- money services business, 171
- paper reporting, 187. *See also* **Guideline 3B (paper reporting); Paper reporting**
- penalties for failure to report, 175
- real estate brokers, 172
- reasonable grounds, 22–23
- reporting entities, 171–72
- requirements, 19–23, 165, 185–87, 197–99
- suspicion, 28–29
- terrorist property, 174
- timelines, 185–86, 197–98
**SWIFT,** 31, 264–65, 269, 303

## T

**Technical filing requirements,** 41
**Terrorist activities,** 38
- *Criminal Code* definition, 29
- list of persons, where reasonable grounds, 24
- *United Nations Suppression of Terrorism Regulations,* 147–48
**Terrorist activity financing offences,** 28–29, 39, 51
**Terrorist financing**
- Canadian legislation, 163–68
- definition, 157
- financial support, 158
- importance of combatting, 155–56, 159
- indicators, 176–77
- international efforts to combat, 156–57, 159–60
- laundering of funds, 158
- methods of, 158
- *vs.* money laundering, 177
- OSFI draft guideline, 286–98
- reporting of, 21, 24
- revenue-generating activities, 158
- suspicion of, 20
- terrorist activity financing offences, 6–7, 38, 51, 170, 172, 173
**Terrorist groups,** 38–39

# Index

**Terrorist property,** 165–66, 174, 221, 244, 256, 268
**Terrorist property reports**
- completion instructions, 222–27
- contents, 221
- *Criminal Code* requirements, 221
- defined, 303
- how to complete, 222
- paper reporting, 221
- requirements, 220–21
- sending to FINTRAC, 222
- when report must be made, 220

**Test of record-keeping system,** 211
**Third parties,** 19–20, 46–47, 53, 80–81, 193–94, 202–03, 226, 251–52, 260–61
**Third-party determination**
- large cash transactions, 238
- life insurance industry, 237–39
- regulations, 115–16

**Timeframe**
- for keeping records, 239
- reporting timeframes, 268

**Training,** 68, 212–13
**Transactions involving accounts,** 181
**Transactions involving areas outside of Canada,** 182
**Transactions involving offshore business activity,** 182–83
**Transfer agent,** 140
**Transfer to government official,** 78
**Traveller's cheques,** 206, 208
*Trust and Loan Companies Act,* 290
**Trust and loan company,** 286–98

## U

*United Nations Act,* 24
**United Nations Security Council,** 147, 177
*United Nations Suppression of Terrorism Regulations,* 24, 160–61, 174
- assisting, 148
- causing, 148
- certificate, 149
- coming into force, 149
- directors' liability, 149
- disclosure, 149
- duty to determine, 148
- freezing property, 148, 256
- indictment, 149
- interpretation, 147
- list, 147–148
- listed person, 148
- offences and punishment, 149
- officers' liability, 149
- promoting, 148
- providing or collecting funds, 148
- summary conviction, 149

**United Nations (UN) Conventions,** 160–61

## V

**Verification,** 280–81, 292, 297
**ViaSafe,** 278
**Voluntary information,** 166

## W

**Web site reporting,** 187
**Wire transfers,** 293